BLADE
OF THE IMMORTAL

On Silent Wings II

publisher
Mike Richardson

series editor
Rachel Penn

collection editor
Chris Warner

collection designer
Amy Arendts

**English version produced by Studio Proteus
for Dark Horse Comics, Inc.**

This book collects issues twenty-three through
twenty-eight of the Dark Horse comic-book series,
Blade of the Immortal.

Published by
Dark Horse Comics, Inc.
10956 SE Main Street
Milwaukie, OR 97222

First edition: March 2000
ISBN: 1-56971-444-4

3 5 7 9 10 8 6 4 2

Printed in Canada

BLADE
OF THE IMMORTAL

art and story
HIROAKI SAMURA

translation
Dana Lewis & Toren Smith

lettering and retouch
Tomoko Saito

On Silent Wings II

DARK HORSE COMICS®

ABOUT THE TRANSLATION

The Swastika

The main character in *Blade of the Immortal*, Manji, has taken the "crux gammata" as both his name and his personal symbol. This symbol is also known as the *swastika*, a name derived from the Sanskrit *svastika* (meaning "welfare," from su — "well" + asti — "he is"). As a symbol of prosperity and good fortune, the swastika was widely used throughout the ancient world (for example, appearing often on Mesopotamian coinage), including North and South America and has been used in Japan as a symbol of Buddhism since ancient times. To be precise, the symbol generally used by Japanese Buddhists is the *sauvastika*, which moves in a counterclockwise direction, and is called the *manji* in Japanese. The *sauvastika* generally stands for night, and often for magical practices. The *swastika*, whose arms point in a clockwise direction, is generally considered a solar symbol. It was this version (the *hakenkreuz*) that was perverted by the Nazis and used as their symbol. It is important that readers understand that the *swastika* has ancient and honorable origins and it is those that apply to this story, which takes place in the 18th century (ca. 1782-3). *There is no anti-Semitic or pro-Nazi meaning behind the use of the symbol in this story. Those meanings did not exist until after 1910.*

The Artwork

The creator of *Blade of the Immortal* requested that we make an effort to avoid mirror-imaging his artwork. Normally, all of our manga are first copied in a mirror-image in order to facilitate the left-to-right reading of the pages. However, Mr. Samura decided that he would rather see his pages reversed via the technique of cutting up the panels and re-pasting them in reverse order. While we feel that this often leads to problems in panel-to-panel continuity, we place primary importance on the wishes of the creator. Therefore, most of *Blade of the Immortal* has been produced using the "cut and paste" technique. There are, of course, some sequences where it was impossible to do this, and mirror-imaged panels or pages were used.

The Sound Effects & Dialogue

Since some of Mr. Samura's sound effects are integral parts of the artwork, we decided to leave those in their original Japanese. When it was crucial to the understanding of the panel that the sound effect be in English, however, Mr. Samura chose to redraw the panel. We hope readers will view the unretouched sound effects as essential portions of Mr. Samura's extraordinary artwork. In addition, Mr. Samura's treatment of dialogue is quite different from that featured in average samurai manga and is considered to be one of the things that has made *Blade* such a hit in Japan. Mr. Samura has mixed a variety of linguistic styles in this fantasy story, where some characters speak in the mannered style of old Japan, while others speak as if they were street-corner punks from a bad area of modern-day Tokyo. The anachronistic slang used by some of the characters in the English translation reflects the unusual mix of speech patterns from the original Japanese text.

ON SILENT WINGS
Part 3

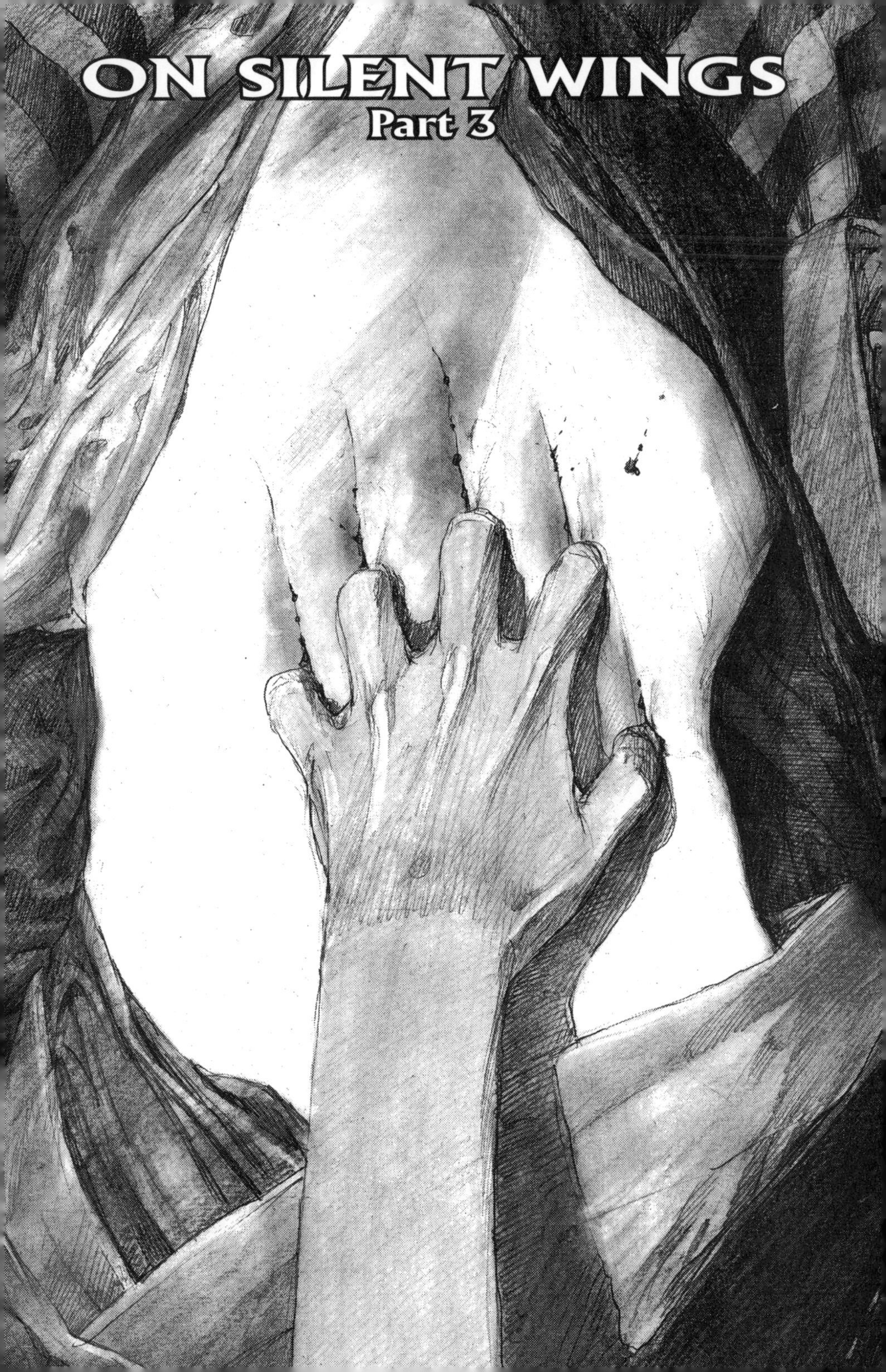

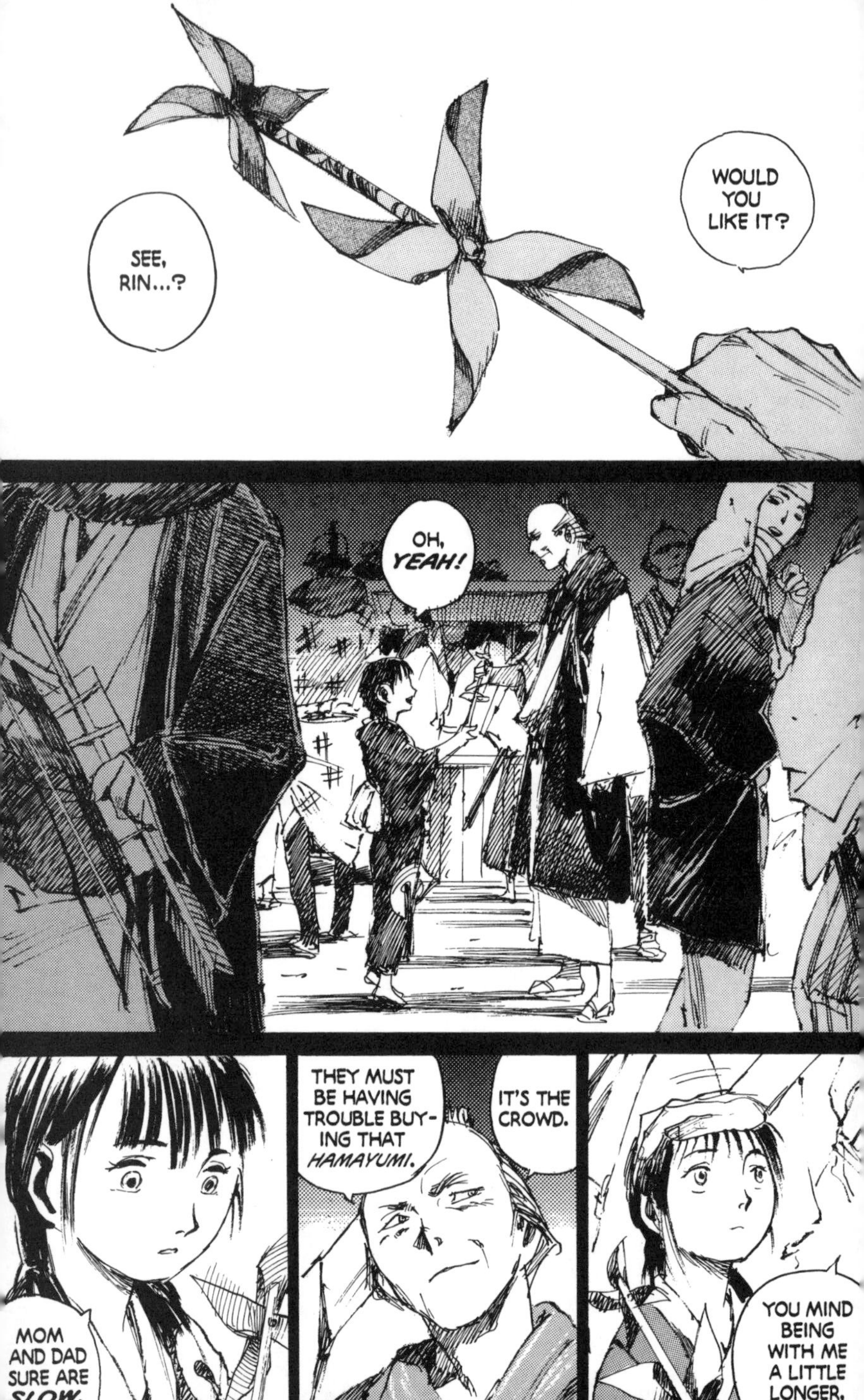
SEE, RIN...?
WOULD YOU LIKE IT?
OH, *YEAH!*
MOM AND DAD SURE ARE *SLOW*, HUH?
THEY MUST BE HAVING TROUBLE BUY-ING THAT *HAMAYUMI*.
IT'S THE CROWD.
YOU MIND BEING WITH ME A LITTLE LONGER, RIN?

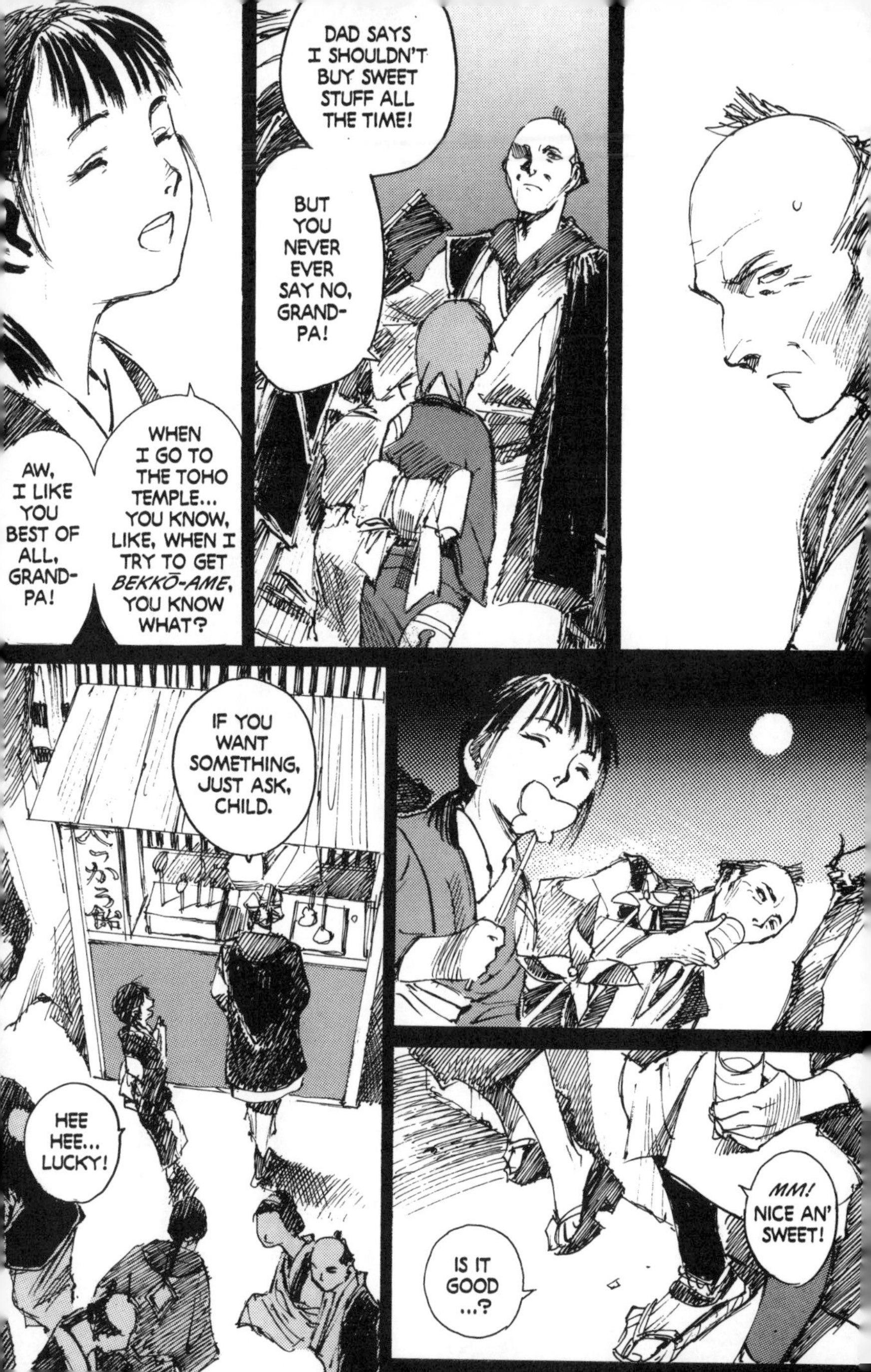

WHEN I GO TO THE TOHO TEMPLE... YOU KNOW, LIKE, WHEN I TRY TO GET *BEKKŌ-AME*, YOU KNOW WHAT?
DAD SAYS I SHOULDN'T BUY SWEET STUFF ALL THE TIME!
BUT YOU NEVER EVER SAY NO, GRAND-PA!
AW, I LIKE YOU BEST OF ALL, GRAND-PA!
IF YOU WANT SOMETHING, JUST ASK, CHILD.
HEE HEE... LUCKY!
IS IT GOOD ...?
MM! NICE AN' SWEET!

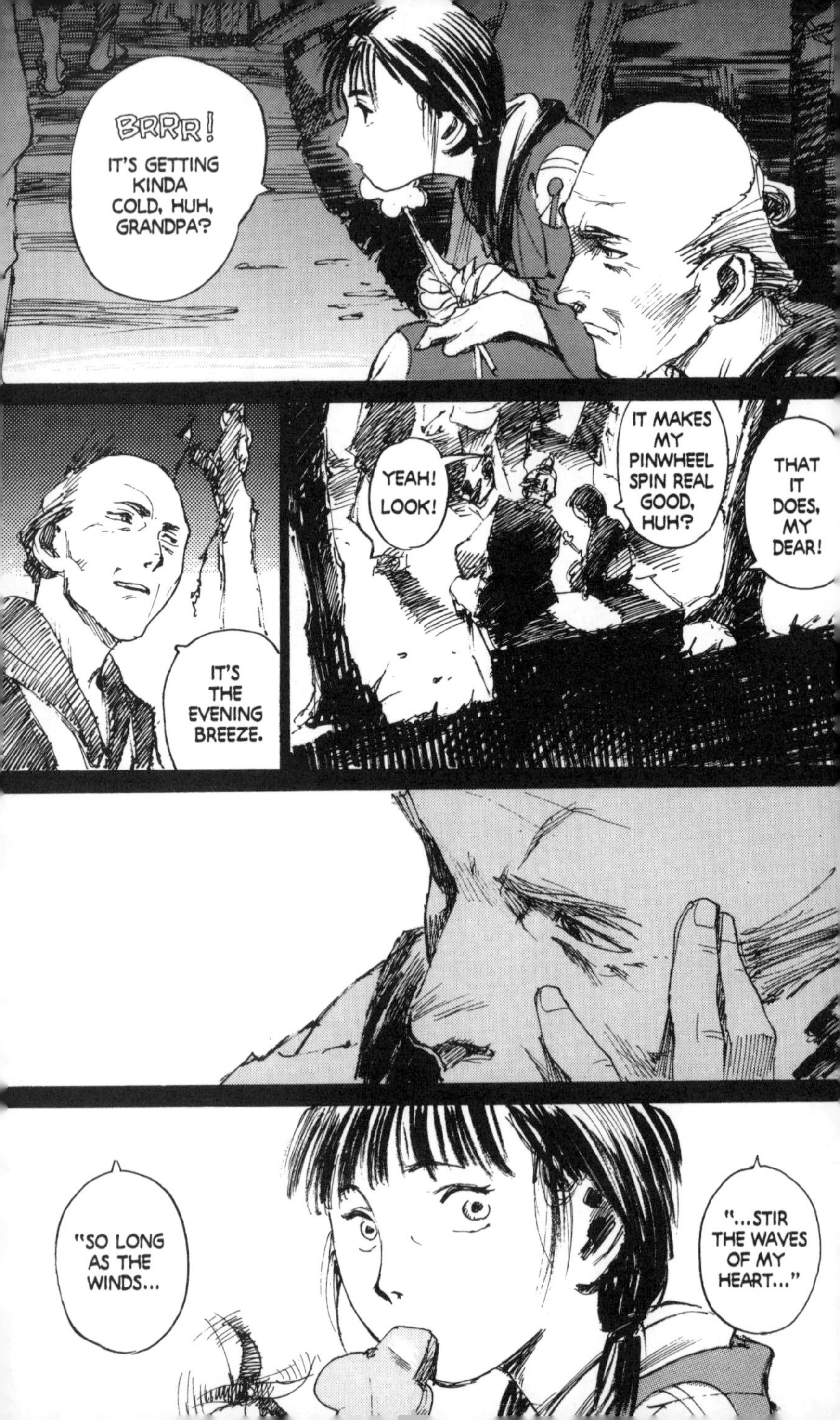
BRRRR!
IT'S GETTING KINDA COLD, HUH, GRANDPA?
IT'S THE EVENING BREEZE.
YEAH! LOOK!
IT MAKES MY PINWHEEL SPIN REAL GOOD, HUH?
THAT IT DOES, MY DEAR!
"SO LONG AS THE WINDS...
"...STIR THE WAVES OF MY HEART..."

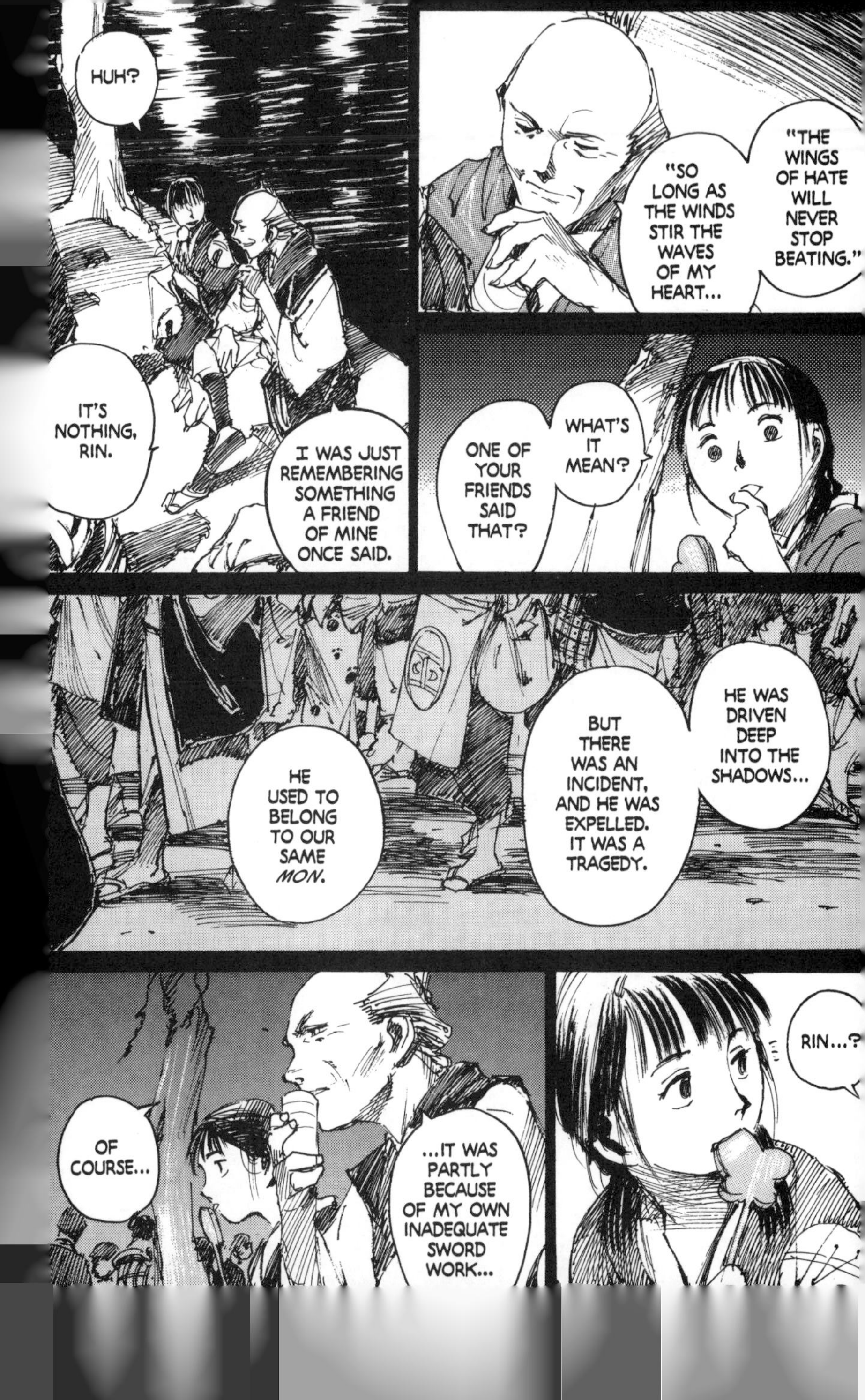
HUH?
IT'S NOTHING, RIN.
I WAS JUST REMEMBERING SOMETHING A FRIEND OF MINE ONCE SAID.
"SO LONG AS THE WINDS STIR THE WAVES OF MY HEART...
"THE WINGS OF HATE WILL NEVER STOP BEATING."
WHAT'S IT MEAN?
ONE OF YOUR FRIENDS SAID THAT?
HE USED TO BELONG TO OUR SAME *MON*.
BUT THERE WAS AN INCIDENT, AND HE WAS EXPELLED. IT WAS A TRAGEDY.
HE WAS DRIVEN DEEP INTO THE SHADOWS...
OF COURSE...
...IT WAS PARTLY BECAUSE OF MY OWN INADEQUATE SWORD WORK...
RIN...?

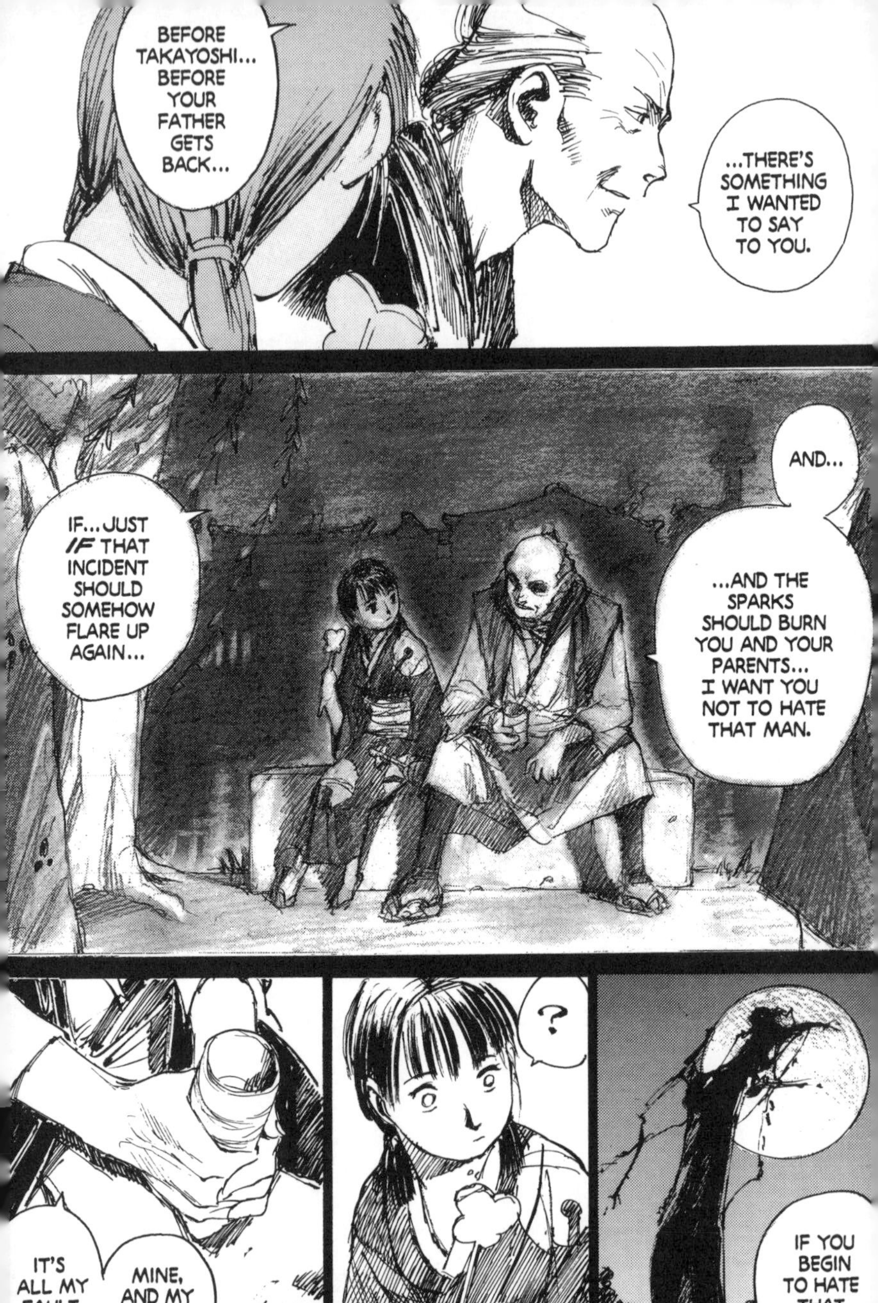
BEFORE TAKAYOSHI... BEFORE YOUR FATHER GETS BACK...
...THERE'S SOMETHING I WANTED TO SAY TO YOU.
IF...JUST IF THAT INCIDENT SHOULD SOMEHOW FLARE UP AGAIN...
AND...
...AND THE SPARKS SHOULD BURN YOU AND YOUR PARENTS... I WANT YOU NOT TO HATE THAT MAN.
IT'S ALL MY FAULT.
MINE, AND MY FATHER.
?
IF YOU BEGIN TO HATE THAT MAN...

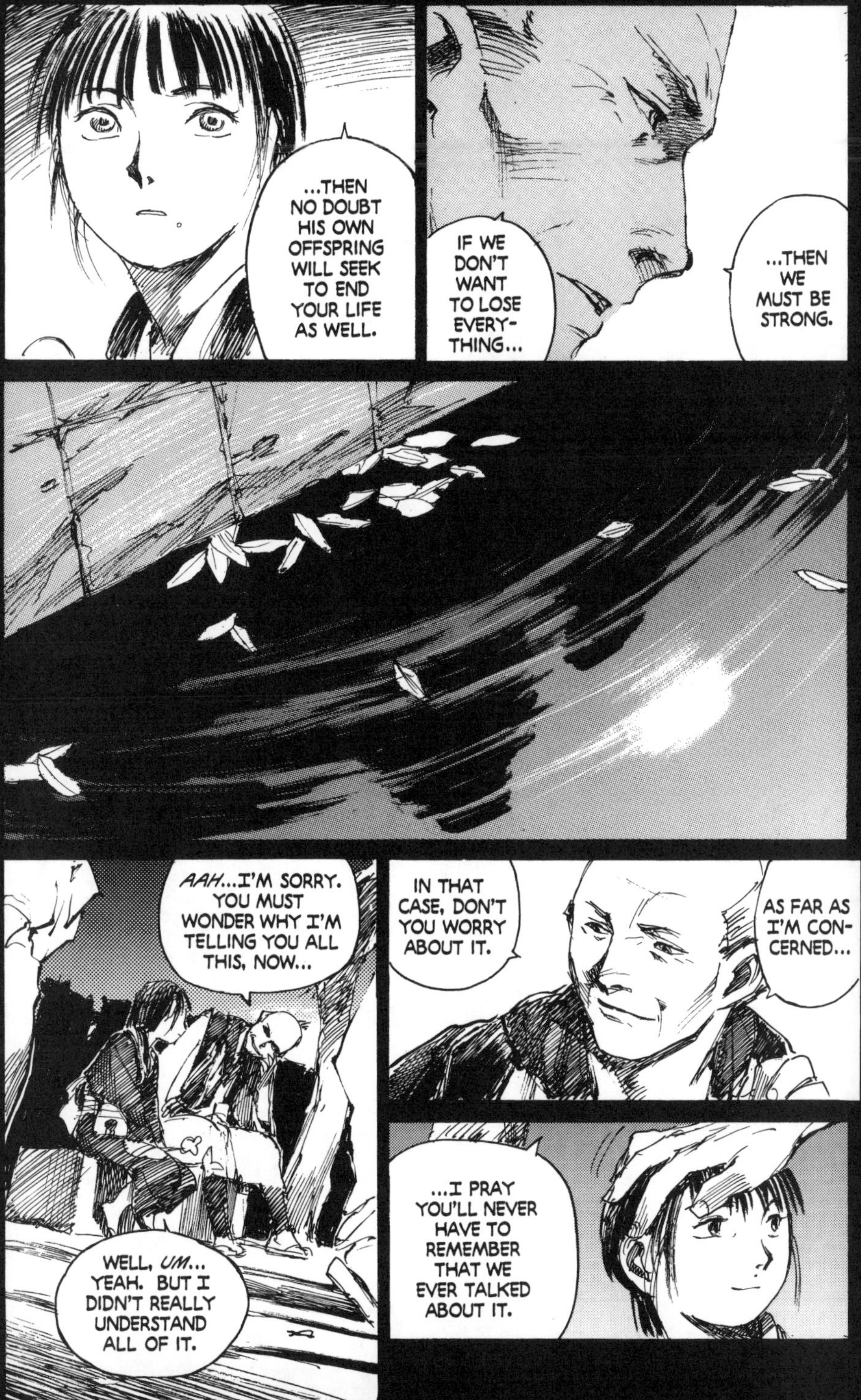
...THEN NO DOUBT HIS OWN OFFSPRING WILL SEEK TO END YOUR LIFE AS WELL.
IF WE DON'T WANT TO LOSE EVERY-THING...
...THEN WE MUST BE STRONG.
AAH...I'M SORRY. YOU MUST WONDER WHY I'M TELLING YOU ALL THIS, NOW...
WELL, UM... YEAH. BUT I DIDN'T REALLY UNDERSTAND ALL OF IT.
IN THAT CASE, DON'T YOU WORRY ABOUT IT.
AS FAR AS I'M CON-CERNED...
...I PRAY YOU'LL NEVER HAVE TO REMEMBER THAT WE EVER TALKED ABOUT IT.

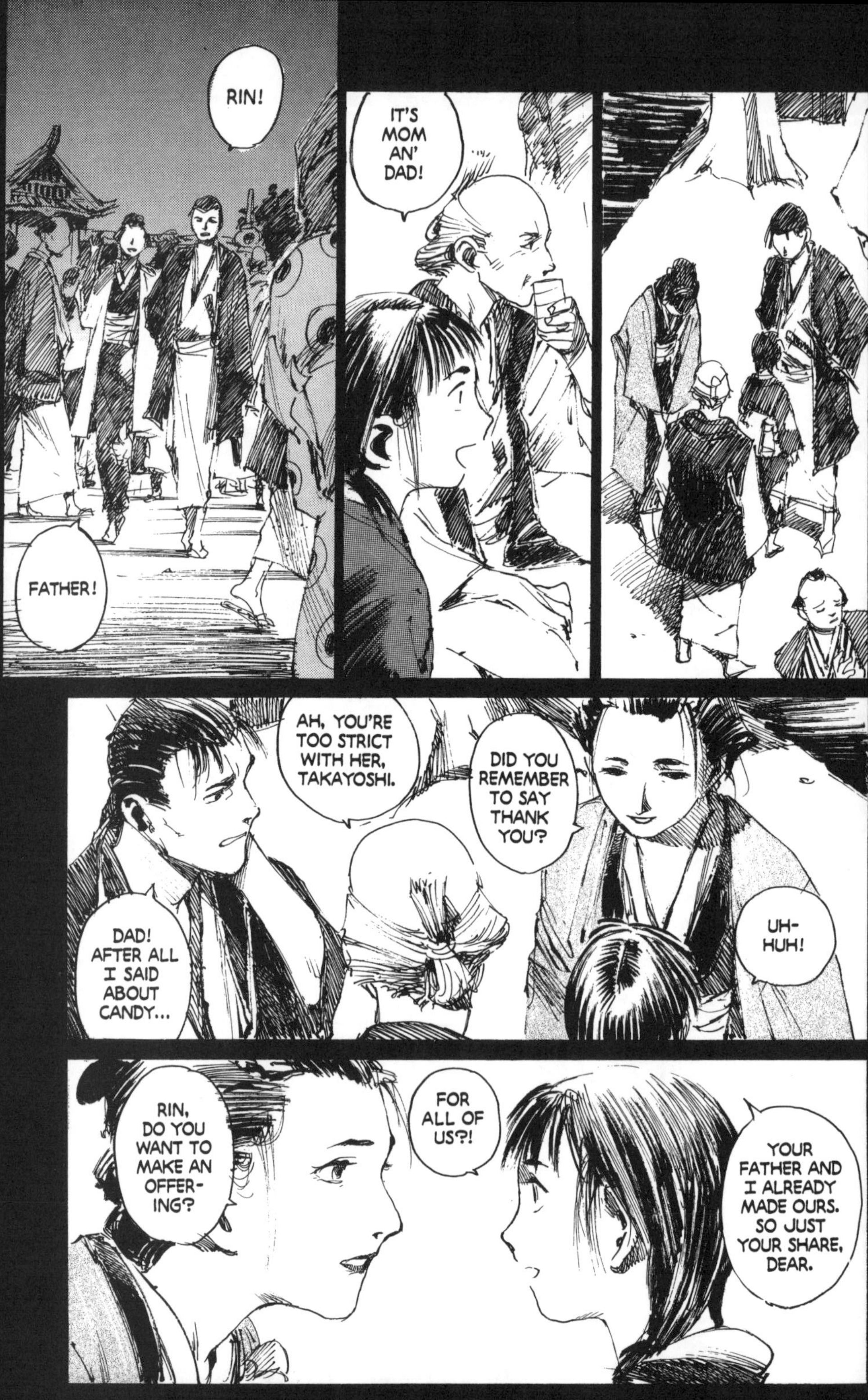
RIN!
FATHER!
IT'S MOM AN' DAD!
DAD! AFTER ALL I SAID ABOUT CANDY...
AH, YOU'RE TOO STRICT WITH HER, TAKAYOSHI.
DID YOU REMEMBER TO SAY THANK YOU?
UH-HUH!
RIN, DO YOU WANT TO MAKE AN OFFER-ING?
FOR ALL OF US?!
YOUR FATHER AND I ALREADY MADE OURS. SO JUST YOUR SHARE, DEAR.

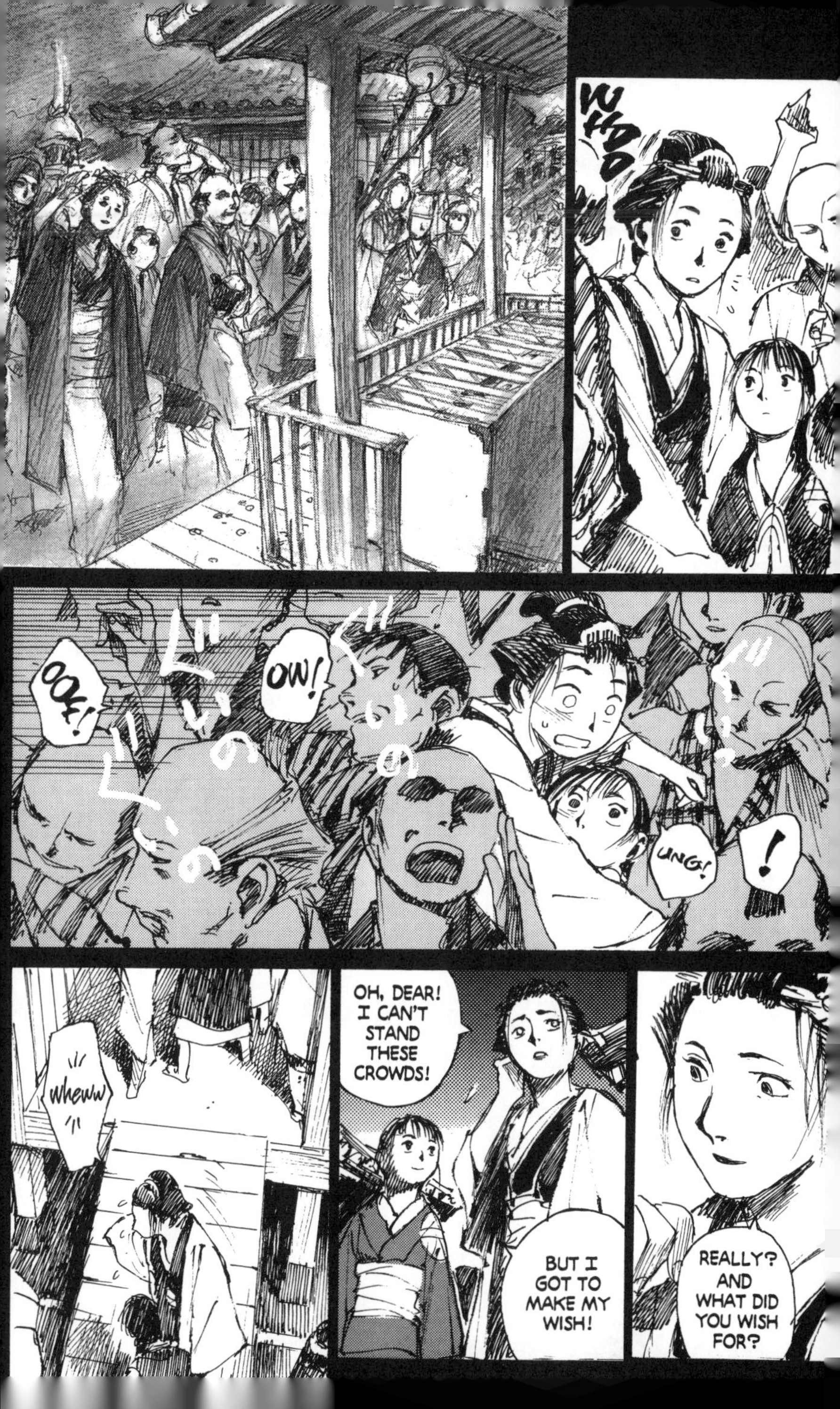
WHOO
!
UNG!
OW!
OOF!
REALLY? AND WHAT DID YOU WISH FOR?
OH, DEAR! I CAN'T STAND THESE CROWDS!
BUT I GOT TO MAKE MY WISH!
wheww

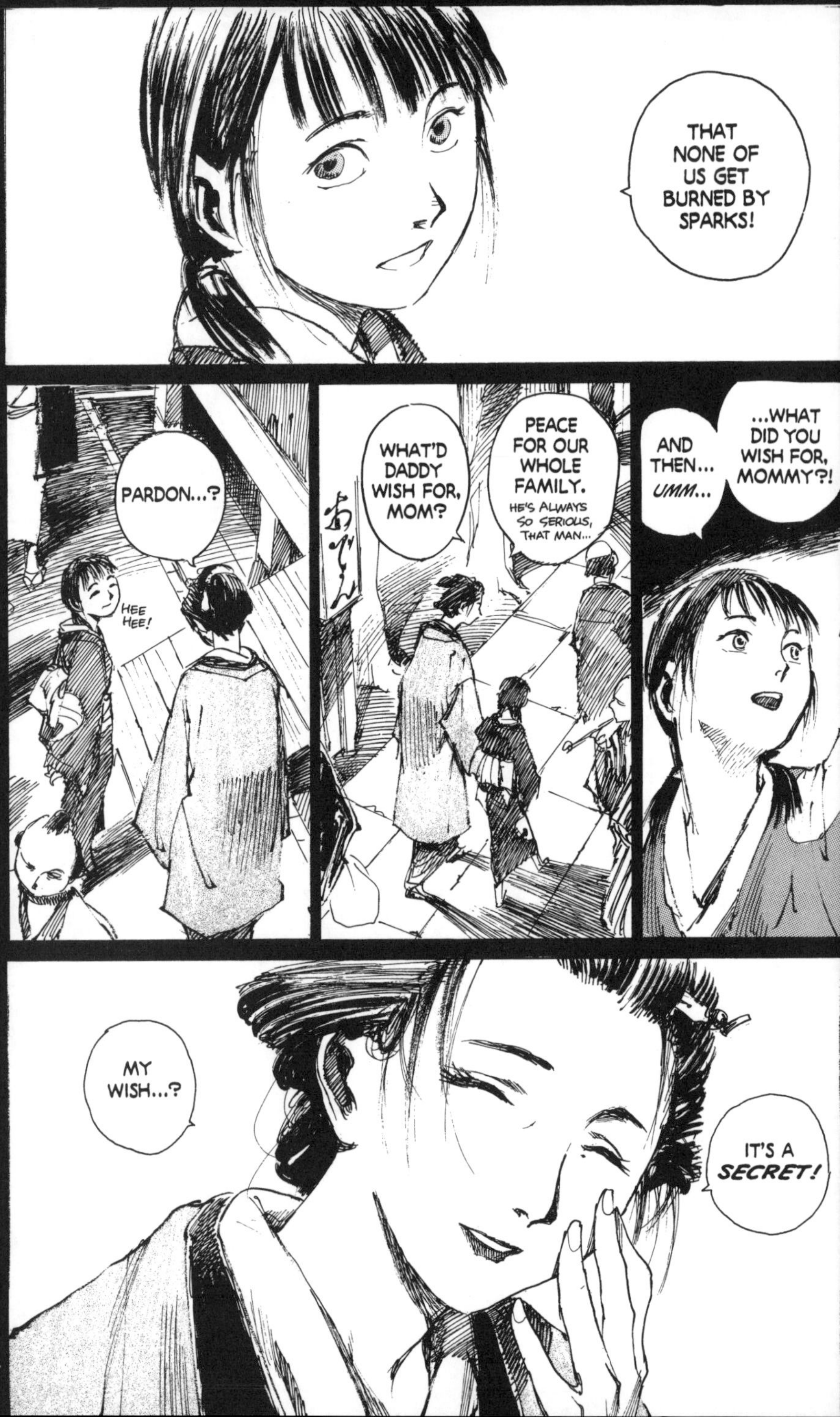
THAT NONE OF US GET BURNED BY SPARKS!
AND THEN... *UMM*...
...WHAT DID YOU WISH FOR, MOMMY?!
WHAT'D DADDY WISH FOR, MOM?
PEACE FOR OUR WHOLE FAMILY.
HE'S ALWAYS SO SERIOUS, THAT MAN...
PARDON...?
HEE HEE!
MY WISH...?
IT'S A *SECRET!*

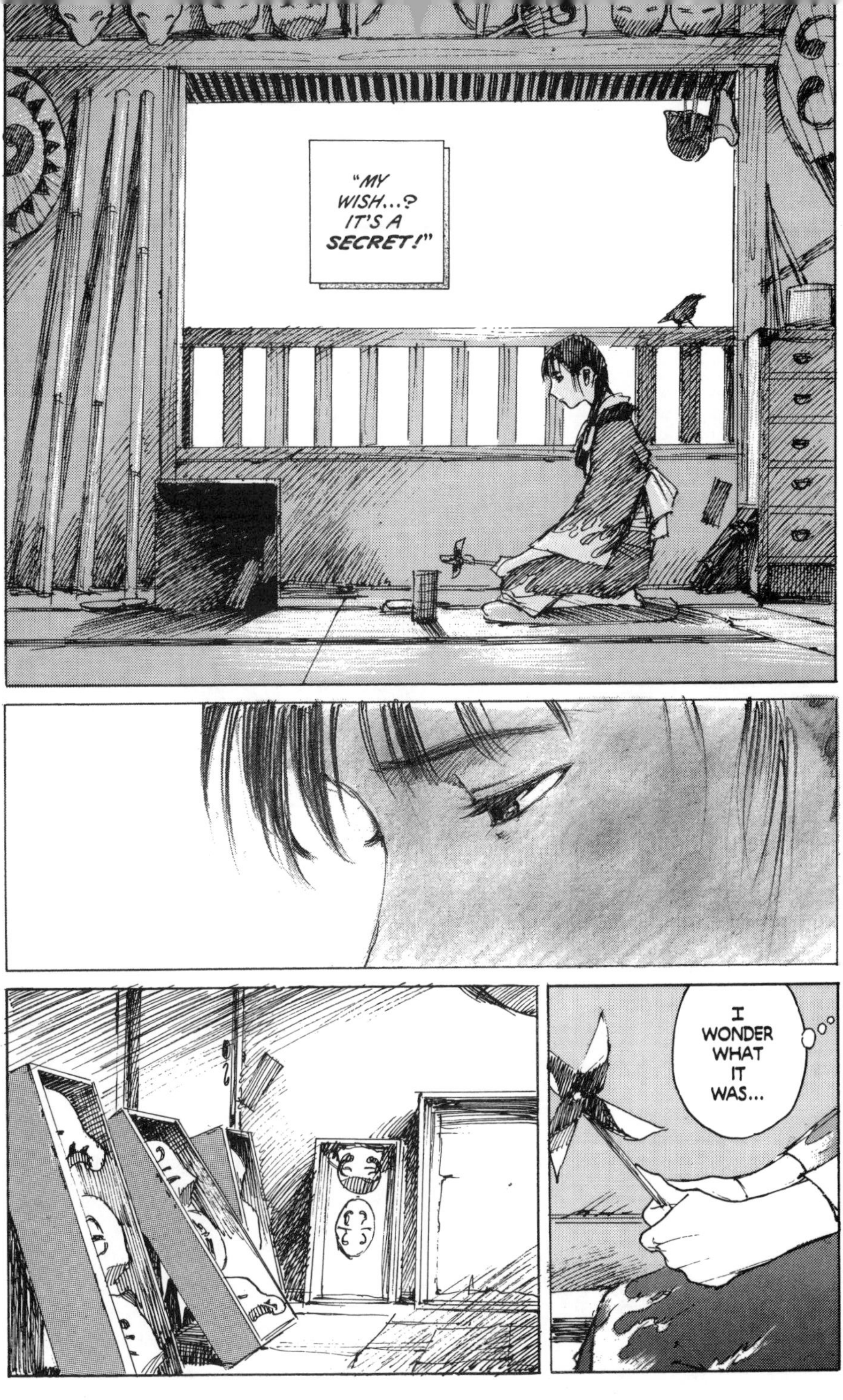
"MY WISH...? IT'S A SECRET!"
I WONDER WHAT IT WAS...

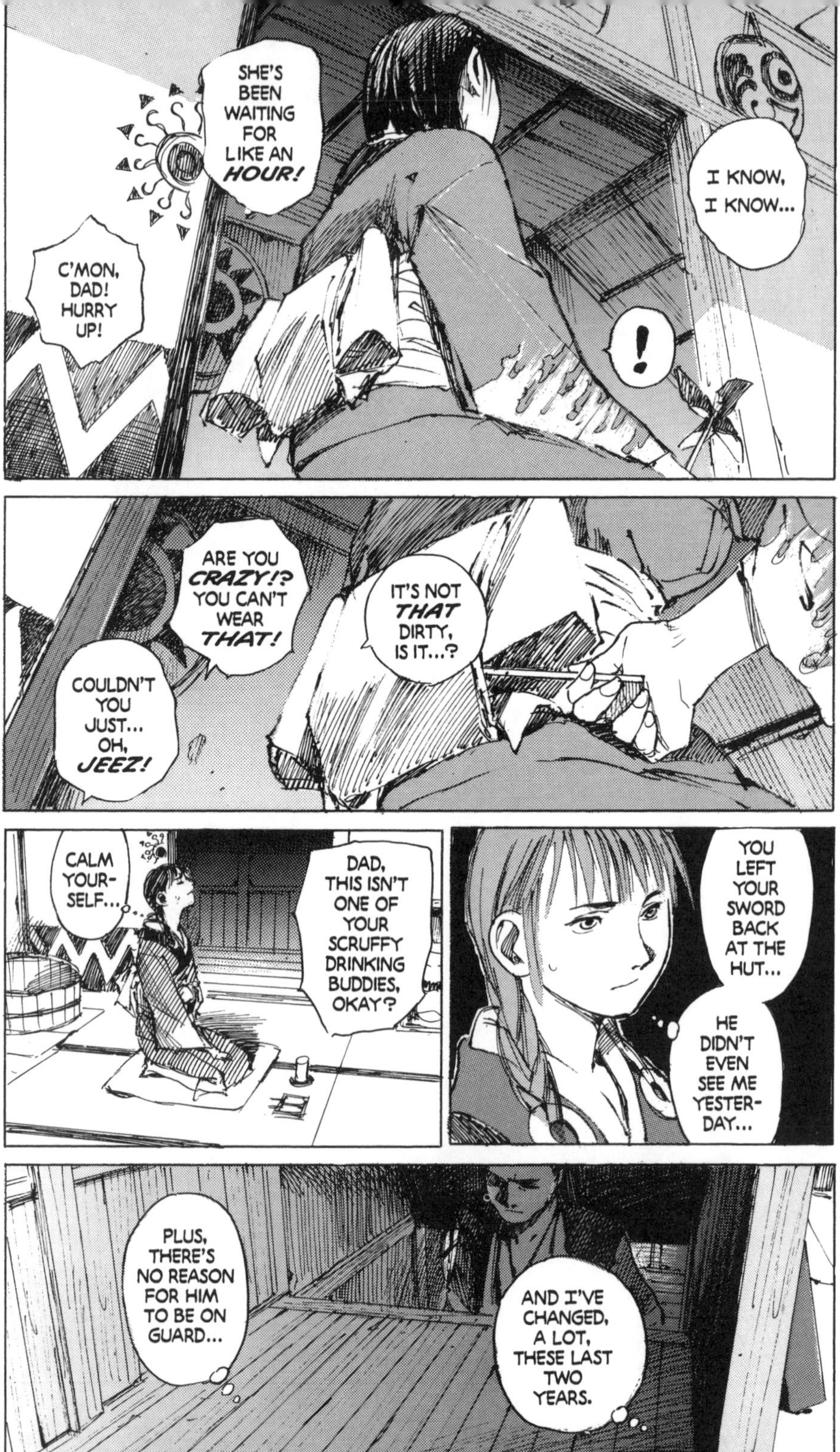
SHE'S BEEN WAITING FOR LIKE AN *HOUR!*
I KNOW, I KNOW...
C'MON, DAD! HURRY UP!
!
ARE YOU *CRAZY!?* YOU CAN'T WEAR *THAT!*
IT'S NOT *THAT* DIRTY, IS IT...?
COULDN'T YOU JUST... OH, *JEEZ!*
CALM YOUR-SELF...
DAD, THIS ISN'T ONE OF YOUR SCRUFFY DRINKING BUDDIES, OKAY?
YOU LEFT YOUR SWORD BACK AT THE HUT...
HE DIDN'T EVEN SEE ME YESTER-DAY...
PLUS, THERE'S NO REASON FOR HIM TO BE ON GUARD...
AND I'VE CHANGED, A LOT, THESE LAST TWO YEARS.

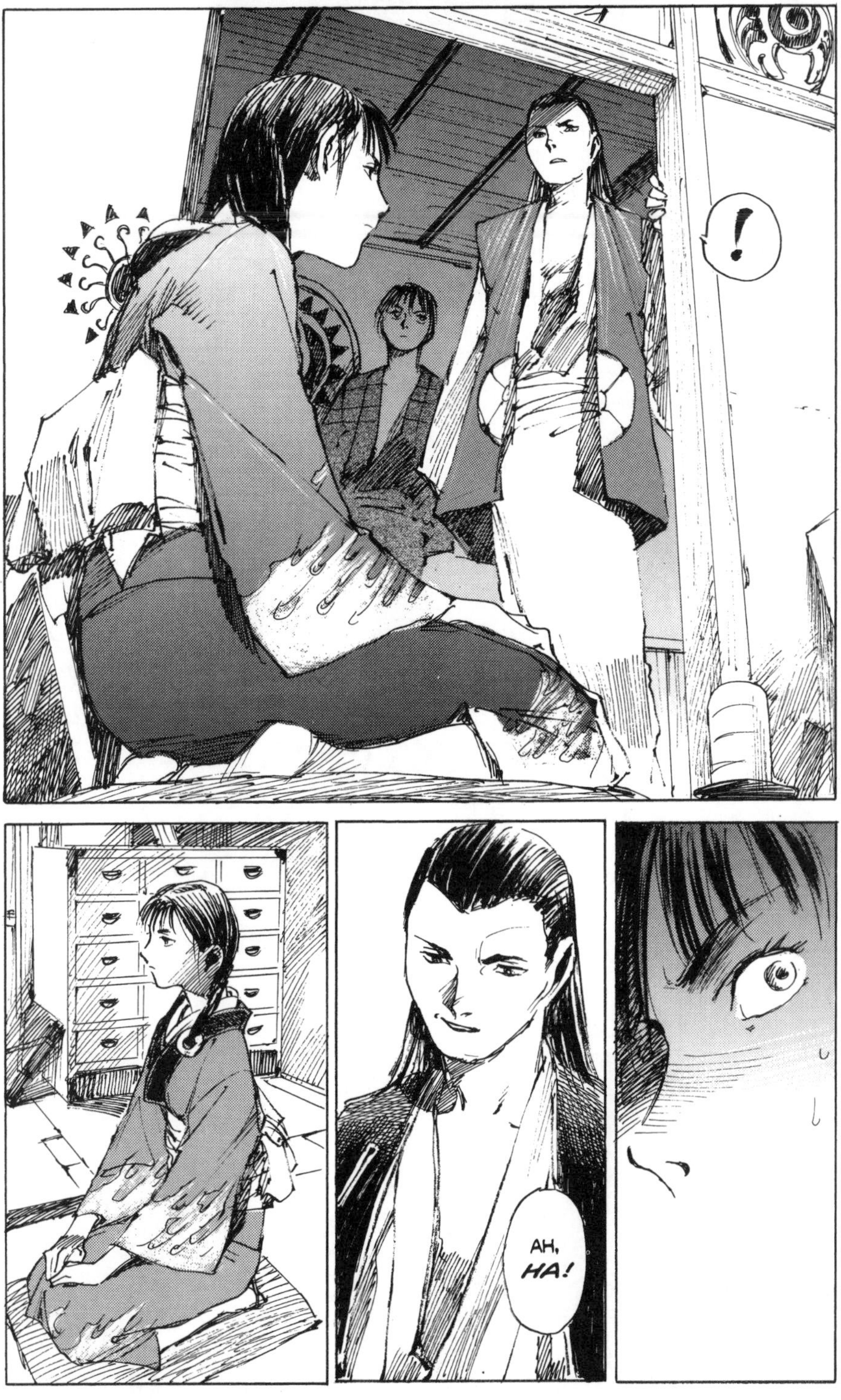
!
AH, HA!

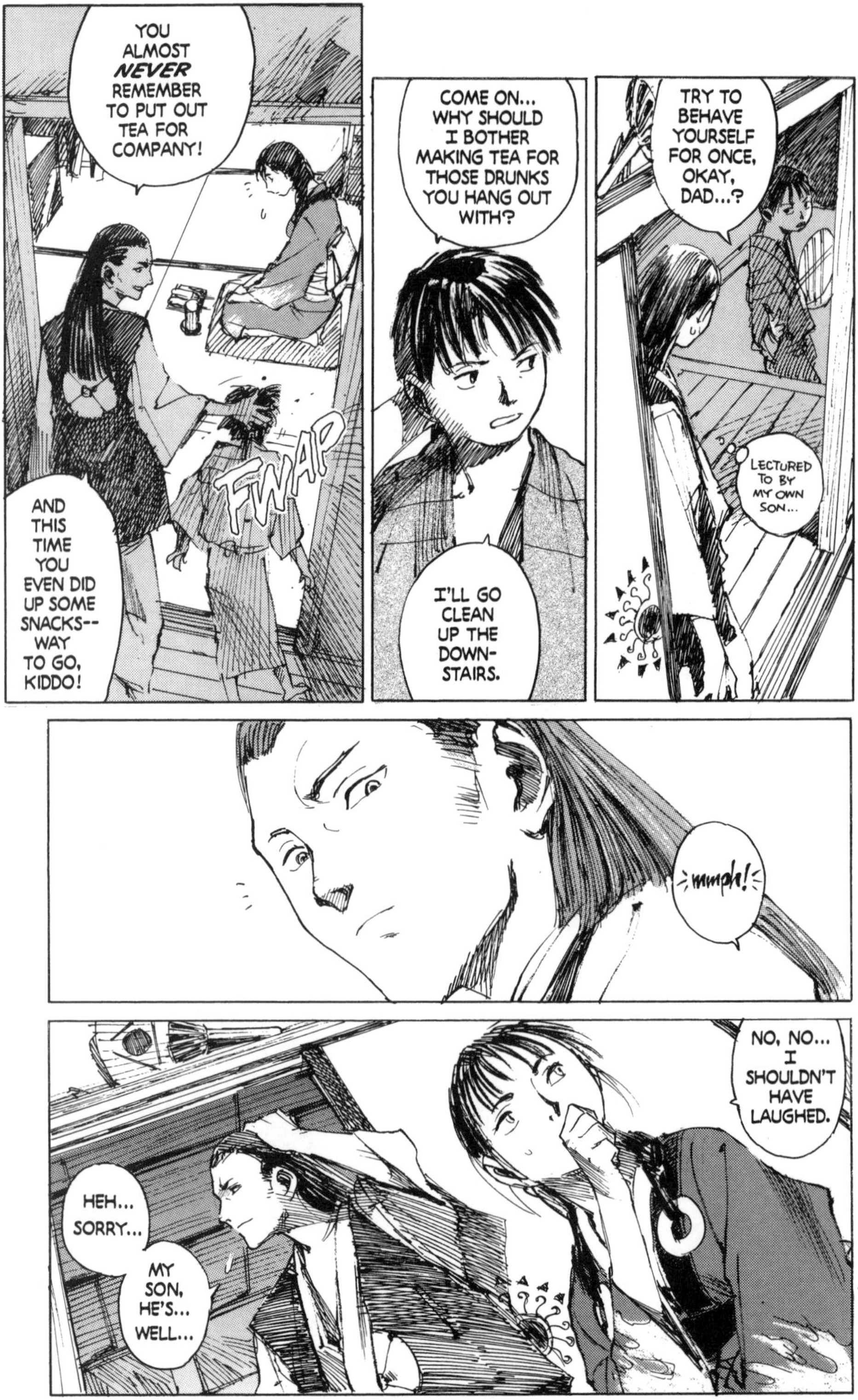
YOU ALMOST *NEVER* REMEMBER TO PUT OUT TEA FOR COMPANY!
FWAP
AND THIS TIME YOU EVEN DID UP SOME SNACKS-- WAY TO GO, KIDDO!
COME ON... WHY SHOULD I BOTHER MAKING TEA FOR THOSE DRUNKS YOU HANG OUT WITH?
I'LL GO CLEAN UP THE DOWN-STAIRS.
TRY TO BEHAVE YOURSELF FOR ONCE, OKAY, DAD...?
LECTURED TO BY MY OWN SON...
mmph!
HEH... SORRY...
MY SON, HE'S... WELL...
NO, NO... I SHOULDN'T HAVE LAUGHED.

THE AMAZING THING IS...

...THIS IS THE CLEANEST ROOM IN THE HOUSE. YOU MUST BE SHOCKED.

OH, NO, NO.

THIS IS WHERE I MAKE ALL MY MASKS...

...SO AT LEAST THERE'S AN EXCUSE FOR THE MESS.

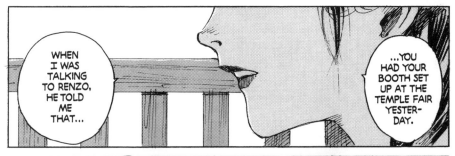

WHEN I WAS TALKING TO RENZO, HE TOLD ME THAT...

...YOU HAD YOUR BOOTH SET UP AT THE TEMPLE FAIR YESTER-DAY.

I WOULDN'T HAVE THOUGHT YOU'D BE BACK AT WORK THE VERY NEXT MORNING.

YEAH... SEEING HOW I LIVE, YOU WOULDN'T BELIEVE IT, BUT I'M A BIT OF A WORK-AHOLIC.

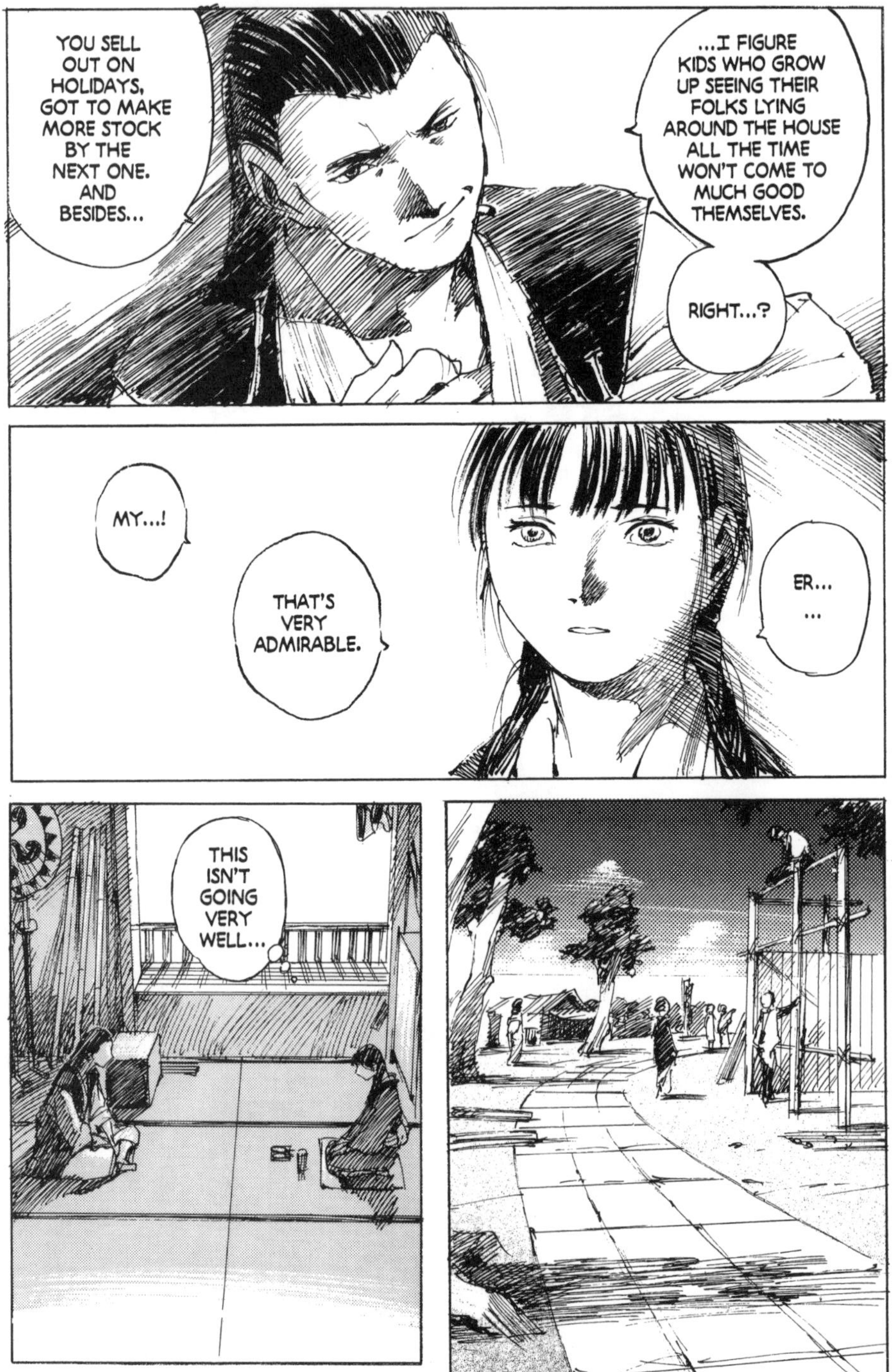
YOU SELL OUT ON HOLIDAYS, GOT TO MAKE MORE STOCK BY THE NEXT ONE. AND BESIDES...
...I FIGURE KIDS WHO GROW UP SEEING THEIR FOLKS LYING AROUND THE HOUSE ALL THE TIME WON'T COME TO MUCH GOOD THEMSELVES.
RIGHT...?
ER... ...
MY...!
THAT'S VERY ADMIRABLE.
THIS ISN'T GOING VERY WELL...

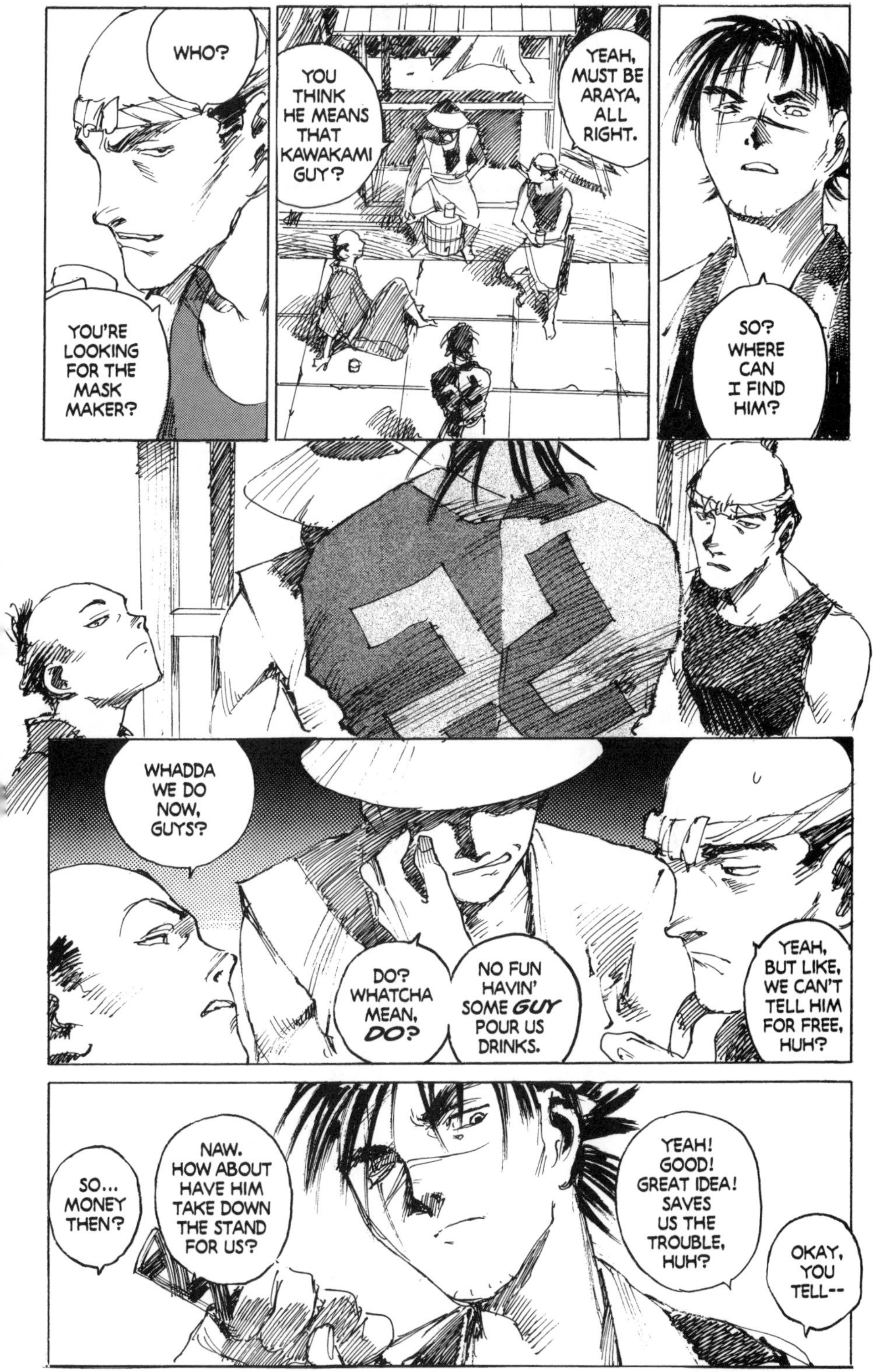
WHO?
YOU'RE LOOKING FOR THE MASK MAKER?
YOU THINK HE MEANS THAT KAWAKAMI GUY?
YEAH, MUST BE ARAYA, ALL RIGHT.
SO? WHERE CAN I FIND HIM?
WHADDA WE DO NOW, GUYS?
DO? WHATCHA MEAN, *DO*?
NO FUN HAVIN' SOME *GUY* POUR US DRINKS.
YEAH, BUT LIKE, WE CAN'T TELL HIM FOR FREE, HUH?
SO... MONEY THEN?
NAW. HOW ABOUT HAVE HIM TAKE DOWN THE STAND FOR US?
YEAH! GOOD! GREAT IDEA! SAVES US THE TROUBLE, HUH?
OKAY, YOU TELL--

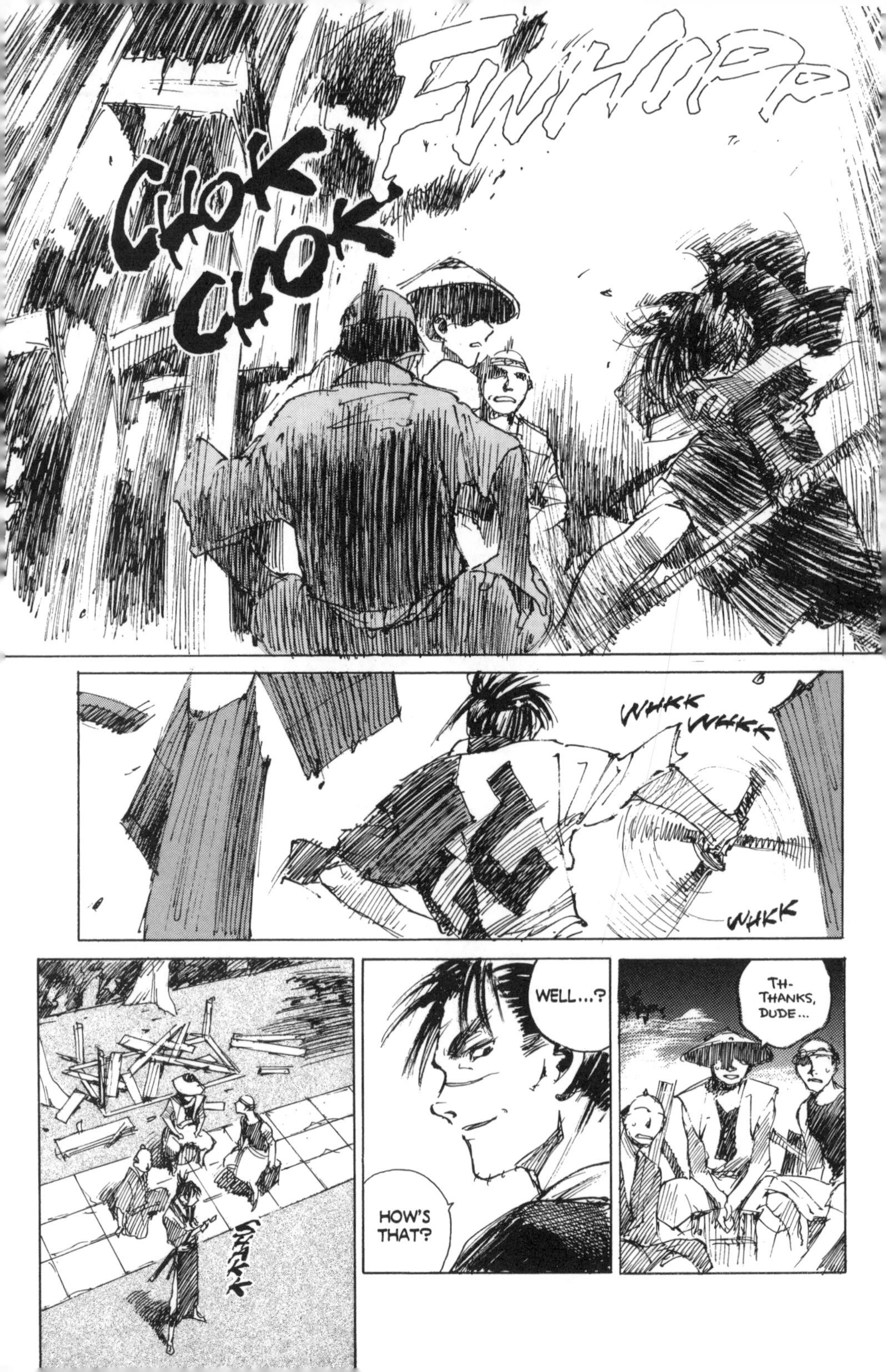
FWHIPP
CHOK
CHOK
WHKK
WHKK
WHKK
WELL...?
HOW'S THAT?
TH-THANKS, DUDE...

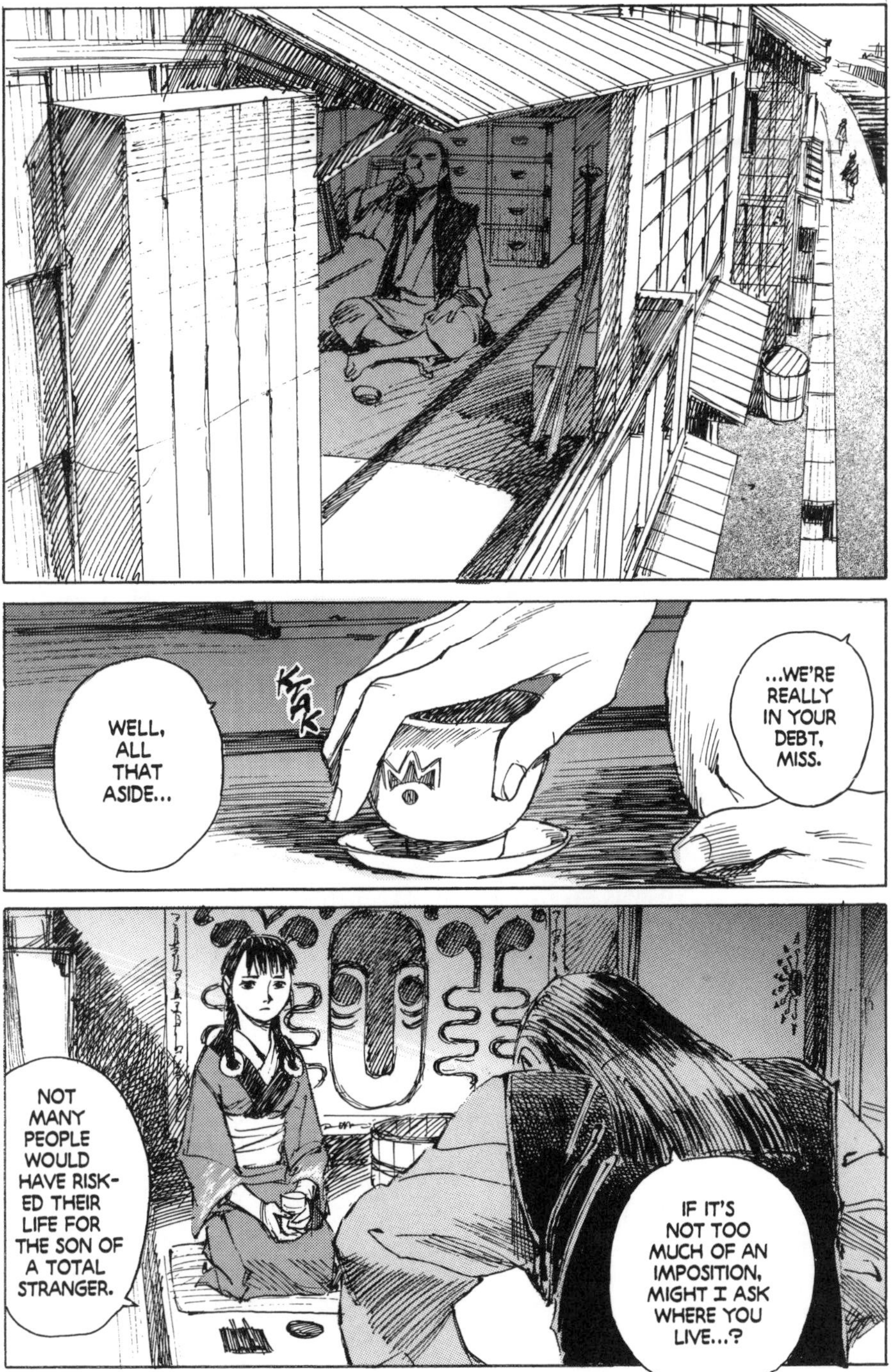
...WE'RE REALLY IN YOUR DEBT, MISS.
KTAK
WELL, ALL THAT ASIDE...
NOT MANY PEOPLE WOULD HAVE RISK-ED THEIR LIFE FOR THE SON OF A TOTAL STRANGER.
IF IT'S NOT TOO MUCH OF AN IMPOSITION, MIGHT I ASK WHERE YOU LIVE...?

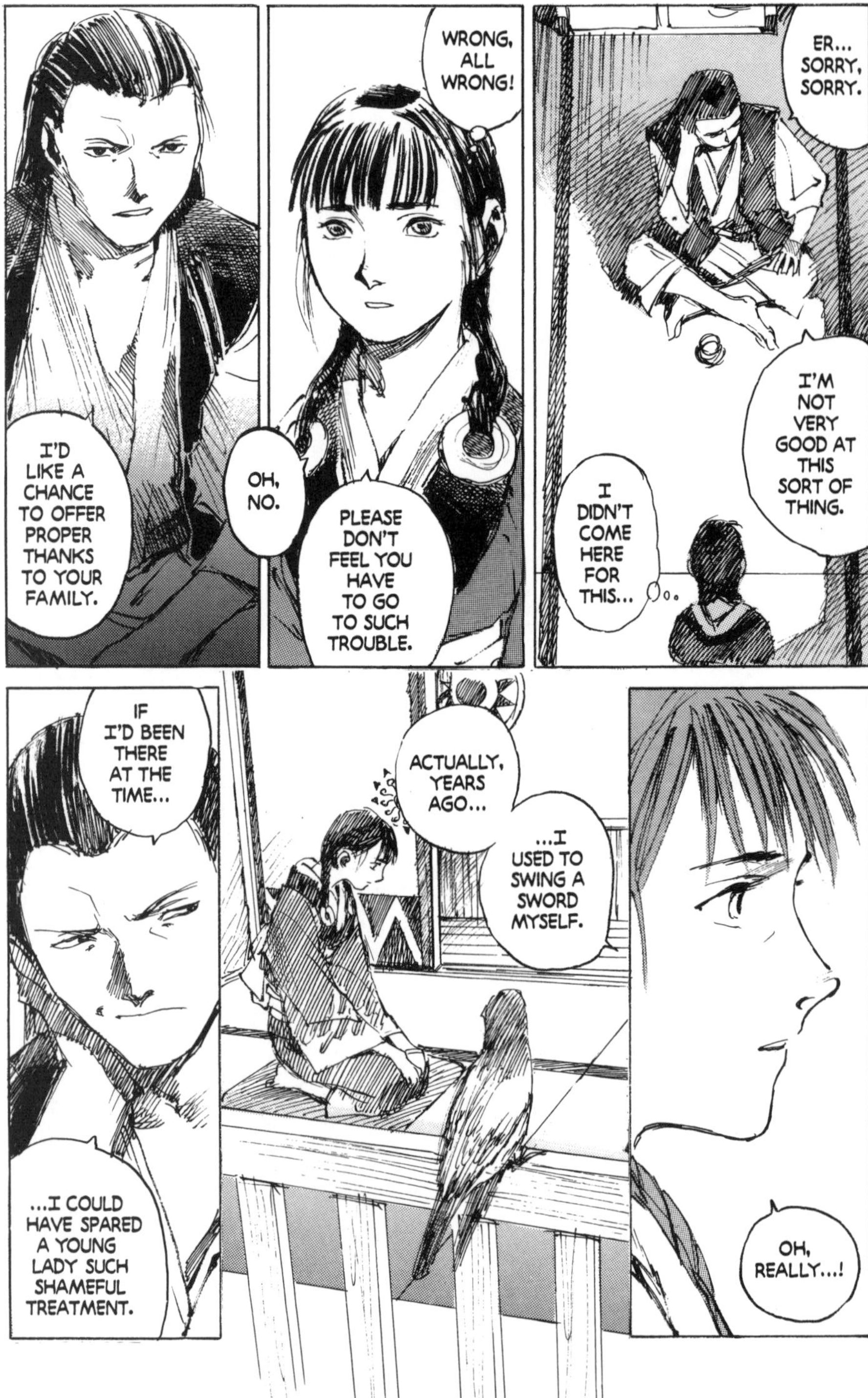
I'D LIKE A CHANCE TO OFFER PROPER THANKS TO YOUR FAMILY.
WRONG, ALL WRONG!
OH, NO.
PLEASE DON'T FEEL YOU HAVE TO GO TO SUCH TROUBLE.
ER... SORRY, SORRY.
I'M NOT VERY GOOD AT THIS SORT OF THING.
I DIDN'T COME HERE FOR THIS...
IF I'D BEEN THERE AT THE TIME...
...I COULD HAVE SPARED A YOUNG LADY SUCH SHAMEFUL TREATMENT.
ACTUALLY, YEARS AGO...
...I USED TO SWING A SWORD MYSELF.
OH, REALLY...!

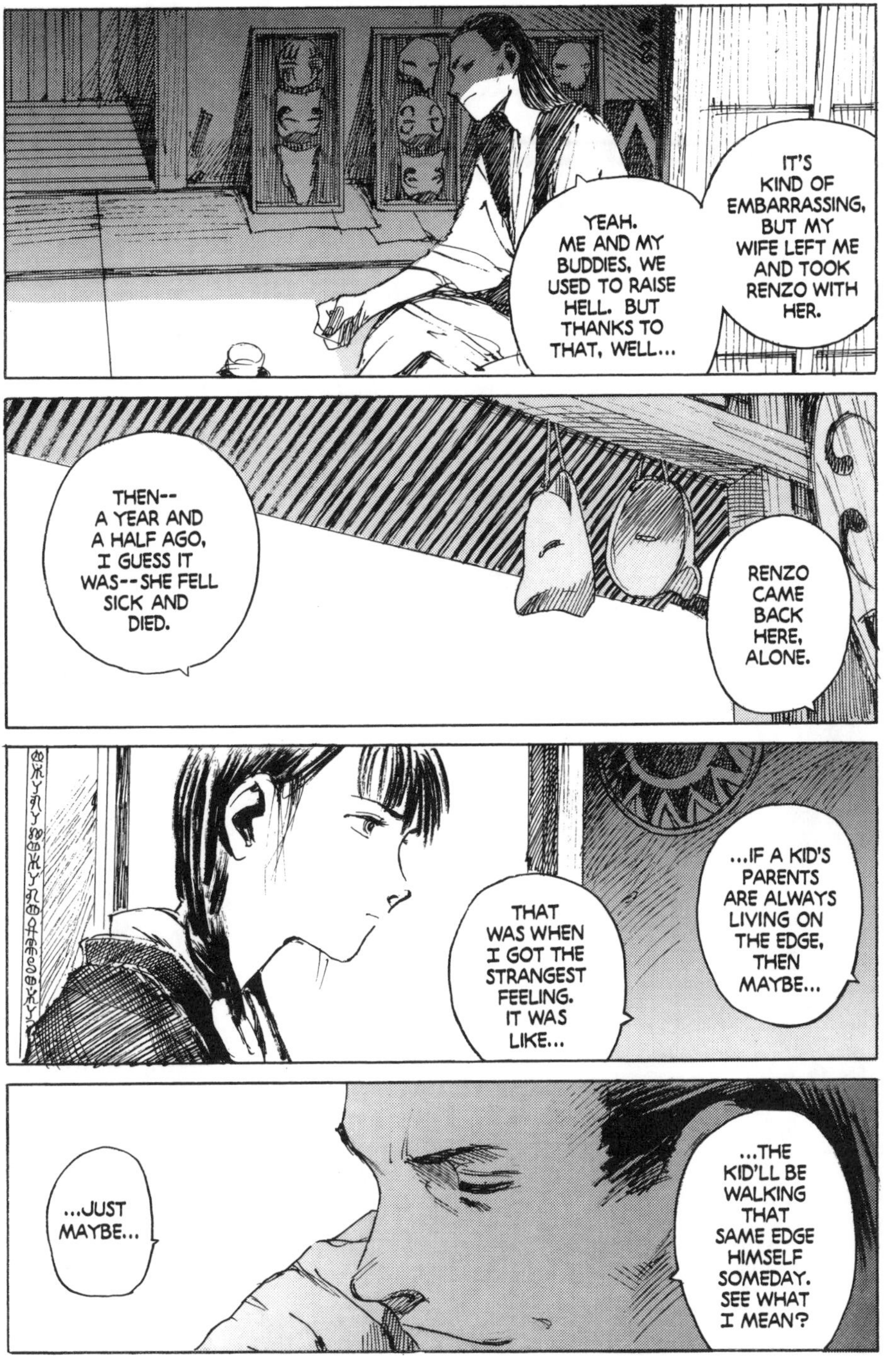
YEAH. ME AND MY BUDDIES, WE USED TO RAISE HELL. BUT THANKS TO THAT, WELL...
IT'S KIND OF EMBARRASSING, BUT MY WIFE LEFT ME AND TOOK RENZO WITH HER.
THEN-- A YEAR AND A HALF AGO, I GUESS IT WAS--SHE FELL SICK AND DIED.
RENZO CAME BACK HERE, ALONE.
THAT WAS WHEN I GOT THE STRANGEST FEELING. IT WAS LIKE...
...IF A KID'S PARENTS ARE ALWAYS LIVING ON THE EDGE, THEN MAYBE...
...JUST MAYBE...
...THE KID'LL BE WALKING THAT SAME EDGE HIMSELF SOMEDAY. SEE WHAT I MEAN?

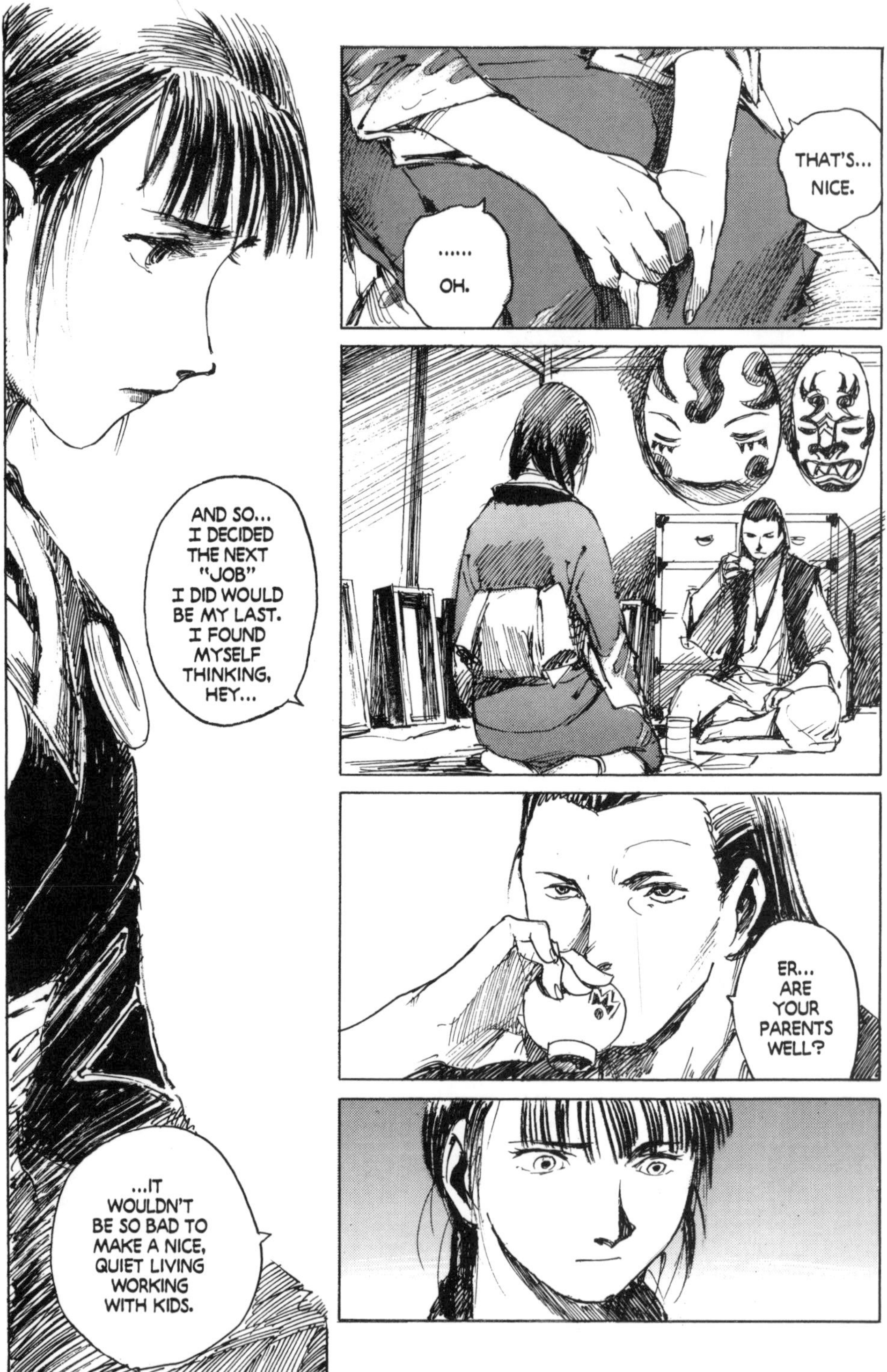
AND SO... I DECIDED THE NEXT "JOB" I DID WOULD BE MY LAST. I FOUND MYSELF THINKING, HEY...
...IT WOULDN'T BE SO BAD TO MAKE A NICE, QUIET LIVING WORKING WITH KIDS.
...... OH.
THAT'S... NICE.
ER... ARE YOUR PARENTS WELL?

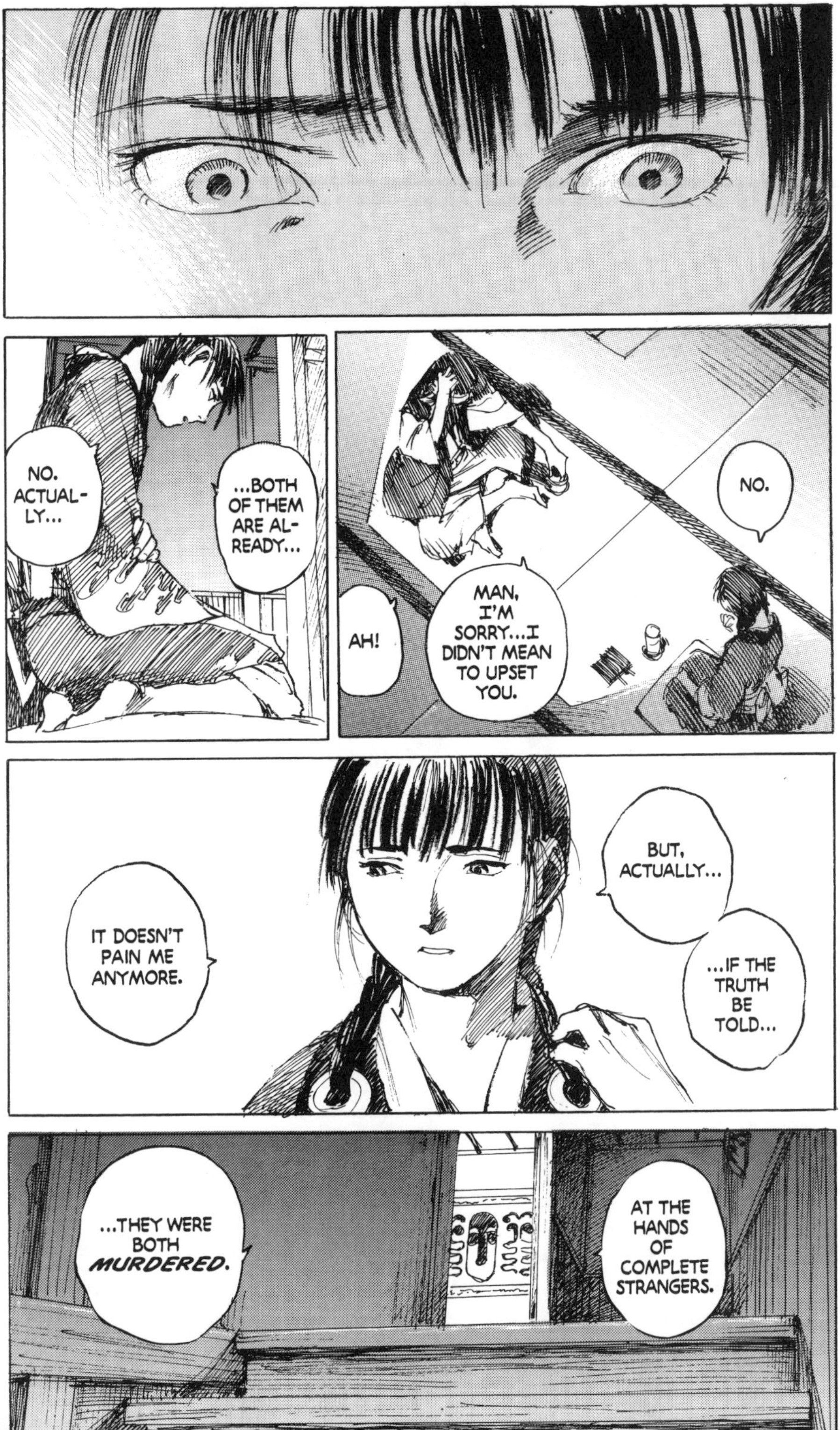
NO. ACTUAL-LY...
...BOTH OF THEM ARE AL-READY...
AH!
MAN, I'M SORRY...I DIDN'T MEAN TO UPSET YOU.
NO.
IT DOESN'T PAIN ME ANYMORE.
BUT, ACTUALLY...
...IF THE TRUTH BE TOLD...
...THEY WERE BOTH *MURDERED*.
AT THE HANDS OF COMPLETE STRANGERS.

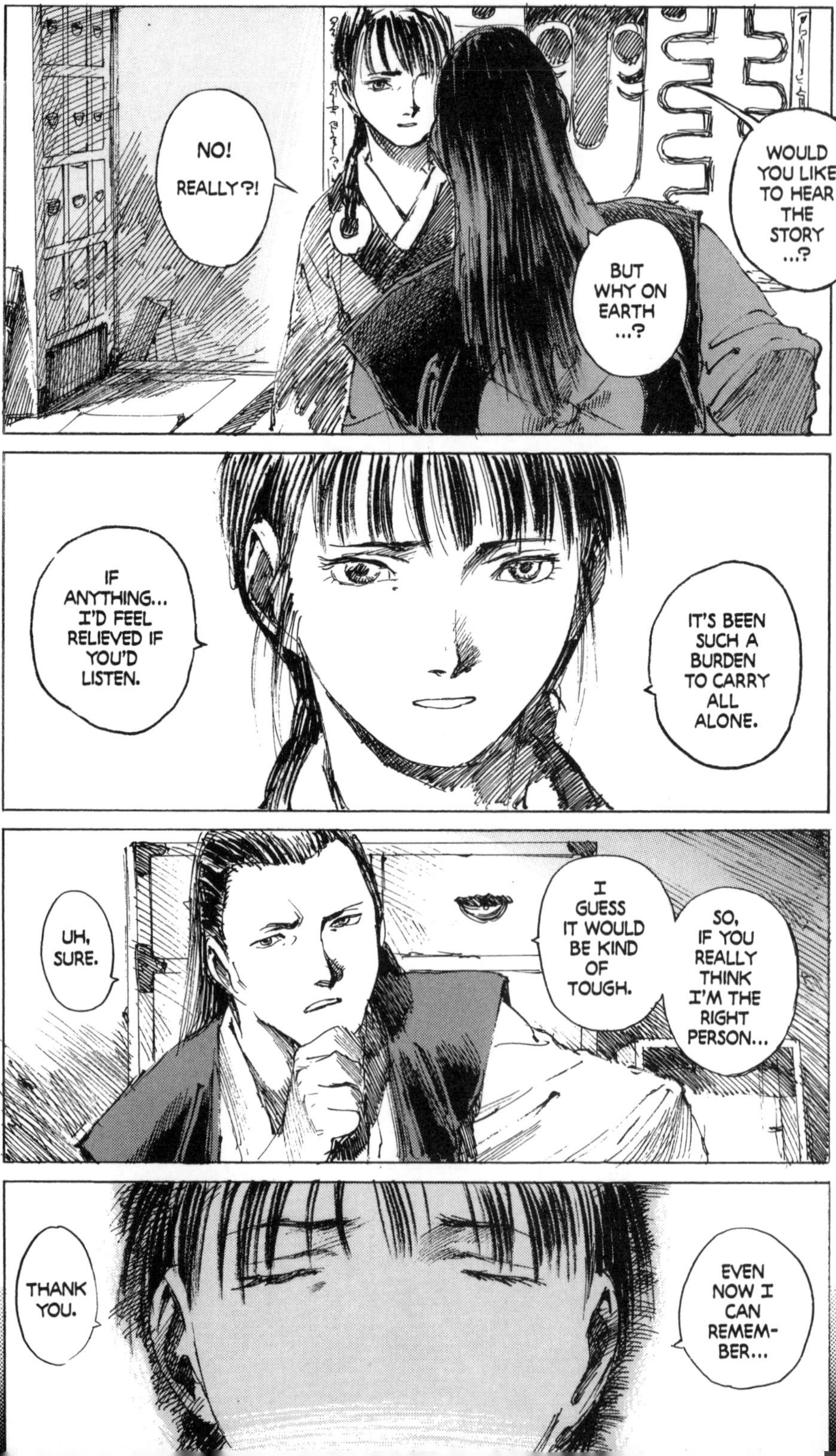
WOULD YOU LIKE TO HEAR THE STORY ...?
BUT WHY ON EARTH ...?
NO! REALLY?!
IT'S BEEN SUCH A BURDEN TO CARRY ALL ALONE.
IF ANYTHING... I'D FEEL RELIEVED IF YOU'D LISTEN.
SO, IF YOU REALLY THINK I'M THE RIGHT PERSON...
I GUESS IT WOULD BE KIND OF TOUGH.
UH, SURE.
EVEN NOW I CAN REMEM-BER...
THANK YOU.

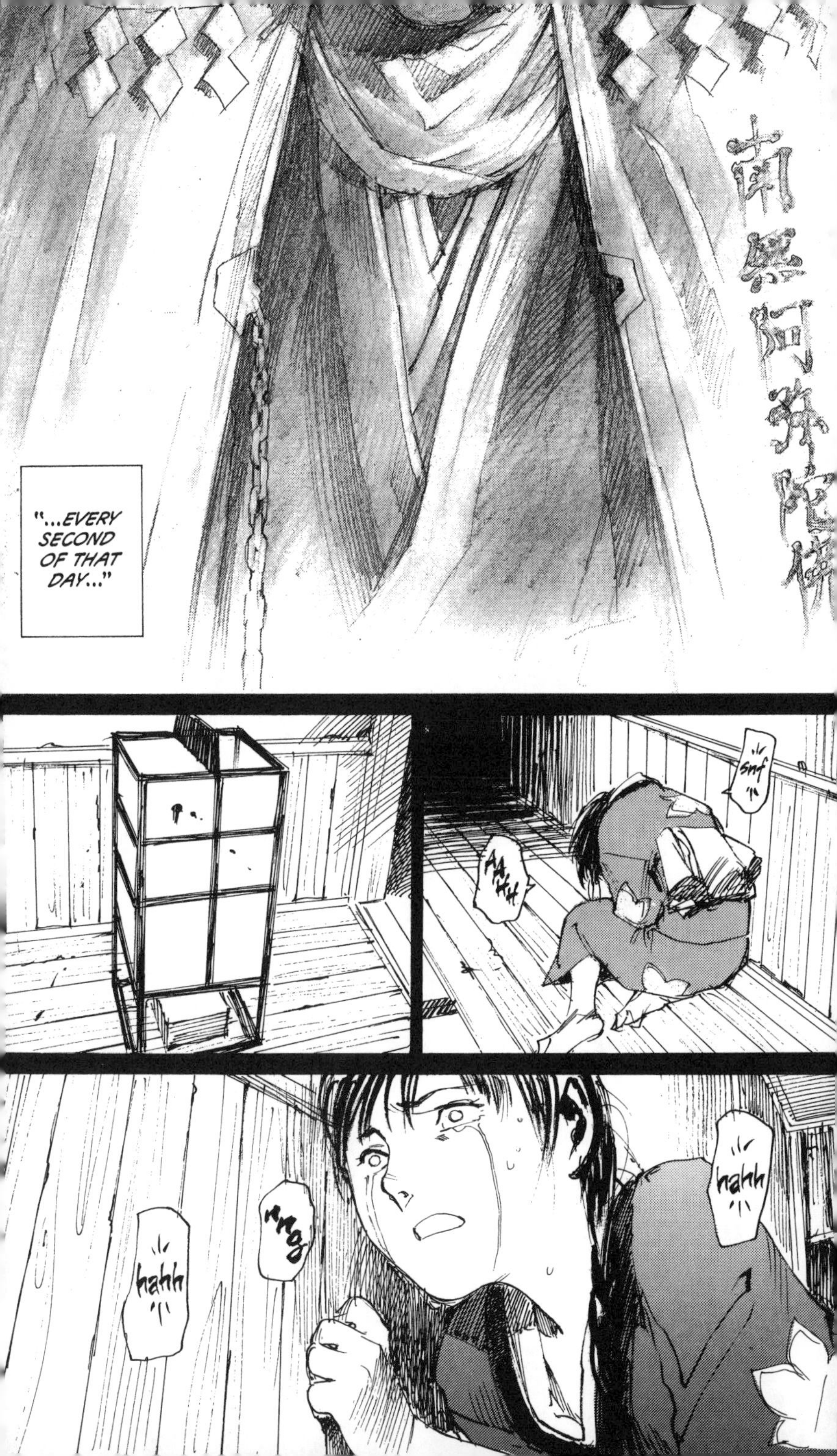
南無阿弥陀仏
"...EVERY SECOND OF THAT DAY..."
snf
AAHH
hahh
rrog
hahh

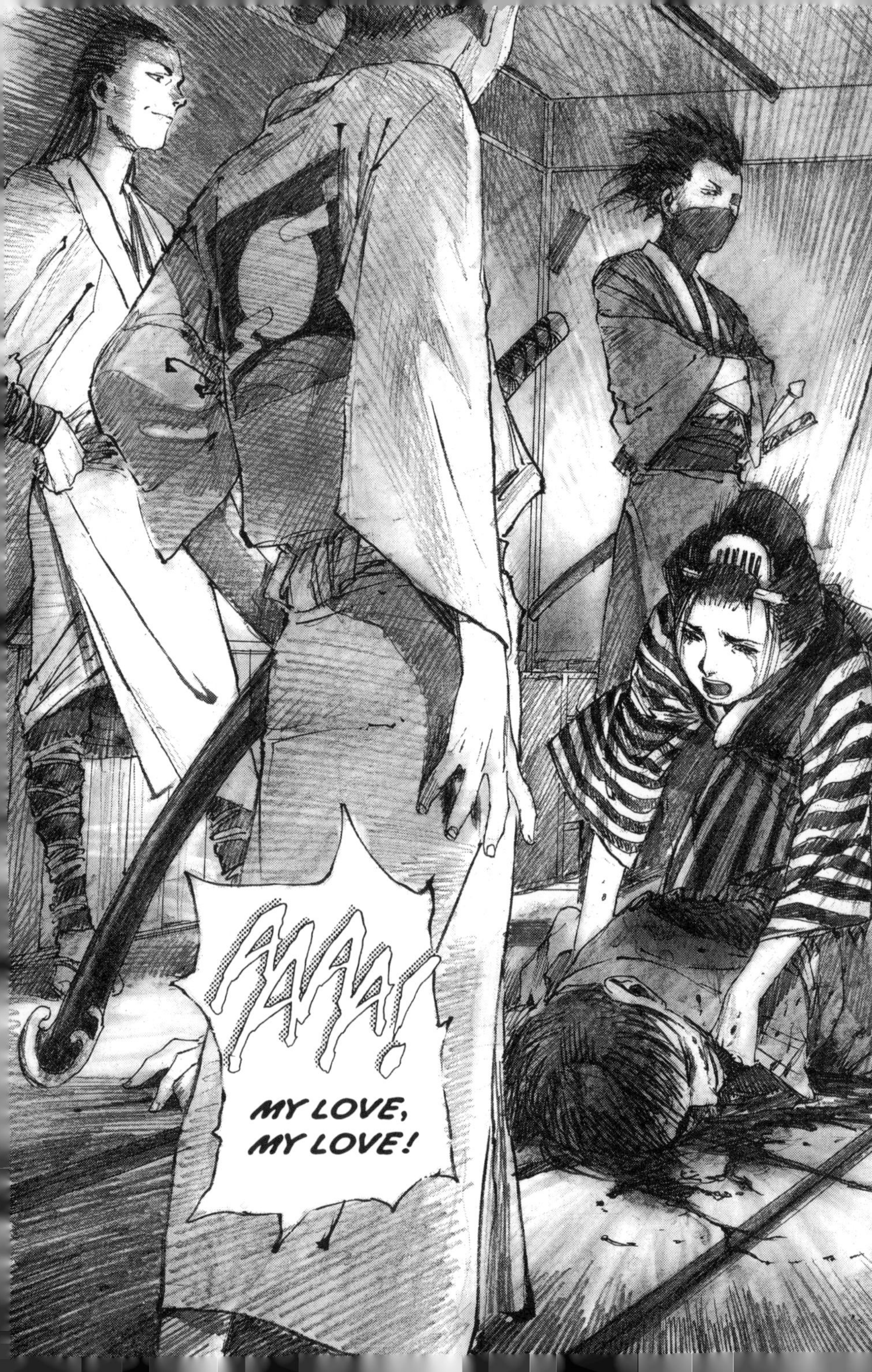
AAAA!
MY LOVE, MY LOVE!

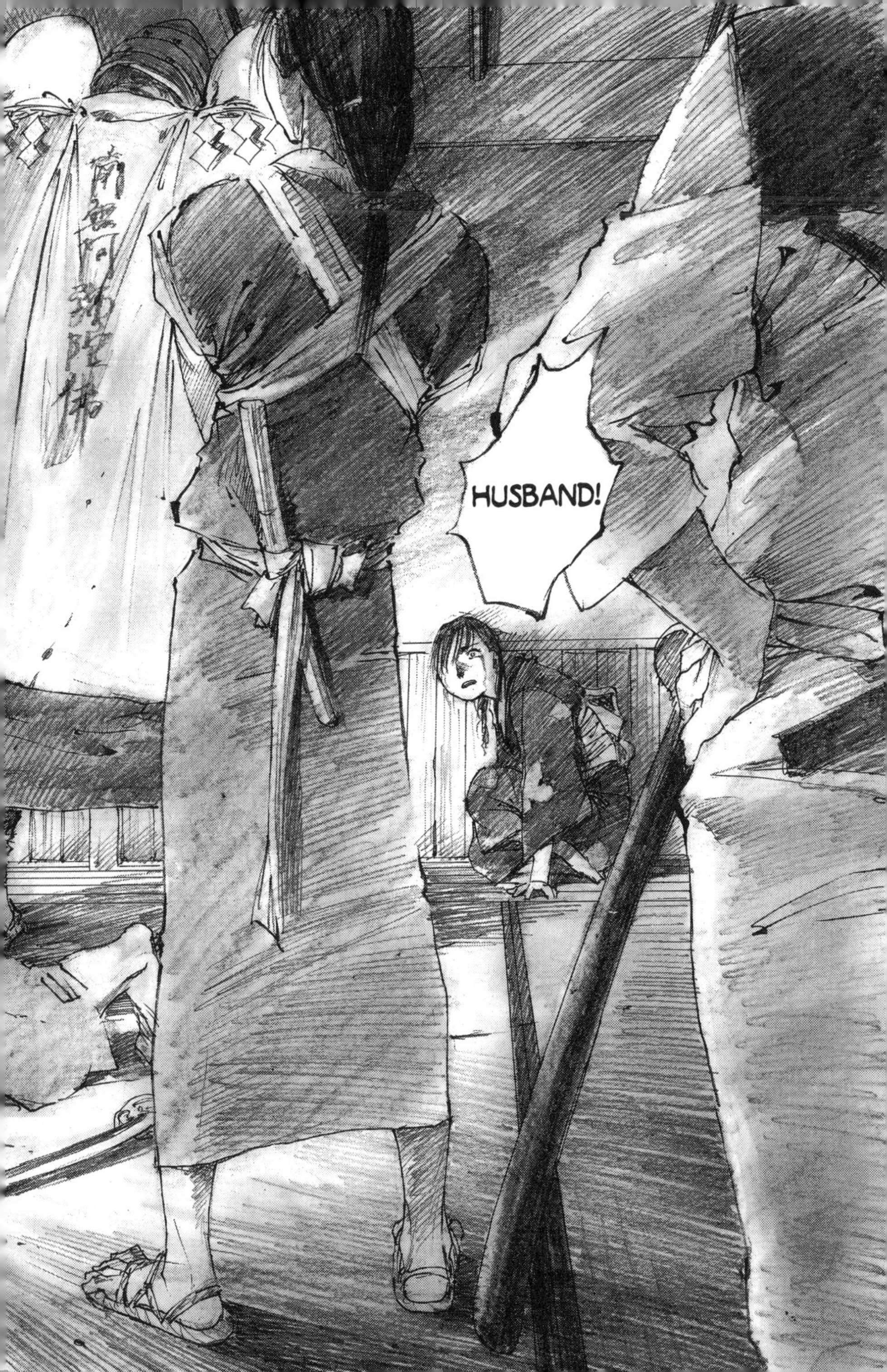
HUSBAND!

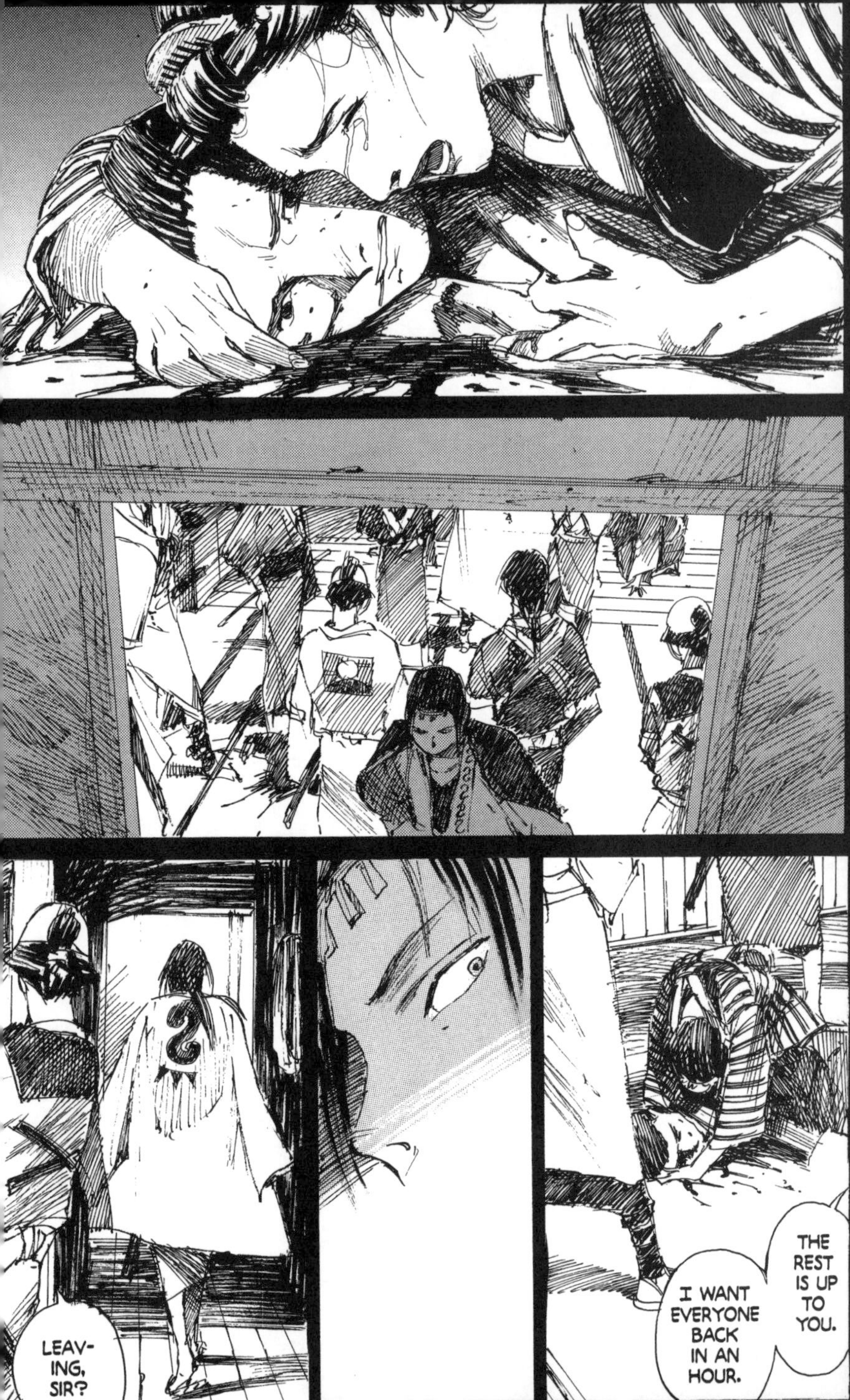
THE REST IS UP TO YOU.
I WANT EVERYONE BACK IN AN HOUR.
LEAV-ING, SIR?

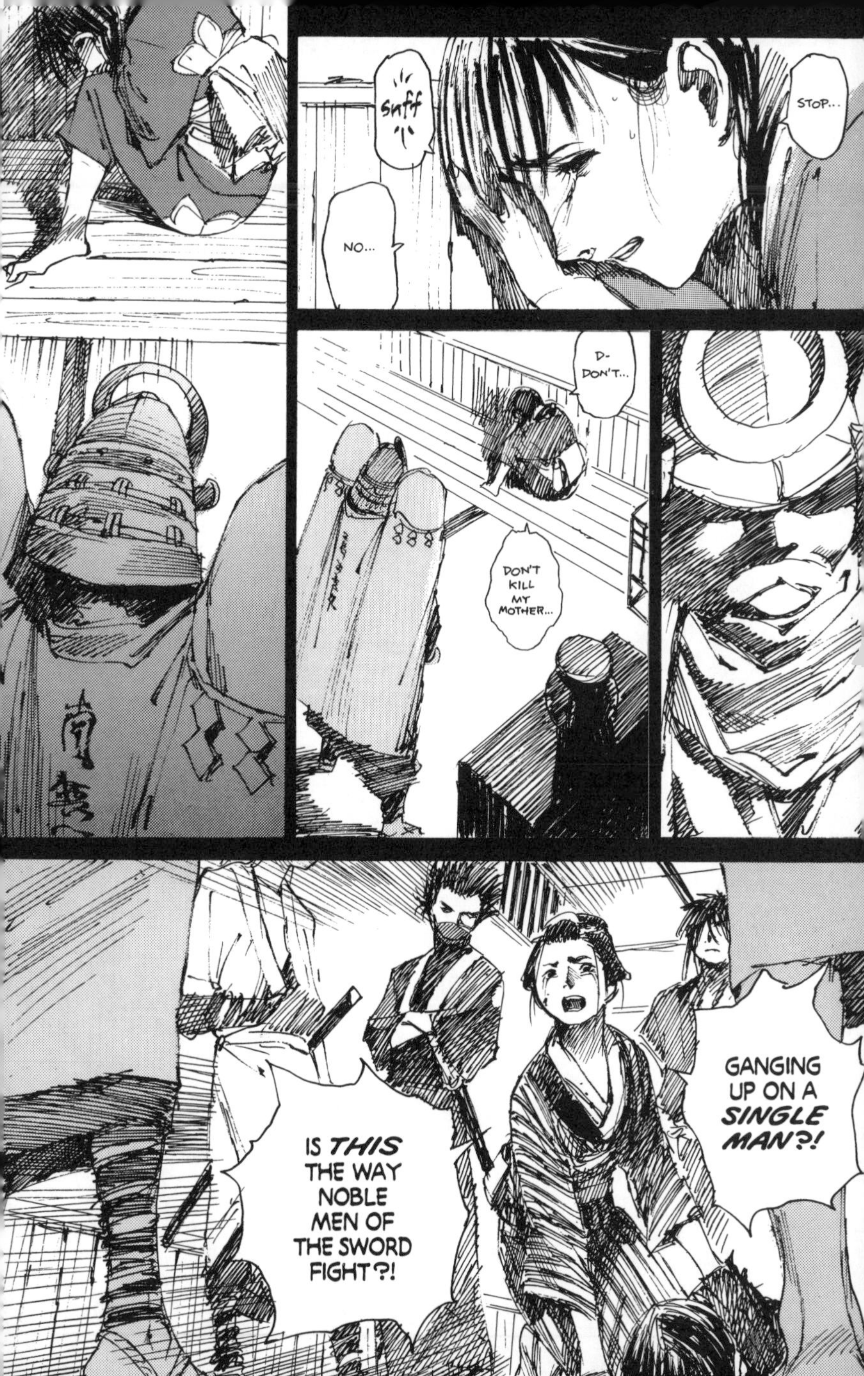
STOP...
snff
NO...
D- DON'T...
DON'T KILL MY MOTHER...
GANGING UP ON A *SINGLE MAN*?!
IS *THIS* THE WAY NOBLE MEN OF THE SWORD FIGHT?!

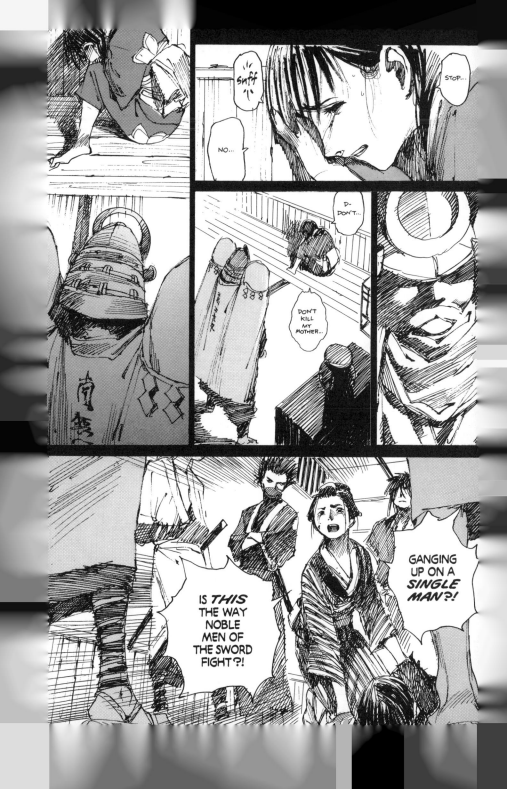

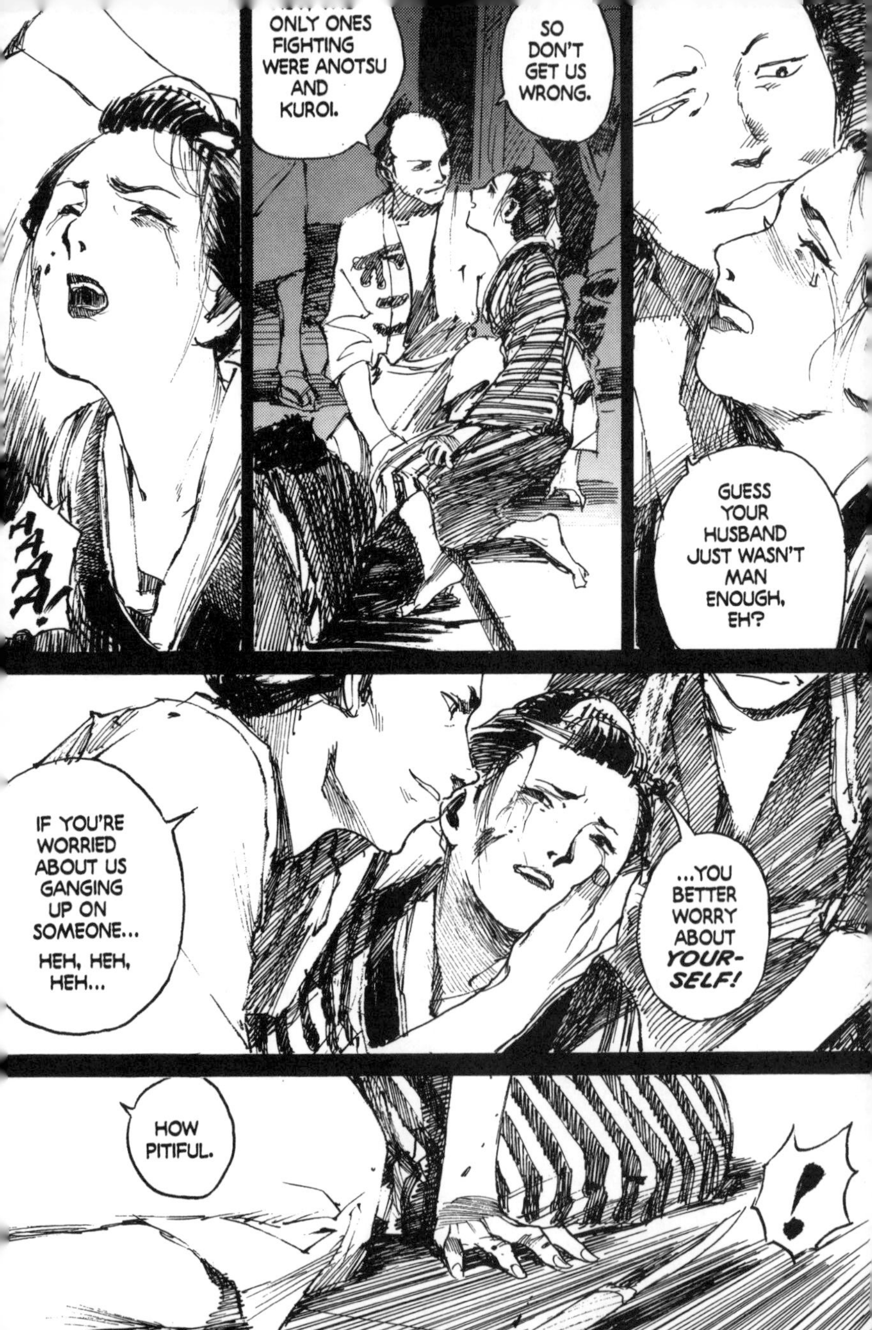
AAAA!
ONLY ONES FIGHTING WERE ANOTSU AND KUROI.
SO DON'T GET US WRONG.
GUESS YOUR HUSBAND JUST WASN'T MAN ENOUGH, EH?
IF YOU'RE WORRIED ABOUT US GANGING UP ON SOMEONE... HEH, HEH, HEH...
...YOU BETTER WORRY ABOUT ***YOURSELF!***
HOW PITIFUL.
!

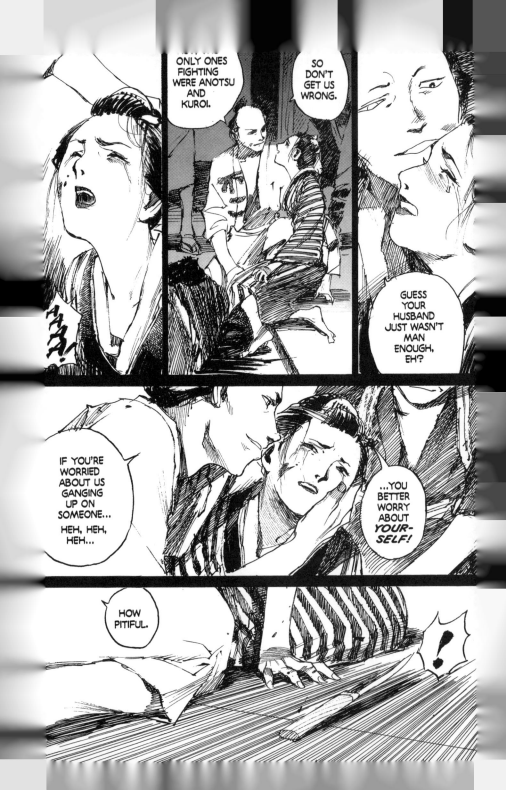

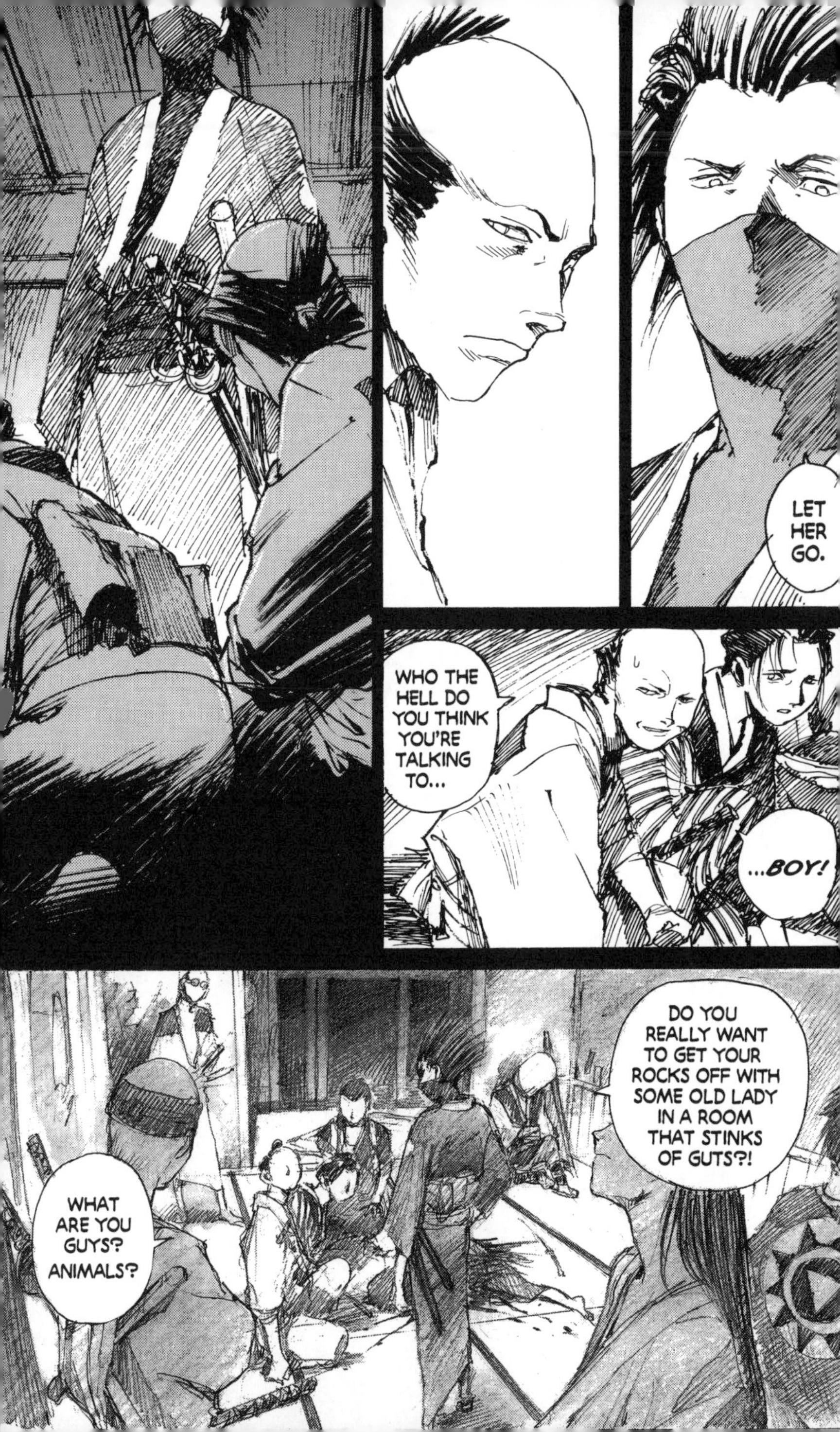
LET HER GO.
WHO THE HELL DO YOU THINK YOU'RE TALKING TO...
...BOY!
DO YOU REALLY WANT TO GET YOUR ROCKS OFF WITH SOME OLD LADY IN A ROOM THAT STINKS OF GUTS?!
WHAT ARE YOU GUYS? ANIMALS?

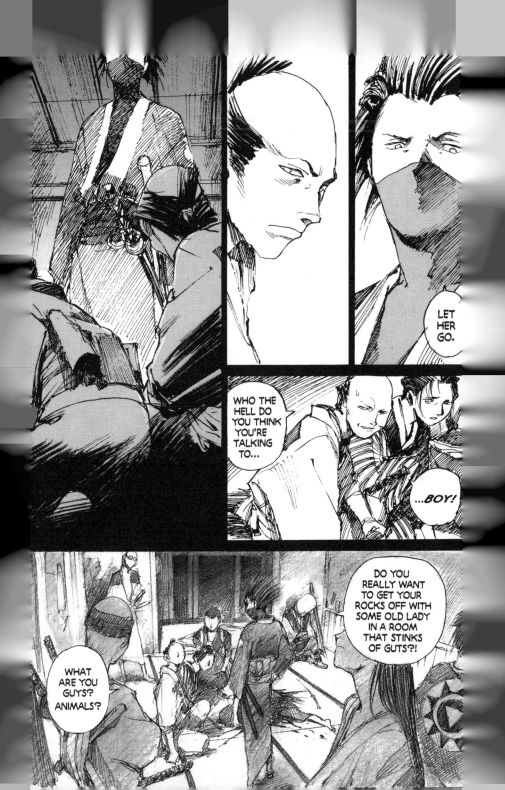

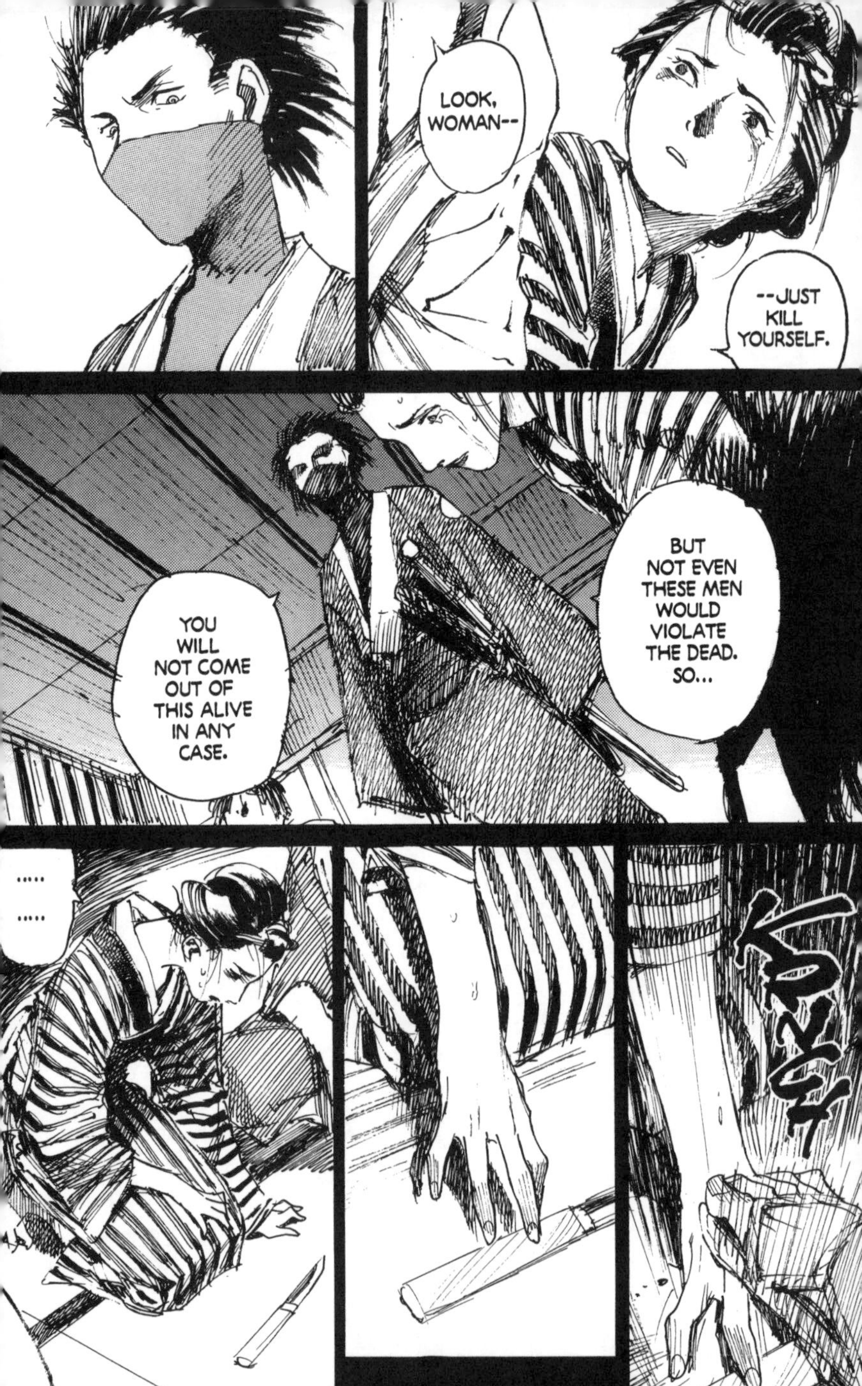
LOOK, WOMAN--
--JUST KILL YOURSELF.
BUT NOT EVEN THESE MEN WOULD VIOLATE THE DEAD. SO...
YOU WILL NOT COME OUT OF THIS ALIVE IN ANY CASE.
.....
.....

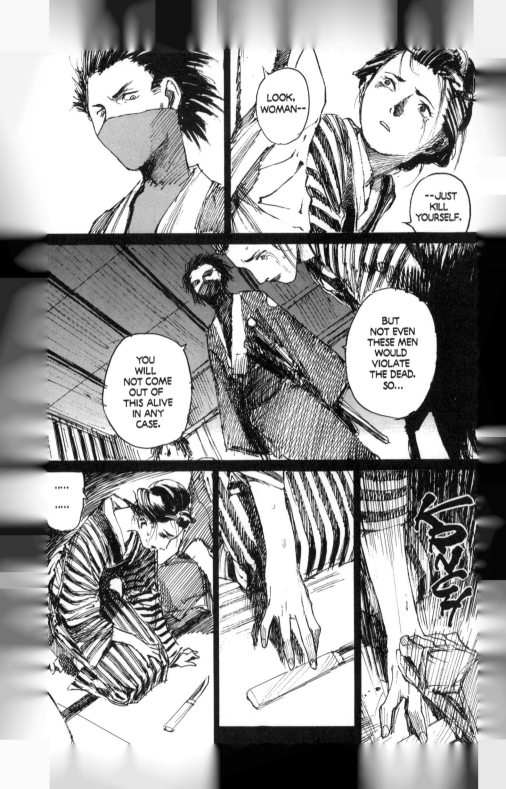

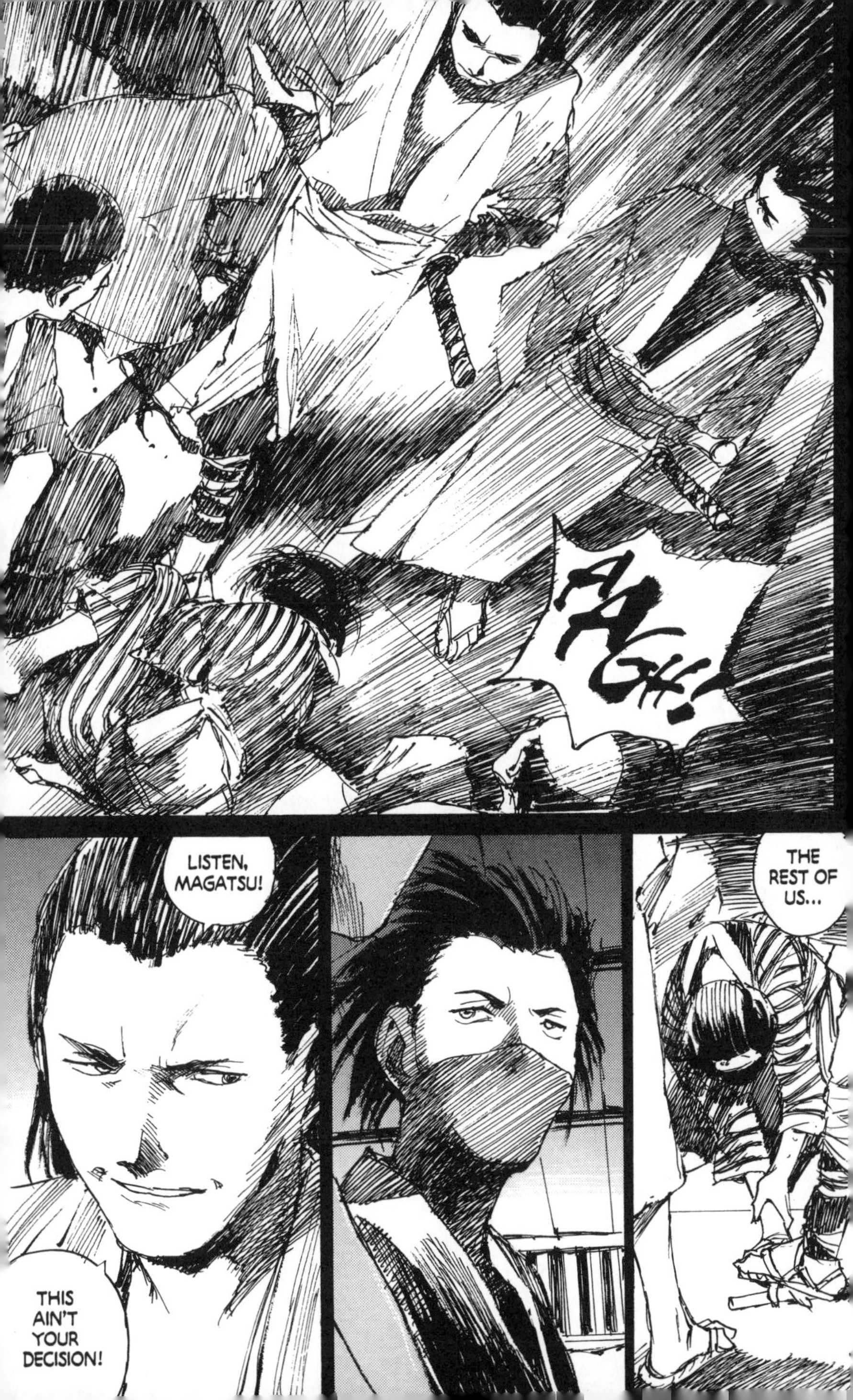
AGH!
THE REST OF US...
LISTEN, MAGATSU!
THIS AIN'T YOUR DECISION!

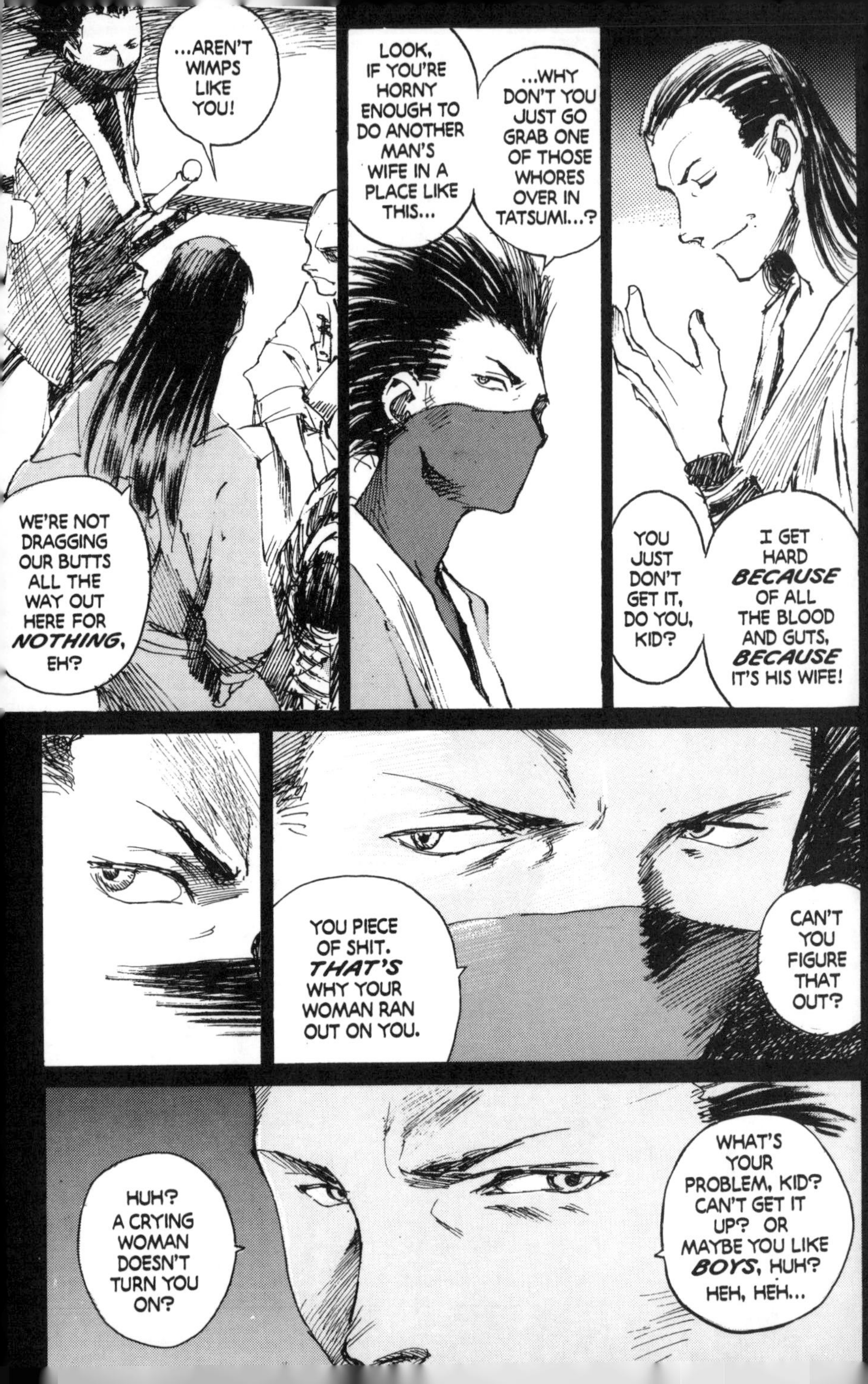
...AREN'T WIMPS LIKE YOU!
WE'RE NOT DRAGGING OUR BUTTS ALL THE WAY OUT HERE FOR ***NOTHING***, EH?
LOOK, IF YOU'RE HORNY ENOUGH TO DO ANOTHER MAN'S WIFE IN A PLACE LIKE THIS...
...WHY DON'T YOU JUST GO GRAB ONE OF THOSE WHORES OVER IN TATSUMI...?
YOU JUST DON'T GET IT, DO YOU, KID?
I GET HARD ***BECAUSE*** OF ALL THE BLOOD AND GUTS, ***BECAUSE*** IT'S HIS WIFE!
YOU PIECE OF SHIT. ***THAT'S*** WHY YOUR WOMAN RAN OUT ON YOU.
CAN'T YOU FIGURE THAT OUT?
HUH? A CRYING WOMAN DOESN'T TURN YOU ON?
WHAT'S YOUR PROBLEM, KID? CAN'T GET IT UP? OR MAYBE YOU LIKE ***BOYS***, HUH? HEH, HEH...

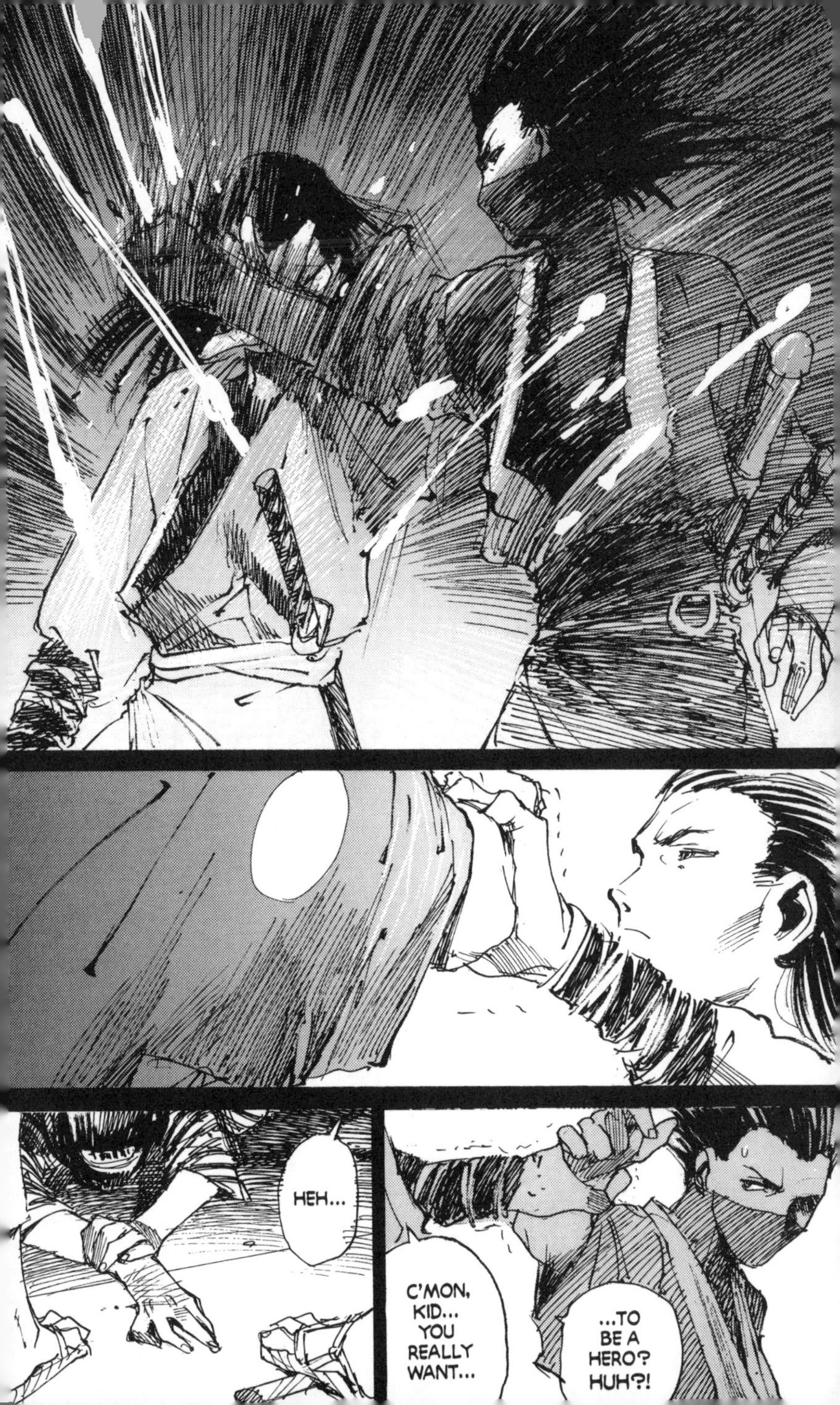
C'MON, KID... YOU REALLY WANT...
...TO BE A HERO? HUH?!
HEH...

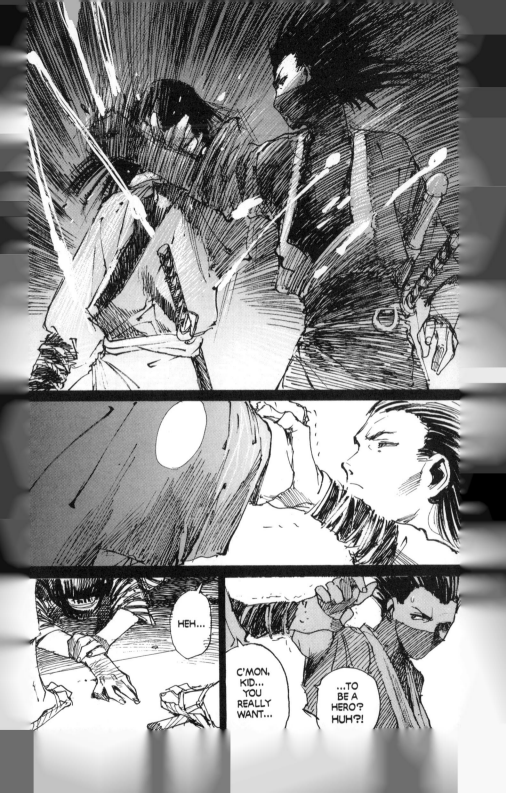

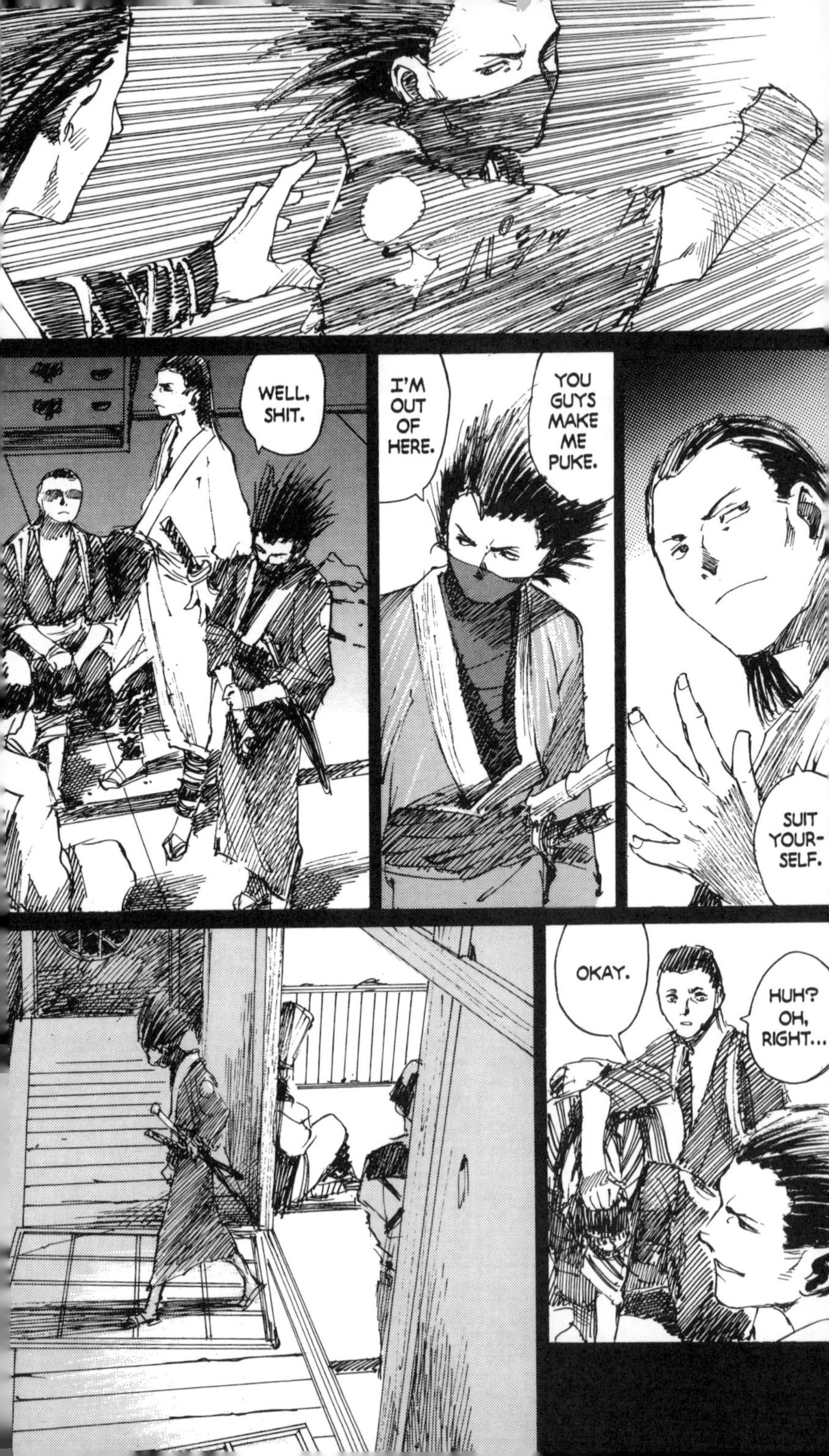
SUIT YOUR-SELF.
YOU GUYS MAKE ME PUKE.
I'M OUT OF HERE.
WELL, SHIT.
OKAY.
HUH? OH, RIGHT...

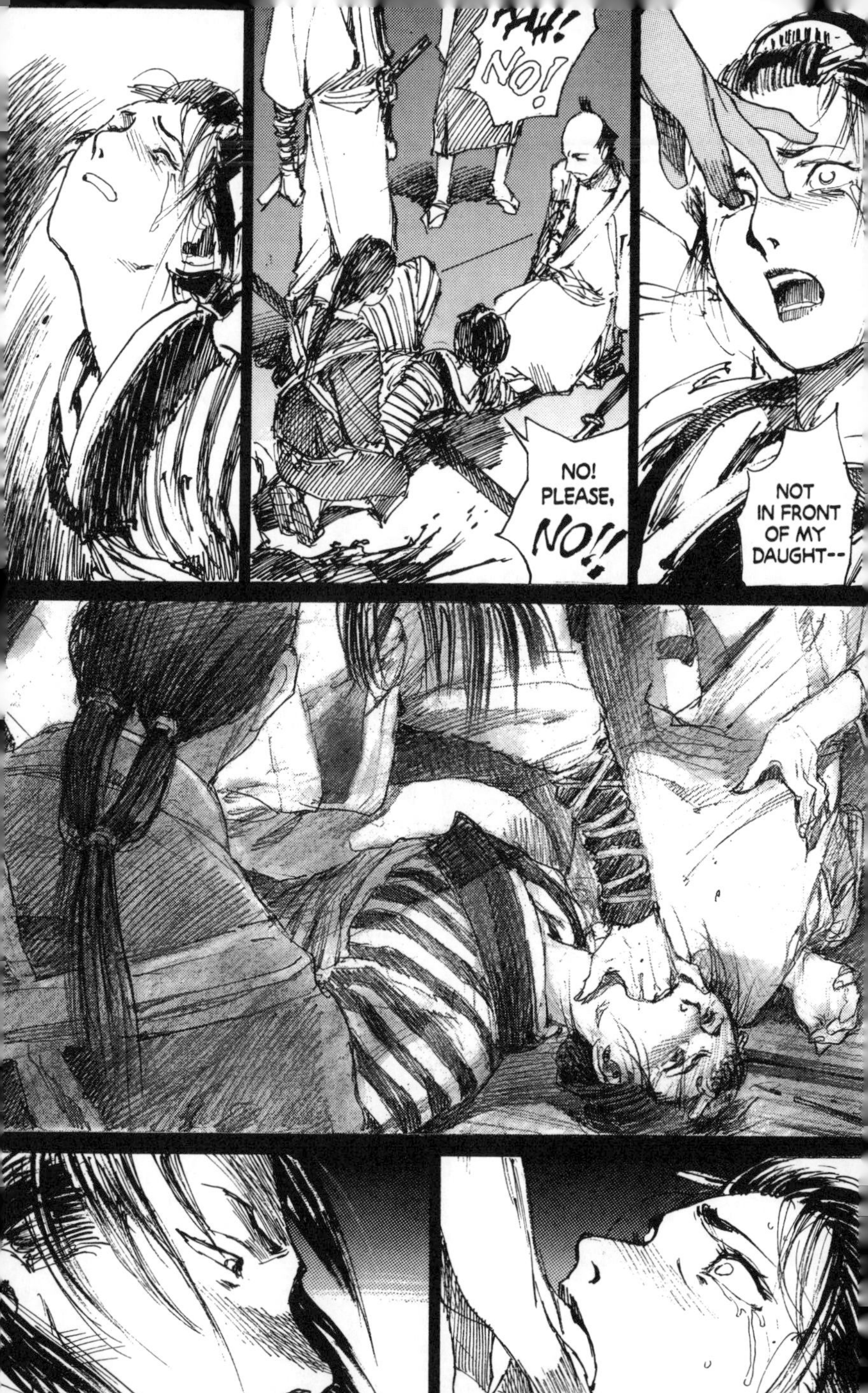
NOT IN FRONT OF MY DAUGHT--
NO!
NO! PLEASE, NO!!

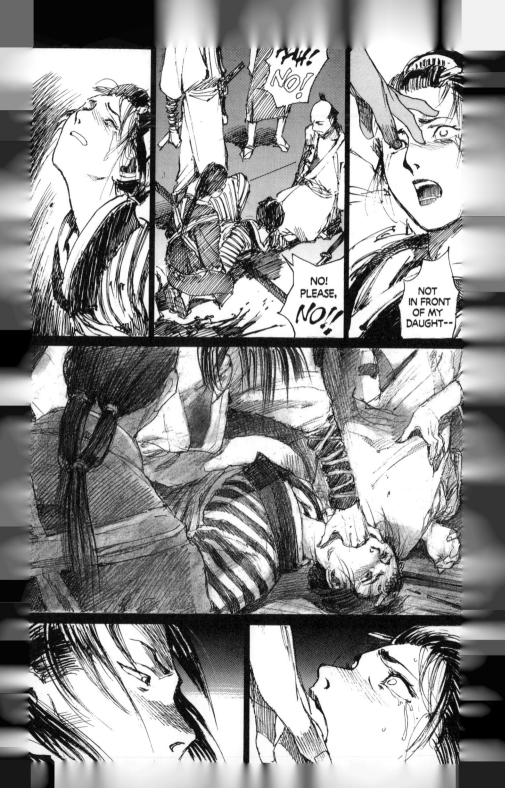

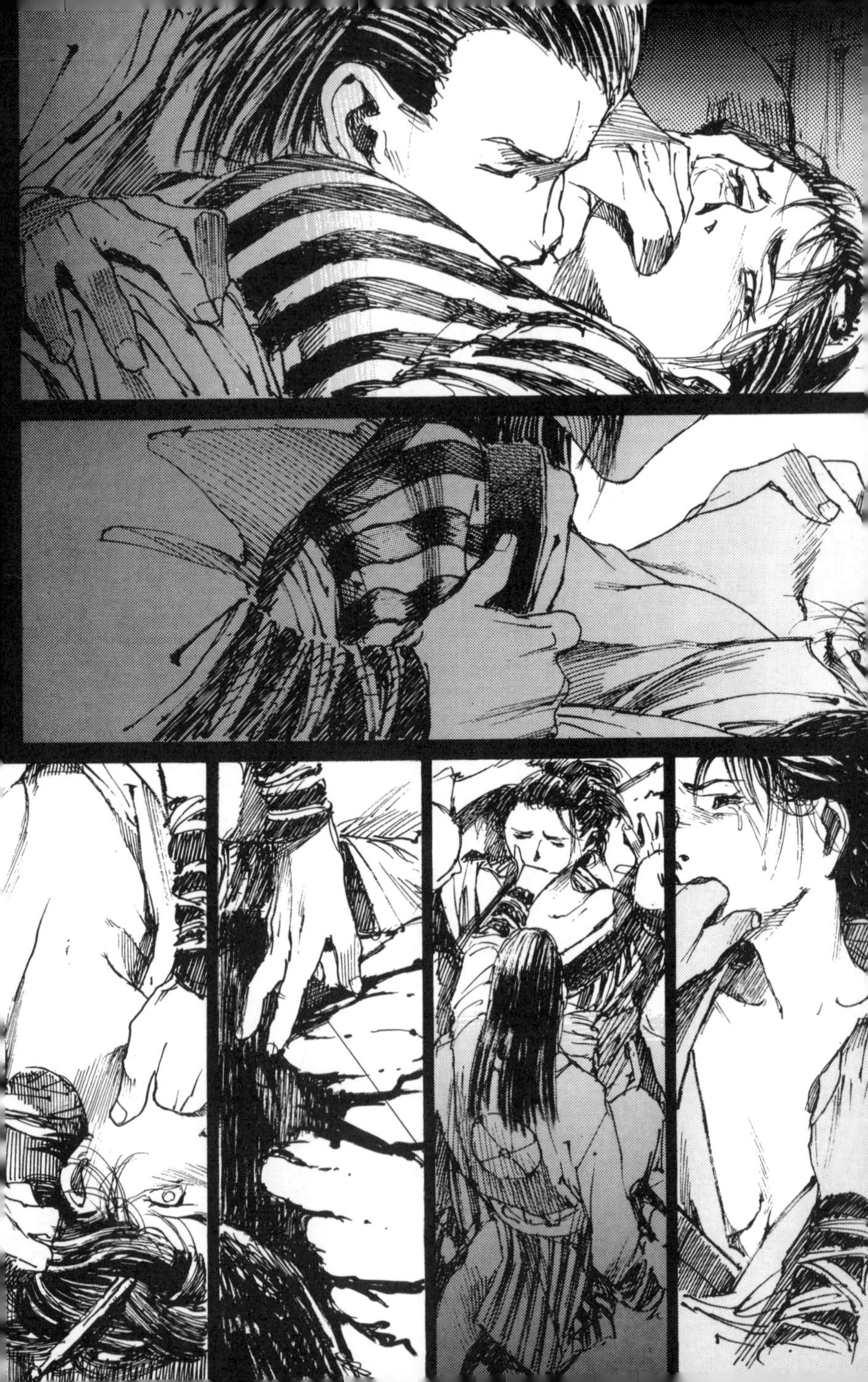

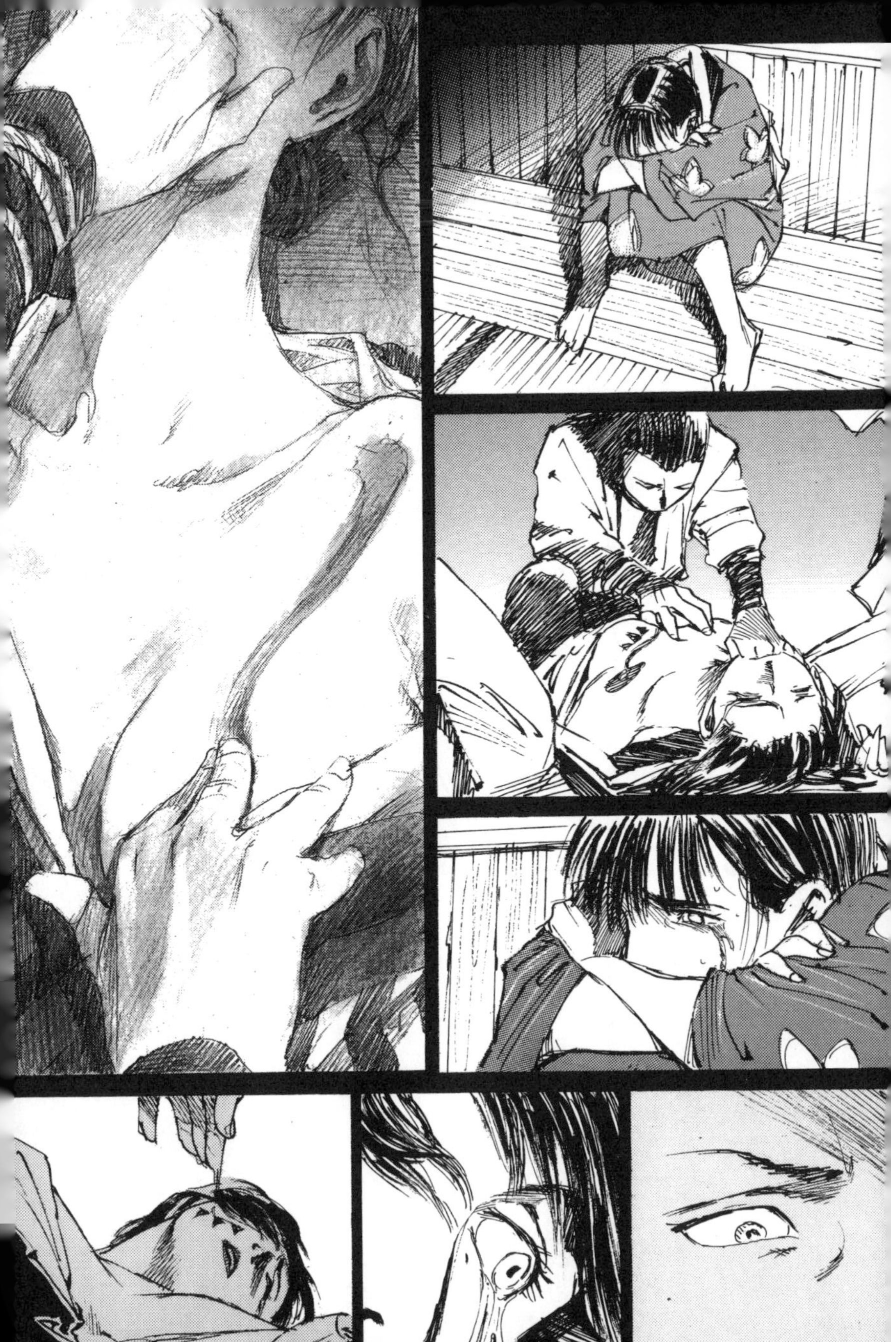

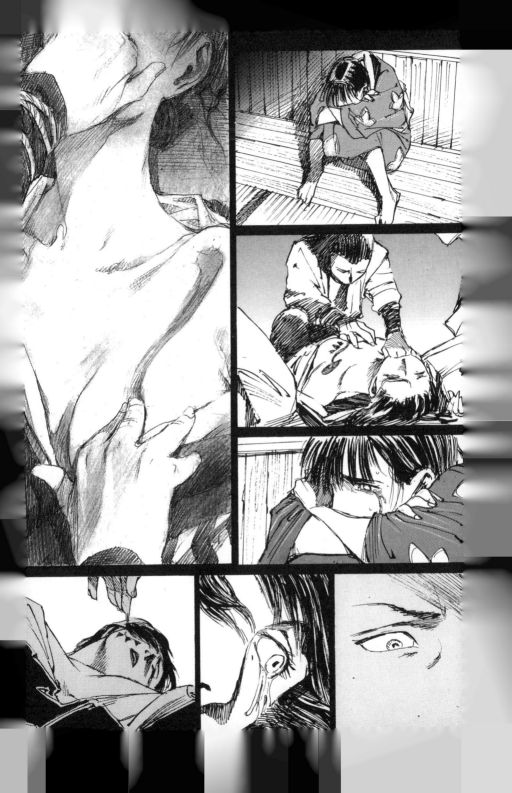

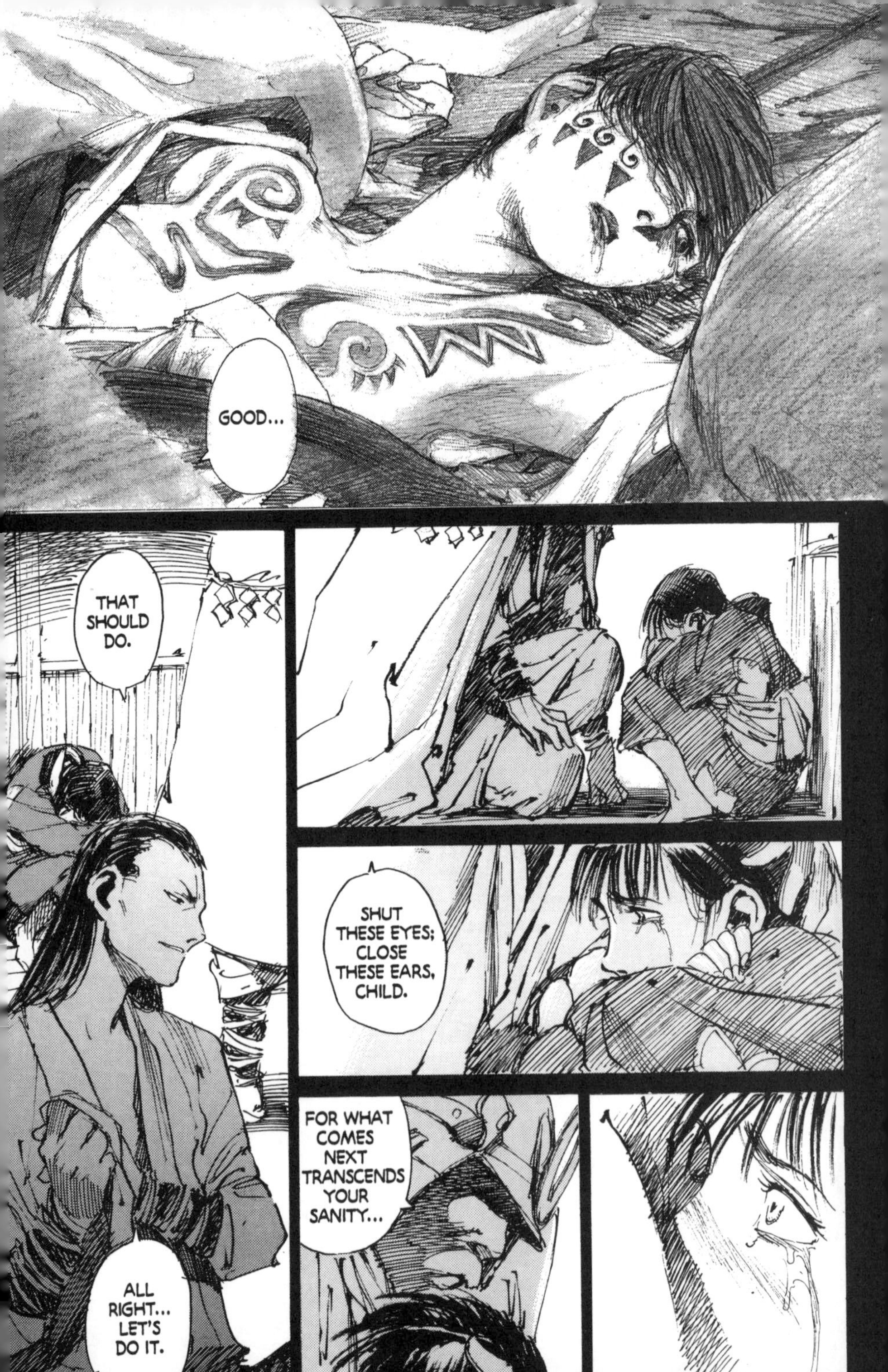
GOOD...
SHUT THESE EYES; CLOSE THESE EARS, CHILD.
FOR WHAT COMES NEXT TRANSCENDS YOUR SANITY...
THAT SHOULD DO.
ALL RIGHT... LET'S DO IT.

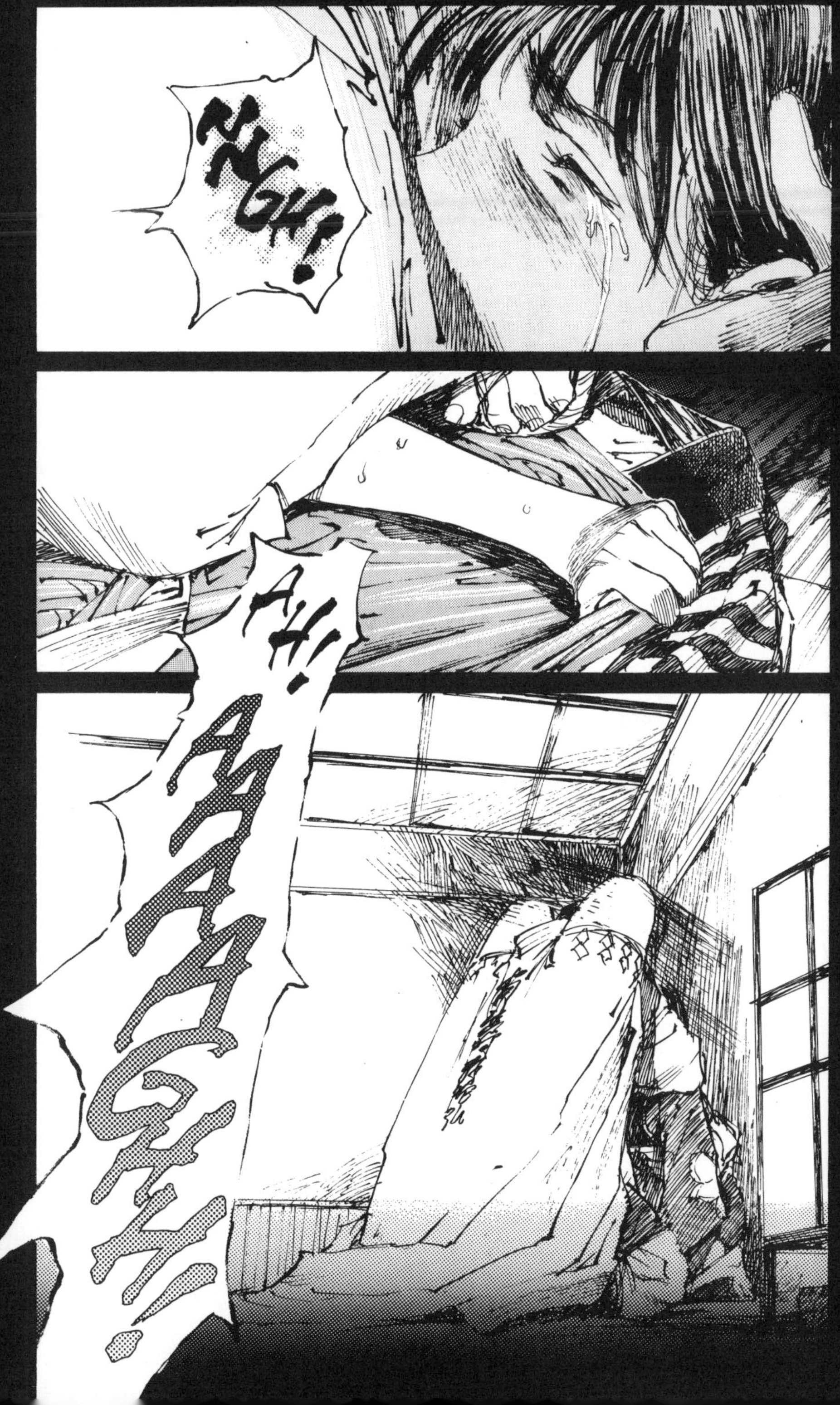
HNGH!
AH!
AAAAAGHH!

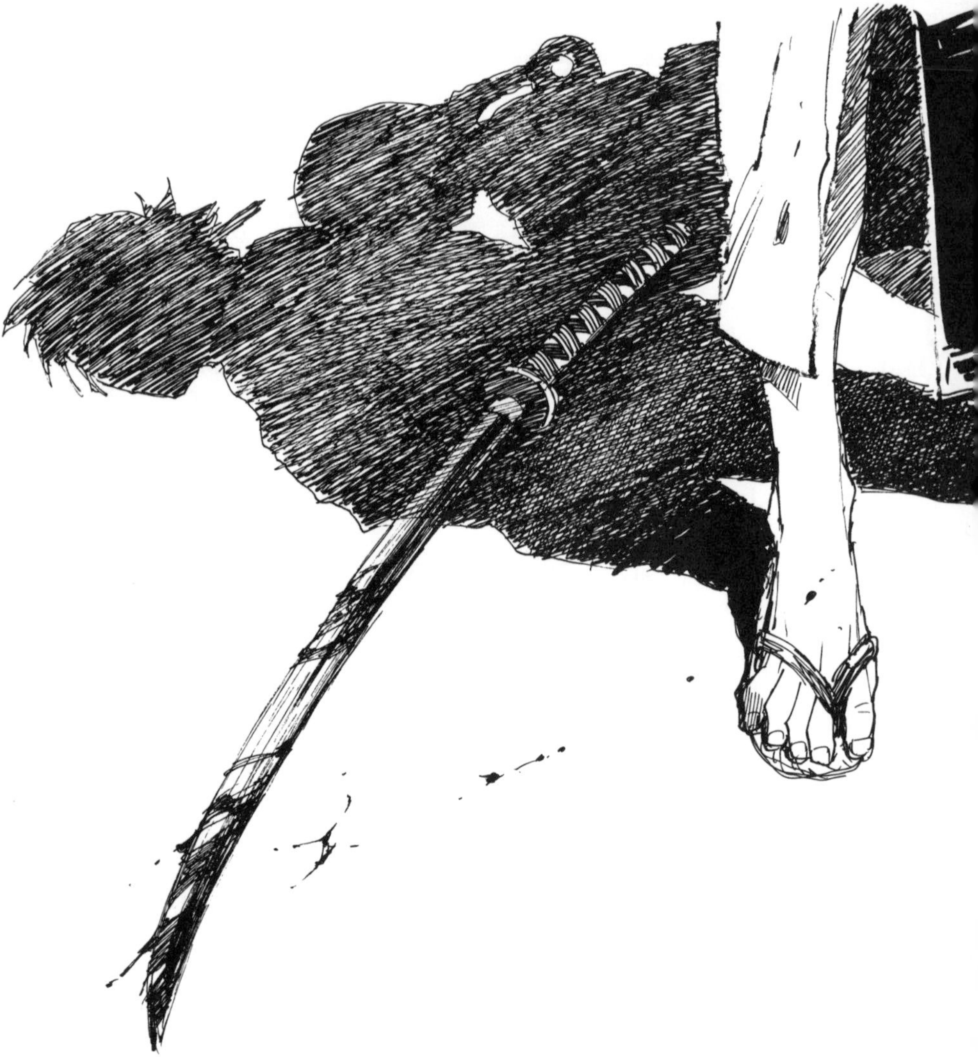

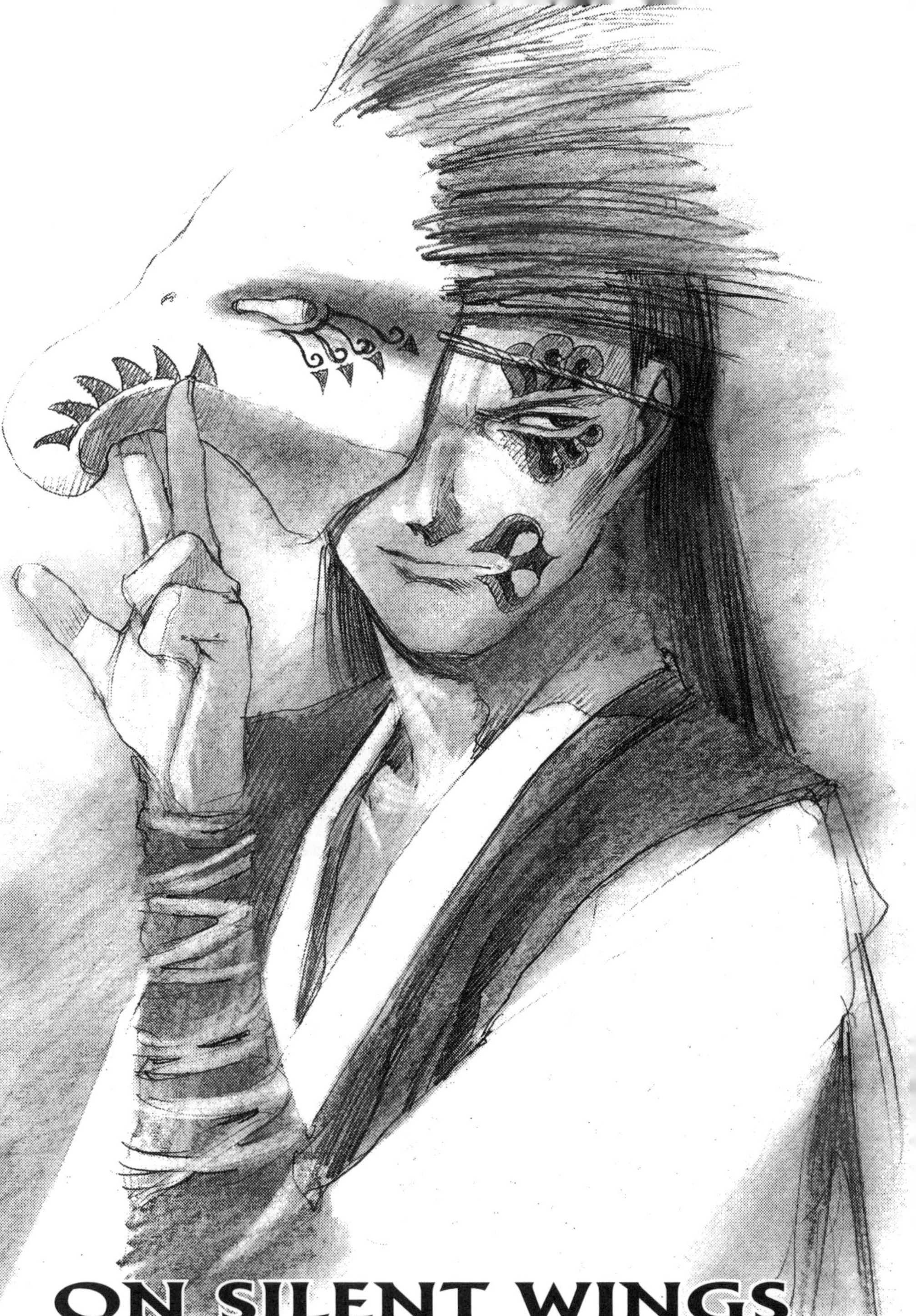

ON SILENT WINGS

Part 4

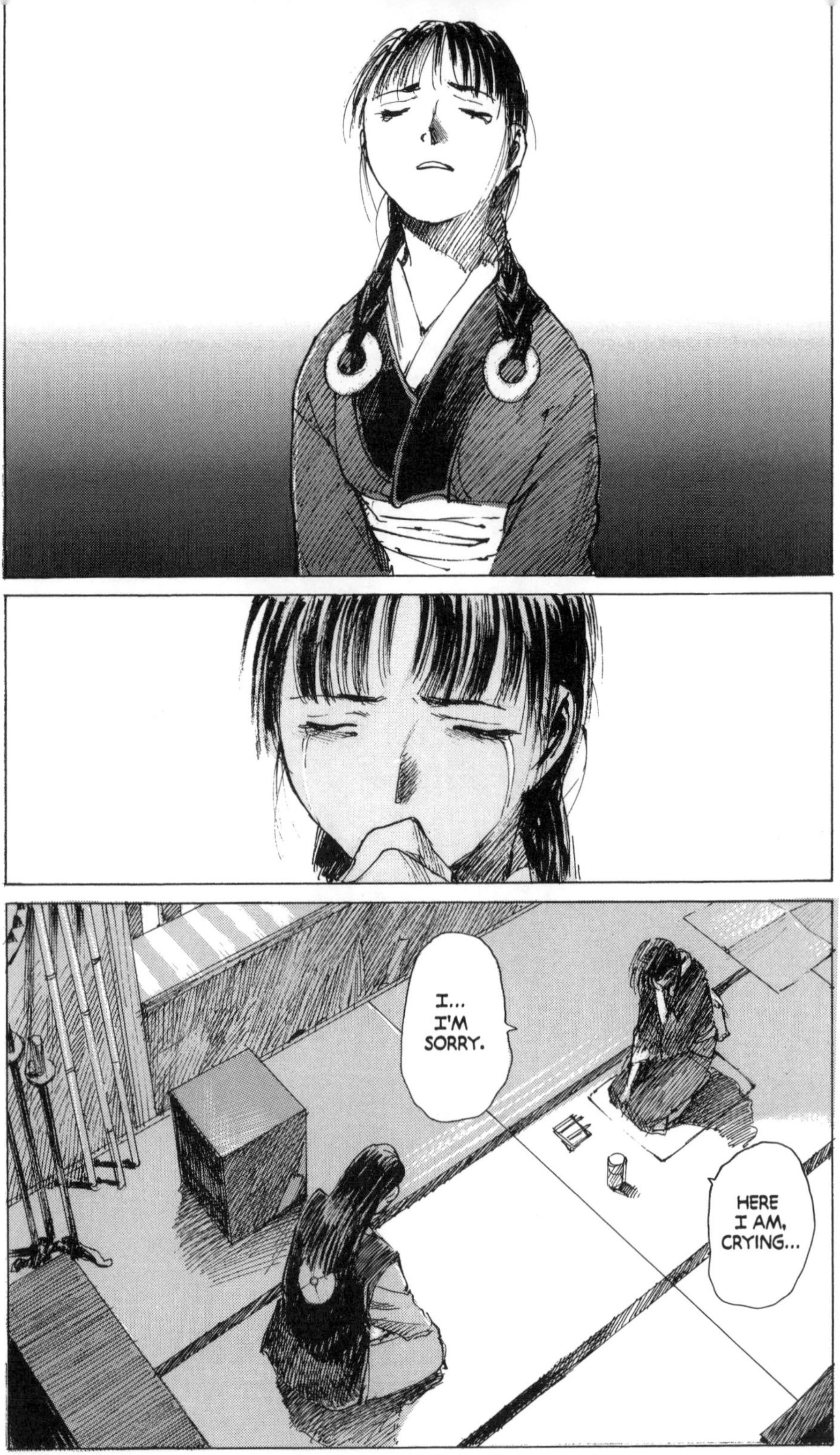
I... I'M SORRY.
HERE I AM, CRYING...

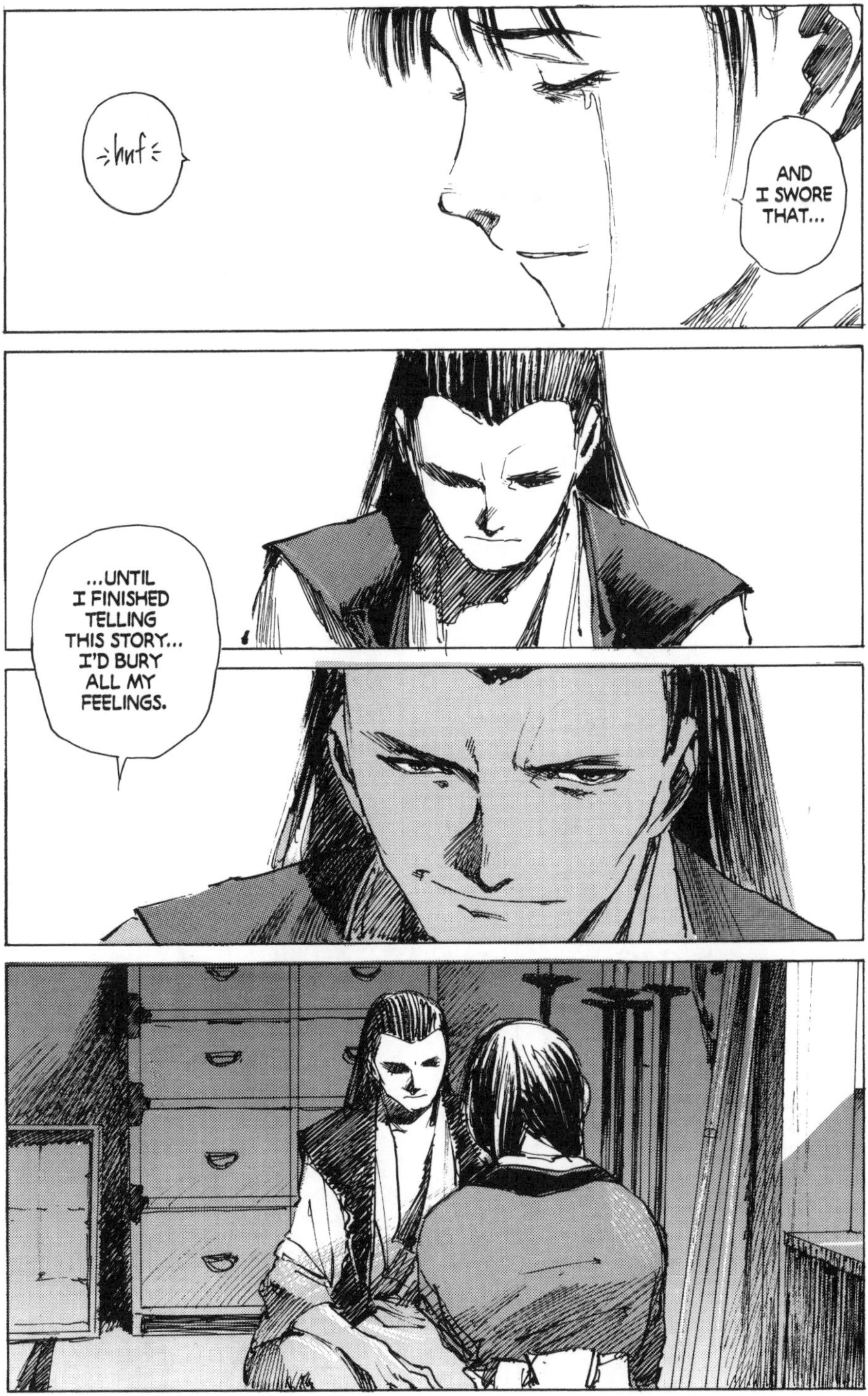
AND I SWORE THAT...
hnf
...UNTIL I FINISHED TELLING THIS STORY... I'D BURY ALL MY FEELINGS.

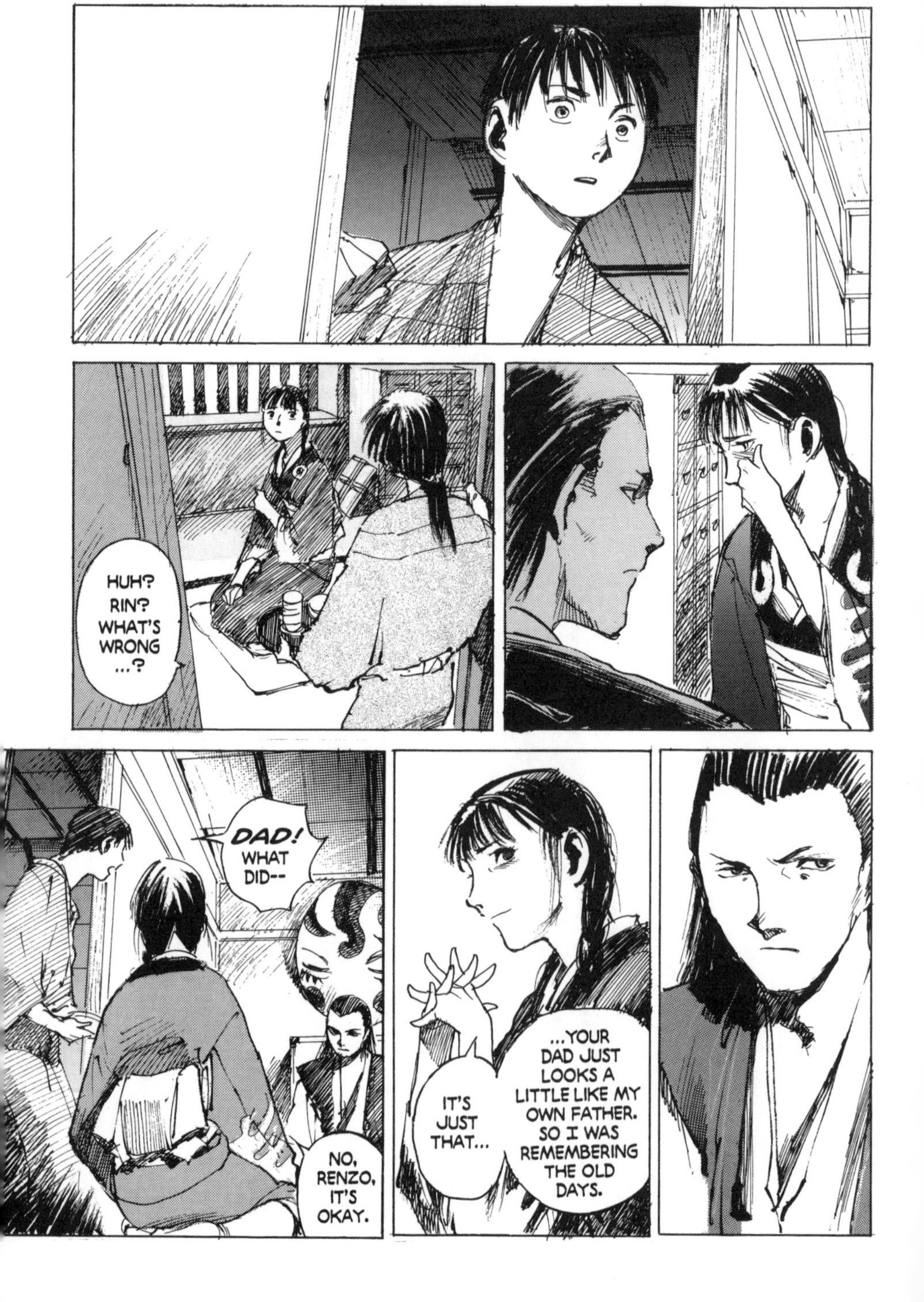
HUH? RIN? WHAT'S WRONG ...?
DAD! WHAT DID--
NO, RENZO, IT'S OKAY.
IT'S JUST THAT...
...YOUR DAD JUST LOOKS A LITTLE LIKE MY OWN FATHER. SO I WAS REMEMBERING THE OLD DAYS.

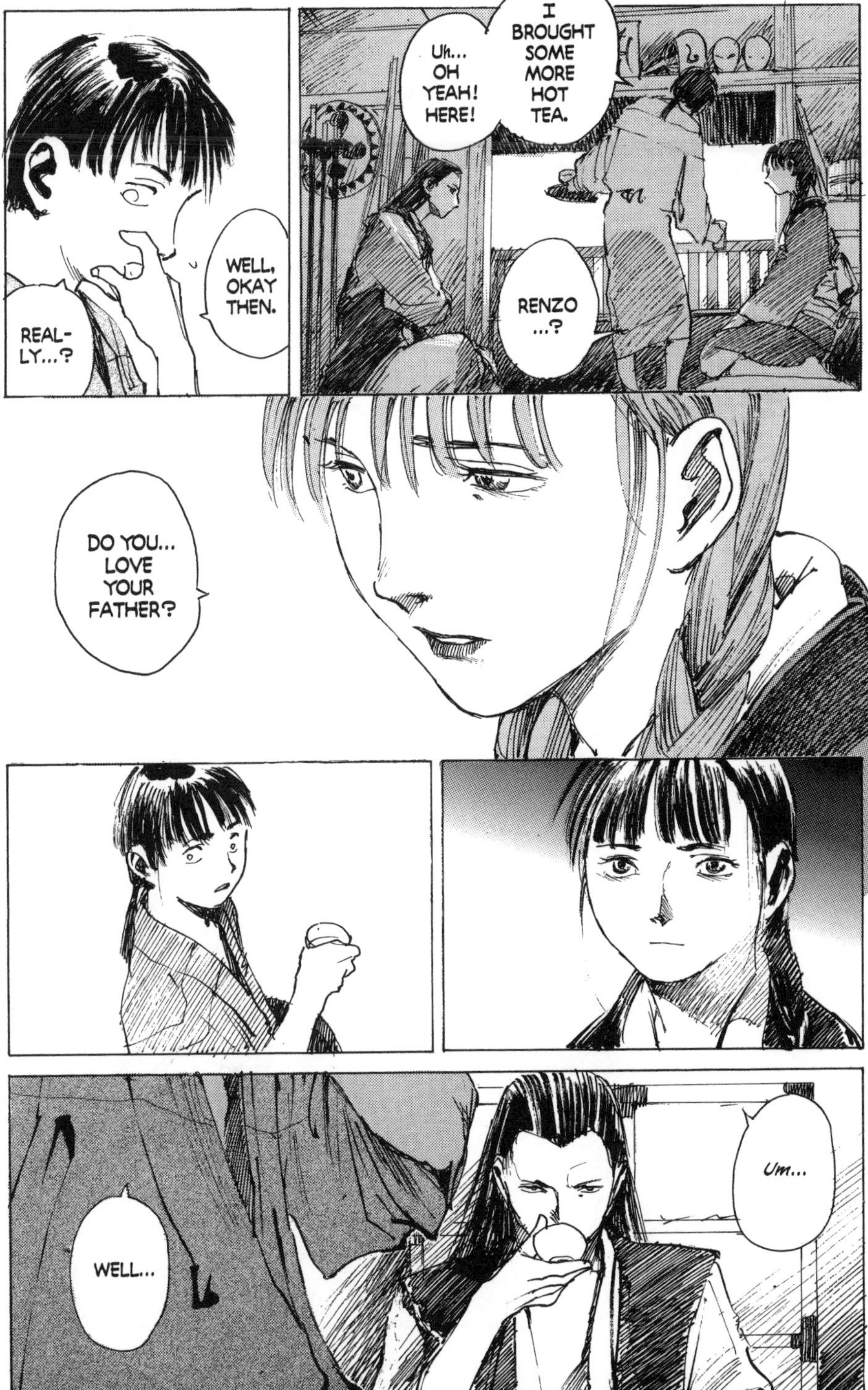
I BROUGHT SOME MORE HOT TEA.
Uh... OH YEAH! HERE!
RENZO ...?
WELL, OKAY THEN.
REAL-LY...?
DO YOU... LOVE YOUR FATHER?
Um...
WELL...

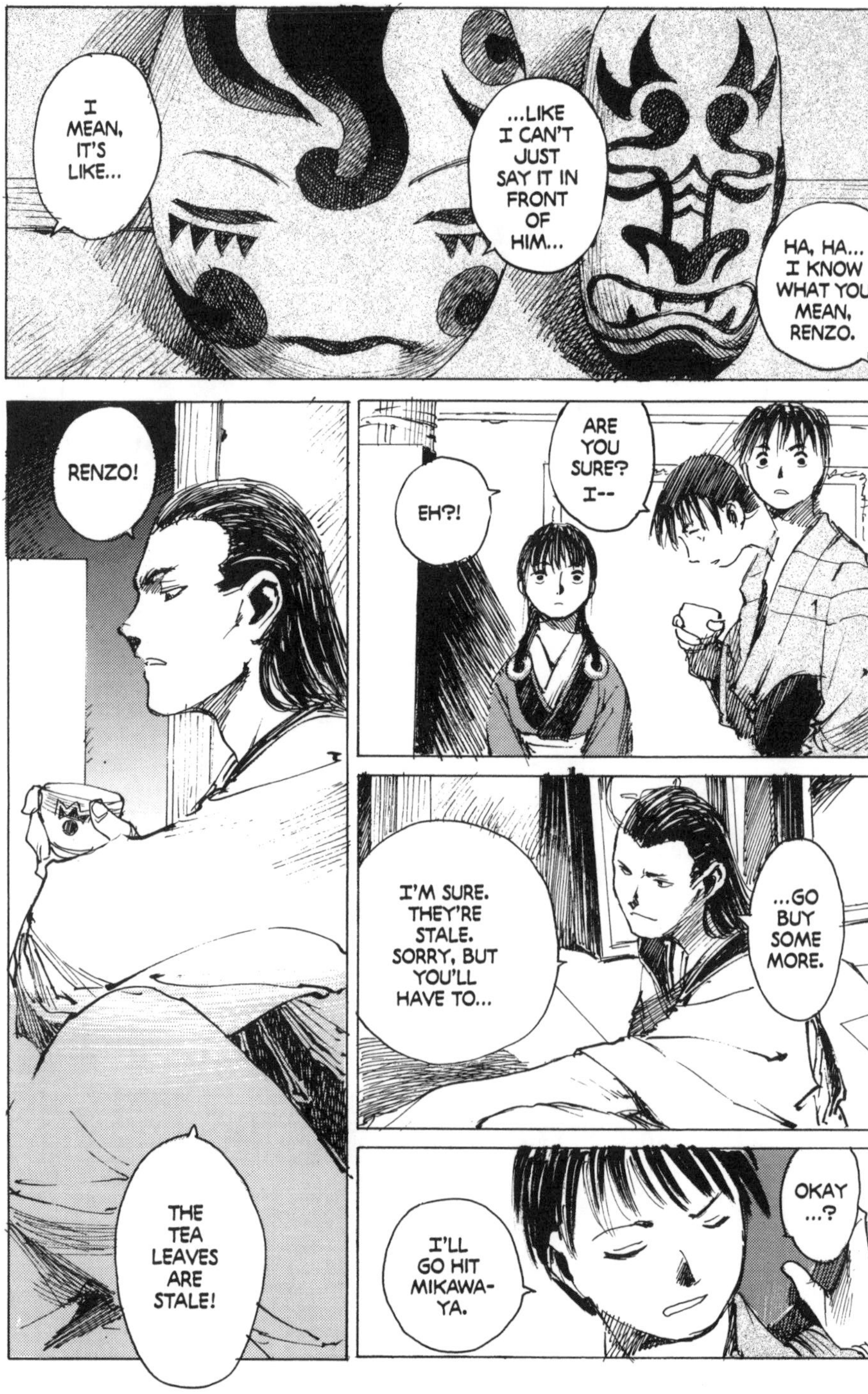
I MEAN, IT'S LIKE...
...LIKE I CAN'T JUST SAY IT IN FRONT OF HIM...
HA, HA... I KNOW WHAT YOU MEAN, RENZO.
RENZO!
THE TEA LEAVES ARE STALE!
EH?!
ARE YOU SURE? I--
I'M SURE. THEY'RE STALE. SORRY, BUT YOU'LL HAVE TO...
...GO BUY SOME MORE.
OKAY ...?
I'LL GO HIT MIKAWA-YA.

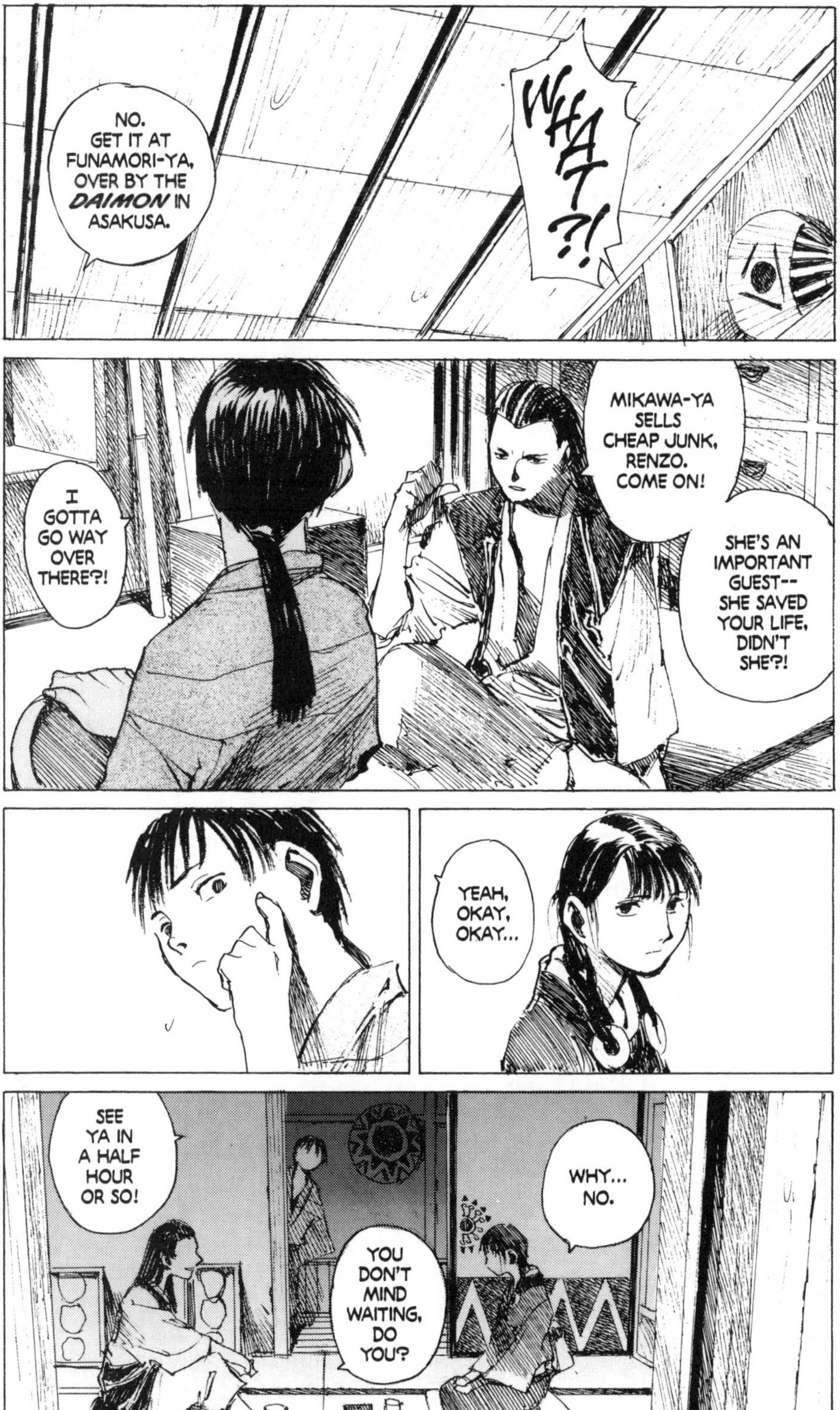
NO. GET IT AT FUNAMORI-YA, OVER BY THE *DAIMON* IN ASAKUSA.
WHAT?!
I GOTTA GO WAY OVER THERE?!
MIKAWA-YA SELLS CHEAP JUNK, RENZO. COME ON!
SHE'S AN IMPORTANT GUEST-- SHE SAVED YOUR LIFE, DIDN'T SHE?!
YEAH, OKAY, OKAY...
SEE YA IN A HALF HOUR OR SO!
YOU DON'T MIND WAITING, DO YOU?
WHY... NO.

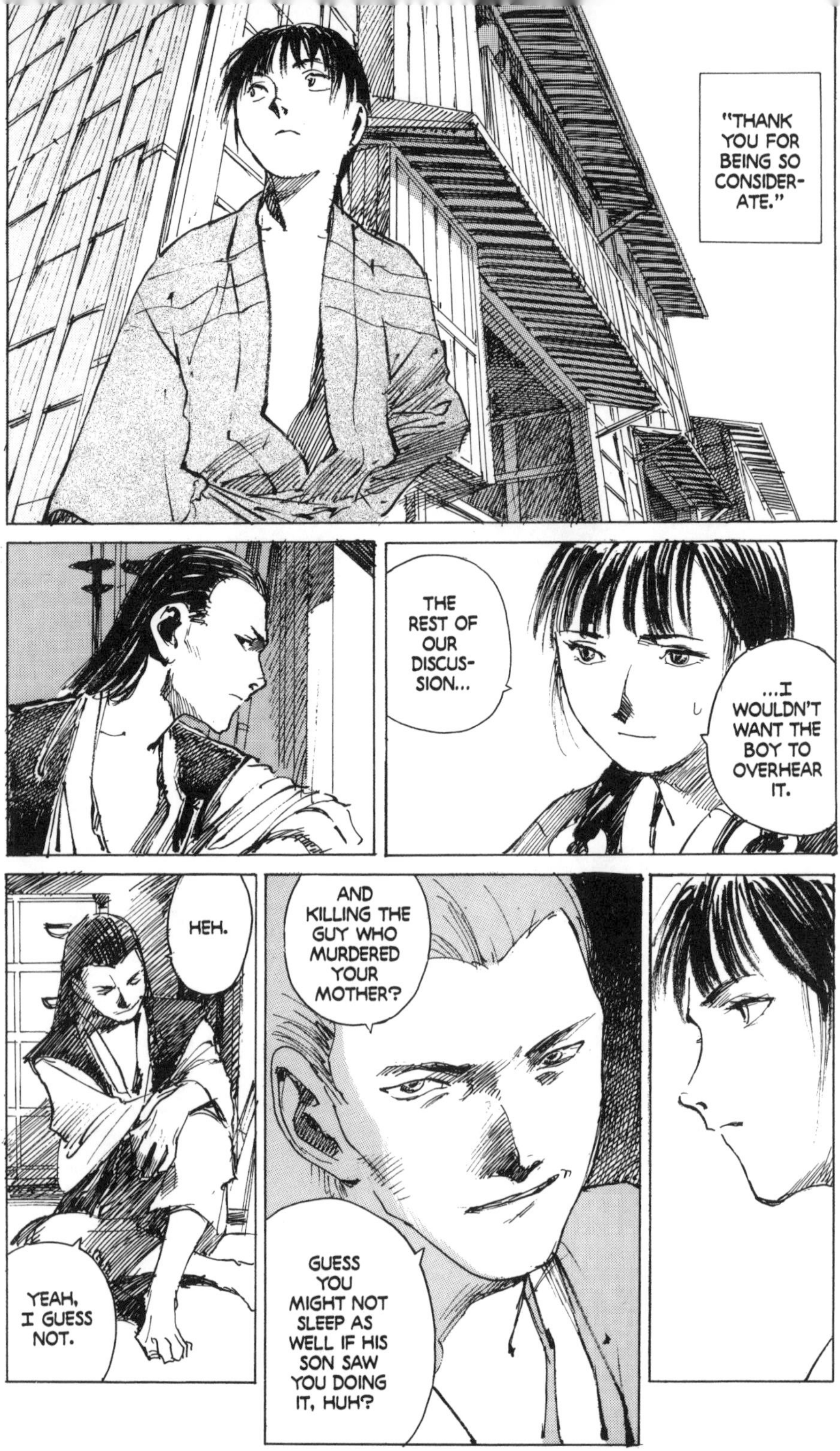
"THANK YOU FOR BEING SO CONSIDER-ATE."
THE REST OF OUR DISCUS-SION...
...I WOULDN'T WANT THE BOY TO OVERHEAR IT.
AND KILLING THE GUY WHO MURDERED YOUR MOTHER?
GUESS YOU MIGHT NOT SLEEP AS WELL IF HIS SON SAW YOU DOING IT, HUH?
HEH.
YEAH, I GUESS NOT.

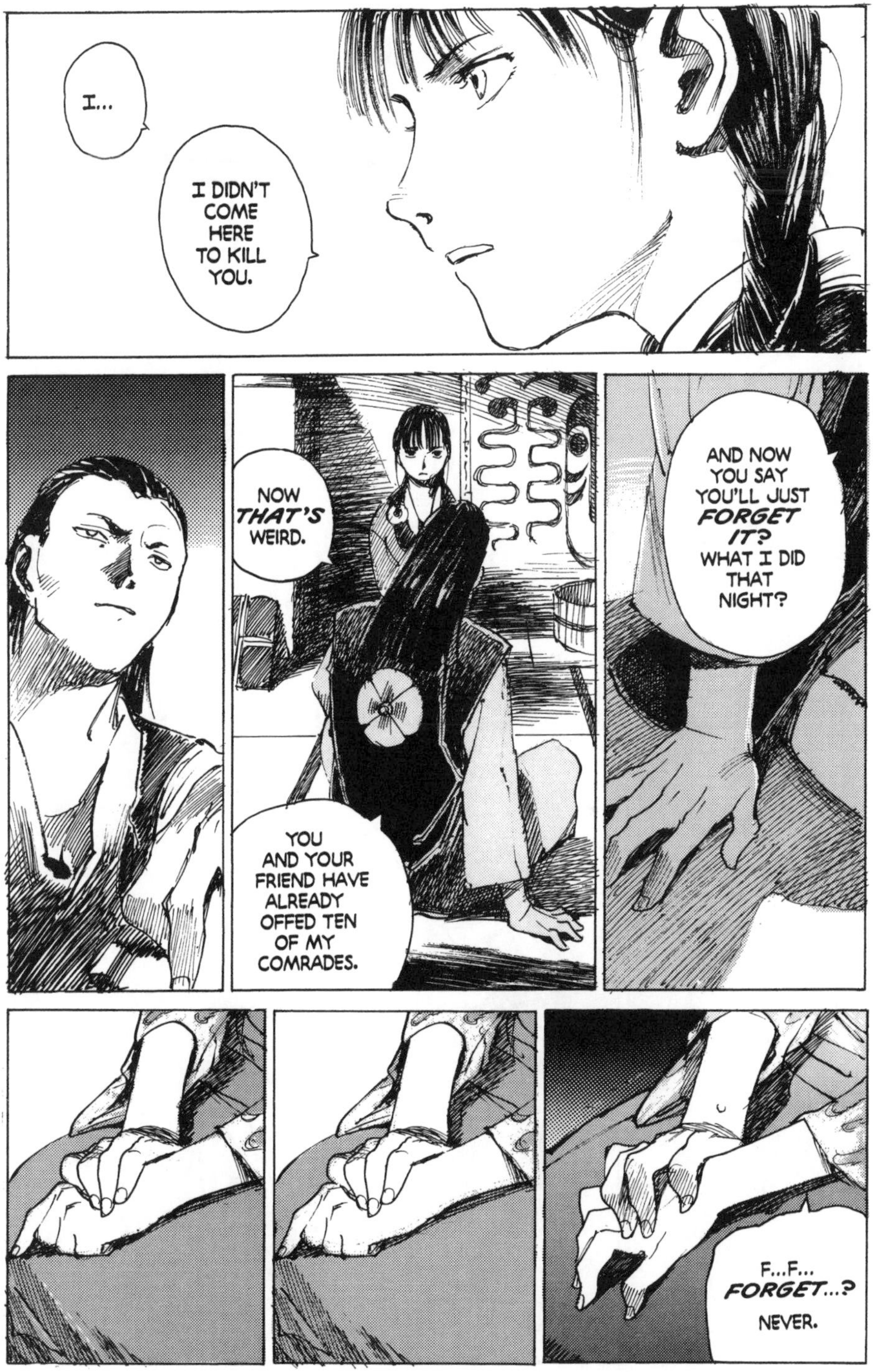
I...
I DIDN'T COME HERE TO KILL YOU.
NOW *THAT'S* WEIRD.
YOU AND YOUR FRIEND HAVE ALREADY OFFED TEN OF MY COMRADES.
AND NOW YOU SAY YOU'LL JUST *FORGET IT?* WHAT I DID THAT NIGHT?
F...F... *FORGET...?* NEVER.

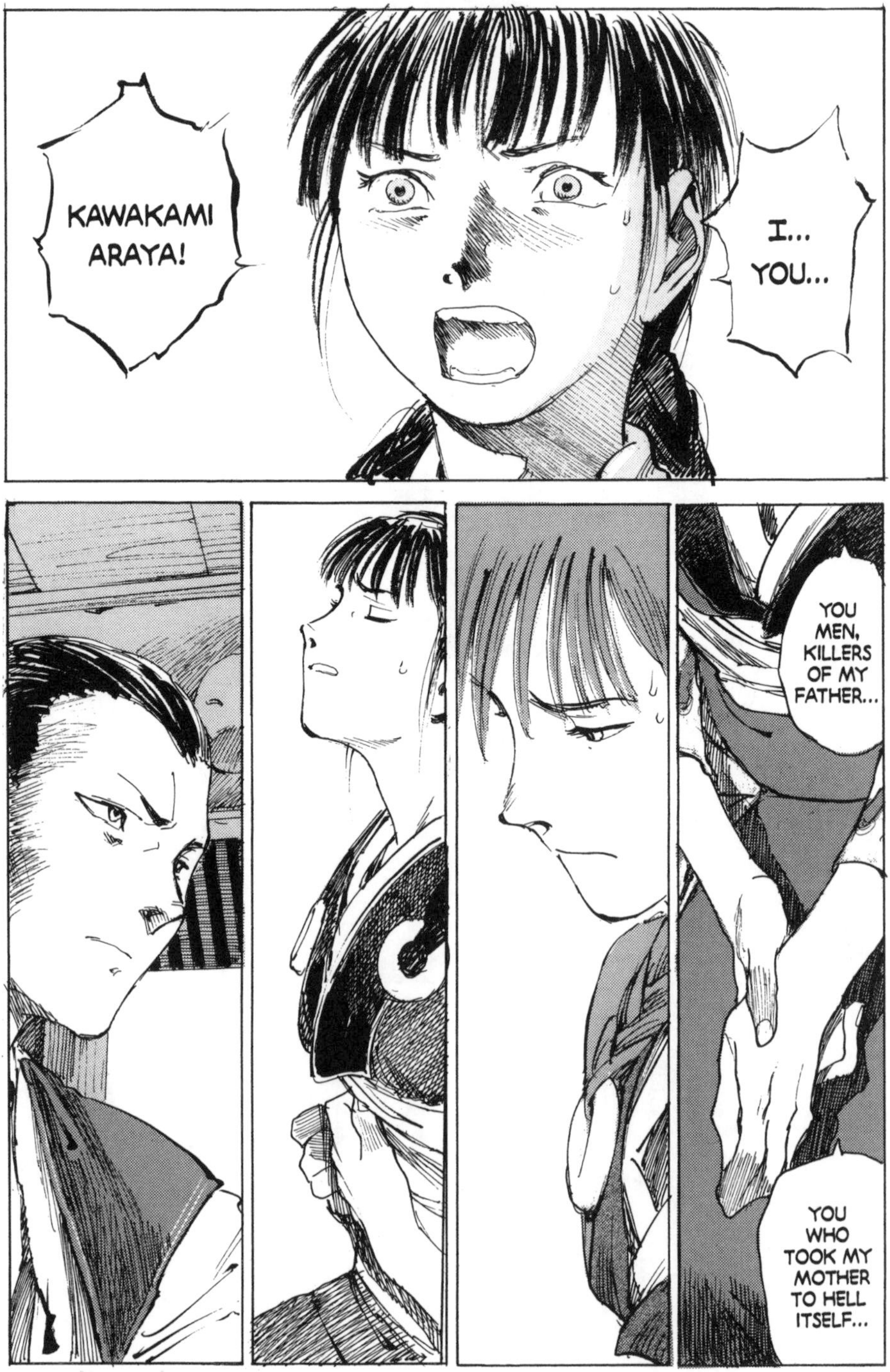
I... YOU...
KAWAKAMI ARAYA!
YOU MEN, KILLERS OF MY FATHER...
YOU WHO TOOK MY MOTHER TO HELL ITSELF...

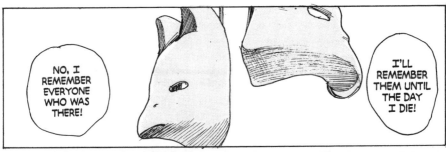

NO, I REMEMBER EVERYONE WHO WAS THERE!

I'LL REMEMBER THEM UNTIL THE DAY I DIE!

YES! YES!! YOU'RE RIGHT!

WE DID KILL YOUR FRIENDS! ALL TEN OF THEM!

BUT SO WHAT?!

THE MUTENICHI-RYU STUDENTS YOU KILLED...? THERE WERE A LOT MORE THAN TEN! WAY MORE!

SO IT'S JUSTICE, RIGHT?!

THERE!! YOU ASKED FOR IT-- THAT'S HOW I FEEL!

AND SO? THEN WHAT DO YOU DO...

...ABOUT ME?

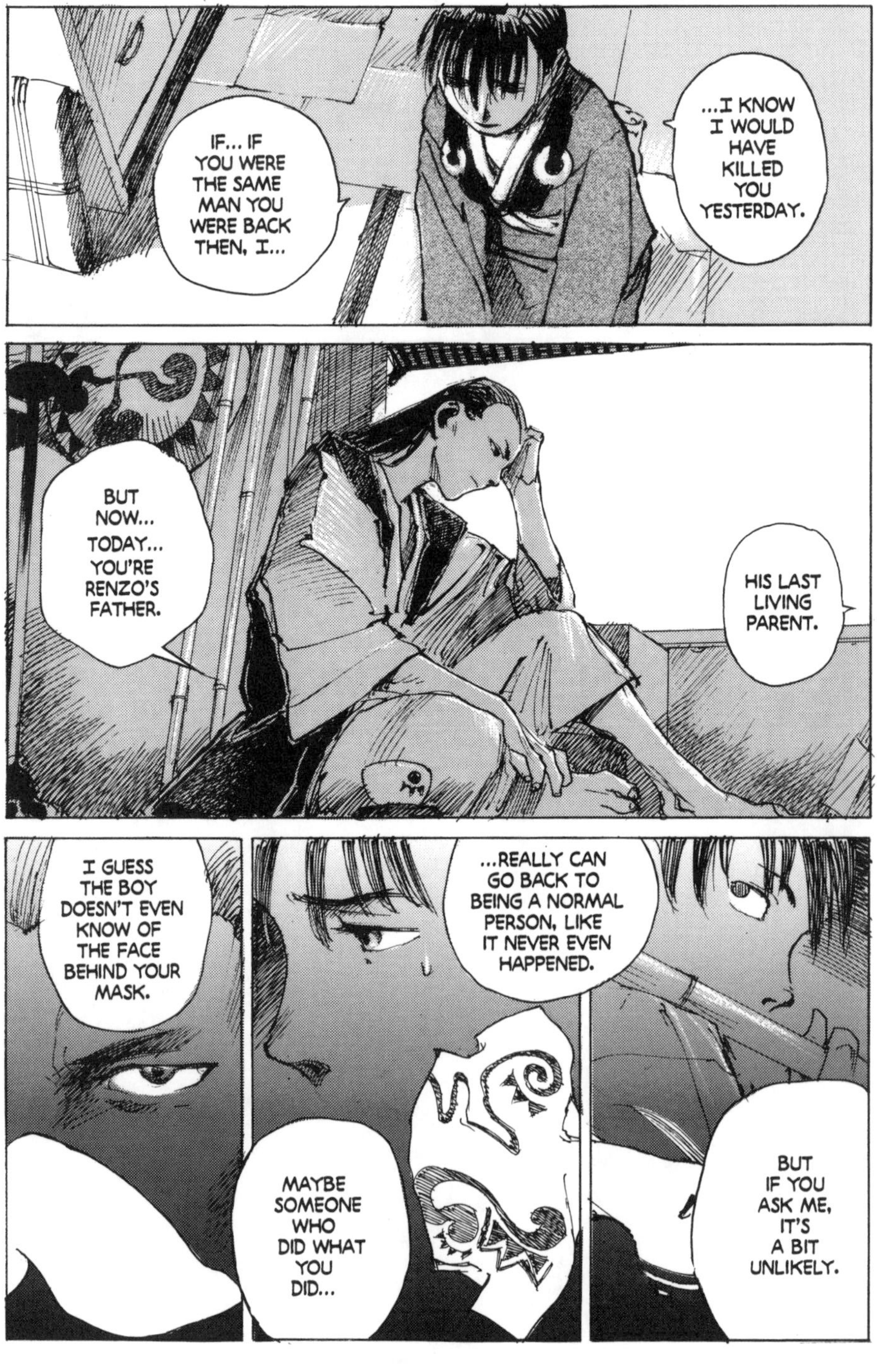
IF... IF YOU WERE THE SAME MAN YOU WERE BACK THEN, I...
...I KNOW I WOULD HAVE KILLED YOU YESTERDAY.
BUT NOW... TODAY... YOU'RE RENZO'S FATHER.
HIS LAST LIVING PARENT.
I GUESS THE BOY DOESN'T EVEN KNOW OF THE FACE BEHIND YOUR MASK.
MAYBE SOMEONE WHO DID WHAT YOU DID...
...REALLY CAN GO BACK TO BEING A NORMAL PERSON, LIKE IT NEVER EVEN HAPPENED.
BUT IF YOU ASK ME, IT'S A BIT UNLIKELY.

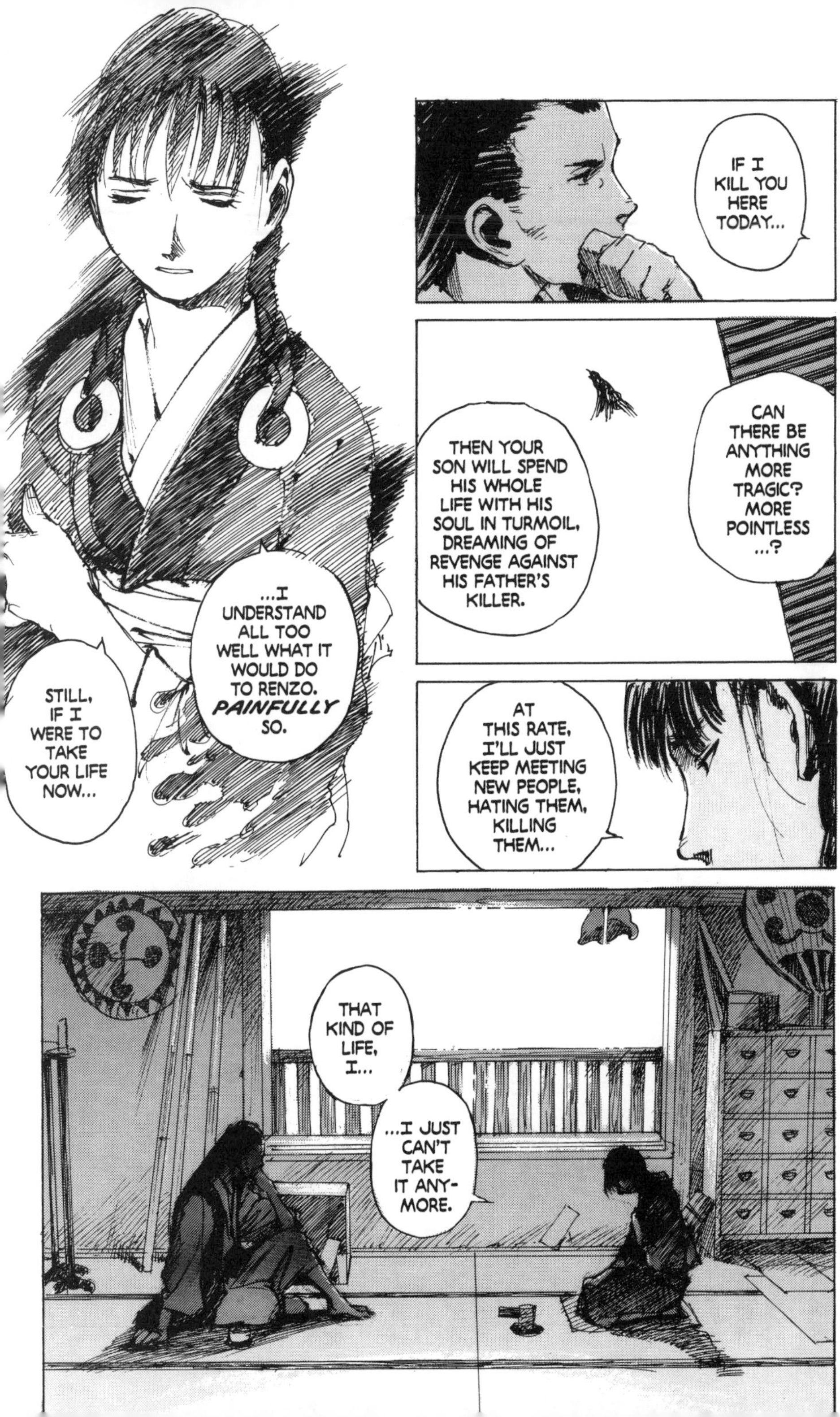
IF I KILL YOU HERE TODAY...
THEN YOUR SON WILL SPEND HIS WHOLE LIFE WITH HIS SOUL IN TURMOIL, DREAMING OF REVENGE AGAINST HIS FATHER'S KILLER.
CAN THERE BE ANYTHING MORE TRAGIC? MORE POINTLESS ...?
AT THIS RATE, I'LL JUST KEEP MEETING NEW PEOPLE, HATING THEM, KILLING THEM...
...I UNDERSTAND ALL TOO WELL WHAT IT WOULD DO TO RENZO. PAINFULLY SO.
STILL, IF I WERE TO TAKE YOUR LIFE NOW...
THAT KIND OF LIFE, I...
...I JUST CAN'T TAKE IT ANYMORE.

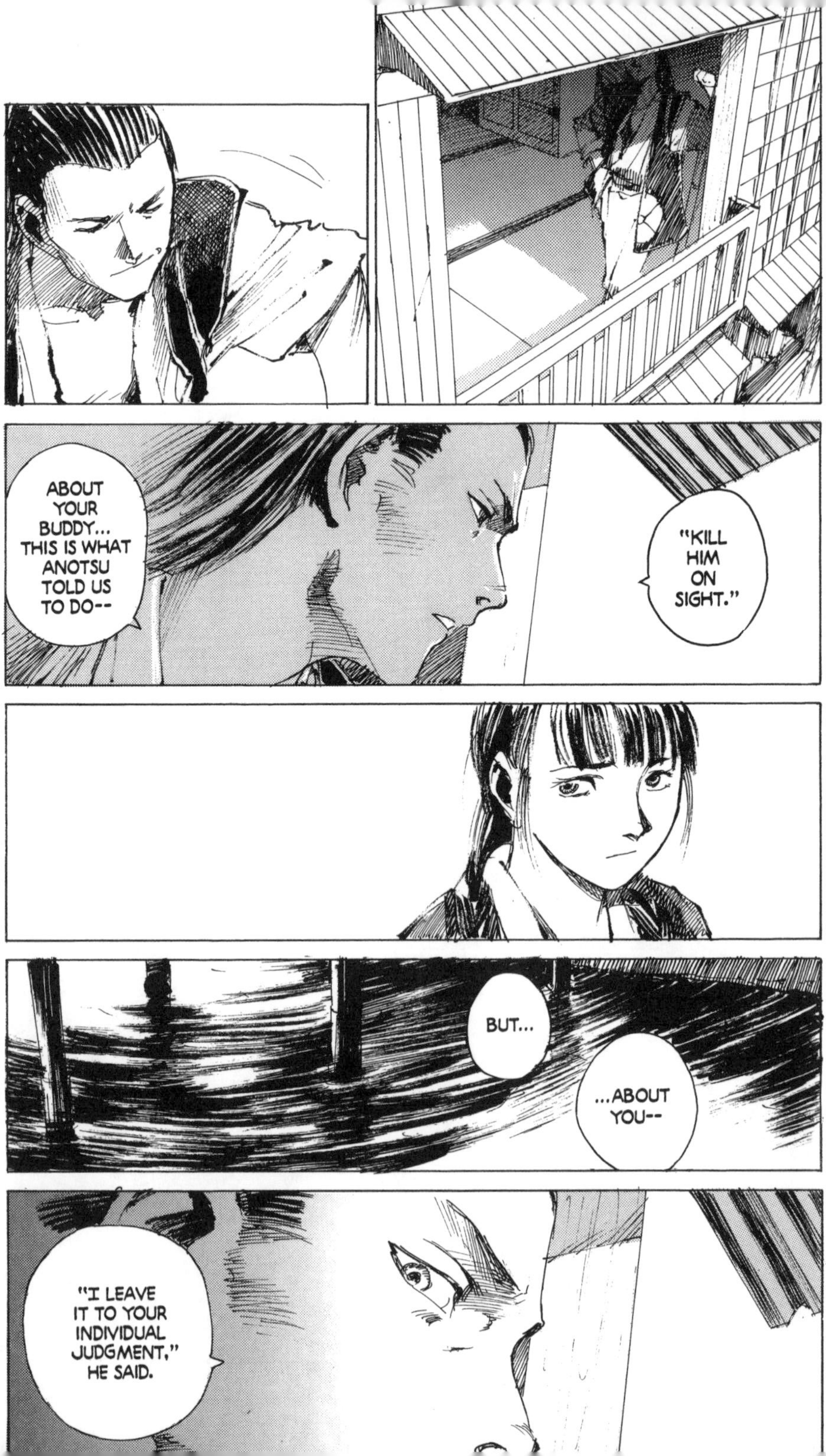
"KILL HIM ON SIGHT."
ABOUT YOUR BUDDY... THIS IS WHAT ANOTSU TOLD US TO DO--
BUT...
...ABOUT YOU--
"I LEAVE IT TO YOUR INDIVIDUAL JUDGMENT," HE SAID.

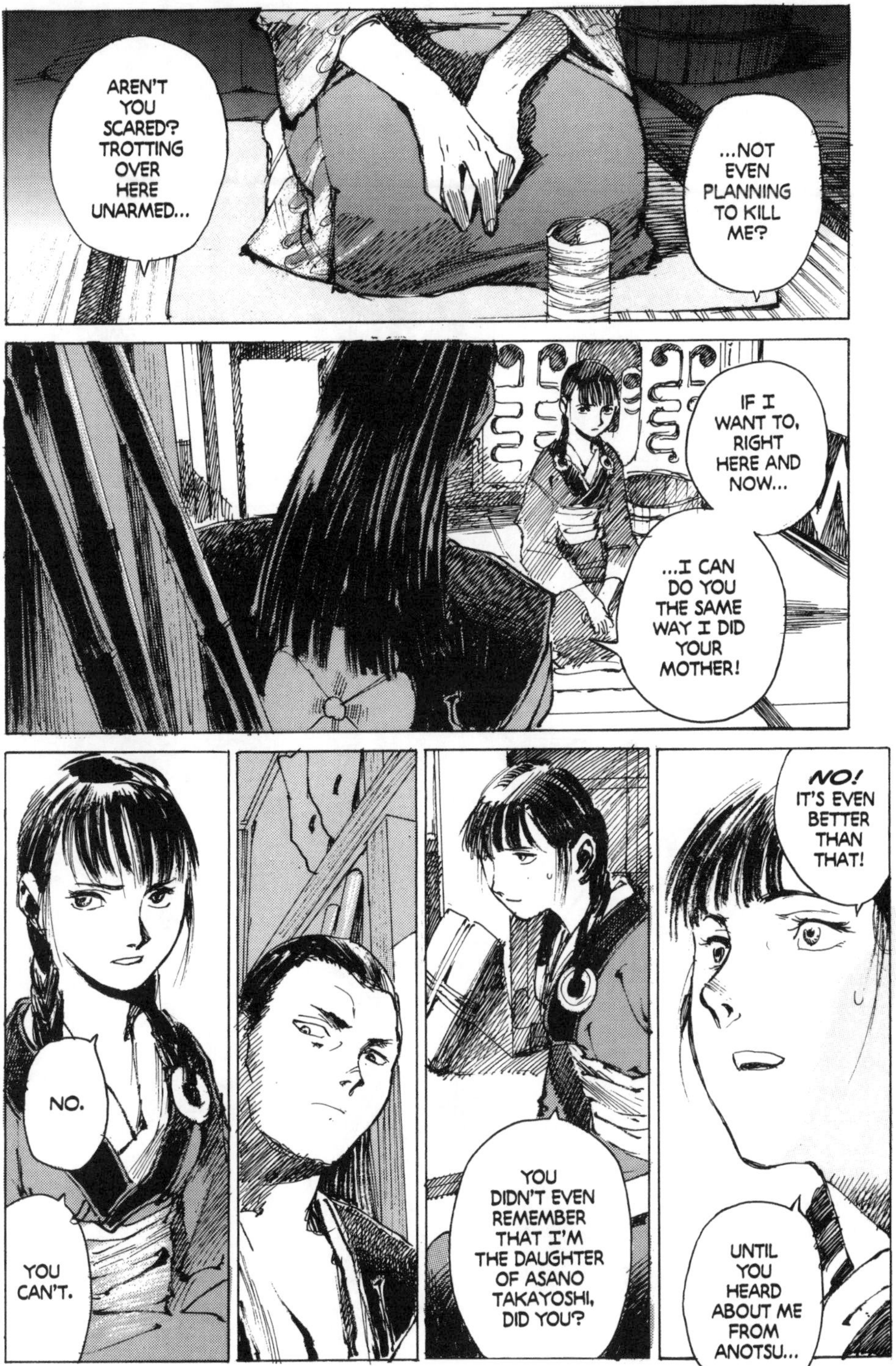
AREN'T YOU SCARED? TROTTING OVER HERE UNARMED...
...NOT EVEN PLANNING TO KILL ME?
IF I WANT TO, RIGHT HERE AND NOW...
...I CAN DO YOU THE SAME WAY I DID YOUR MOTHER!
NO.
YOU CAN'T.
YOU DIDN'T EVEN REMEMBER THAT I'M THE DAUGHTER OF ASANO TAKAYOSHI, DID YOU?
NO! IT'S EVEN BETTER THAN THAT!
UNTIL YOU HEARD ABOUT ME FROM ANOTSU...

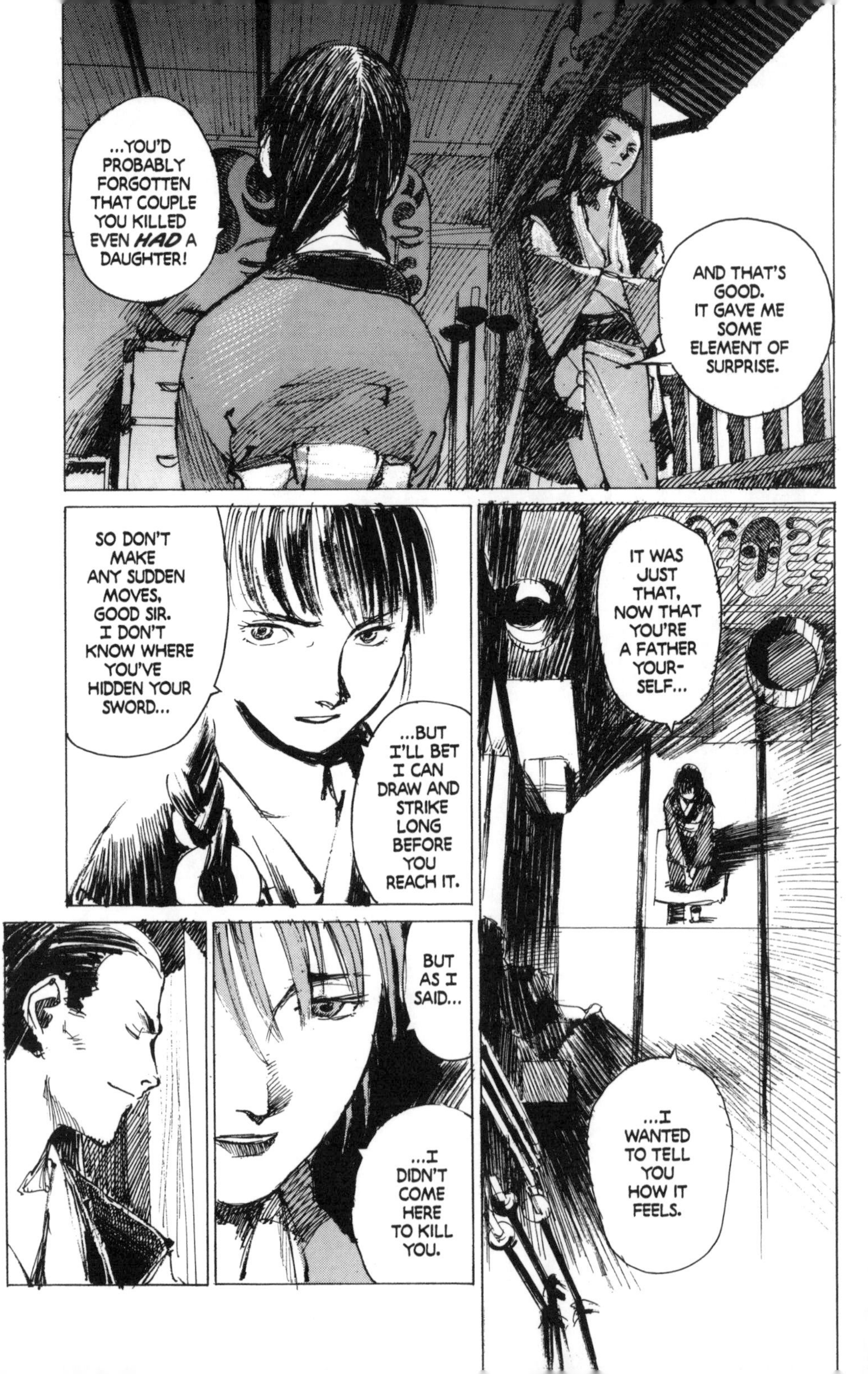
...YOU'D PROBABLY FORGOTTEN THAT COUPLE YOU KILLED EVEN HAD A DAUGHTER!
AND THAT'S GOOD. IT GAVE ME SOME ELEMENT OF SURPRISE.
SO DON'T MAKE ANY SUDDEN MOVES, GOOD SIR. I DON'T KNOW WHERE YOU'VE HIDDEN YOUR SWORD...
...BUT I'LL BET I CAN DRAW AND STRIKE LONG BEFORE YOU REACH IT.
BUT AS I SAID...
...I DIDN'T COME HERE TO KILL YOU.
IT WAS JUST THAT, NOW THAT YOU'RE A FATHER YOURSELF...
...I WANTED TO TELL YOU HOW IT FEELS.

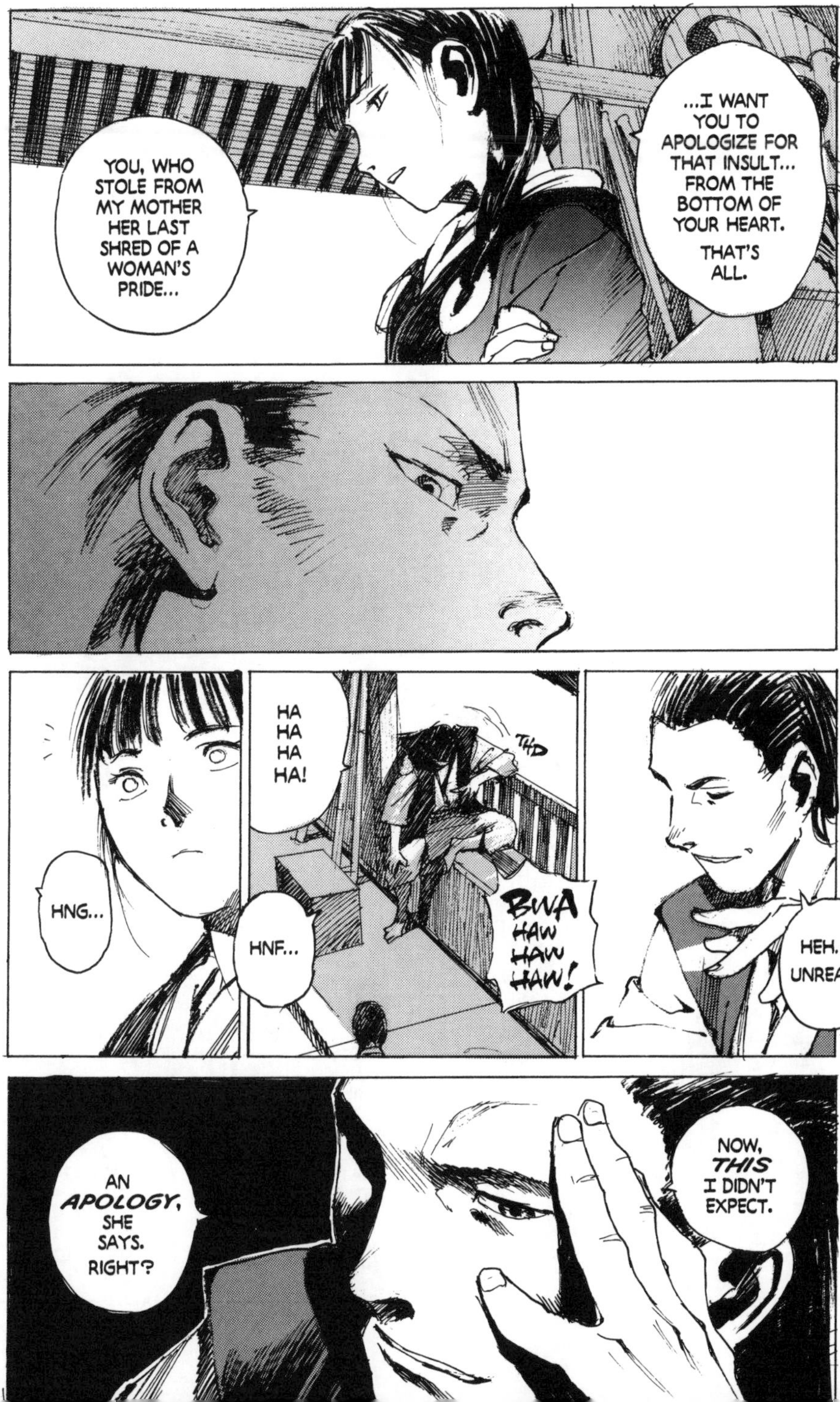
YOU, WHO STOLE FROM MY MOTHER HER LAST SHRED OF A WOMAN'S PRIDE...
...I WANT YOU TO APOLOGIZE FOR THAT INSULT... FROM THE BOTTOM OF YOUR HEART.
THAT'S ALL.
HNG...
HA HA HA HA!
THD
HNF...
BWA HAW HAW HAW!
HEH... UNREAL!
AN APOLOGY, SHE SAYS. RIGHT?
NOW, THIS I DIDN'T EXPECT.

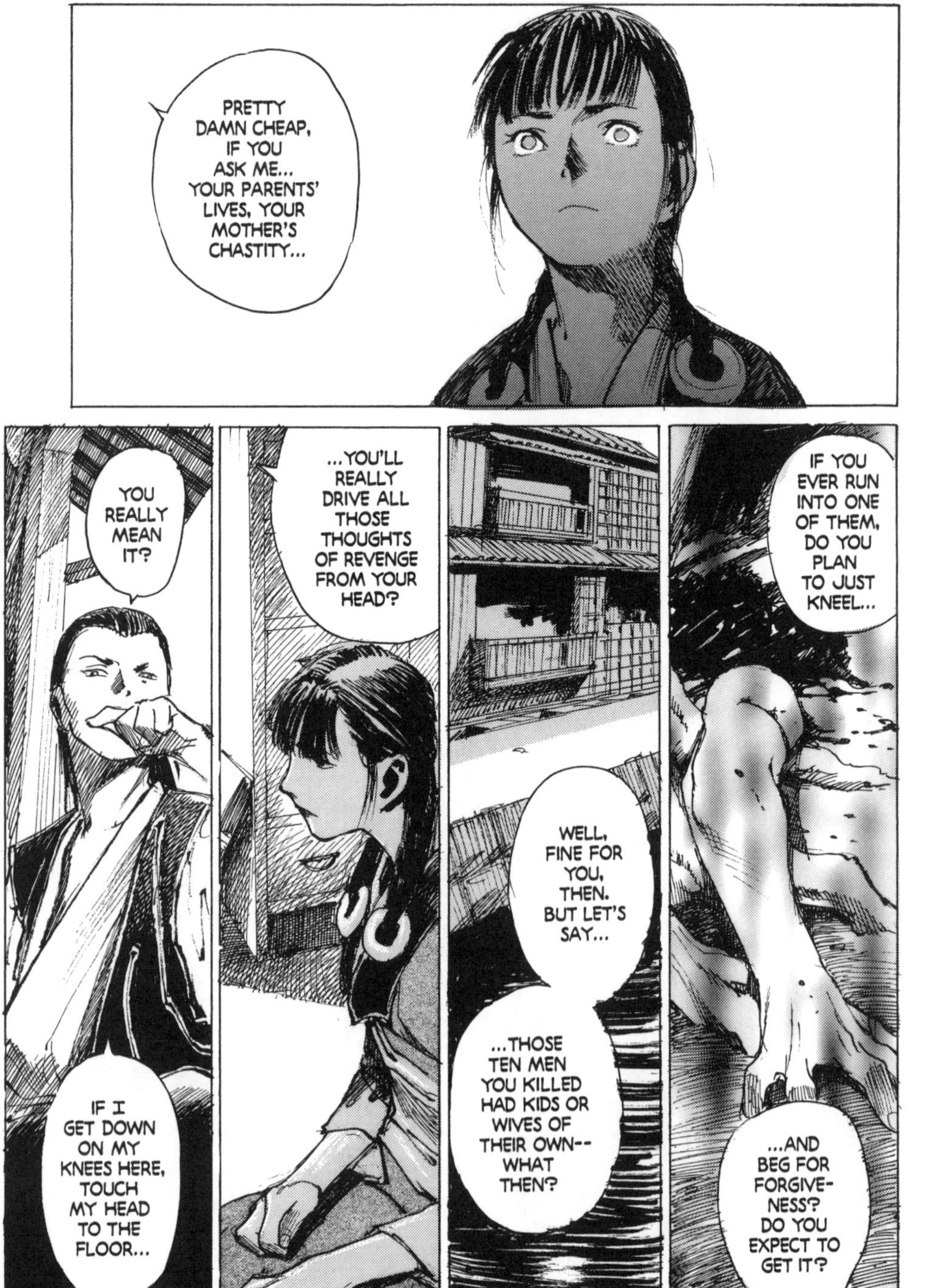
PRETTY DAMN CHEAP, IF YOU ASK ME... YOUR PARENTS' LIVES, YOUR MOTHER'S CHASTITY...
YOU REALLY MEAN IT?
IF I GET DOWN ON MY KNEES HERE, TOUCH MY HEAD TO THE FLOOR...
...YOU'LL REALLY DRIVE ALL THOSE THOUGHTS OF REVENGE FROM YOUR HEAD?
WELL, FINE FOR YOU, THEN. BUT LET'S SAY...
...THOSE TEN MEN YOU KILLED HAD KIDS OR WIVES OF THEIR OWN-- WHAT THEN?
IF YOU EVER RUN INTO ONE OF THEM, DO YOU PLAN TO JUST KNEEL...
...AND BEG FOR FORGIVE-NESS? DO YOU EXPECT TO GET IT?

IN THIS WORLD THERE'S ONLY ONE THING THAT CAN PAY FOR A LIFE.

ANOTHER LIFE! THAT'S ALL.

YOU TOOK THAT BURDEN ON YOURSELF LONG AGO.

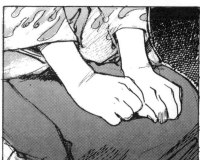

AND IF YOU'RE JUST AFRAID OF BLOOD, AND YOU'RE JUST TRYING TO FOOL YOURSELF...

...THEN THAT'S JUST A BUNCH OF--

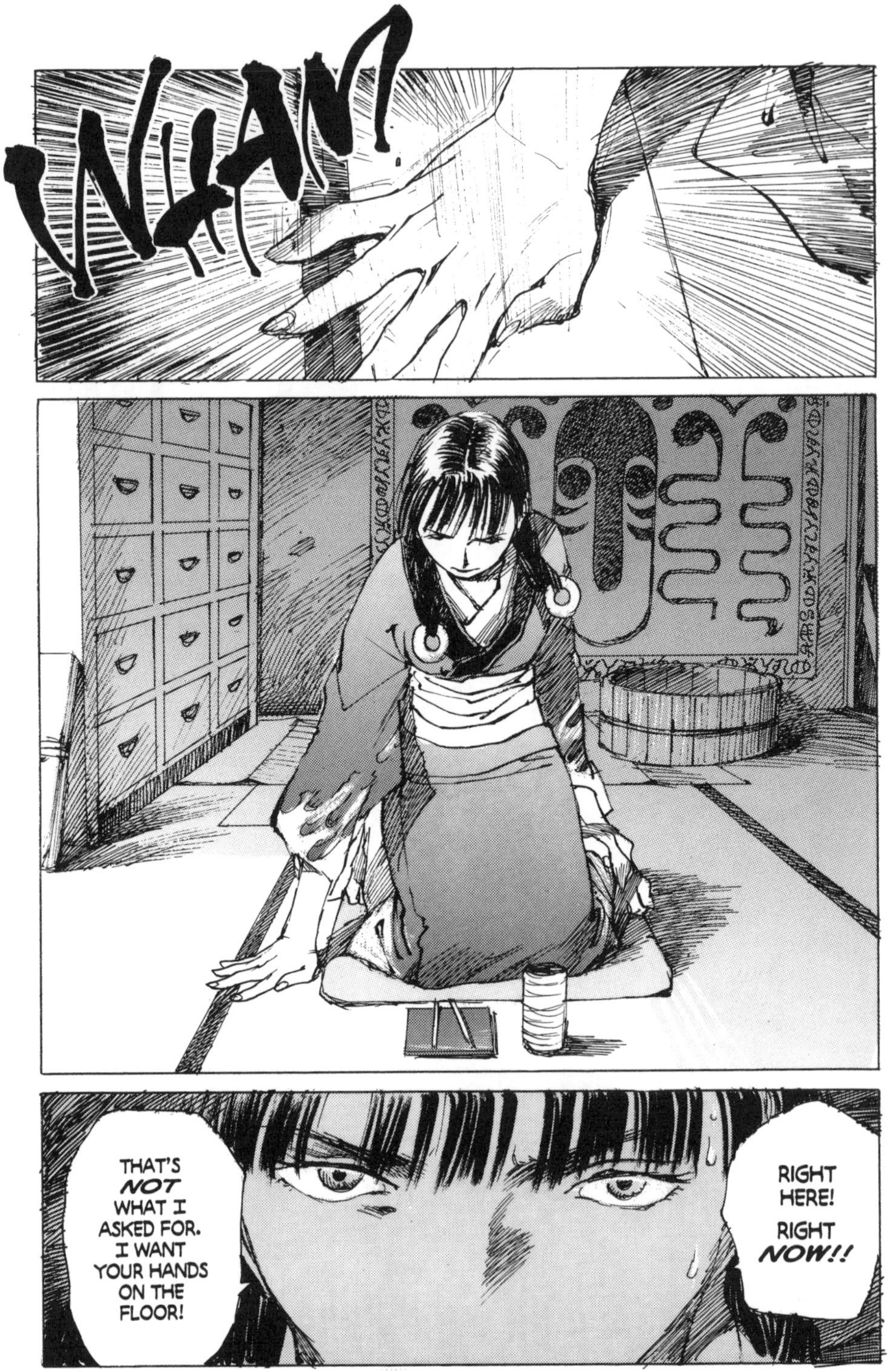
WHAM!
THAT'S NOT WHAT I ASKED FOR. I WANT YOUR HANDS ON THE FLOOR!
RIGHT HERE! RIGHT NOW!!

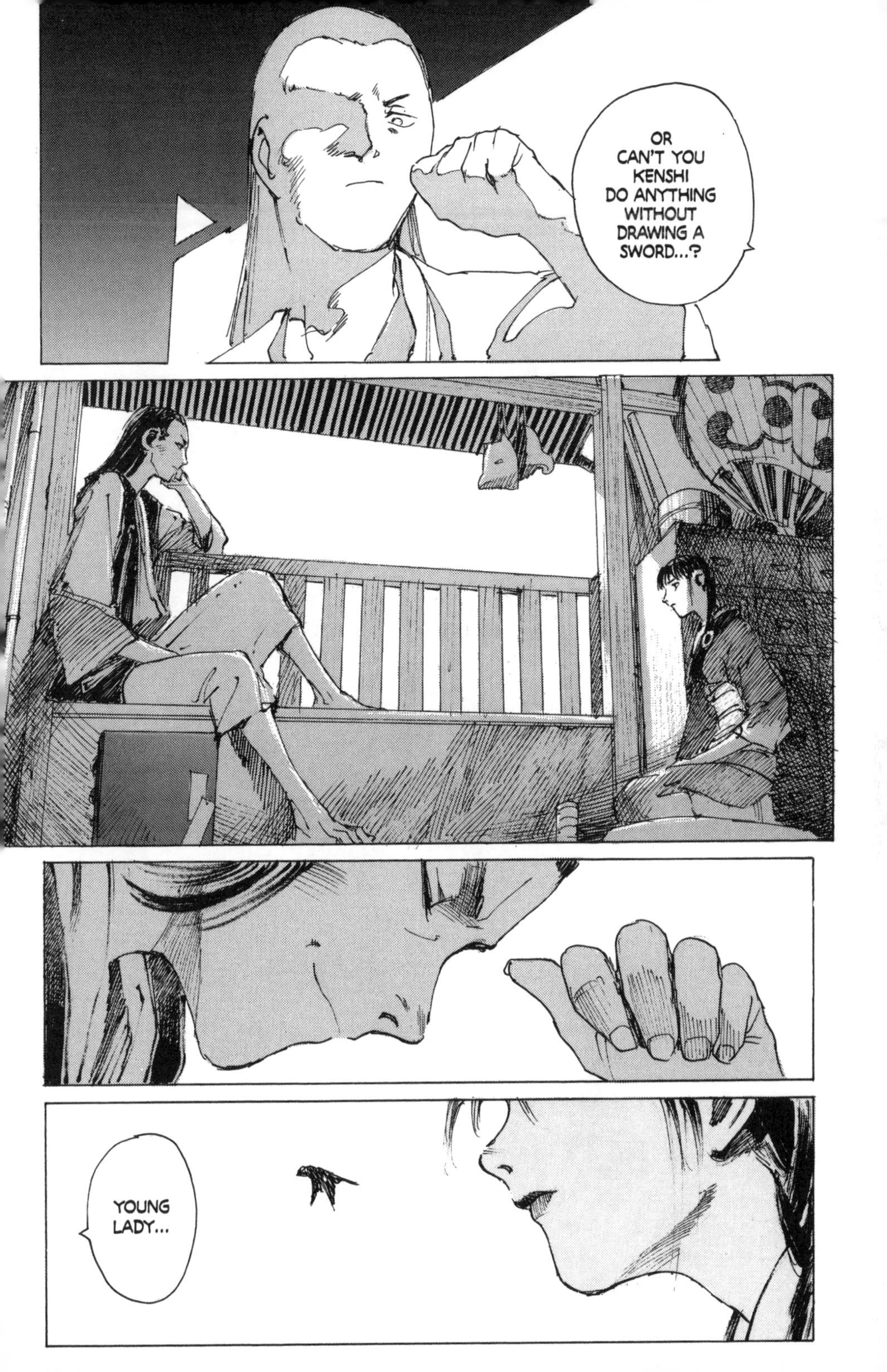
OR CAN'T YOU KENSHI DO ANYTHING WITHOUT DRAWING A SWORD...?
YOUNG LADY...

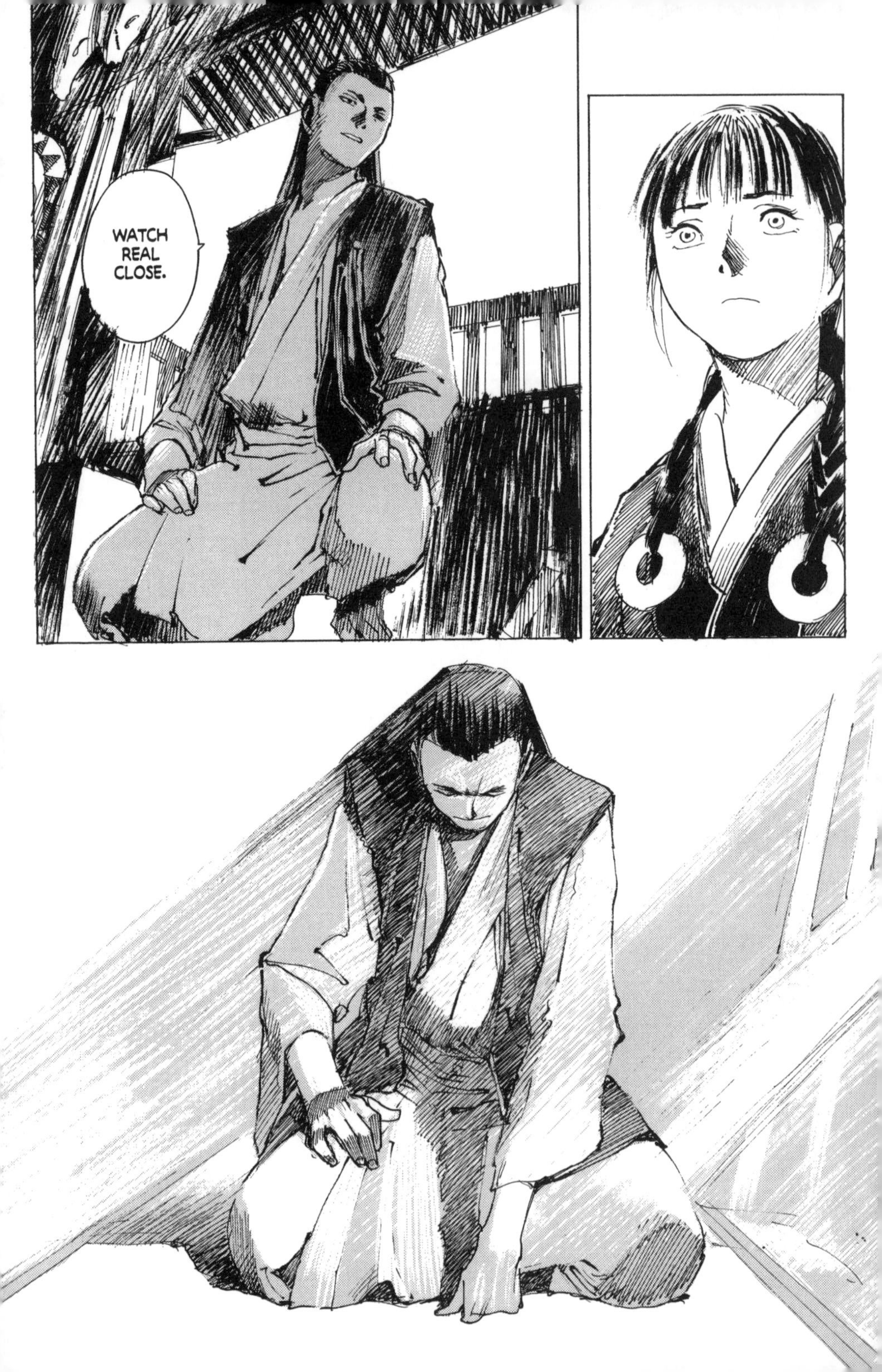
WATCH REAL CLOSE.

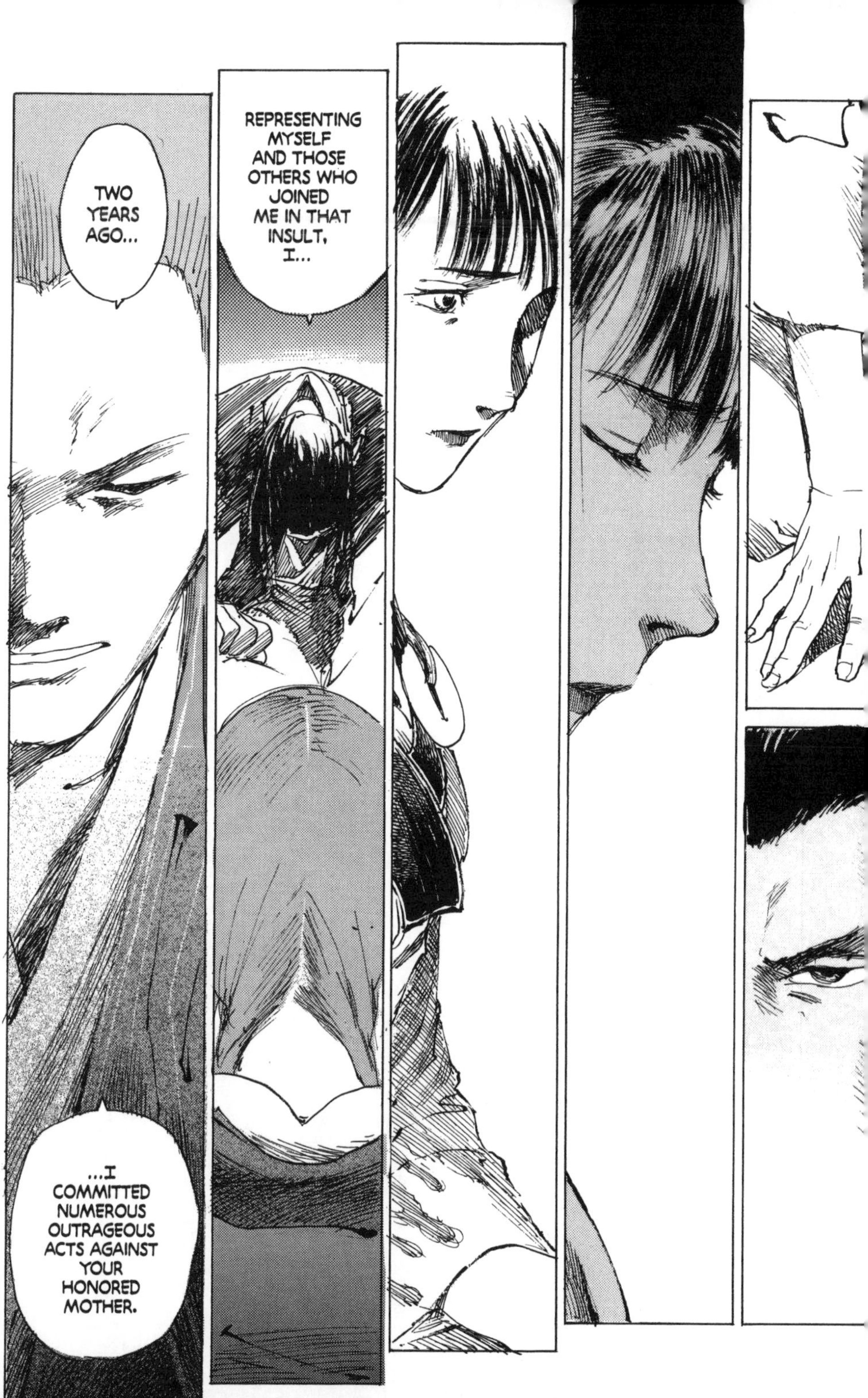
TWO YEARS AGO...
REPRESENTING MYSELF AND THOSE OTHERS WHO JOINED ME IN THAT INSULT, I...
...I COMMITTED NUMEROUS OUTRAGEOUS ACTS AGAINST YOUR HONORED MOTHER.

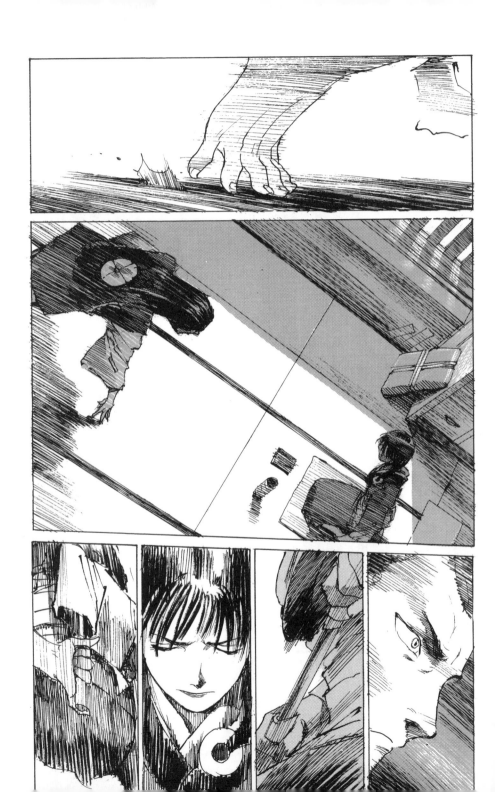

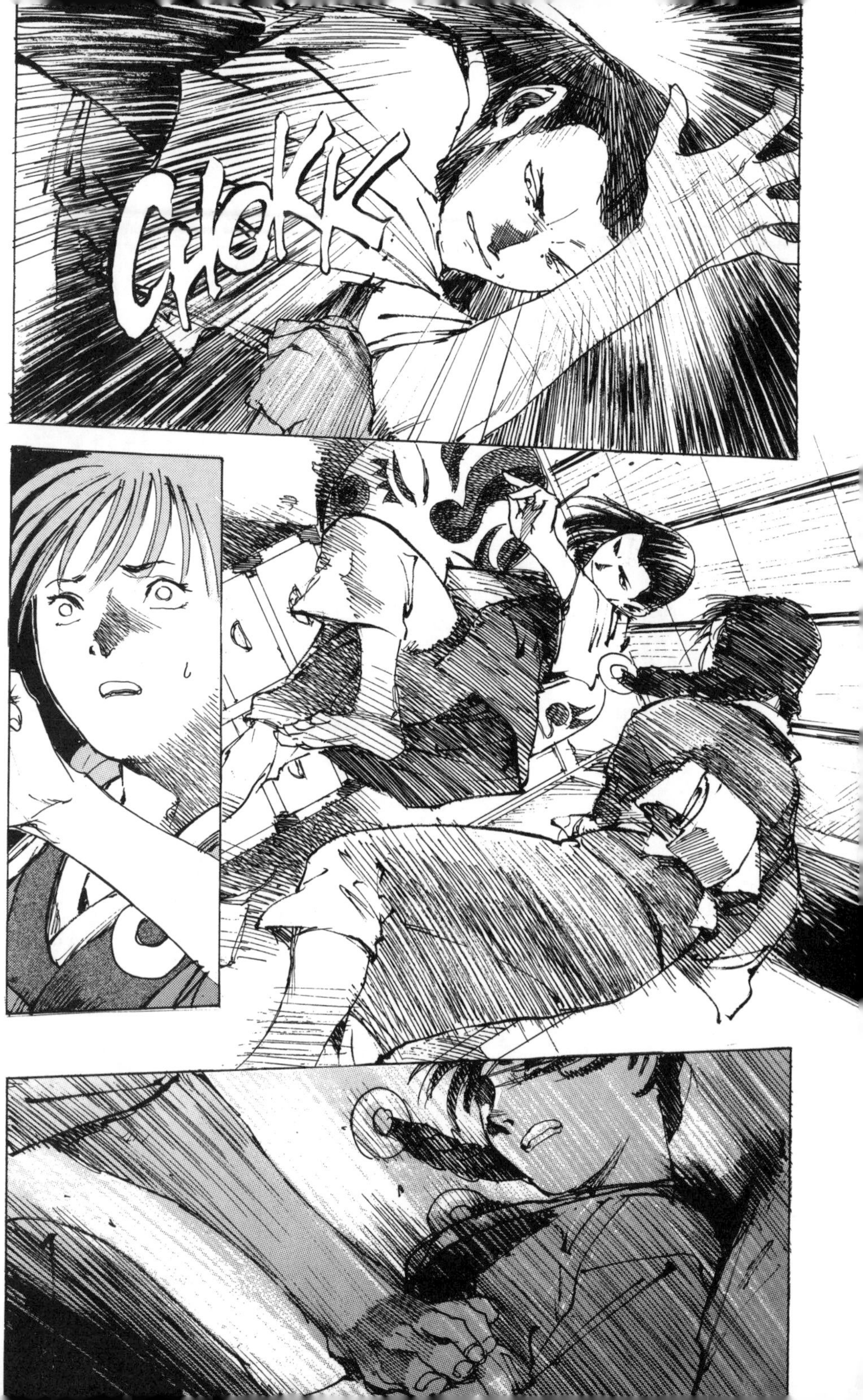
CHOKK

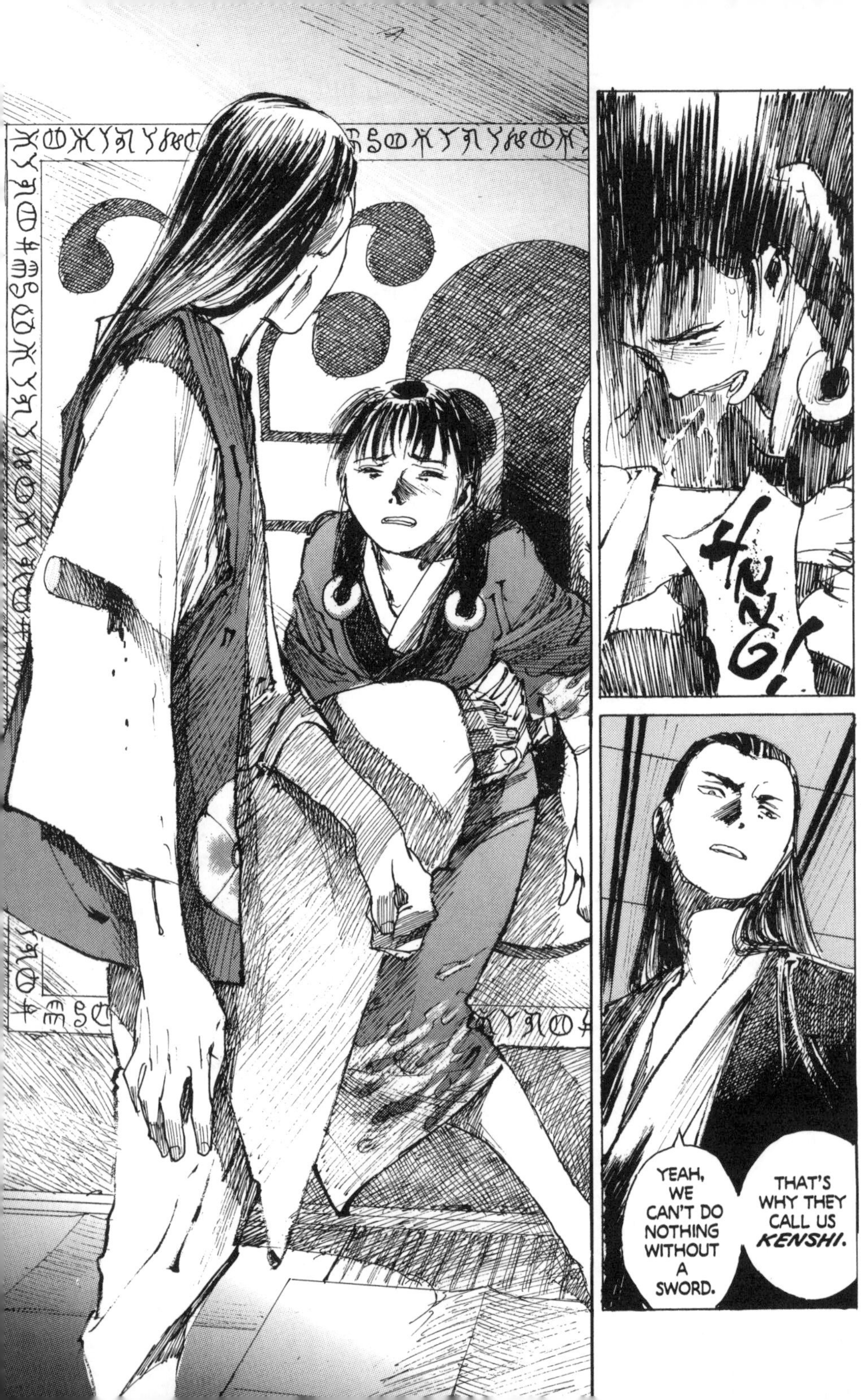
HNG!
THAT'S WHY THEY CALL US *KENSHI*.
YEAH, WE CAN'T DO NOTHING WITHOUT A SWORD.

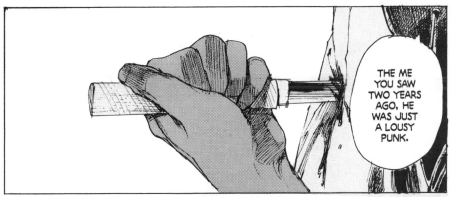

THE ME YOU SAW TWO YEARS AGO, HE WAS JUST A LOUSY PUNK.

MAYBE I DON'T UNDERSTAND THE NORMAL WORLD MUCH, BUT...

WHEN RENZO CAME BACK TO ME, I FIGURED MAYBE NOW I COULD FINALLY WASH MY HANDS OF ALL THAT KILLING.

I DON'T WANT RENZO TO KNOW THE REAL ME. NOT MY ONLY SON.

BUT WHO COULD HAVE IMAGINED...

...THAT *YOU* WOULD BEFRIEND HIM?!

SORRY, GIRL. BUT...

...I'VE GOT TO NIP THIS IN THE BUD.

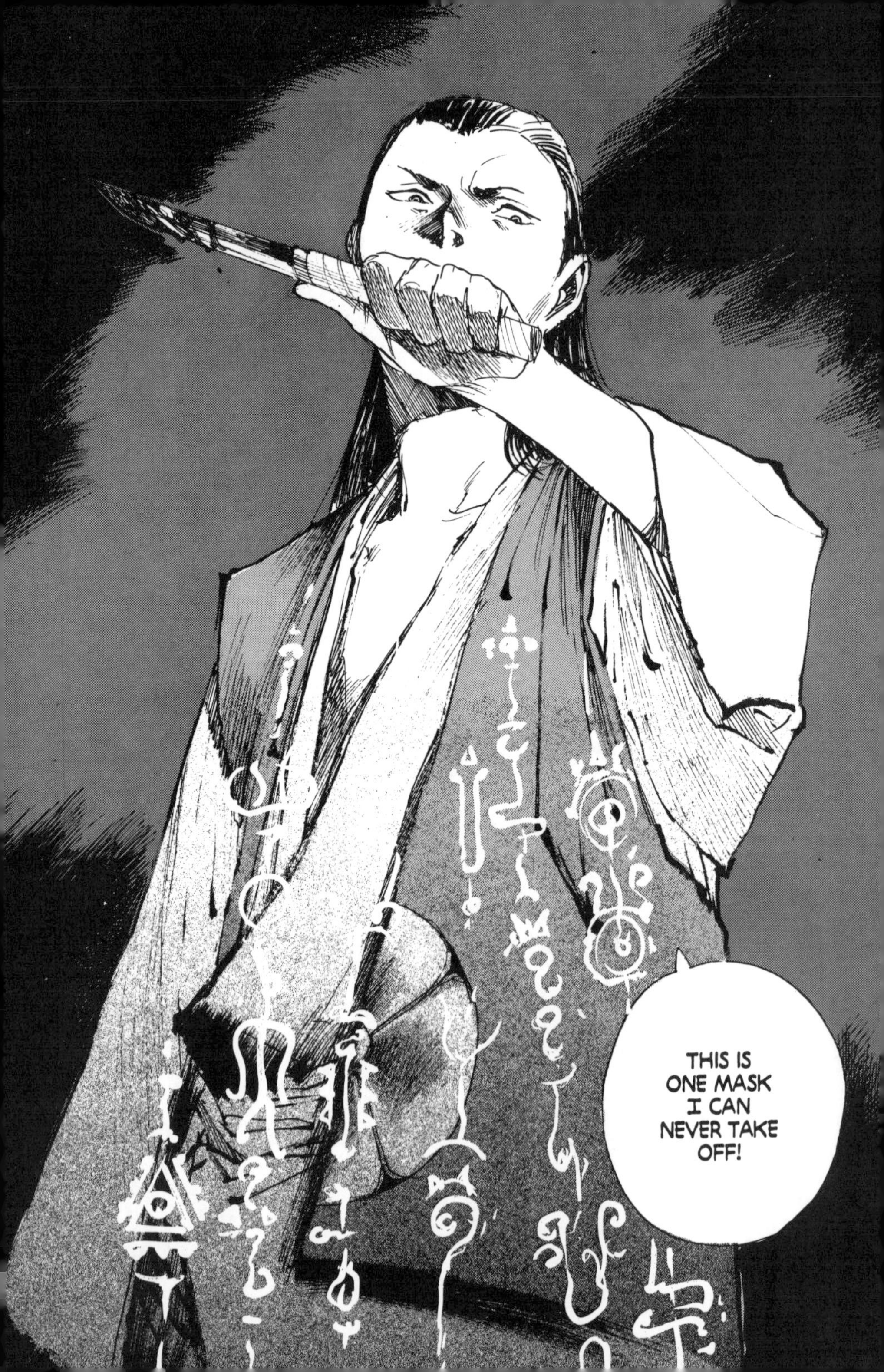
THIS IS ONE MASK I CAN NEVER TAKE OFF!

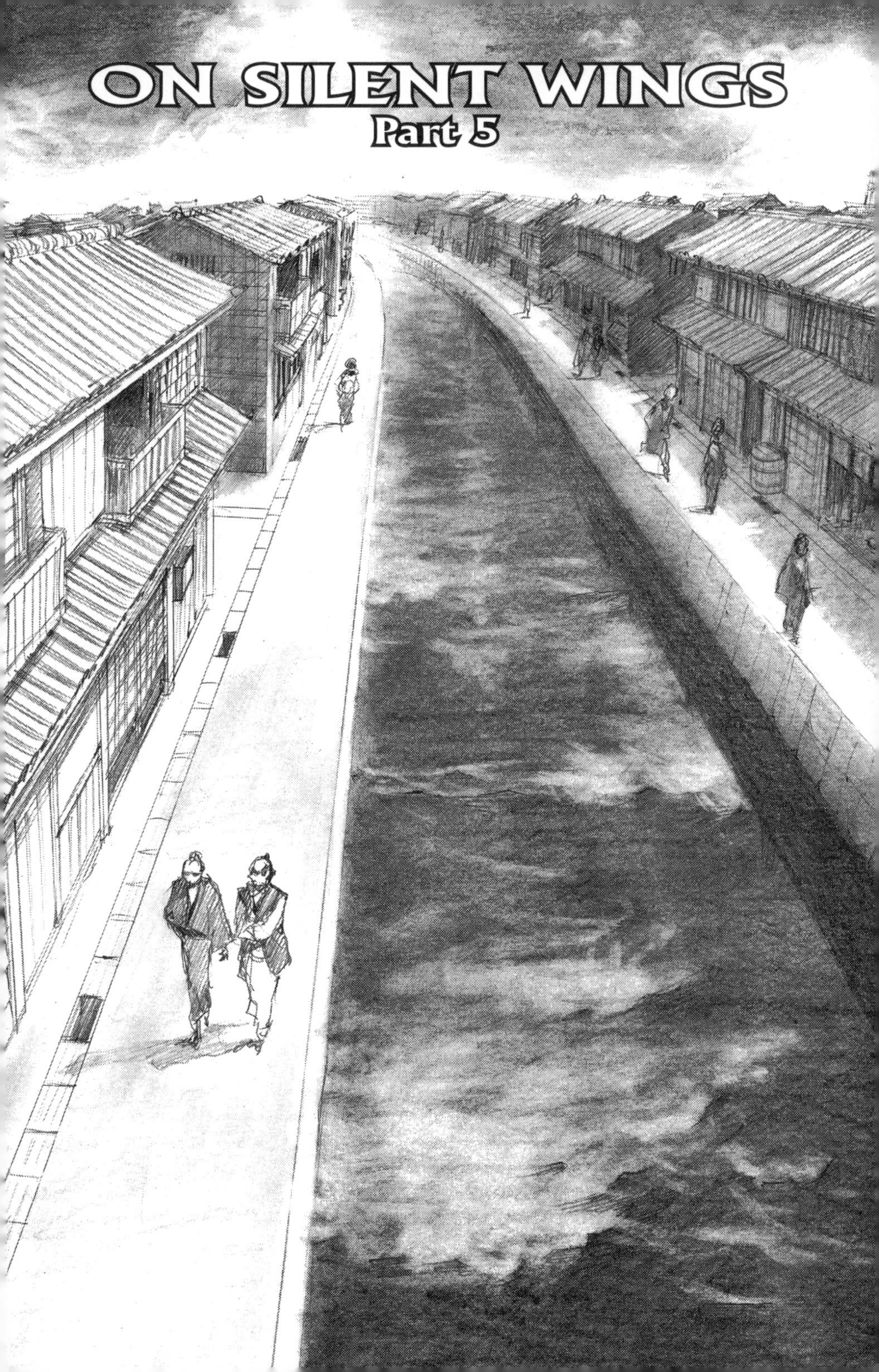
ON SILENT WINGS
Part 5

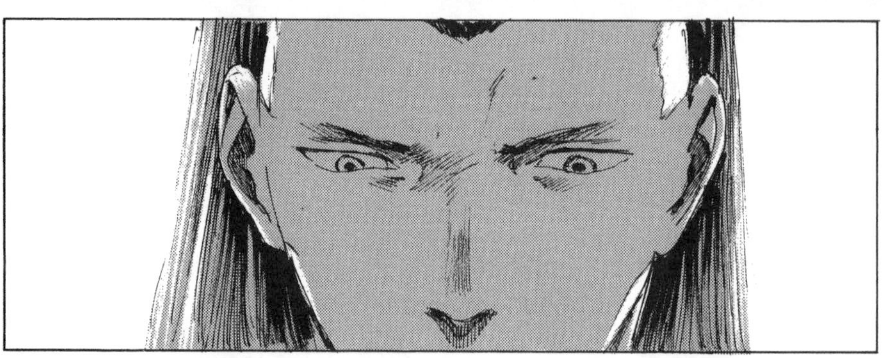
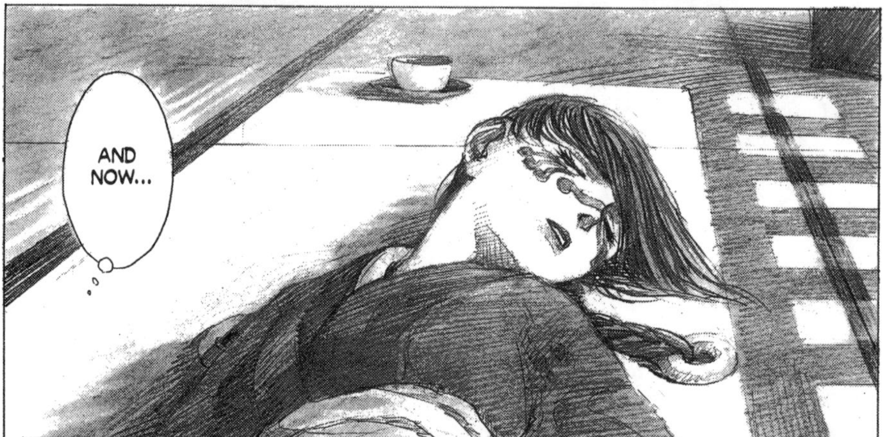
AND NOW...
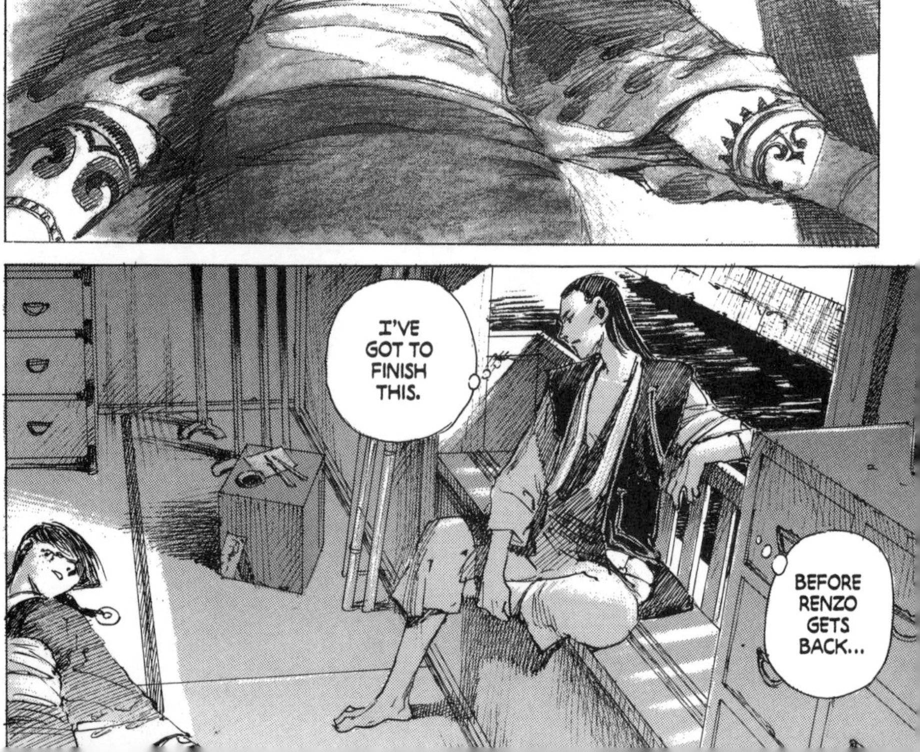
I'VE GOT TO FINISH THIS.
BEFORE RENZO GETS BACK...

HMM...
SHE
NEEDS A
LITTLE
MORE...
LIKE
THIS...

THERE--
THAT'S
GOOD.

NO
BLOOD...
TOO
HARD TO
CLEAN
UP.

SO
THAT
LEAVES...

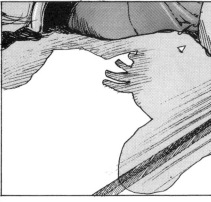

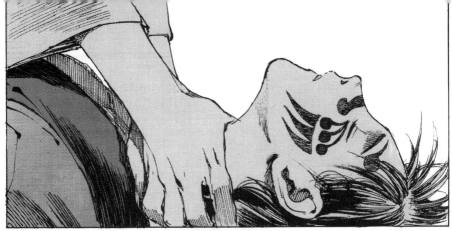

NNG...

SORRY, KID.

BUT THIS IS SOME-THING I JUST HAVE--

HEY, ARAYA ...?!

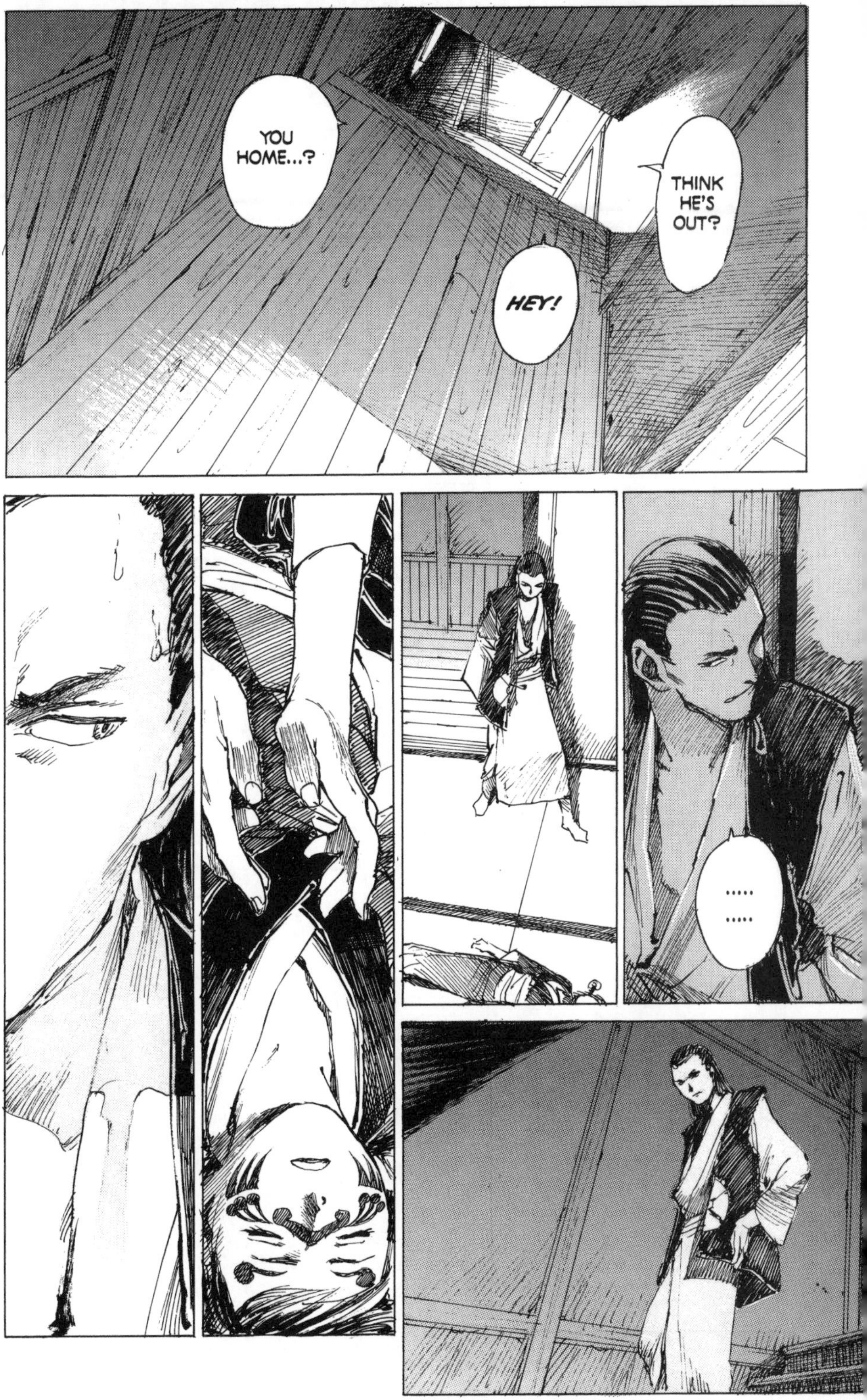
THINK HE'S OUT?
HEY!
YOU HOME...?
....

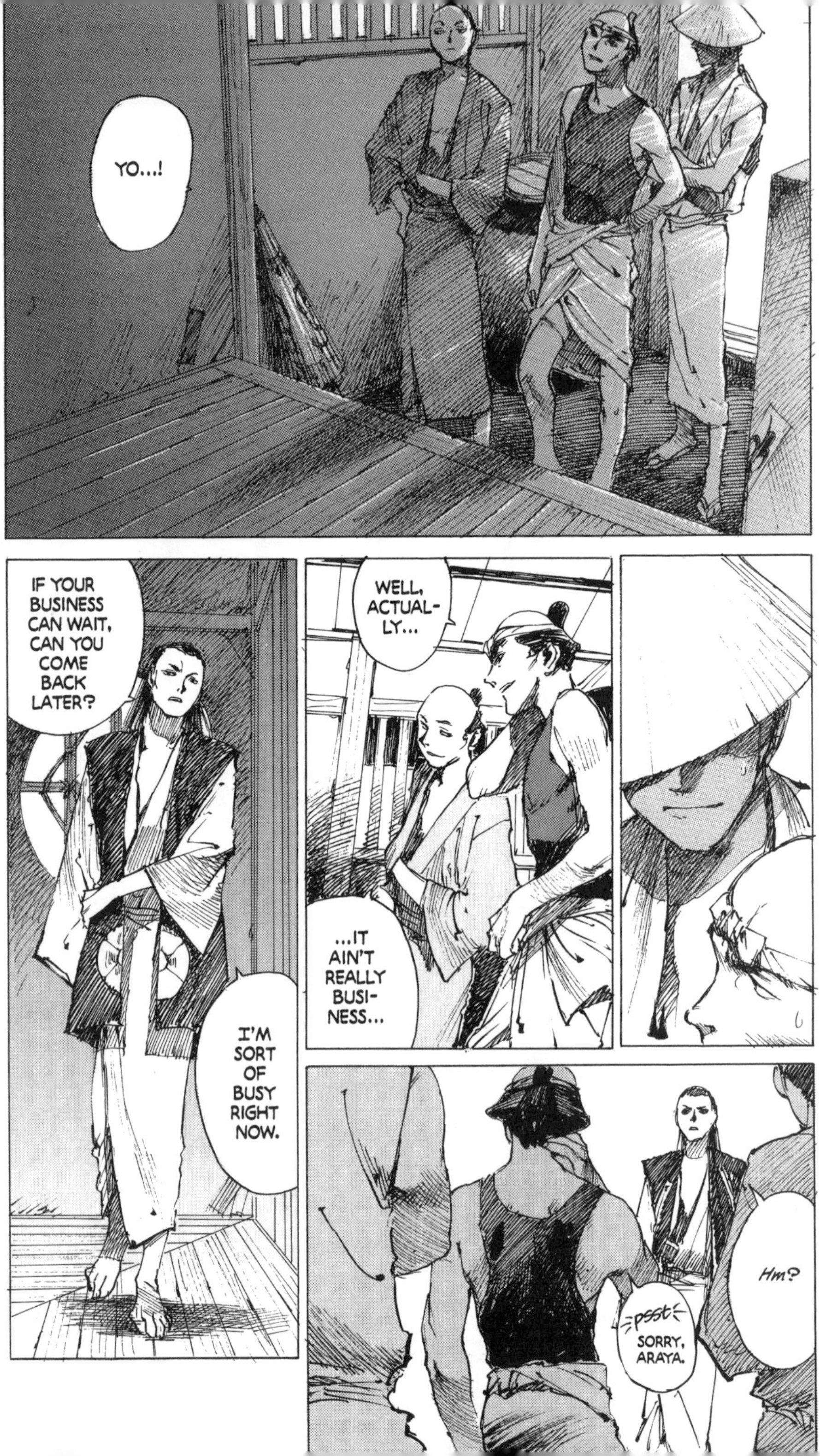
YO...!
IF YOUR BUSINESS CAN WAIT, CAN YOU COME BACK LATER?
I'M SORT OF BUSY RIGHT NOW.
WELL, ACTUALLY...
...IT AIN'T REALLY BUSINESS...
pssst
SORRY, ARAYA.
Hm?

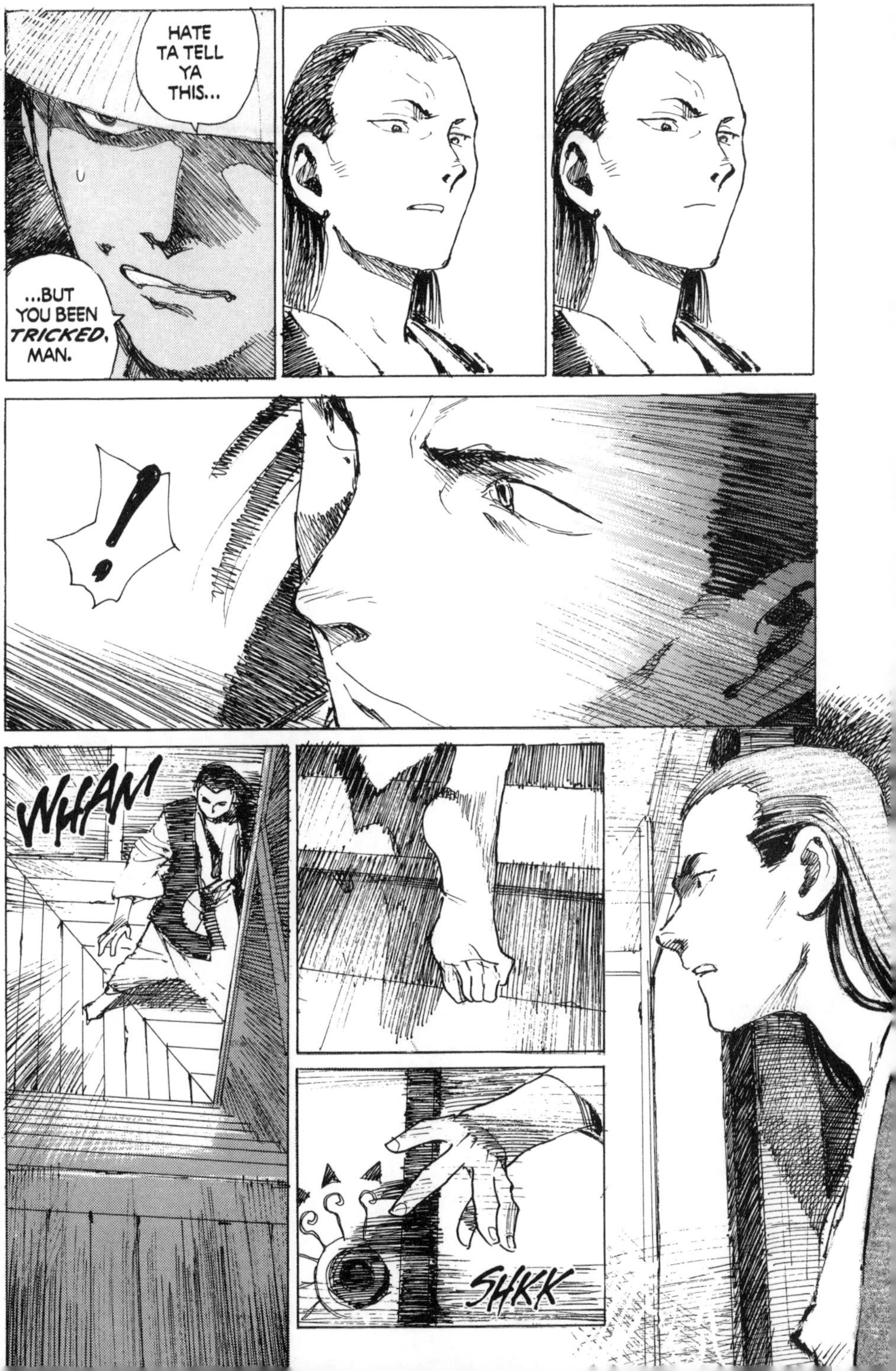
HATE TA TELL YA THIS...
...BUT YOU BEEN *TRICKED*, MAN.
!
WHAM
SHKK

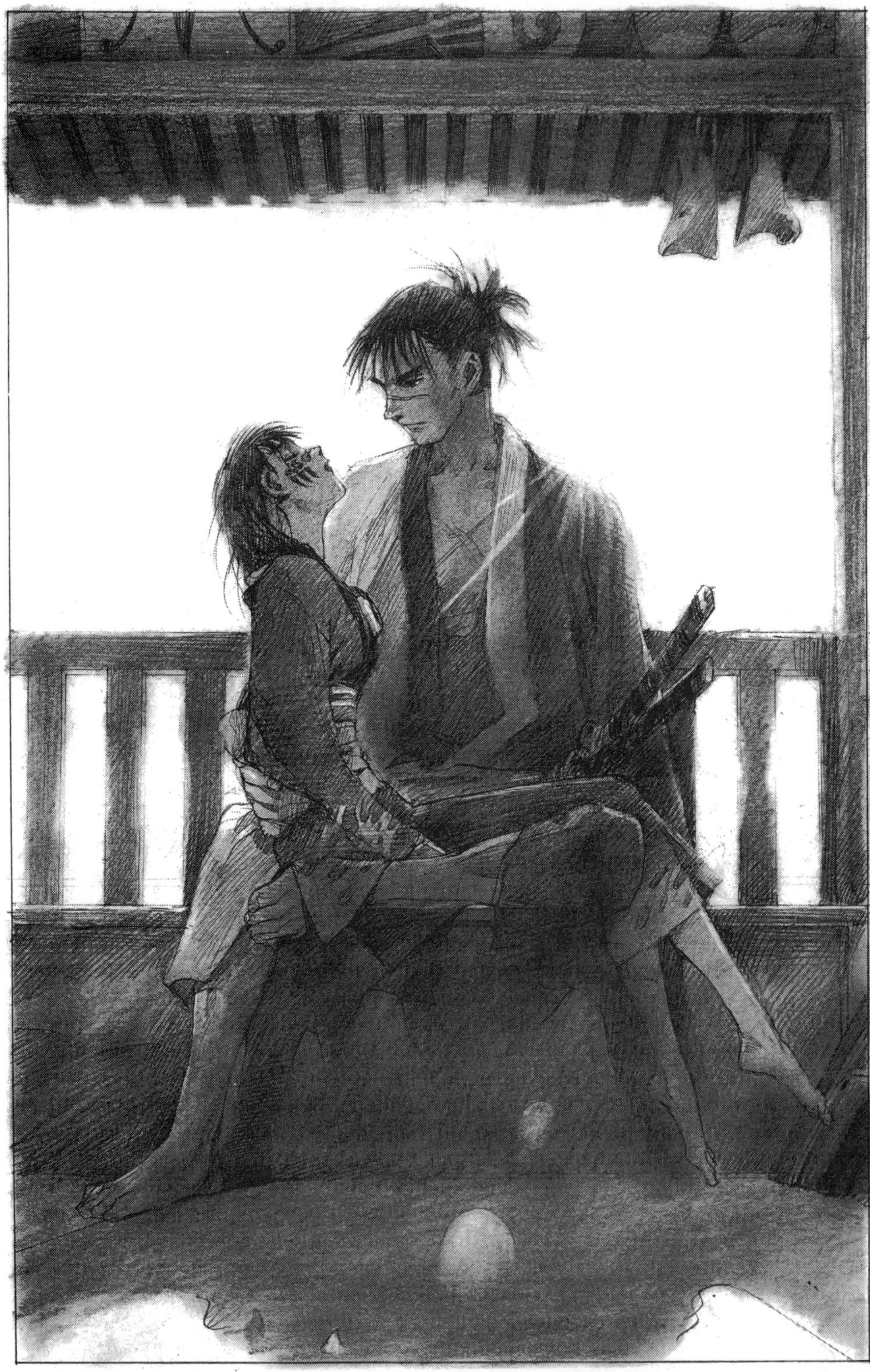

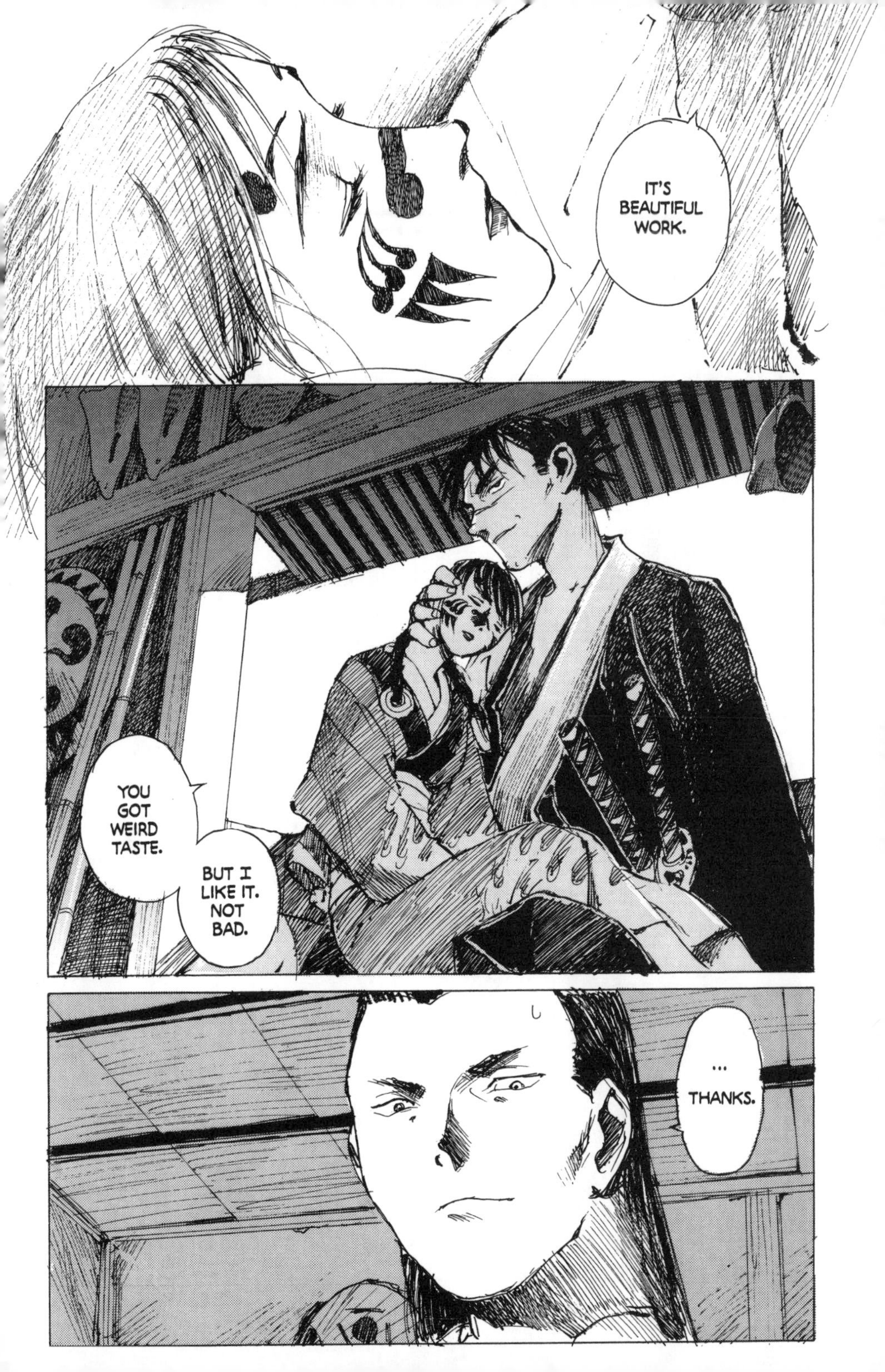
IT'S BEAUTIFUL WORK.
YOU GOT WEIRD TASTE.
BUT I LIKE IT. NOT BAD.
... THANKS.

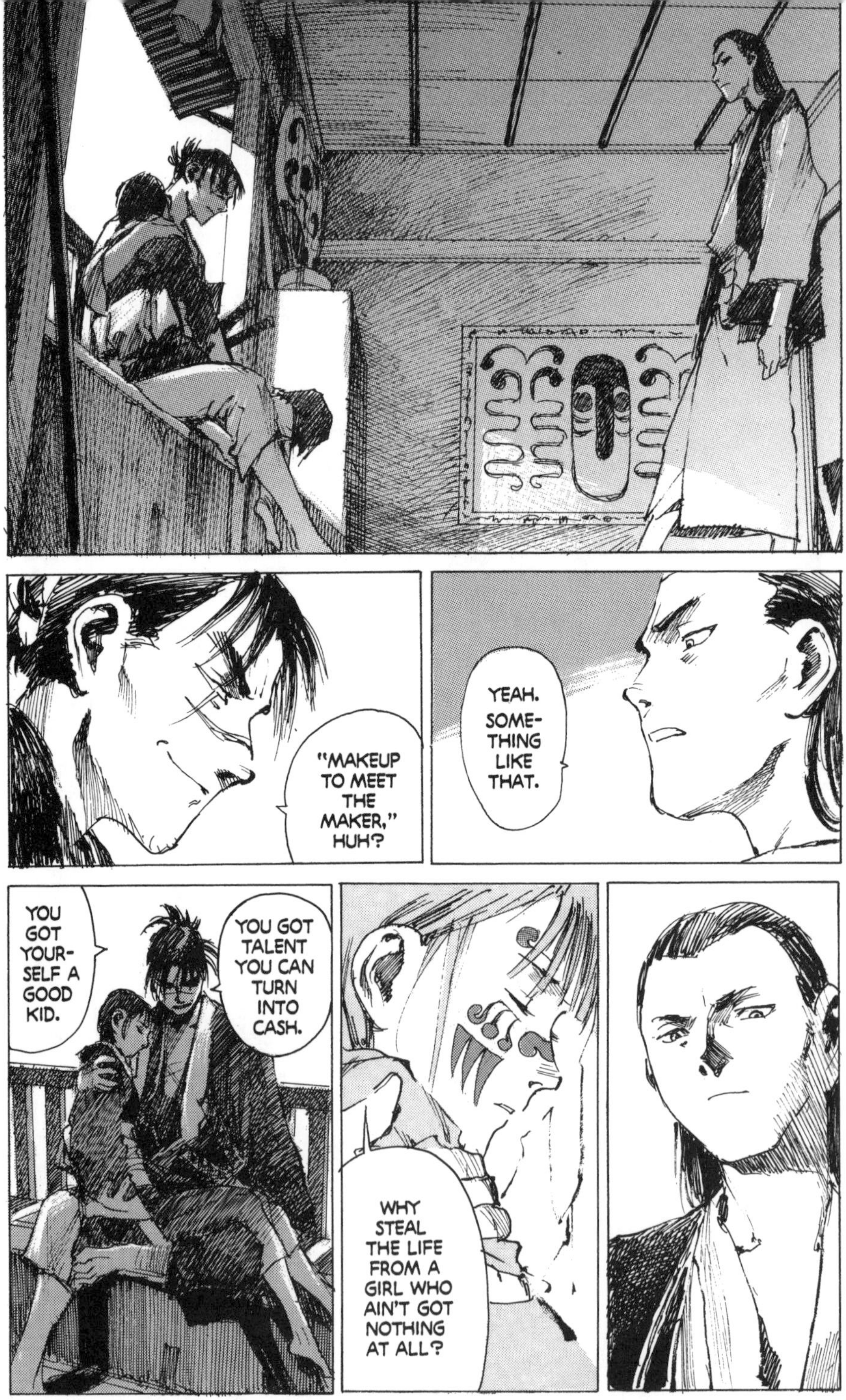
"MAKEUP TO MEET THE MAKER," HUH?
YEAH. SOME-THING LIKE THAT.
YOU GOT YOUR-SELF A GOOD KID.
YOU GOT TALENT YOU CAN TURN INTO CASH.
WHY STEAL THE LIFE FROM A GIRL WHO AIN'T GOT NOTHING AT ALL?

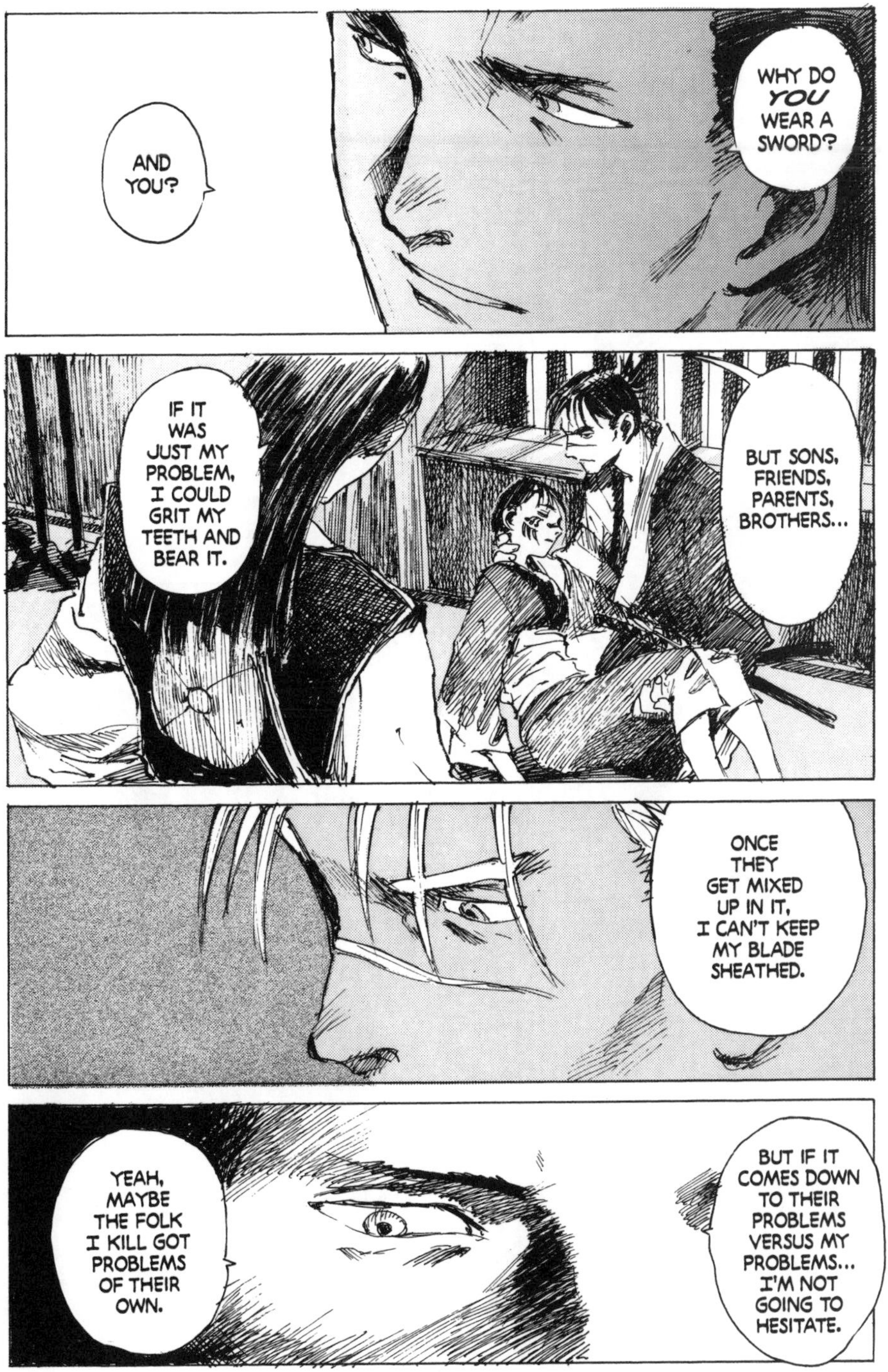
AND YOU?
WHY DO *YOU* WEAR A SWORD?
IF IT WAS JUST MY PROBLEM, I COULD GRIT MY TEETH AND BEAR IT.
BUT SONS, FRIENDS, PARENTS, BROTHERS...
ONCE THEY GET MIXED UP IN IT, I CAN'T KEEP MY BLADE SHEATHED.
YEAH, MAYBE THE FOLK I KILL GOT PROBLEMS OF THEIR OWN.
BUT IF IT COMES DOWN TO THEIR PROBLEMS VERSUS MY PROBLEMS... I'M NOT GOING TO HESITATE.

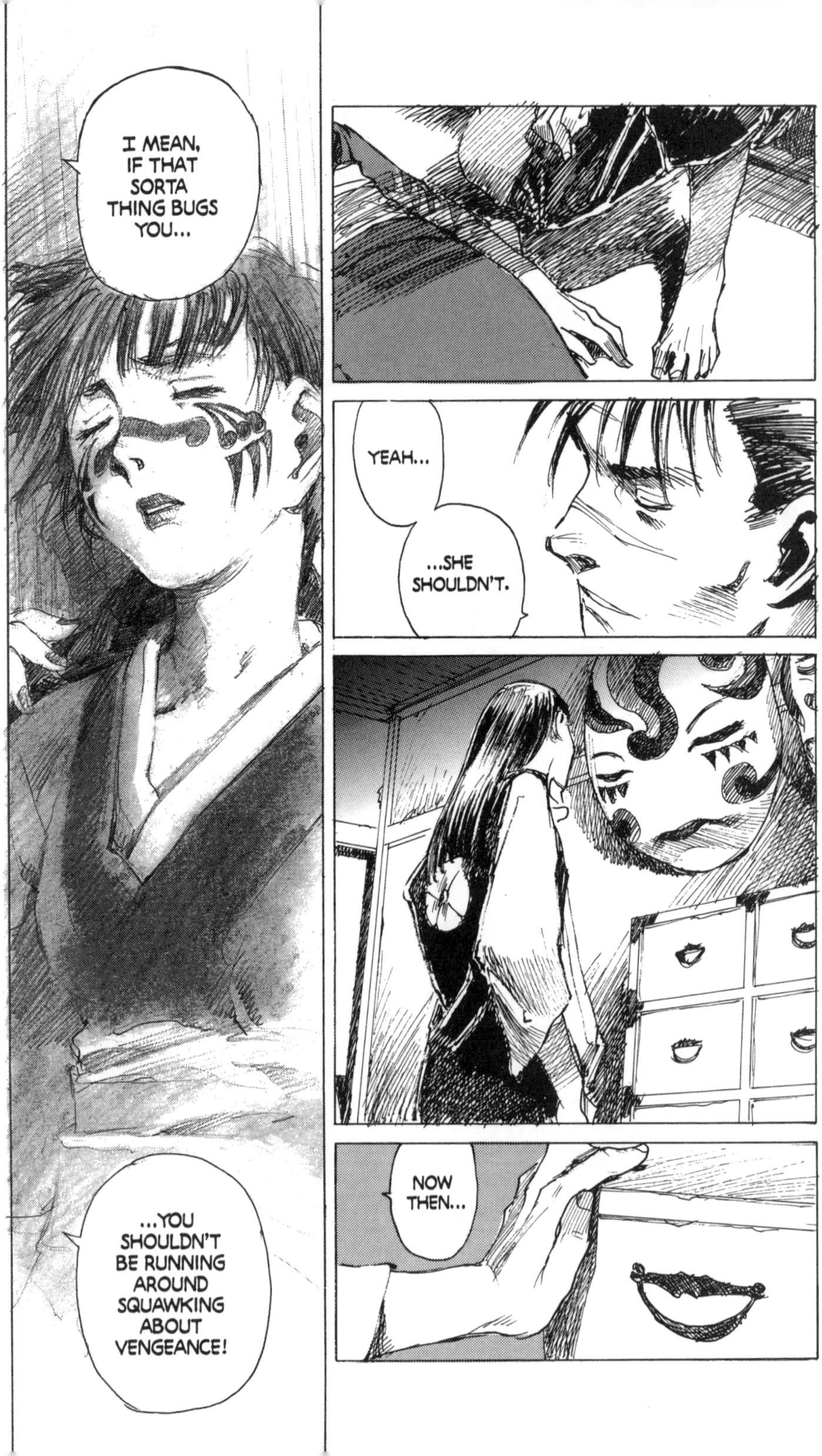
I MEAN, IF THAT SORTA THING BUGS YOU...
...YOU SHOULDN'T BE RUNNING AROUND SQUAWKING ABOUT VENGEANCE!
YEAH...
...SHE SHOULDN'T.
NOW THEN...

HNNF!!

...?

HEY, MANJI.

I'M BUILDING *OUR* RING.

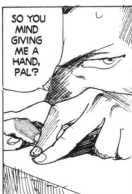

SO YOU MIND GIVING ME A HAND, PAL?

OOOF!!

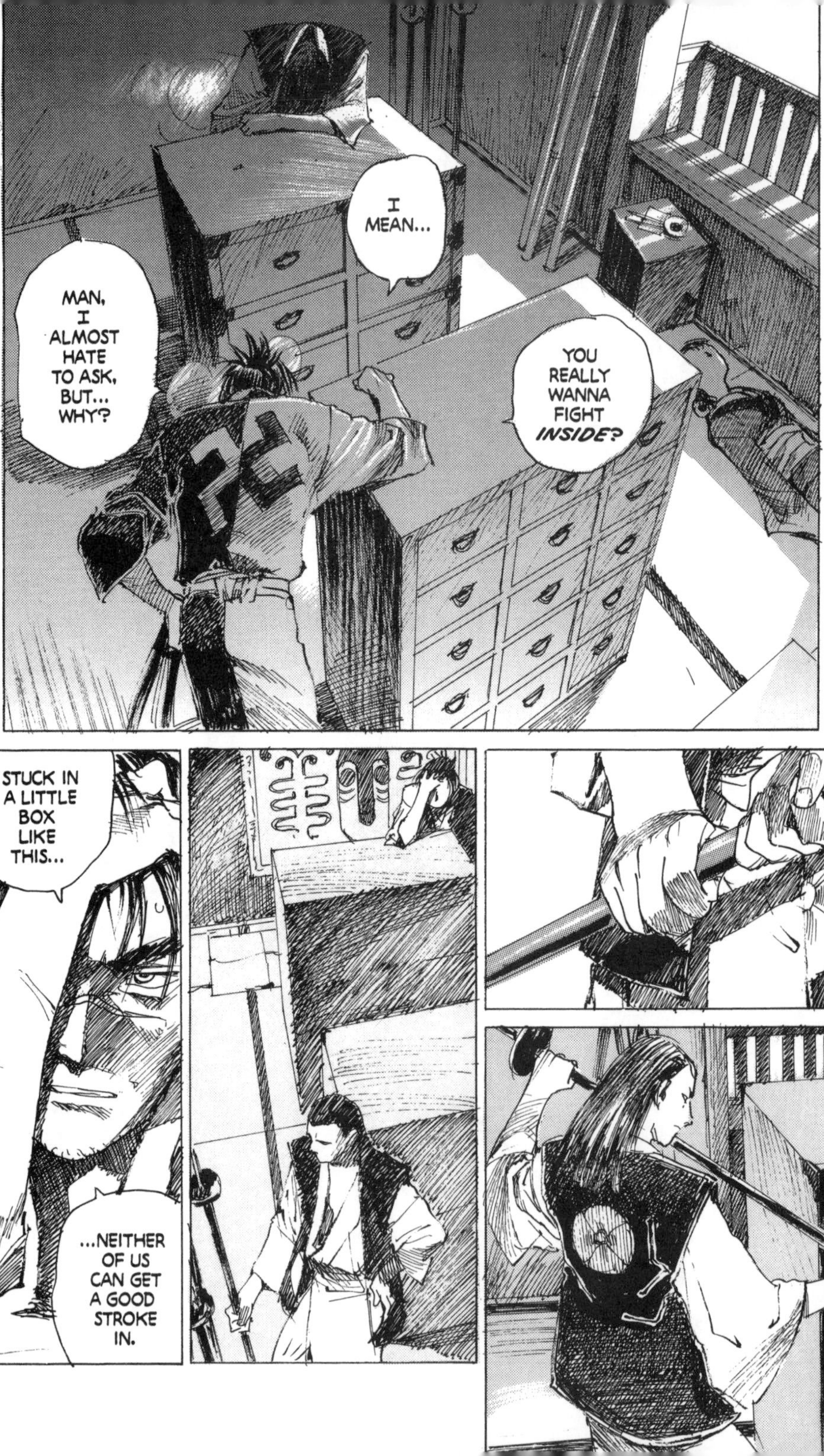
YOU REALLY WANNA FIGHT *INSIDE?*
I MEAN...
MAN, I ALMOST HATE TO ASK, BUT... WHY?
STUCK IN A LITTLE BOX LIKE THIS...
...NEITHER OF US CAN GET A GOOD STROKE IN.

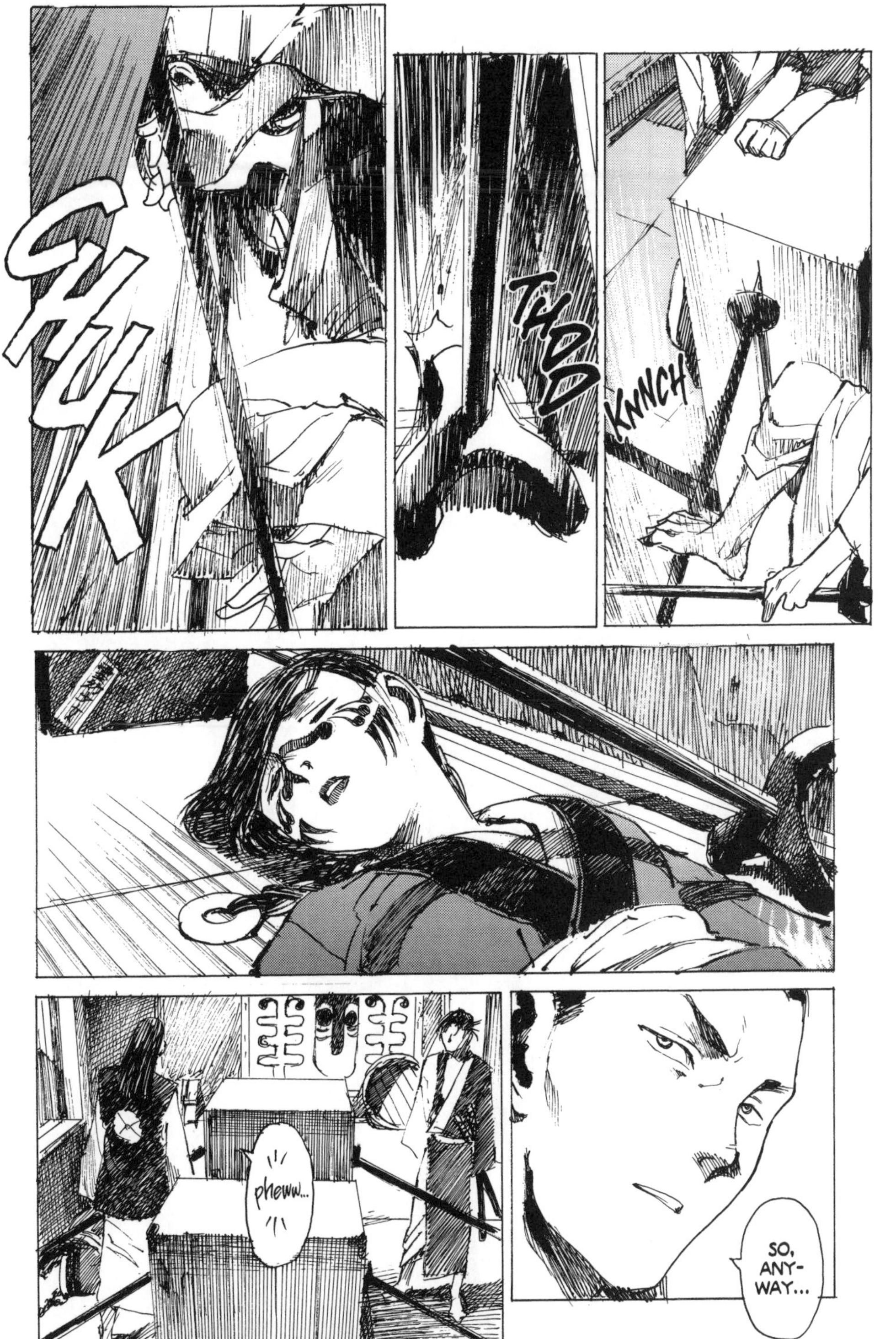
KNNCH
THDD
CHUK
SO, ANY-WAY...
pheww...

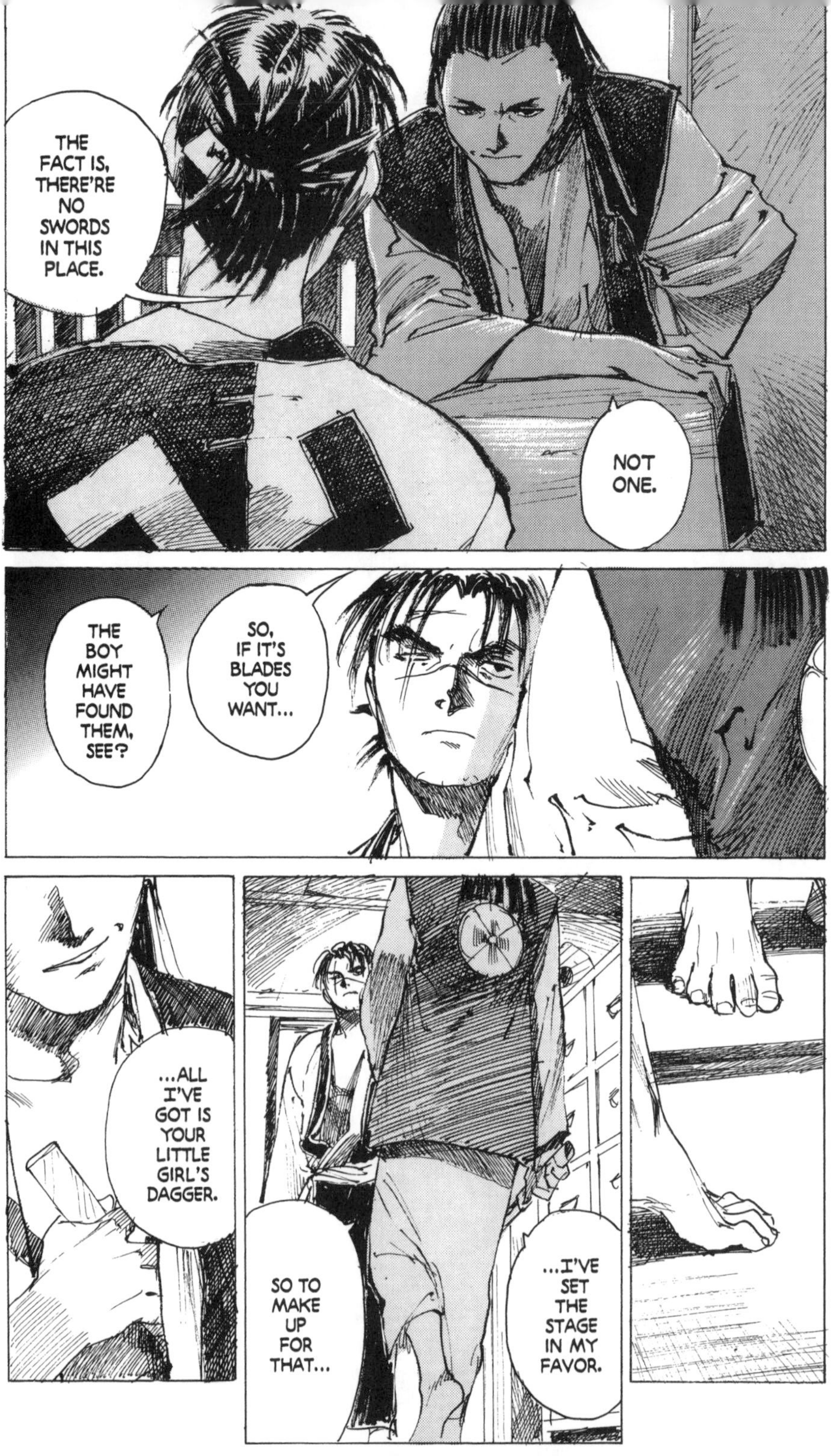
THE FACT IS, THERE'RE NO SWORDS IN THIS PLACE.
NOT ONE.
THE BOY MIGHT HAVE FOUND THEM, SEE?
SO, IF IT'S BLADES YOU WANT...
...ALL I'VE GOT IS YOUR LITTLE GIRL'S DAGGER.
SO TO MAKE UP FOR THAT...
...I'VE SET THE STAGE IN MY FAVOR.

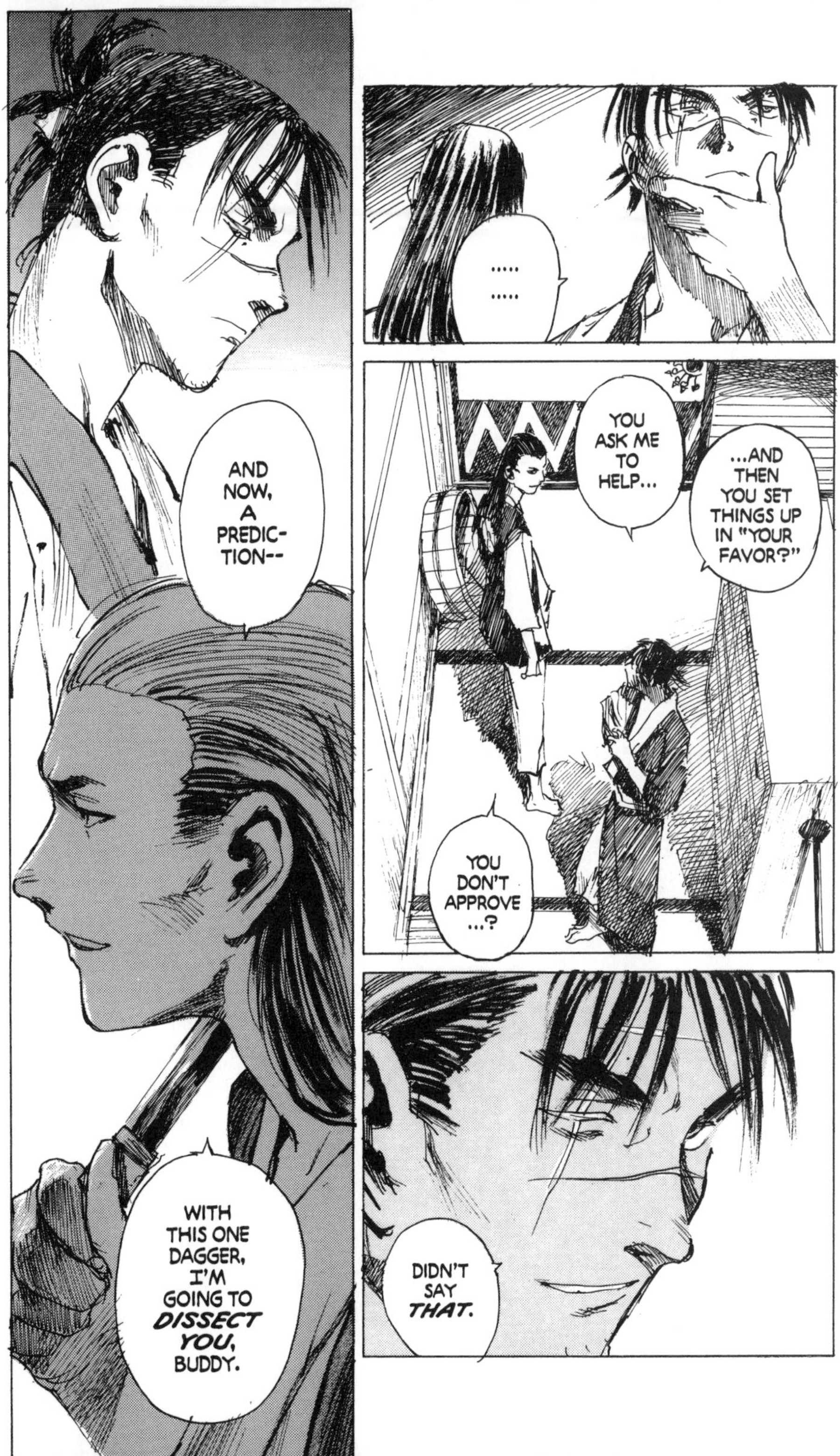
.....
.....
YOU ASK ME TO HELP...
...AND THEN YOU SET THINGS UP IN "YOUR FAVOR?"
YOU DON'T APPROVE ...?
DIDN'T SAY *THAT*.
AND NOW, A PREDICTION--
WITH THIS ONE DAGGER, I'M GOING TO ***DISSECT YOU***, BUDDY.

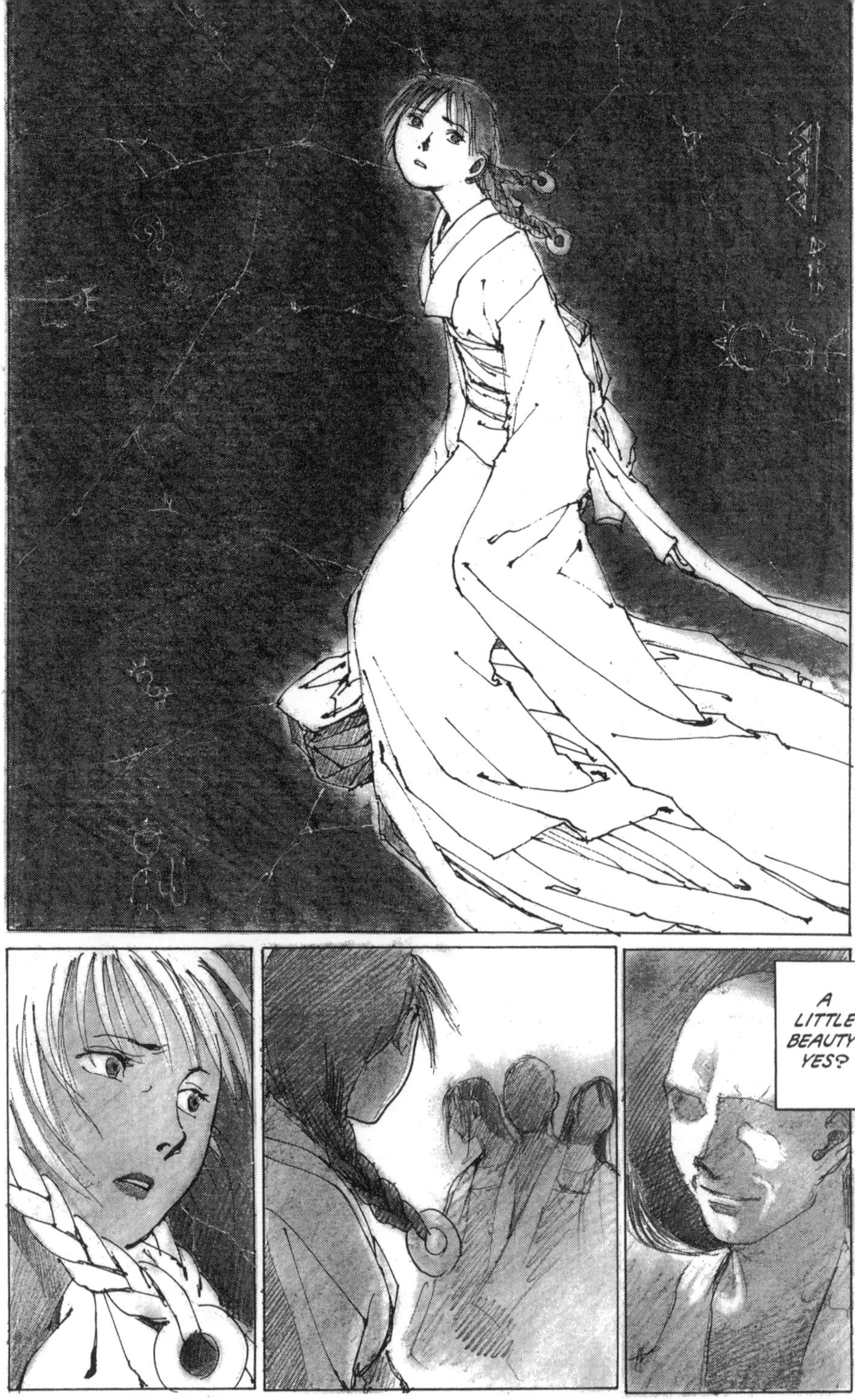
A LITTLE BEAUTY, YES?

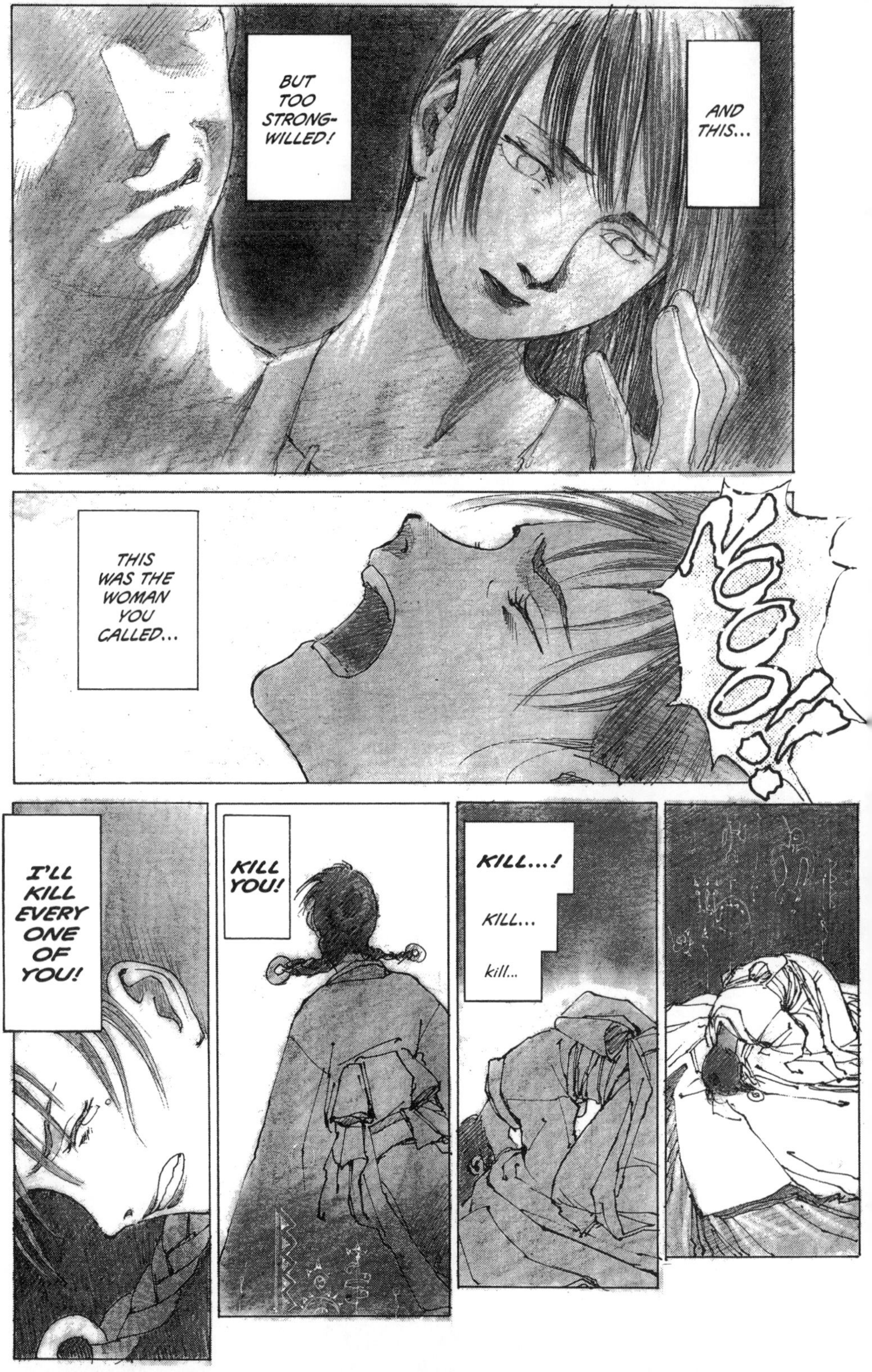
BUT TOO STRONG-WILLED!
AND THIS...
THIS WAS THE WOMAN YOU CALLED...
NOOOO!!
I'LL KILL EVERY ONE OF YOU!
KILL YOU!
KILL...!
KILL...
kill...

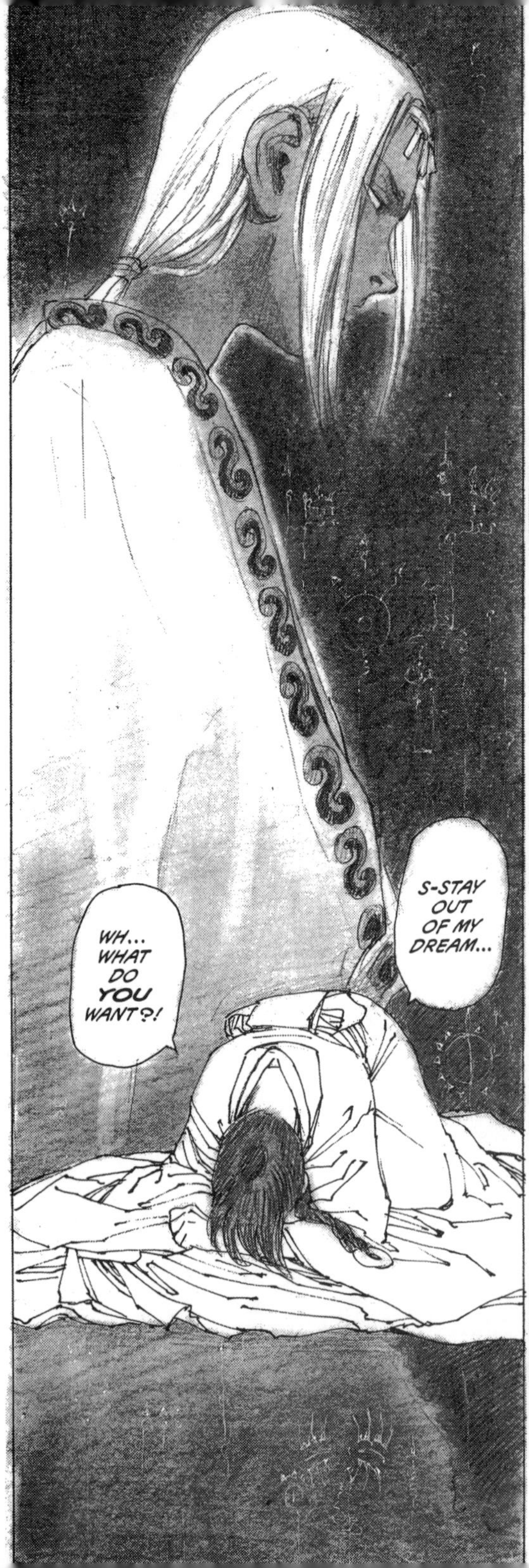
S-STAY OUT OF MY DREAM...
WH... WHAT DO **YOU** WANT?!
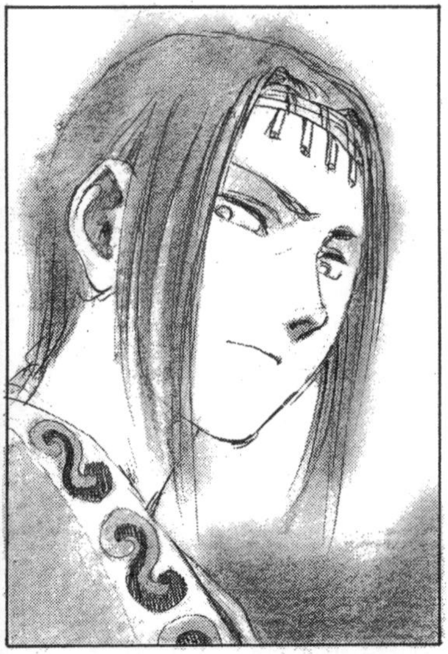
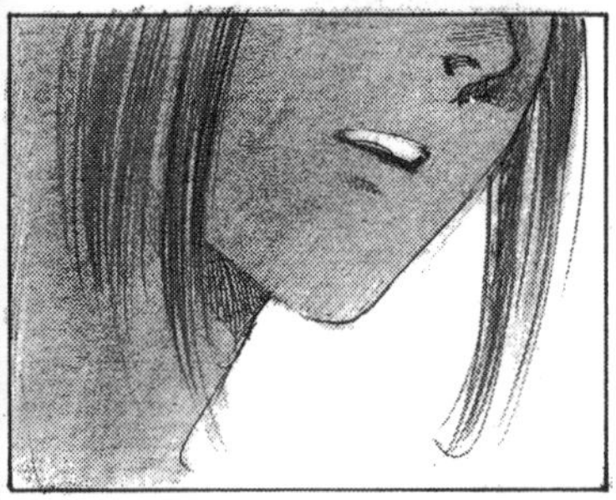
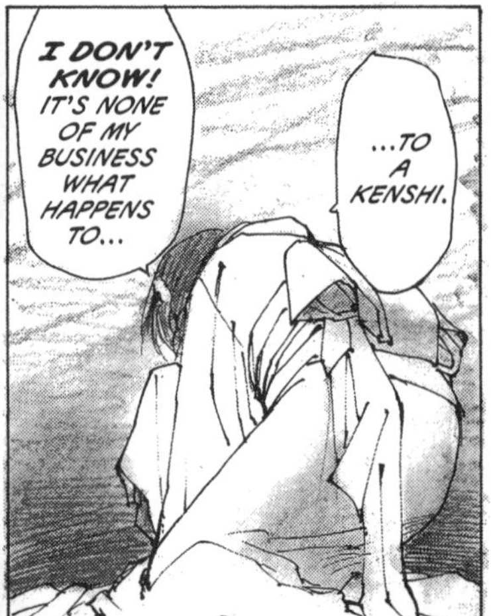
I DON'T KNOW! IT'S NONE OF MY BUSINESS WHAT HAPPENS TO...
...TO A KENSHI.

I JUST...

I JUST WANT TO PUNISH THE GUYS WHO KILLED MY MOTHER, MY FATHER...

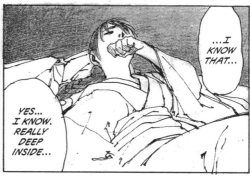

...I KNOW THAT...

YES... I KNOW. REALLY DEEP INSIDE...

...MY HANDS COULD BE **SOAKED** IN BLOOD...

...AND IT STILL WOULDN'T BRING MY MOMMY AND DADDY BACK TO ME.

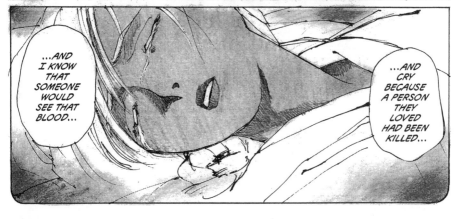

...AND I KNOW THAT SOMEONE WOULD SEE THAT BLOOD...

...AND CRY BECAUSE A PERSON THEY LOVED HAD BEEN KILLED...

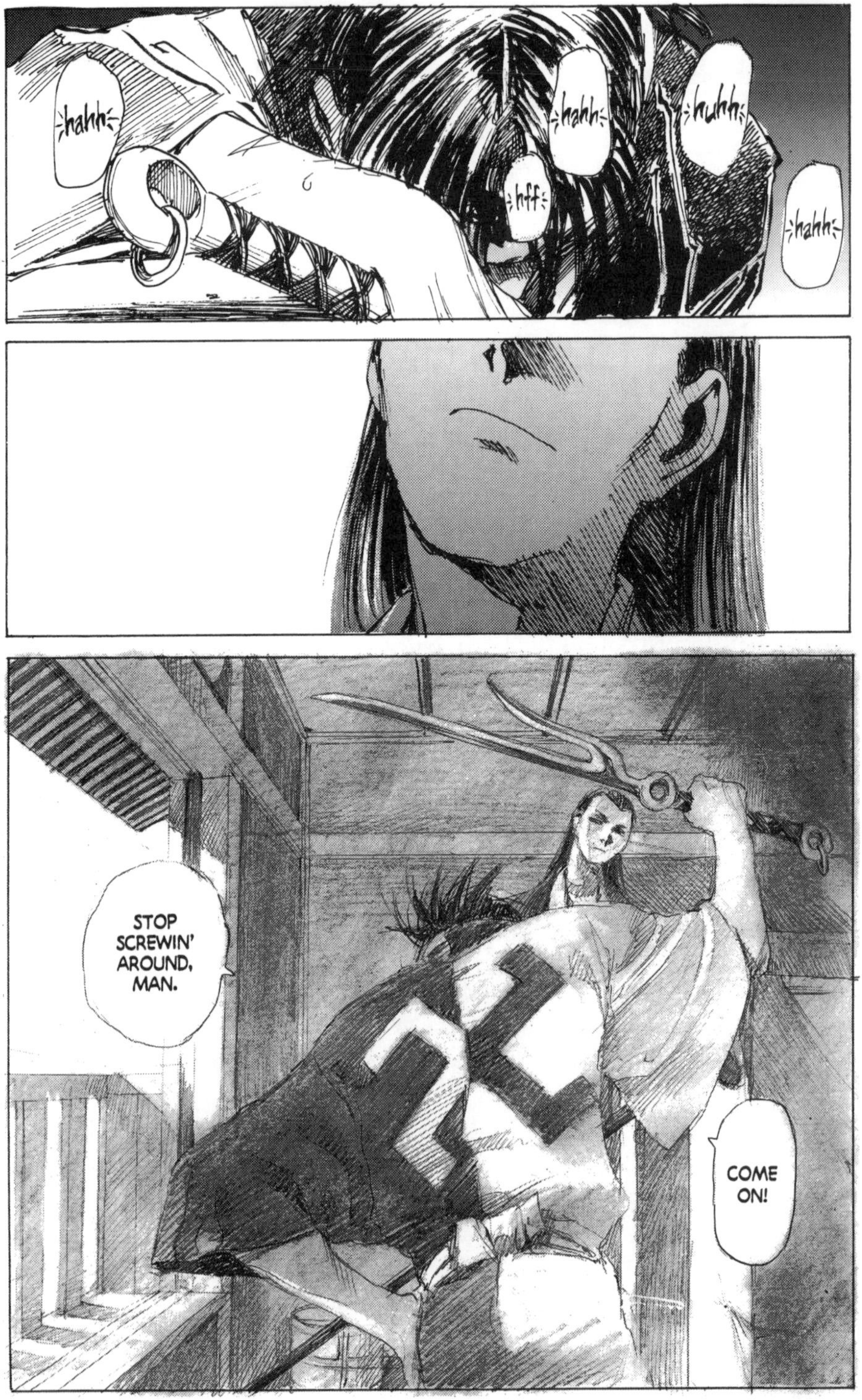
hahh
huhh
hahh
hff
hahh
STOP SCREWIN' AROUND, MAN.
COME ON!

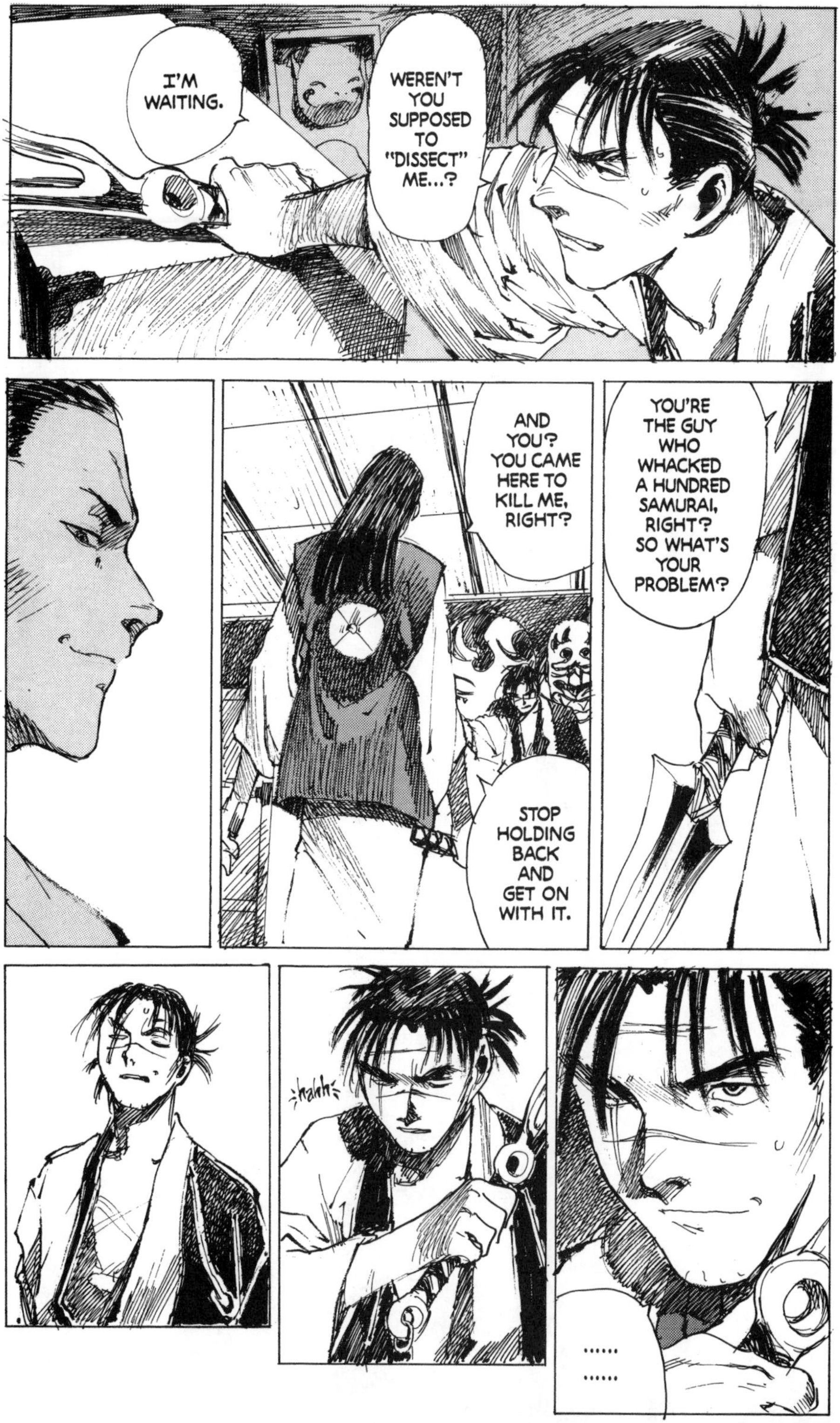
I'M WAITING.
WEREN'T YOU SUPPOSED TO "DISSECT" ME...?
AND YOU? YOU CAME HERE TO KILL ME, RIGHT?
STOP HOLDING BACK AND GET ON WITH IT.
YOU'RE THE GUY WHO WHACKED A HUNDRED SAMURAI, RIGHT? SO WHAT'S YOUR PROBLEM?
hahh
......
......

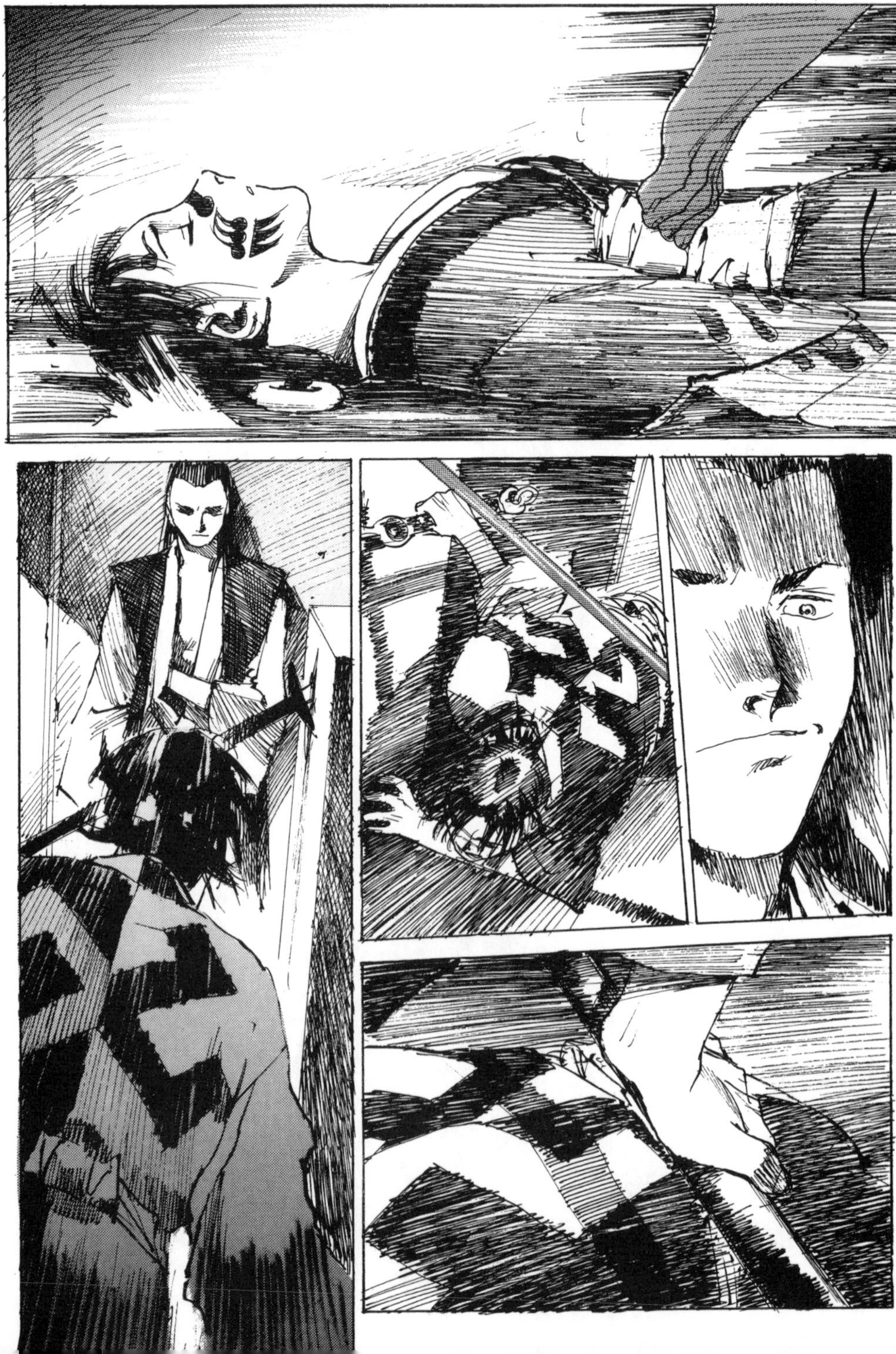

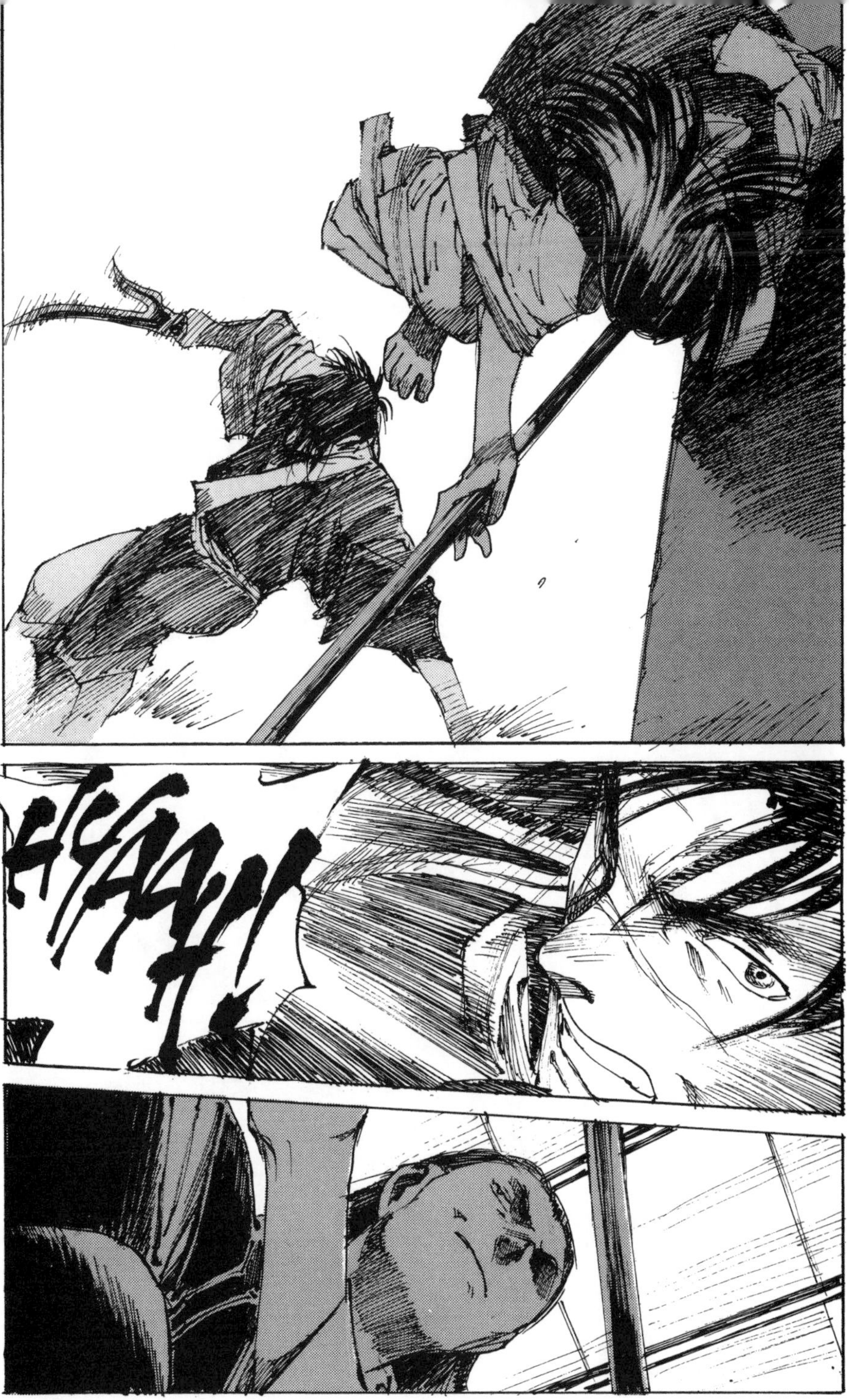
HYAAH!!

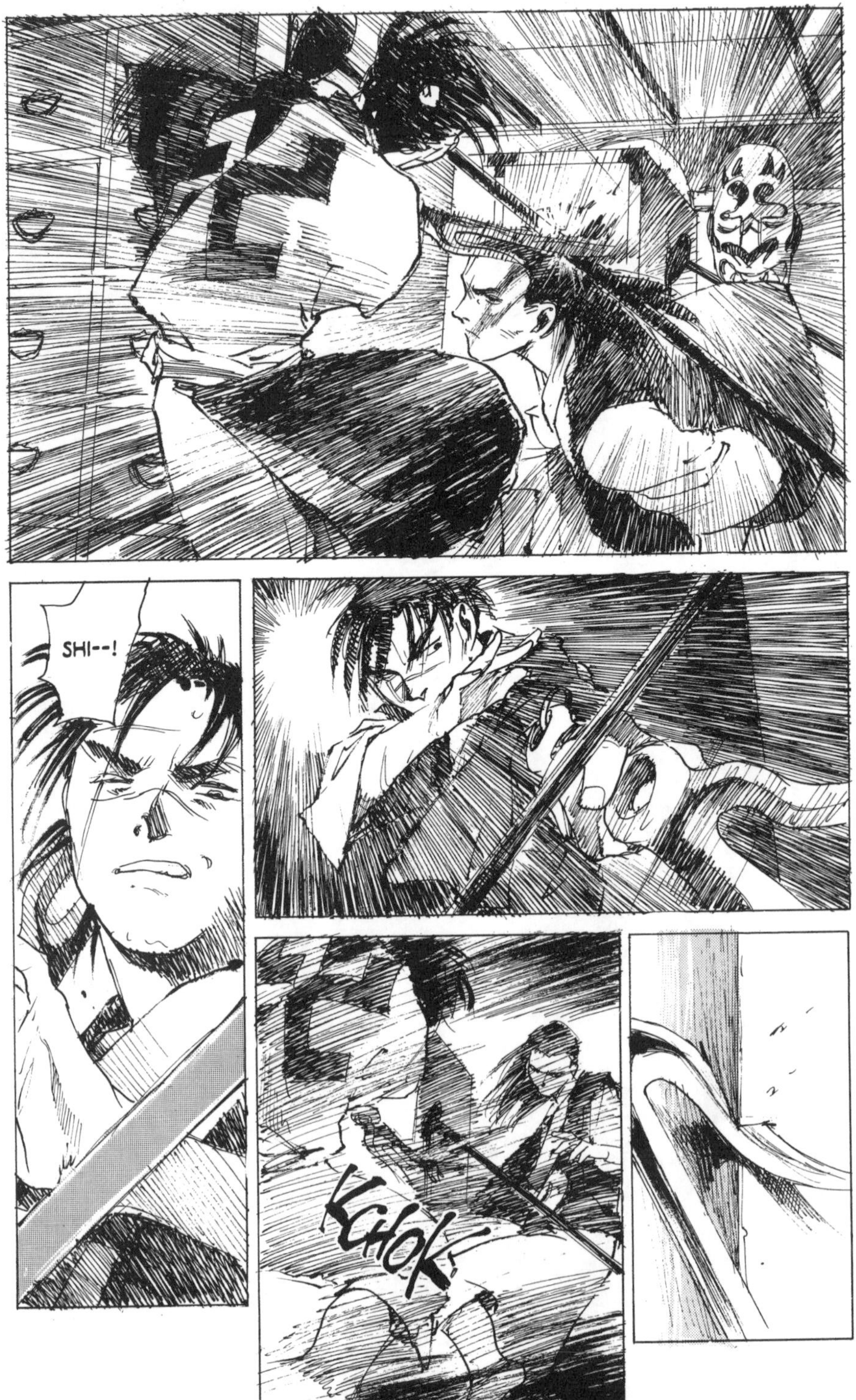
SHI--!
KCHOK!

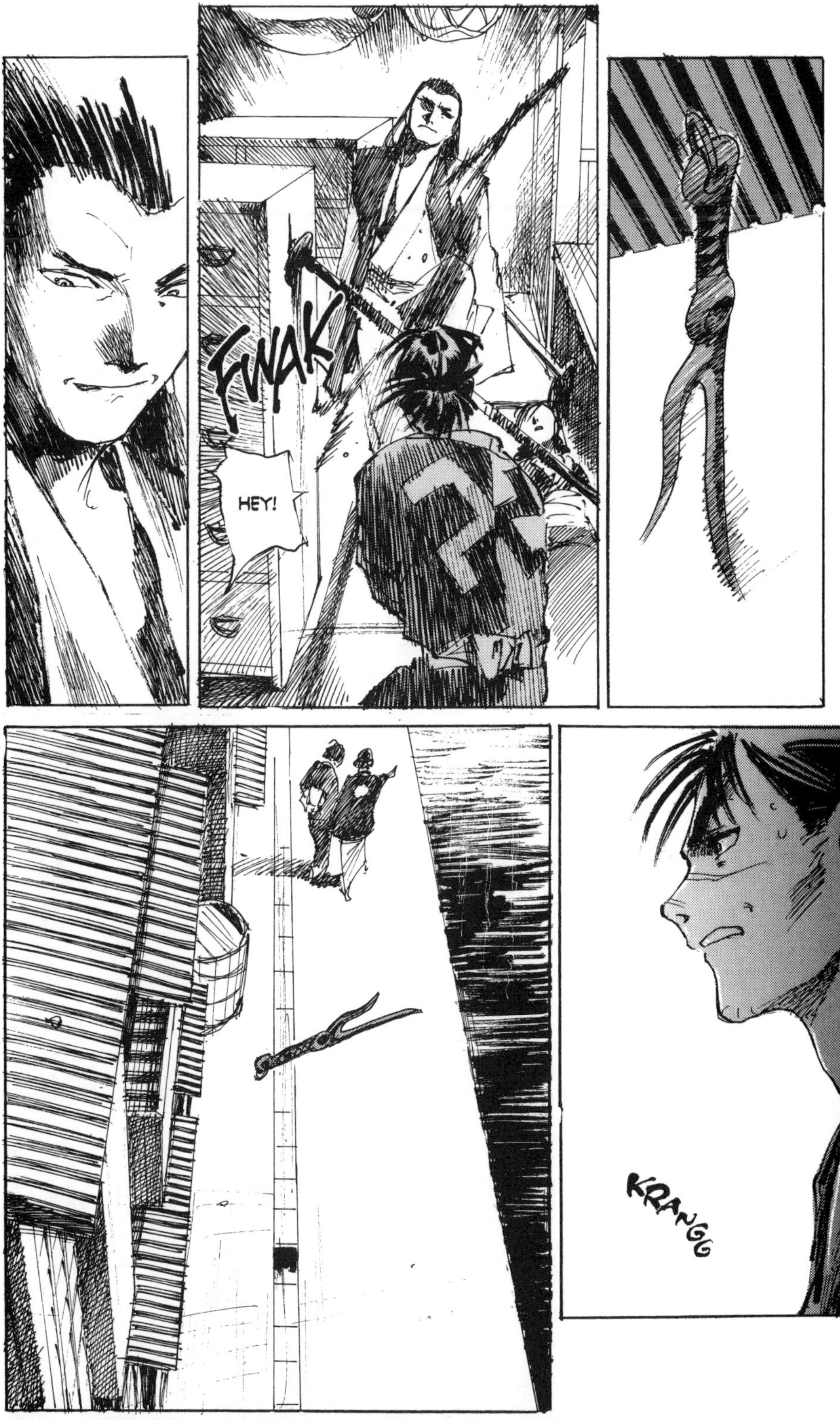
FWAK
HEY!
KRANGG

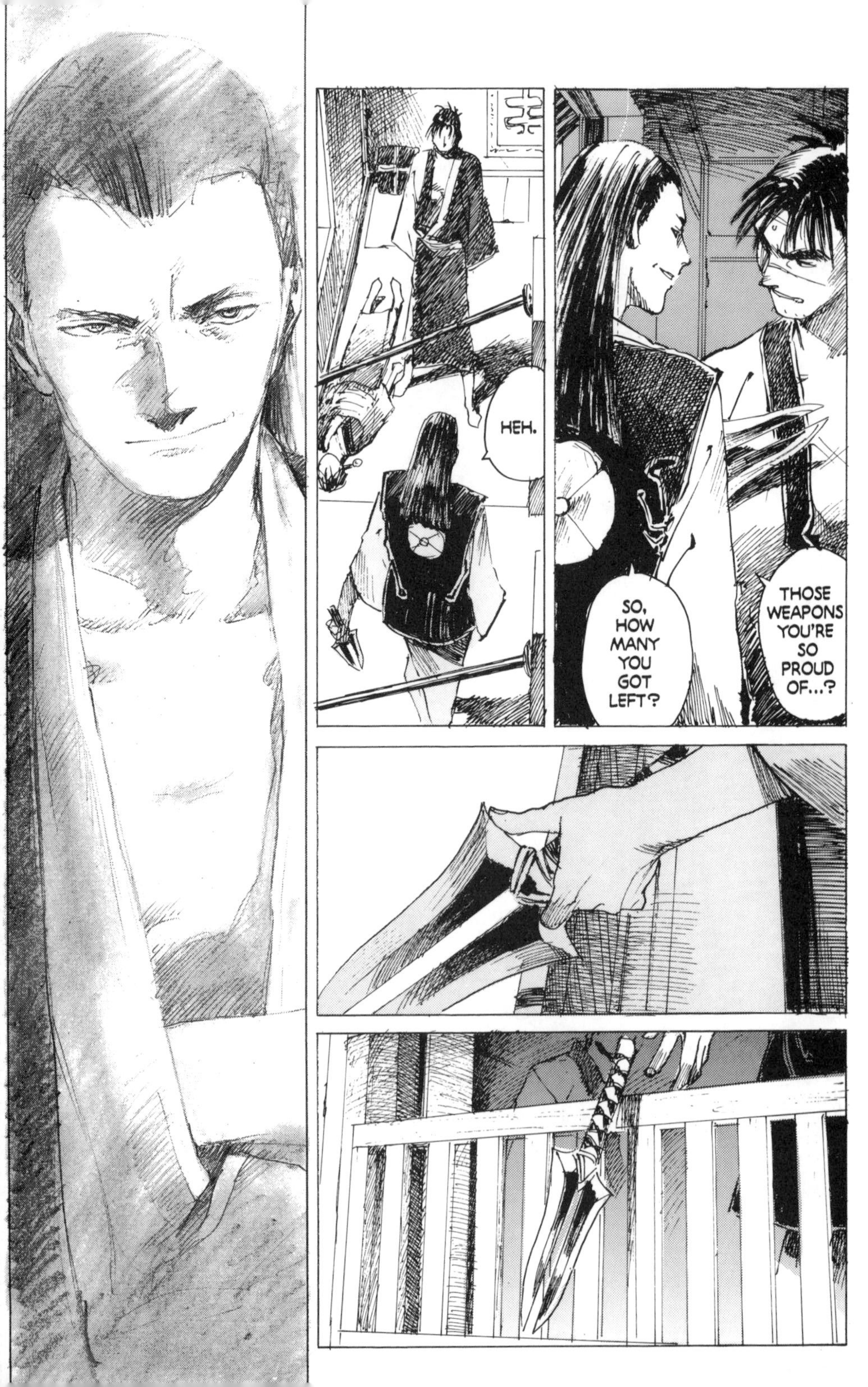
THOSE WEAPONS YOU'RE SO PROUD OF...?
SO, HOW MANY YOU GOT LEFT?
HEH.

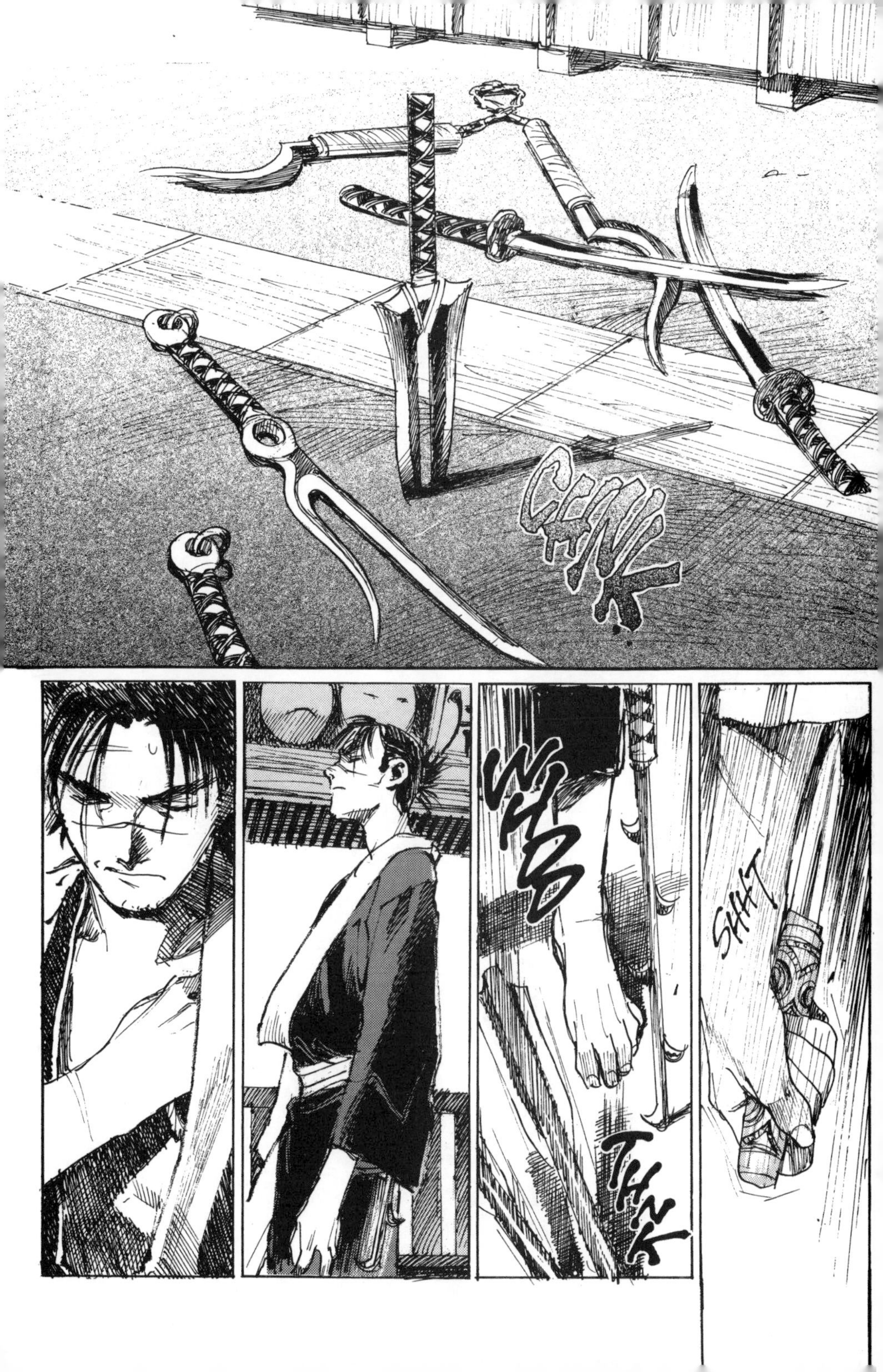
CLINK
SHHT
WHSS
THNK

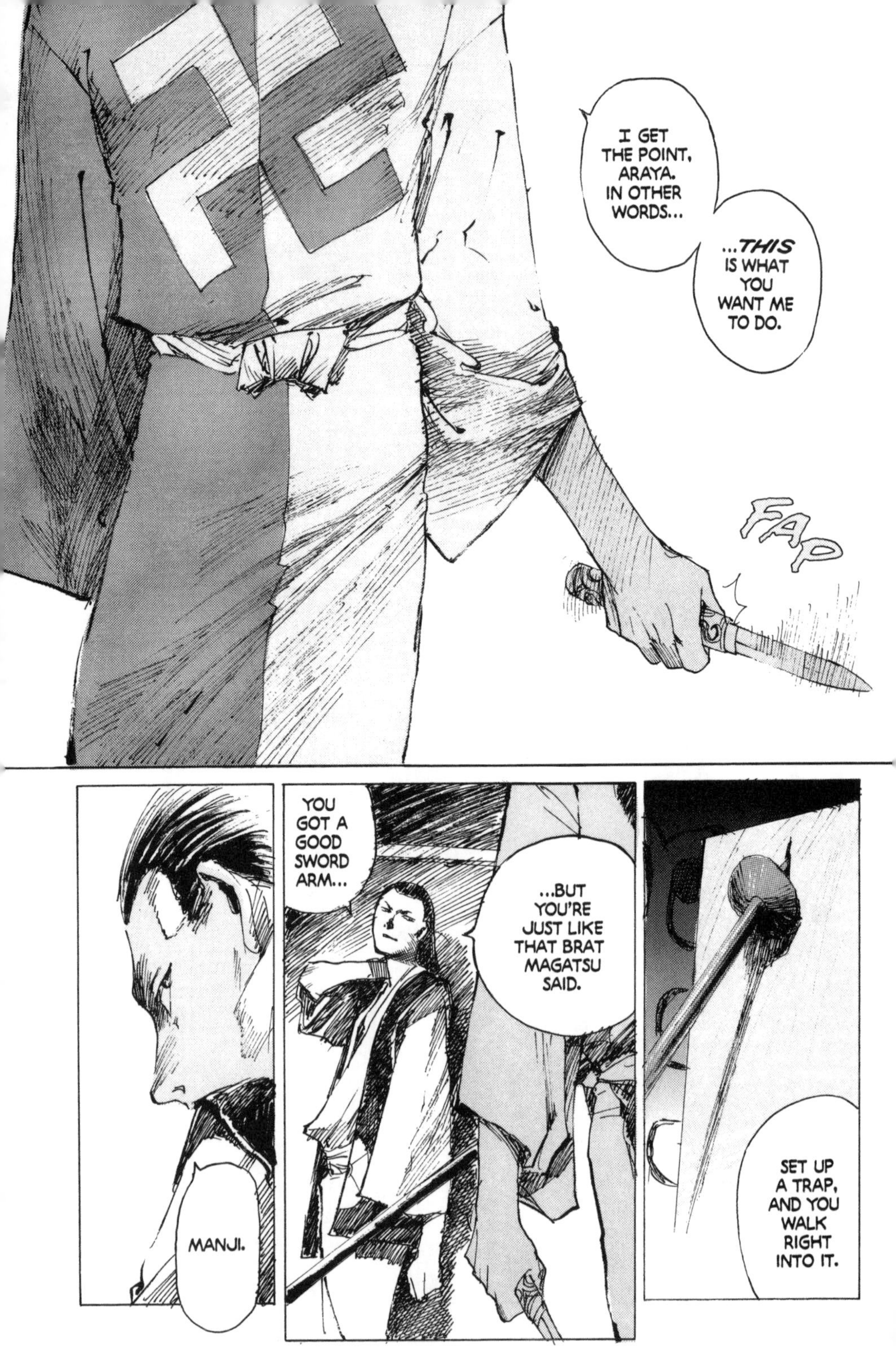
I GET THE POINT, ARAYA. IN OTHER WORDS...
...*THIS* IS WHAT YOU WANT ME TO DO.
FAP
SET UP A TRAP, AND YOU WALK RIGHT INTO IT.
YOU GOT A GOOD SWORD ARM...
...BUT YOU'RE JUST LIKE THAT BRAT MAGATSU SAID.
MANJI.

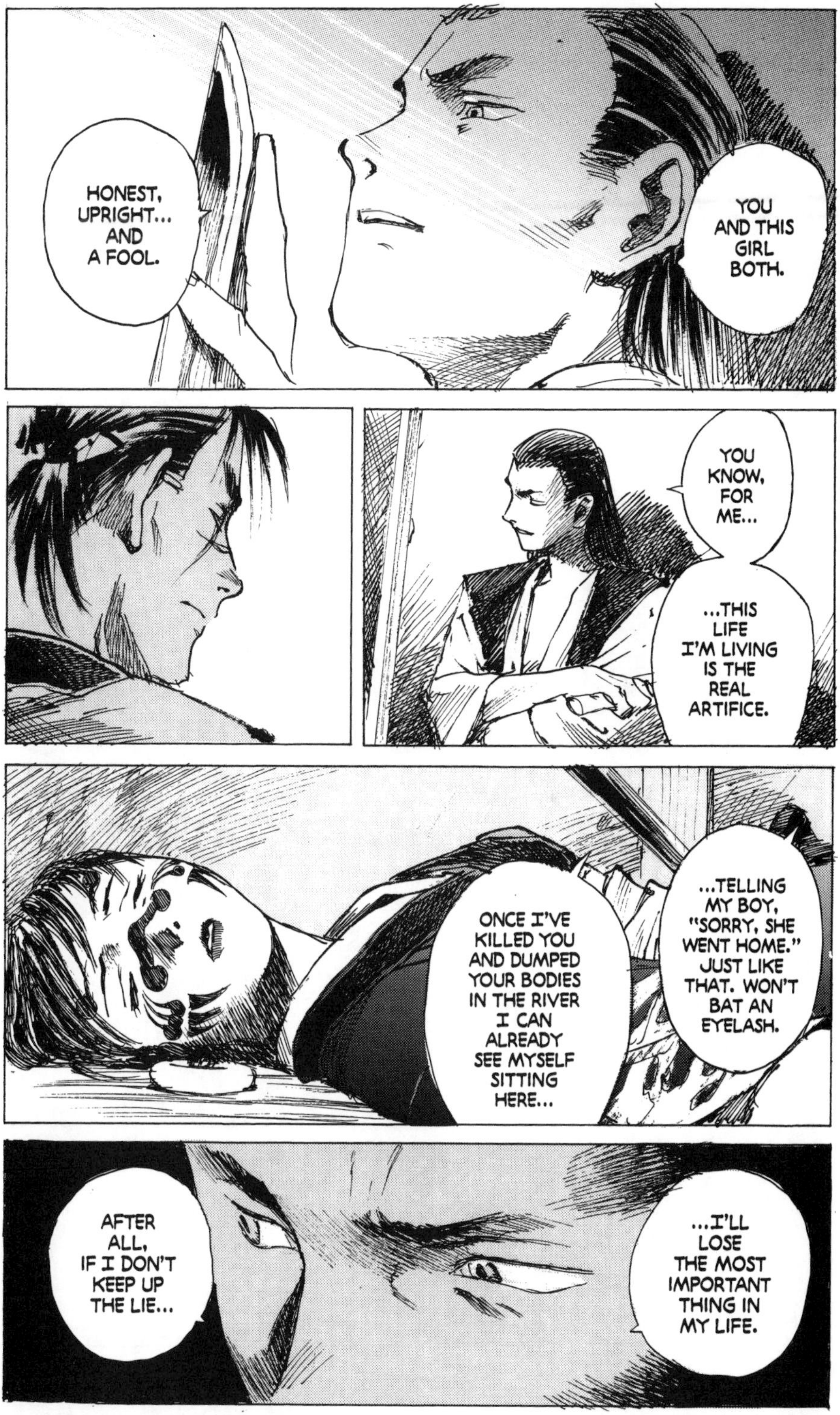
HONEST, UPRIGHT... AND A FOOL.
YOU AND THIS GIRL BOTH.
YOU KNOW, FOR ME...
...THIS LIFE I'M LIVING IS THE REAL ARTIFICE.
ONCE I'VE KILLED YOU AND DUMPED YOUR BODIES IN THE RIVER I CAN ALREADY SEE MYSELF SITTING HERE...
...TELLING MY BOY, "SORRY, SHE WENT HOME." JUST LIKE THAT. WON'T BAT AN EYELASH.
AFTER ALL, IF I DON'T KEEP UP THE LIE...
...I'LL LOSE THE MOST IMPORTANT THING IN MY LIFE.

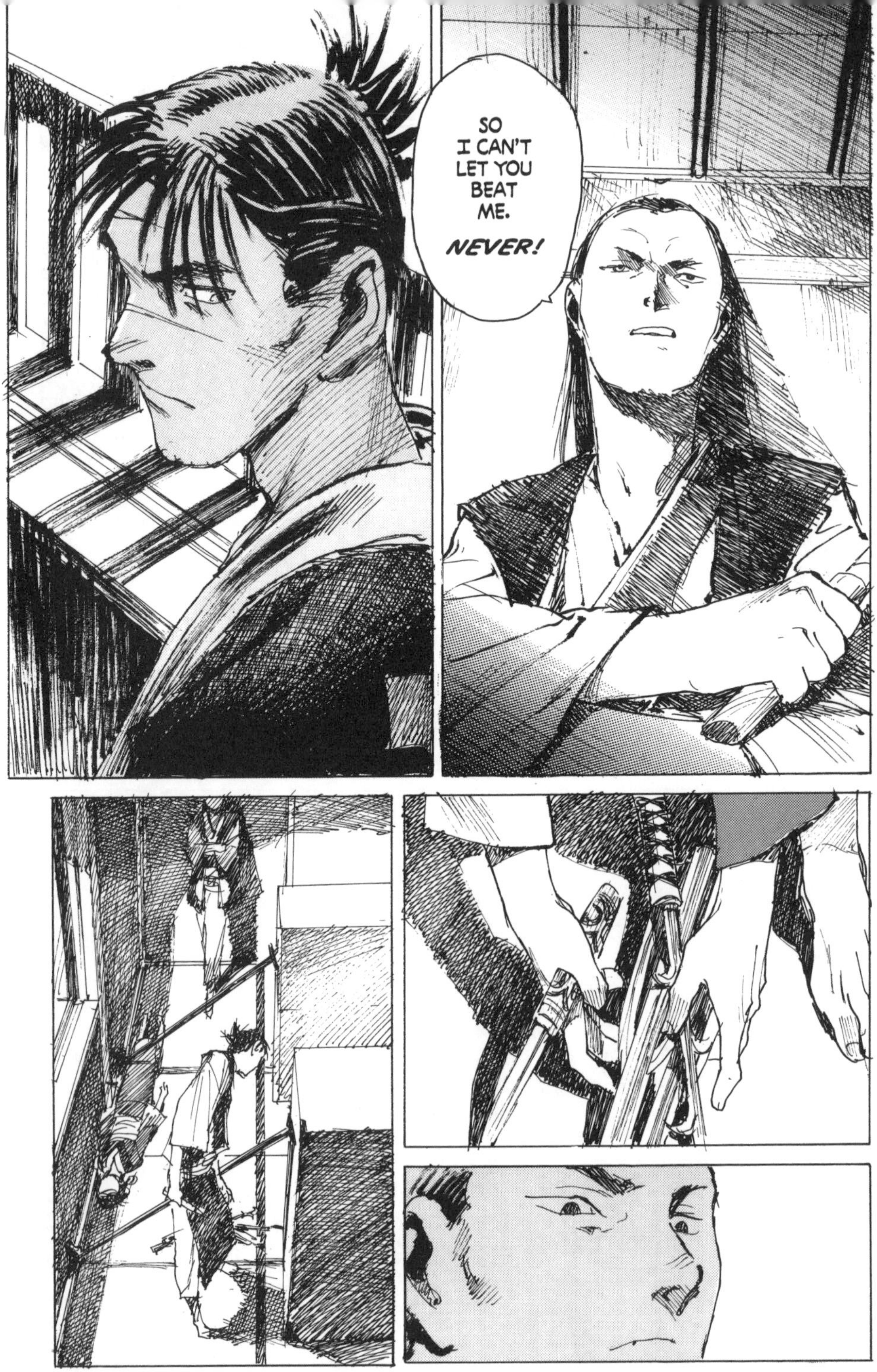
SO I CAN'T LET YOU BEAT ME.
NEVER!

ARAYA...

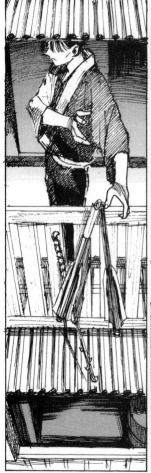

TING

? KATUG

SKIP YOUR LITTLE TRICKS.

WE'RE EVEN NOW.

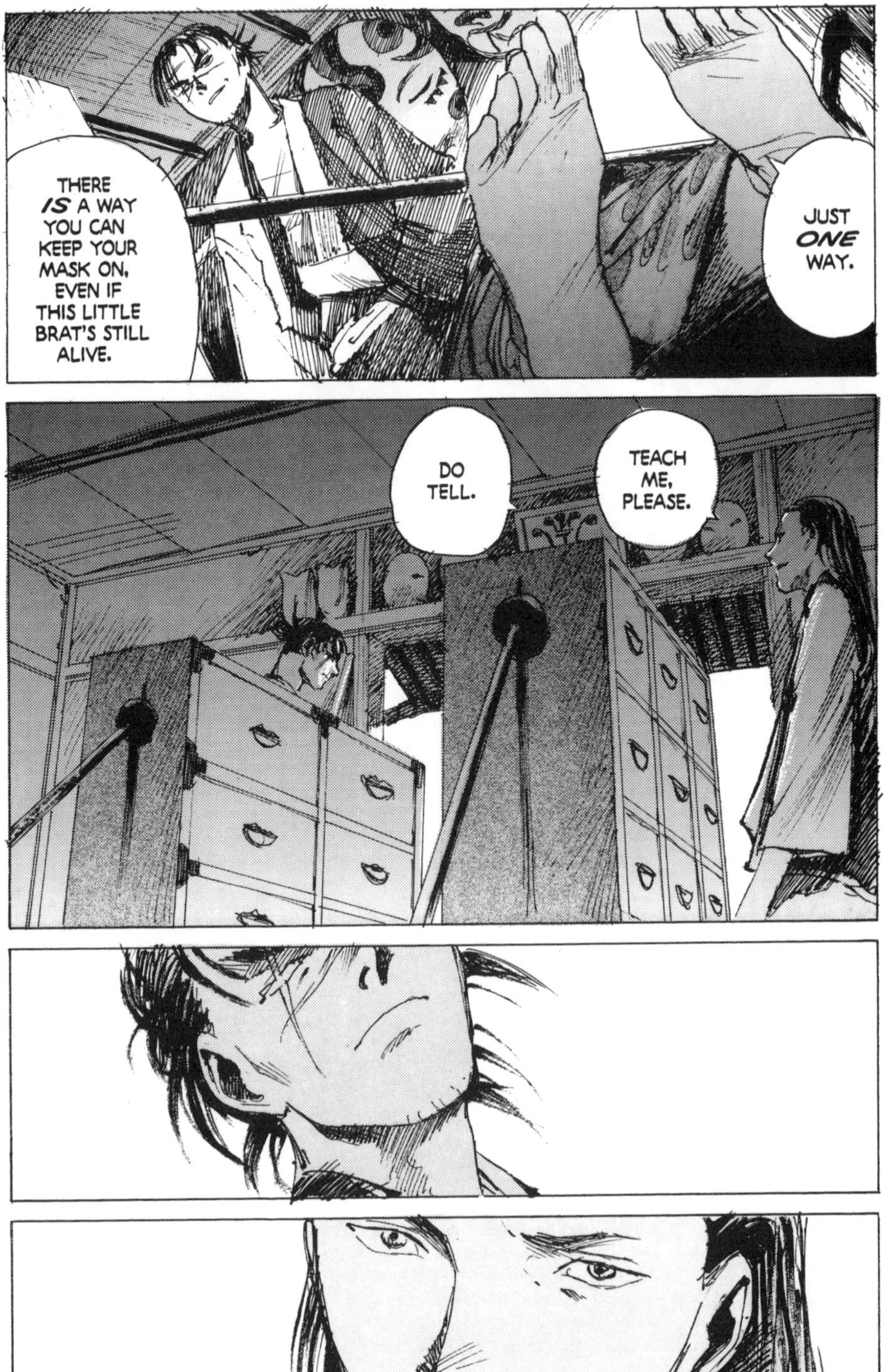
THERE *IS* A WAY YOU CAN KEEP YOUR MASK ON, EVEN IF THIS LITTLE BRAT'S STILL ALIVE.
JUST *ONE* WAY.
DO TELL.
TEACH ME, PLEASE.

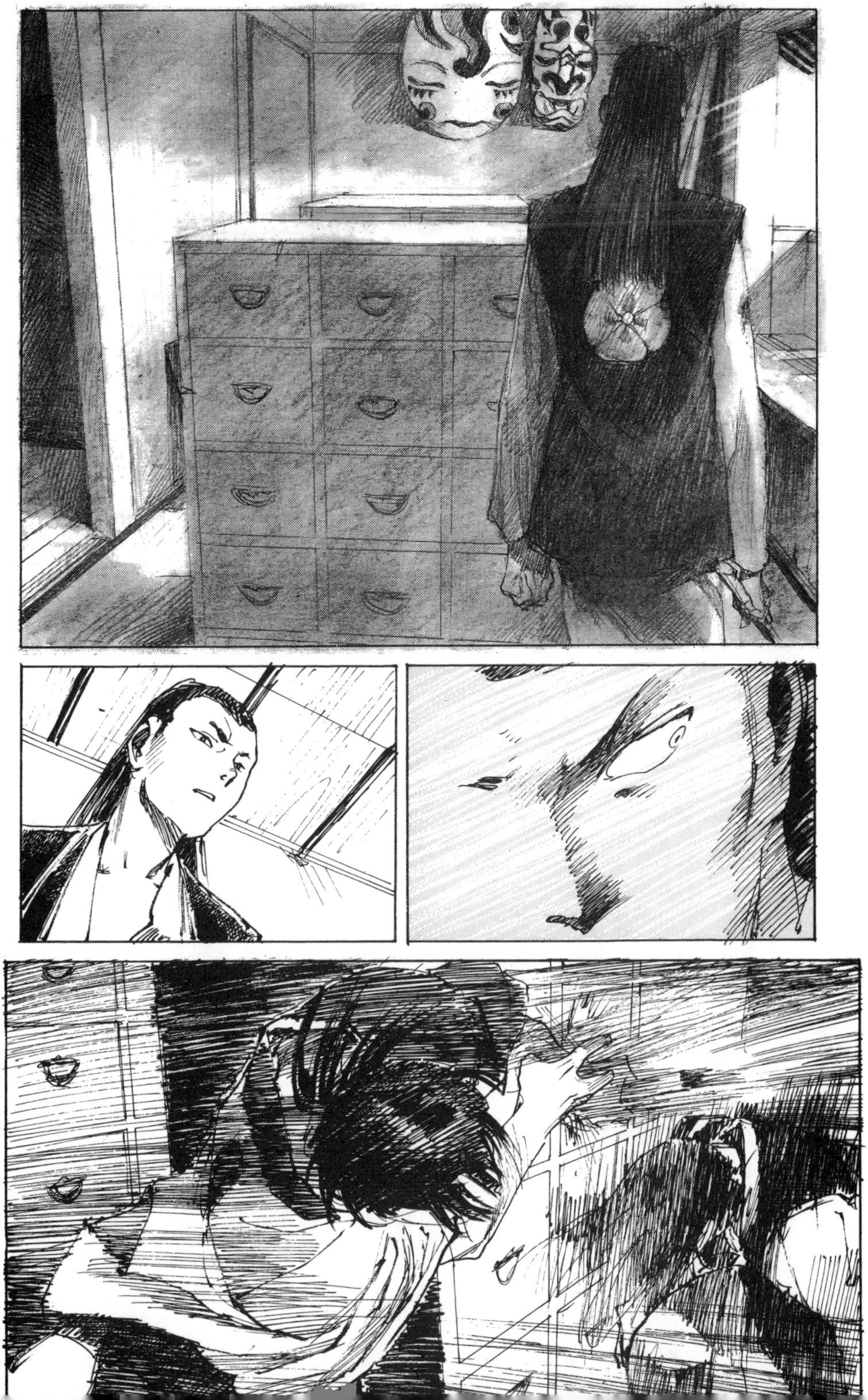

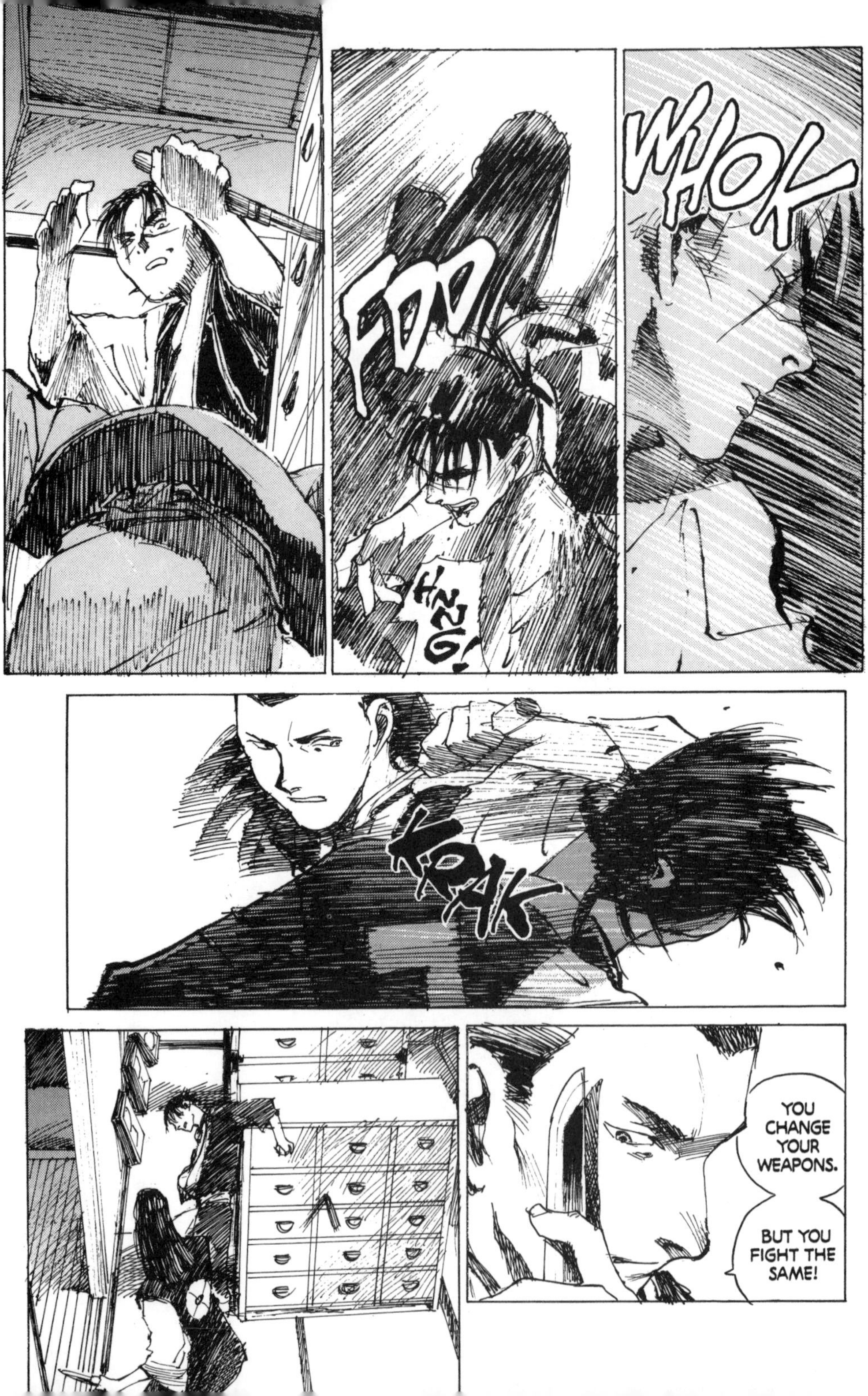
WHOK
FOO
HNNG!
KRAK
YOU CHANGE YOUR WEAPONS.
BUT YOU FIGHT THE SAME!

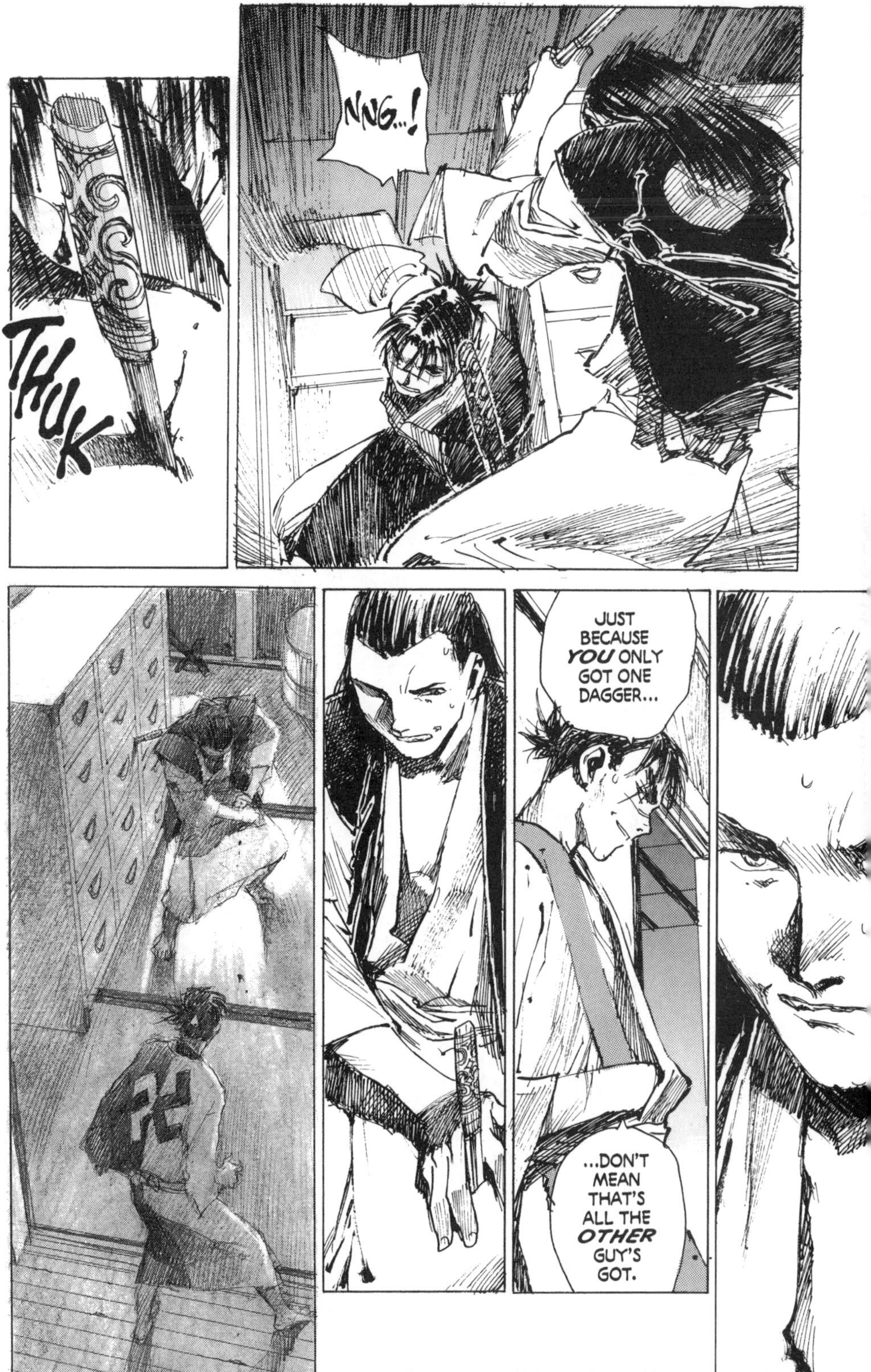
NNG..!
THUK
JUST BECAUSE *YOU* ONLY GOT ONE DAGGER...
...DON'T MEAN THAT'S ALL THE *OTHER* GUY'S GOT.

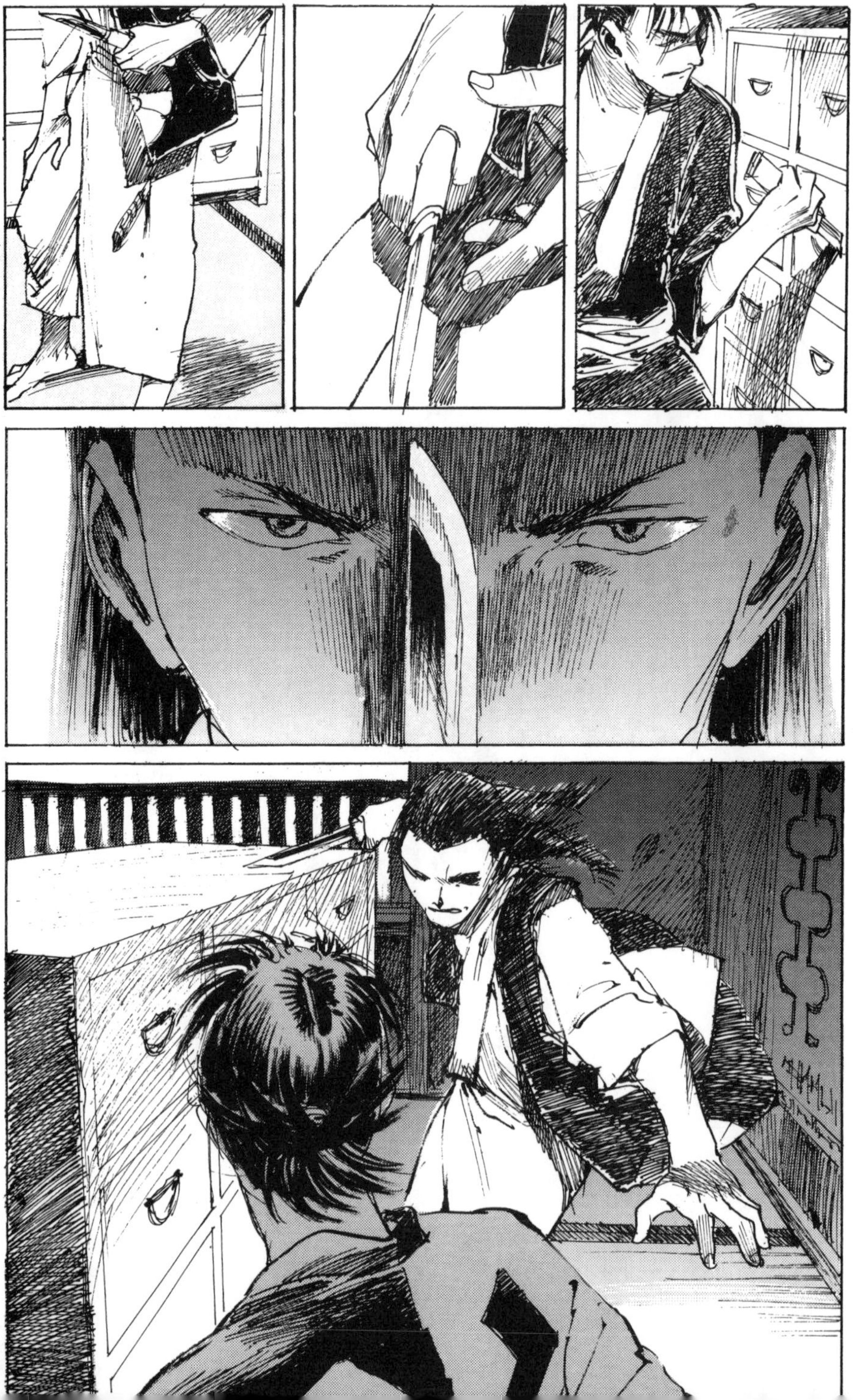

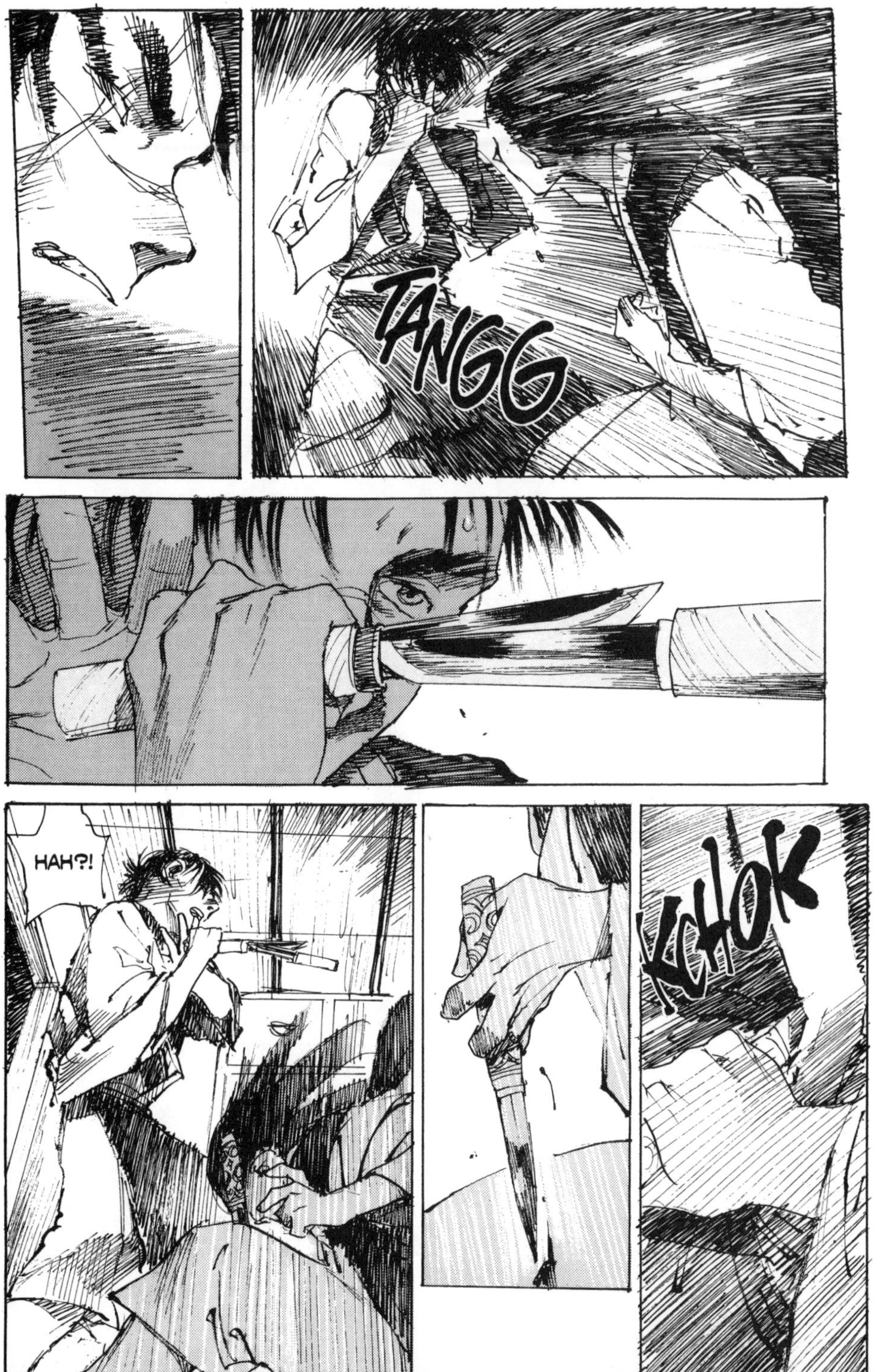
TANGG
KCHOK
HAH?!

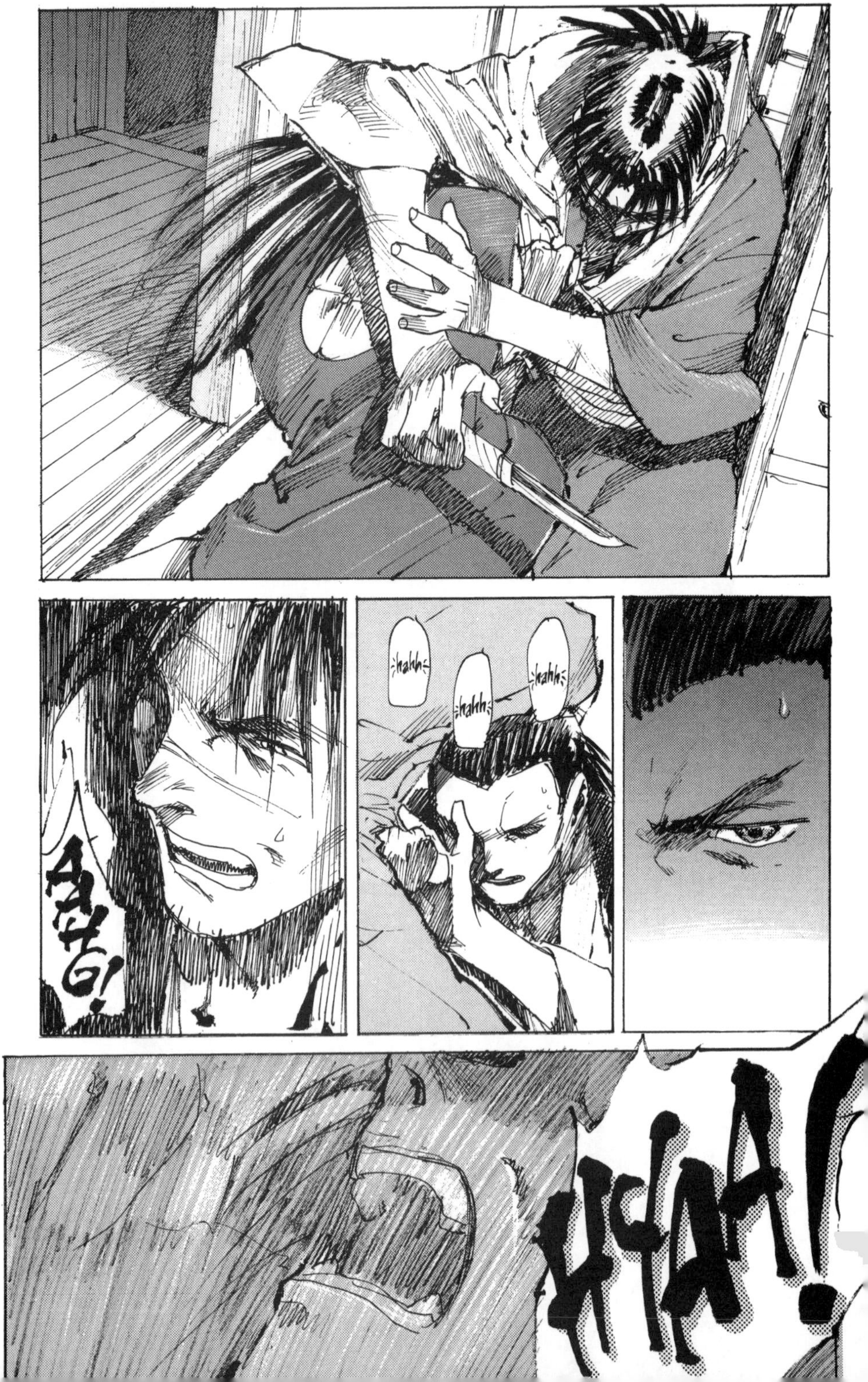
hahh
hahh
hahh
AAHG!
KYAA!

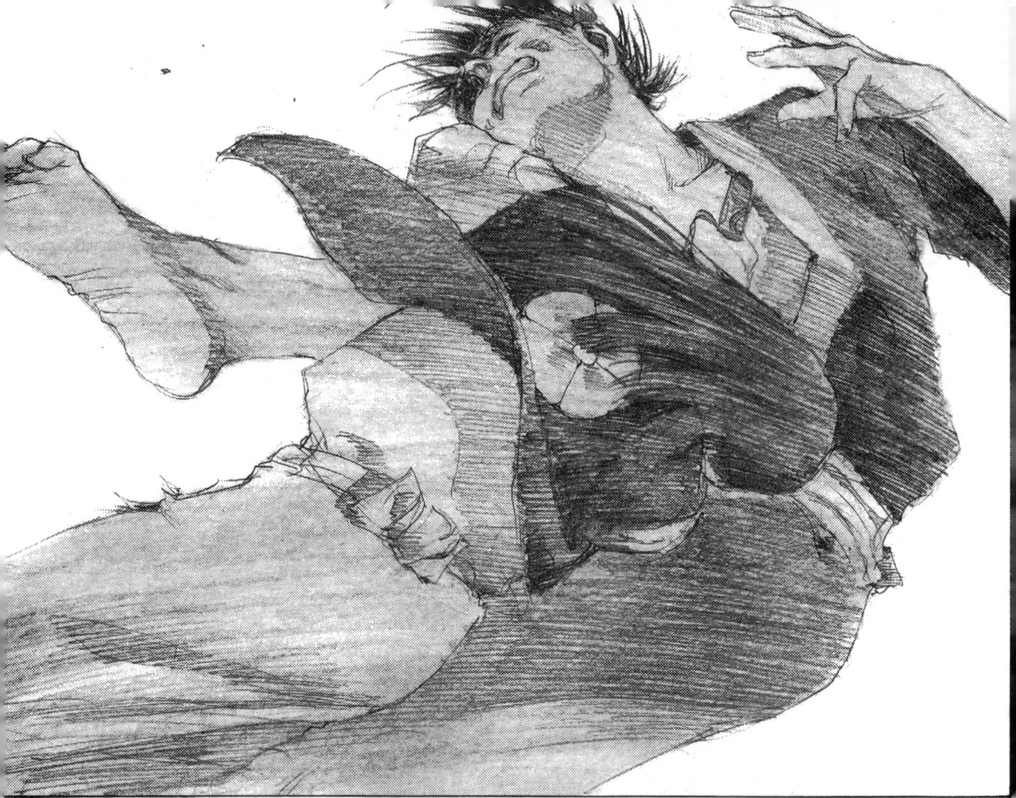
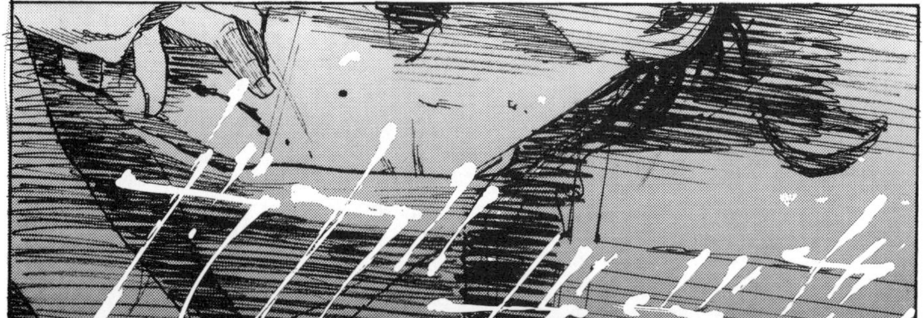
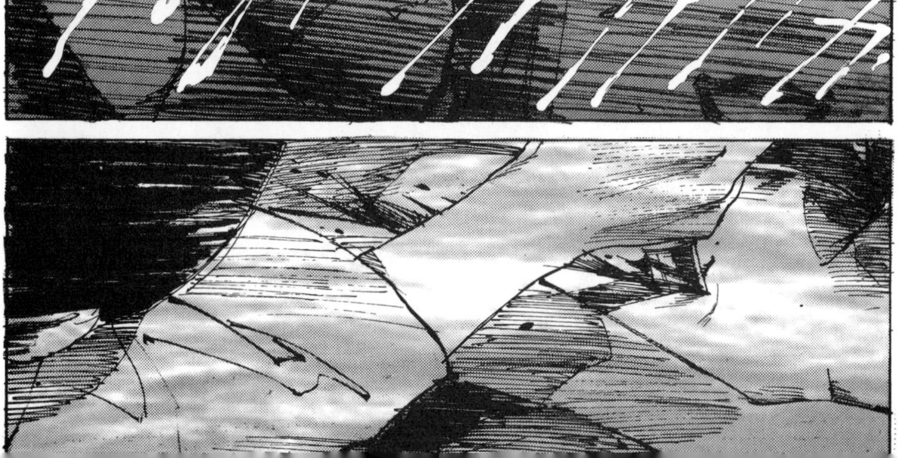

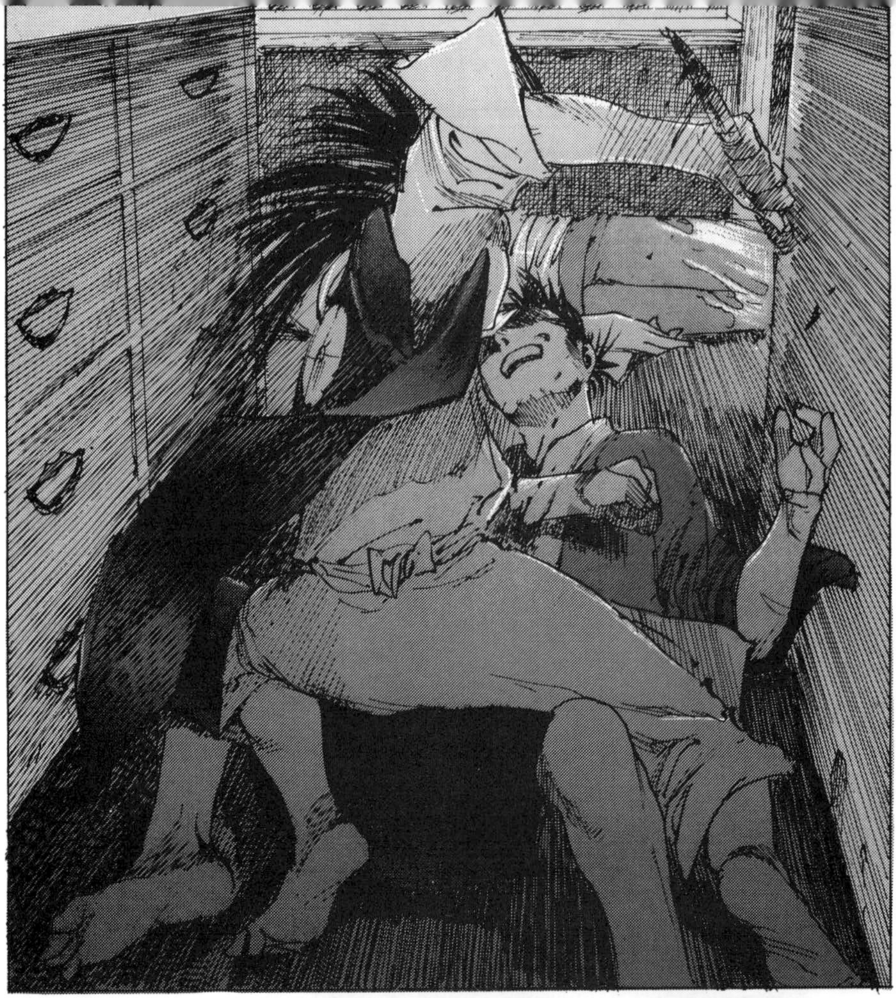

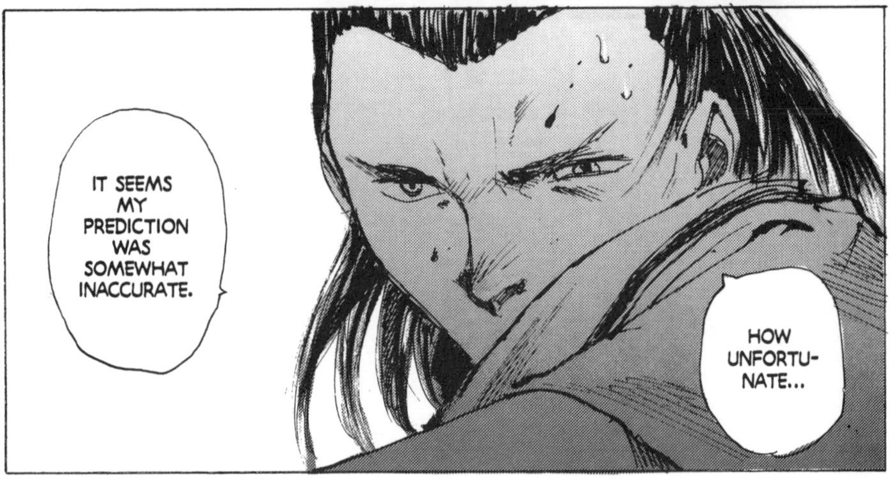
HOW UNFORTU-NATE...
IT SEEMS MY PREDICTION WAS SOMEWHAT INACCURATE.

ON SILENT WINGS
Part 6

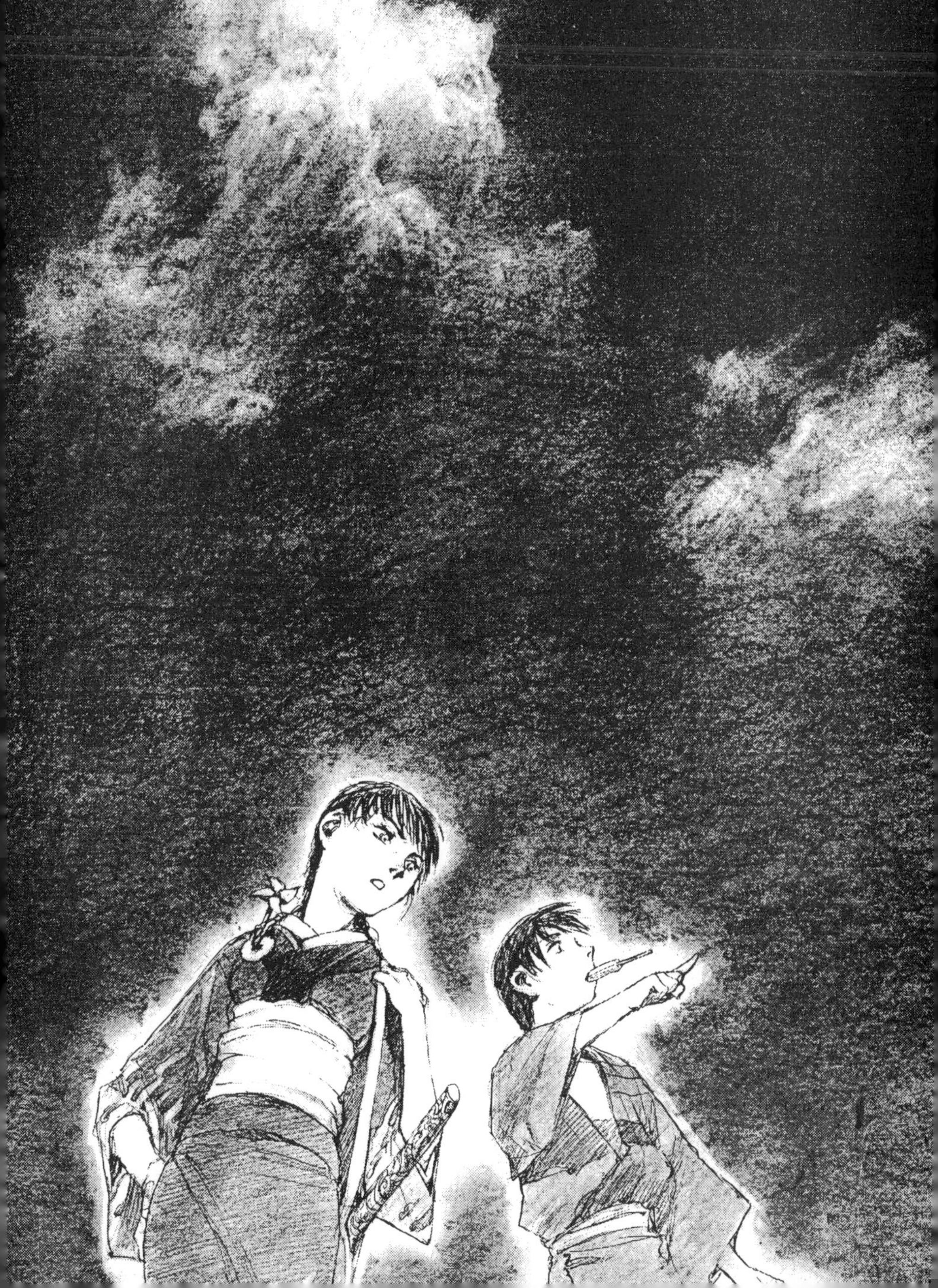

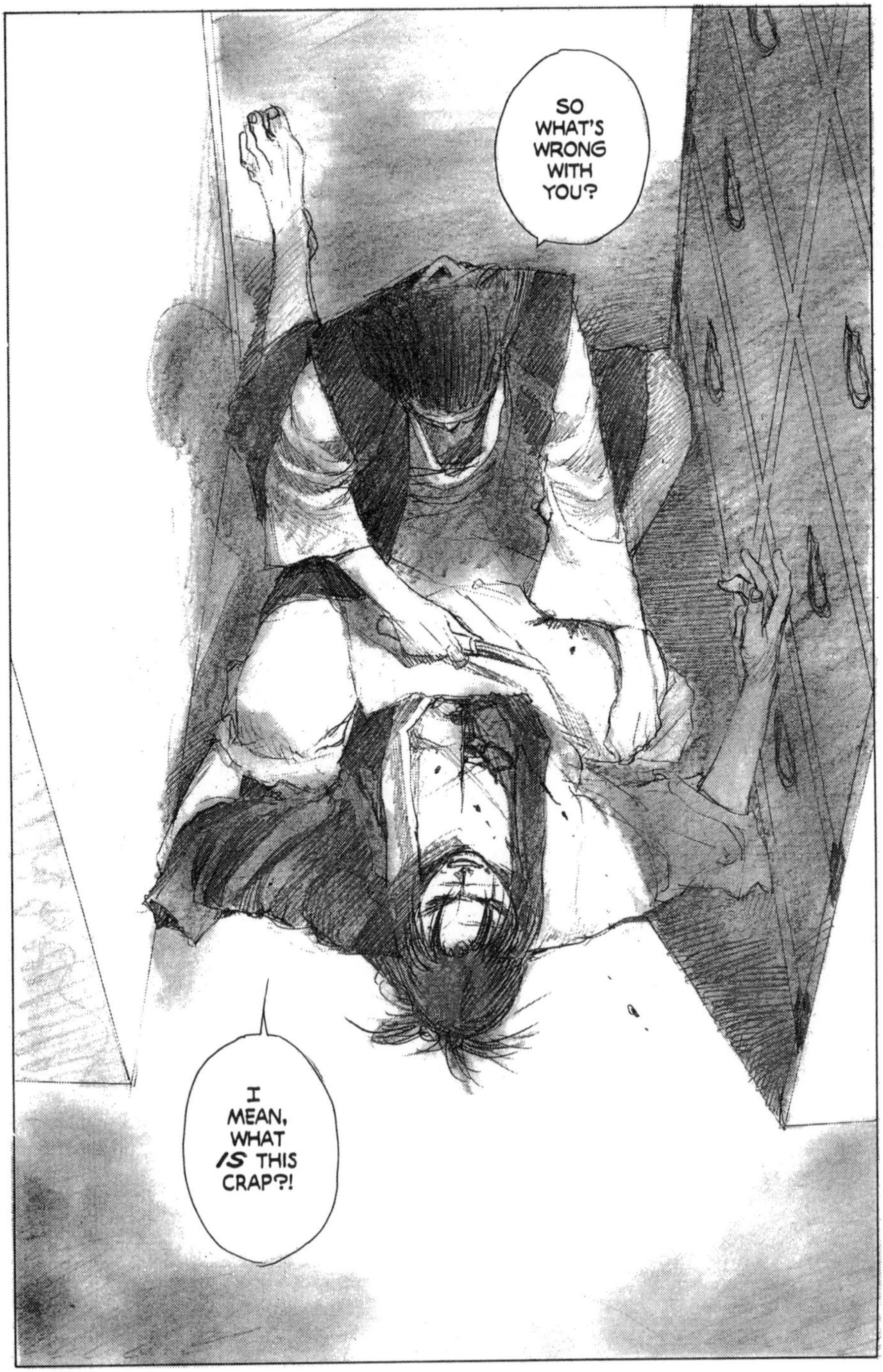
SO WHAT'S WRONG WITH YOU?
I MEAN, WHAT *IS* THIS CRAP?!

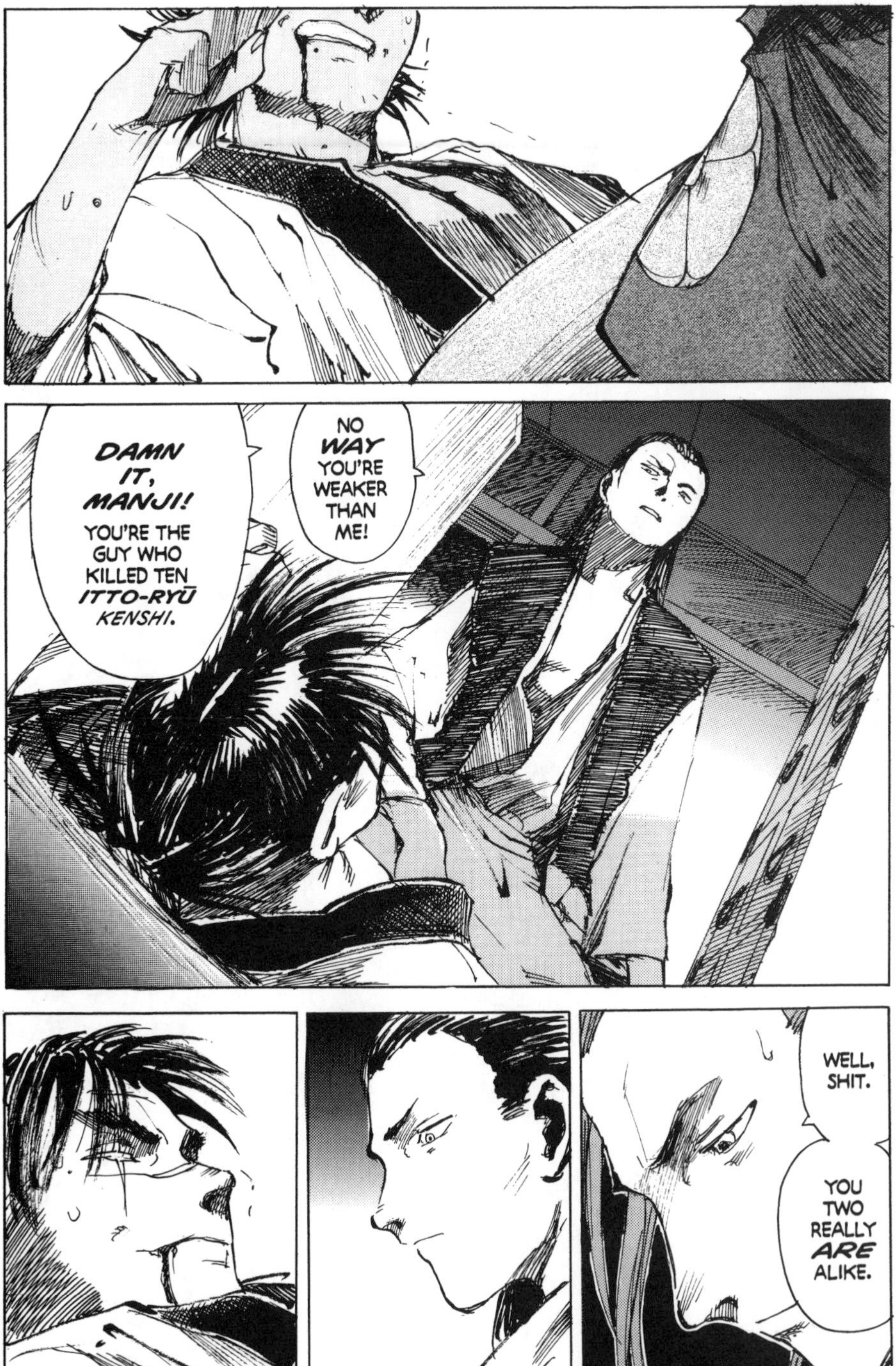
NO *WAY* YOU'RE WEAKER THAN ME!
DAMN IT, MANJI! YOU'RE THE GUY WHO KILLED TEN *ITTO-RYŪ KENSHI*.
WELL, SHIT.
YOU TWO REALLY *ARE* ALIKE.

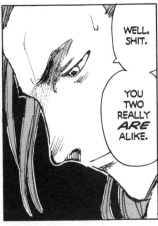

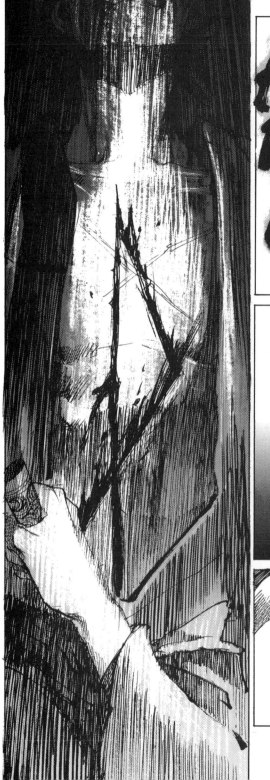

SORRY, MY FRIEND.

BUT I'M OUT OF TIME.

YOU'LL JUST HAVE TO LET ME FINISH YOU OFF.

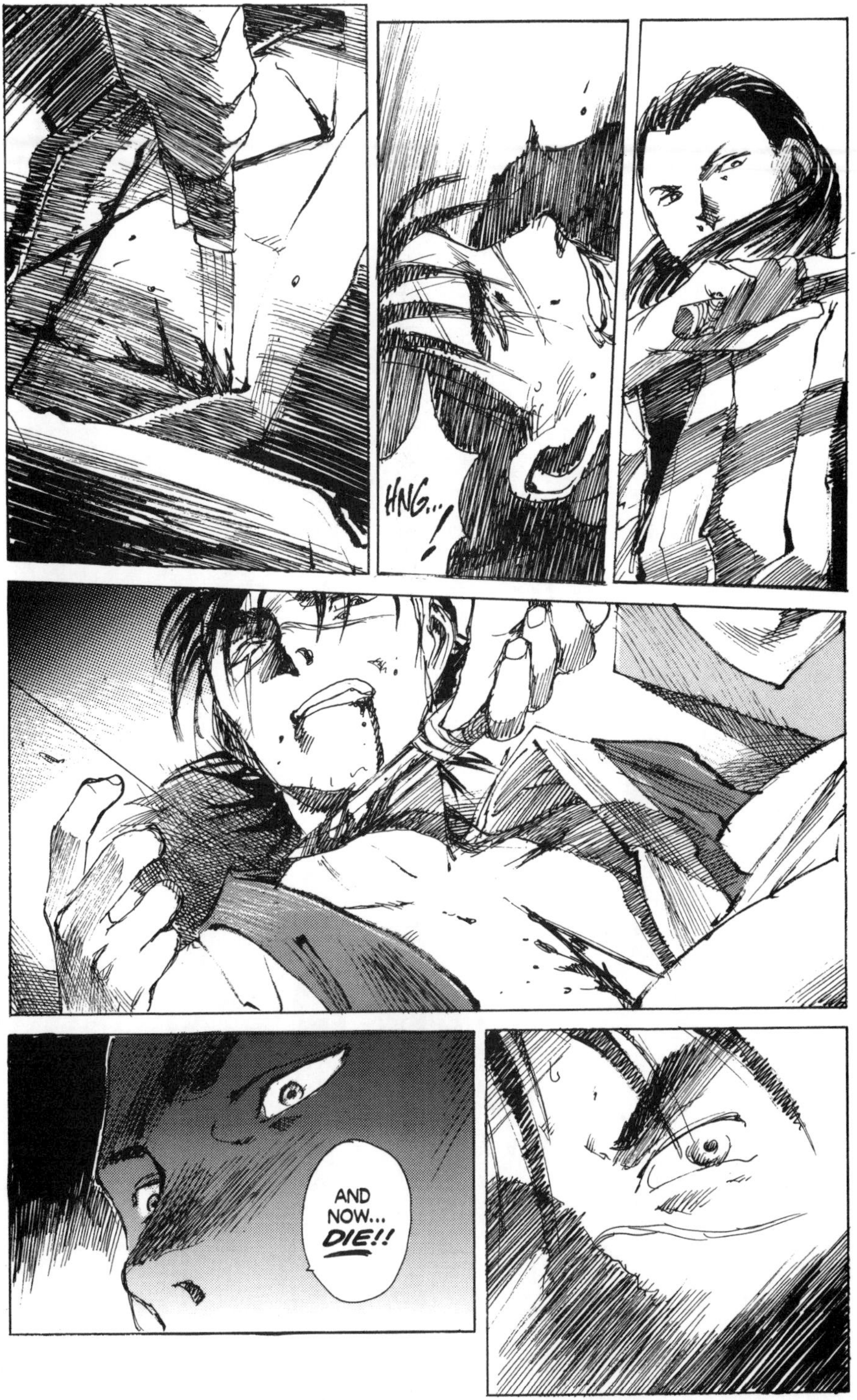
HNG...!
AND NOW... DIE!!

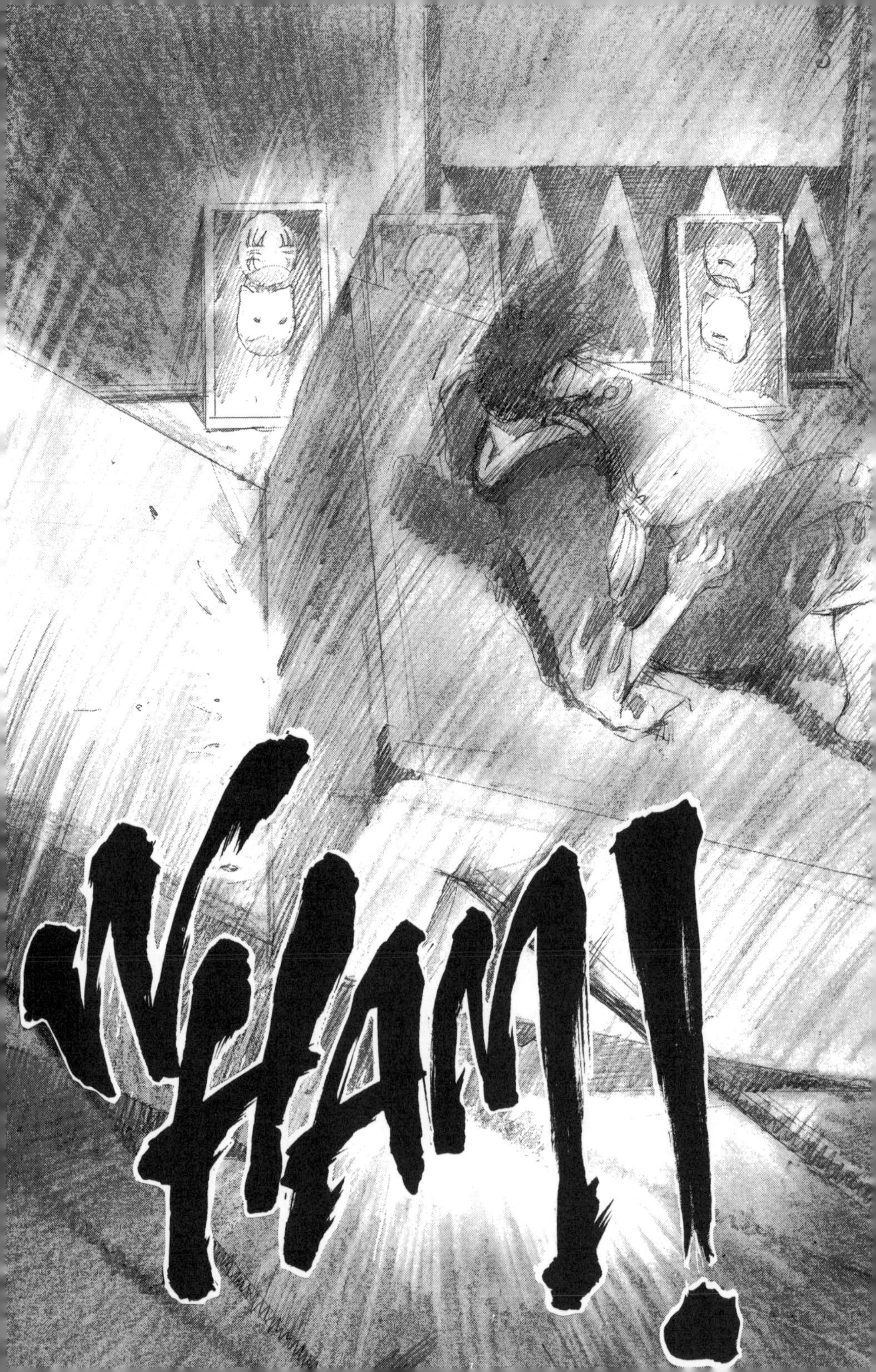
WHAM!

:hahh: :gasp: :hahh:
:hff: :hff:
:hah!: :hahh:

:whew:

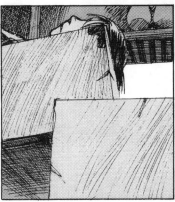

•••••
•••••

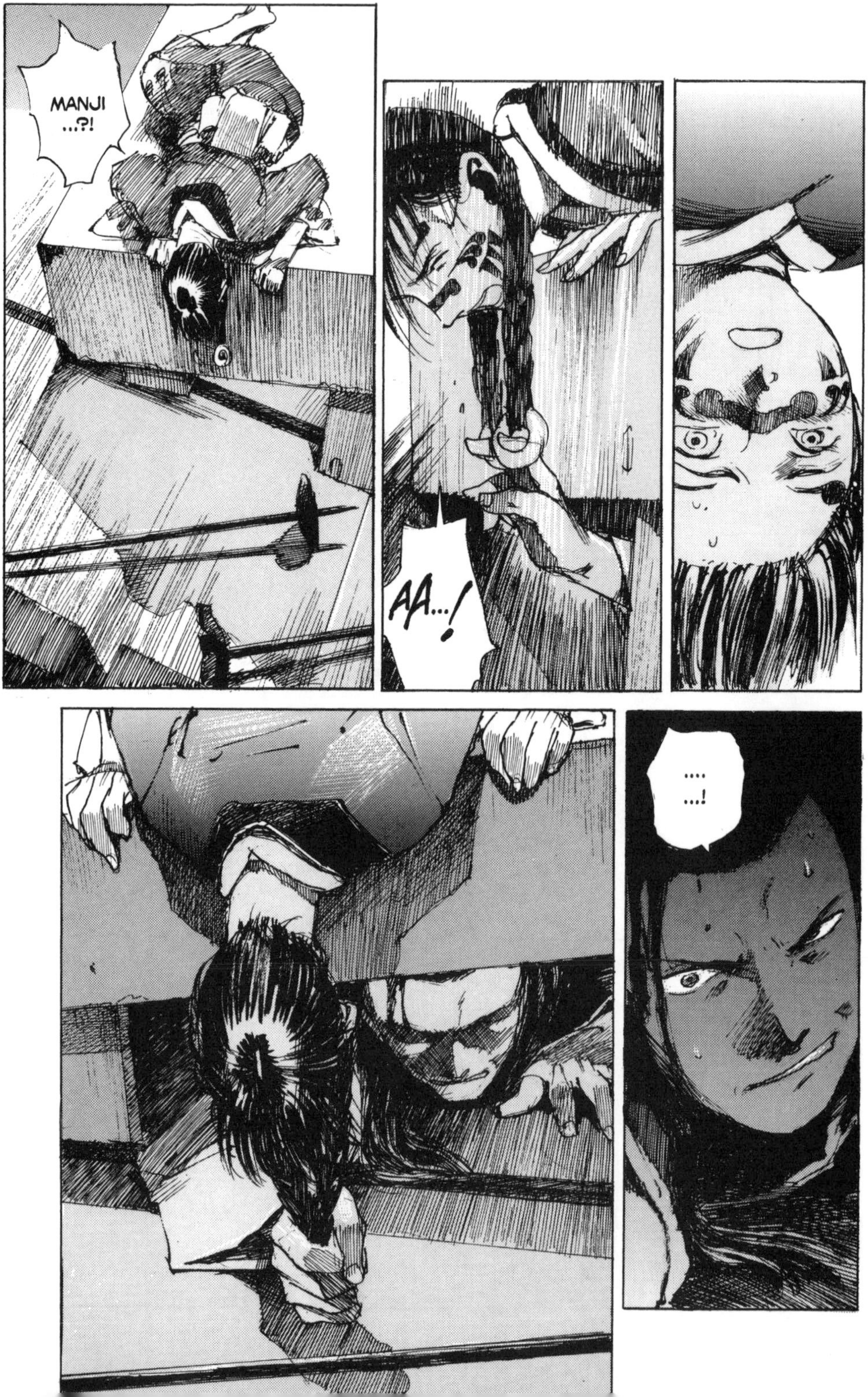
MANJI ...?!
AA...!
....
...!

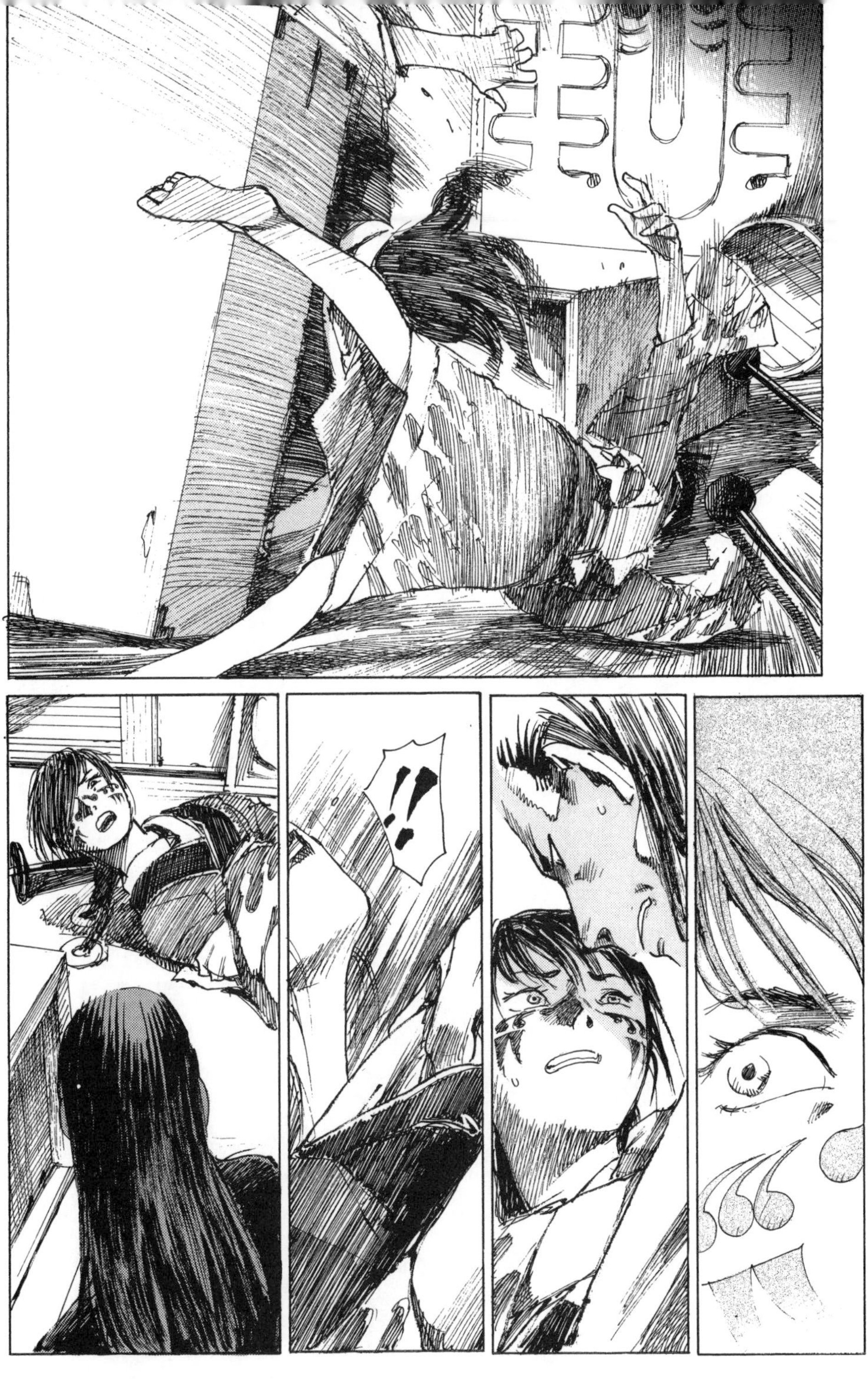
!!

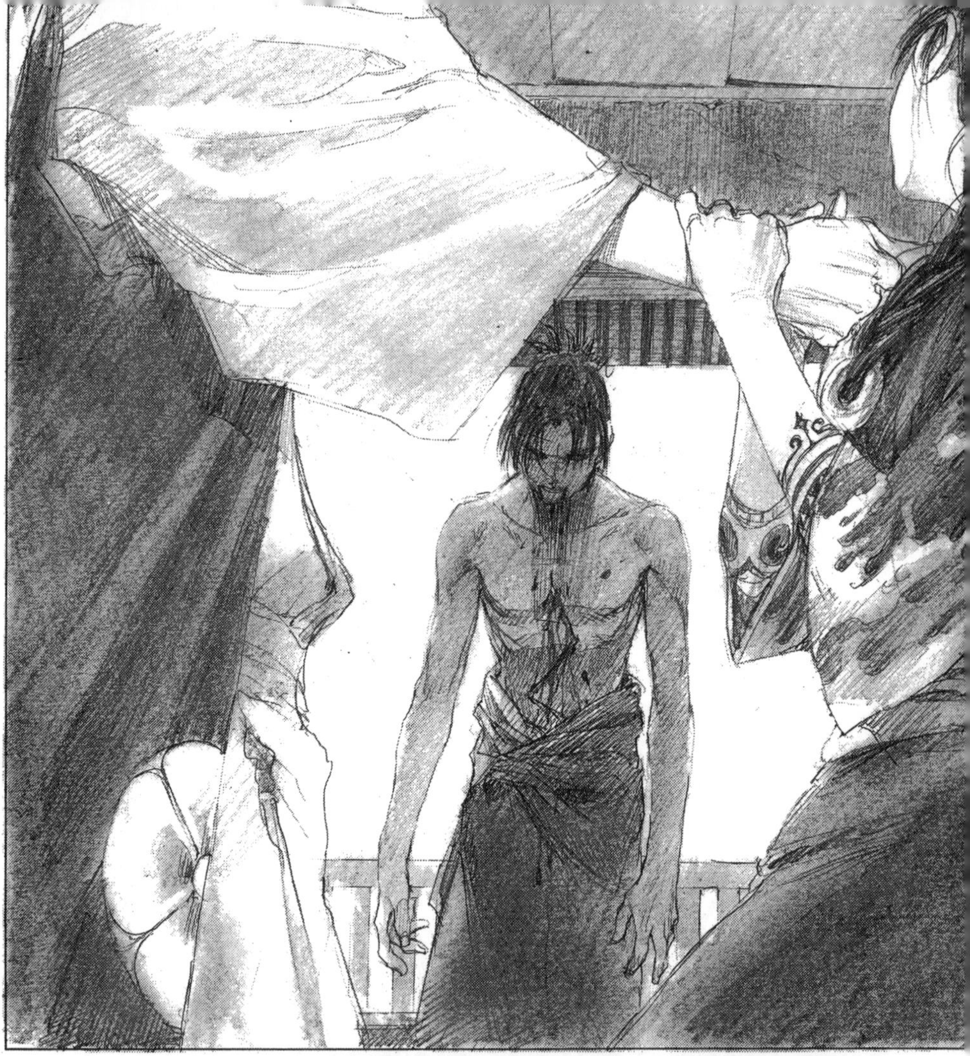
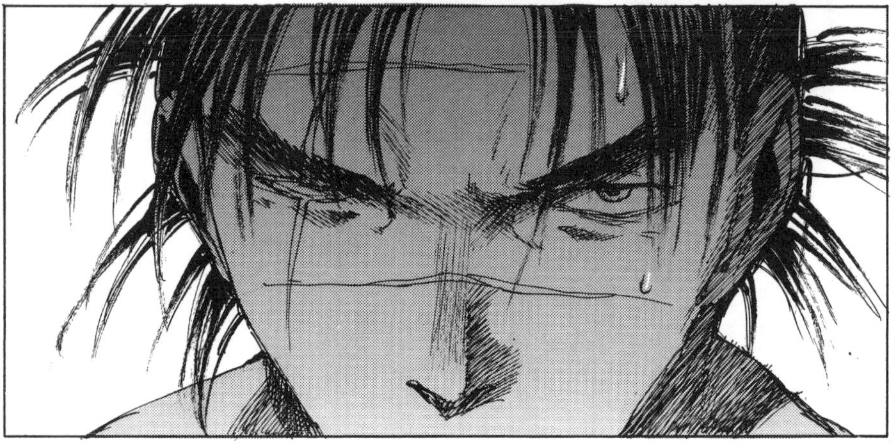

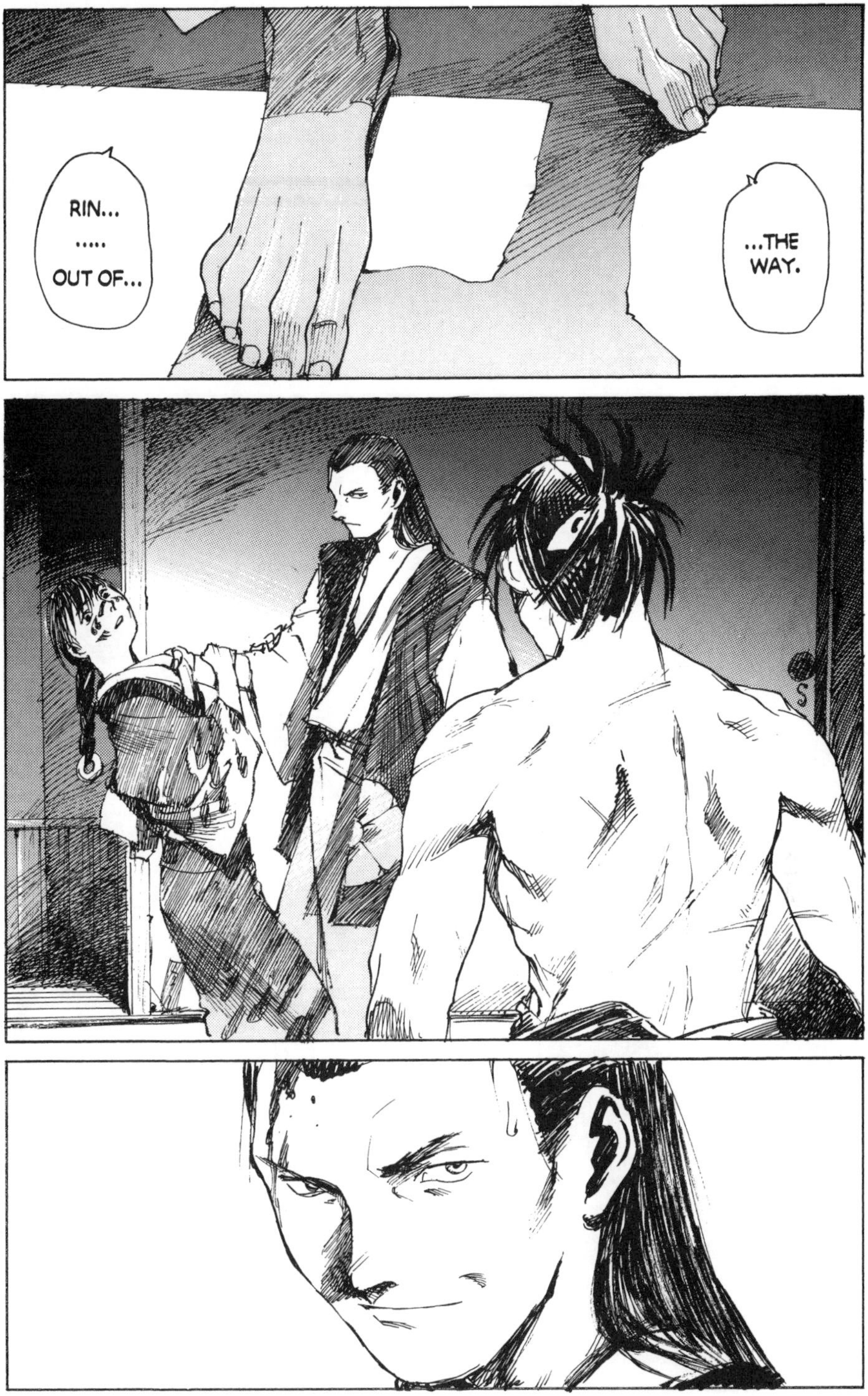
RIN...
.....
OUT OF...
...THE WAY.

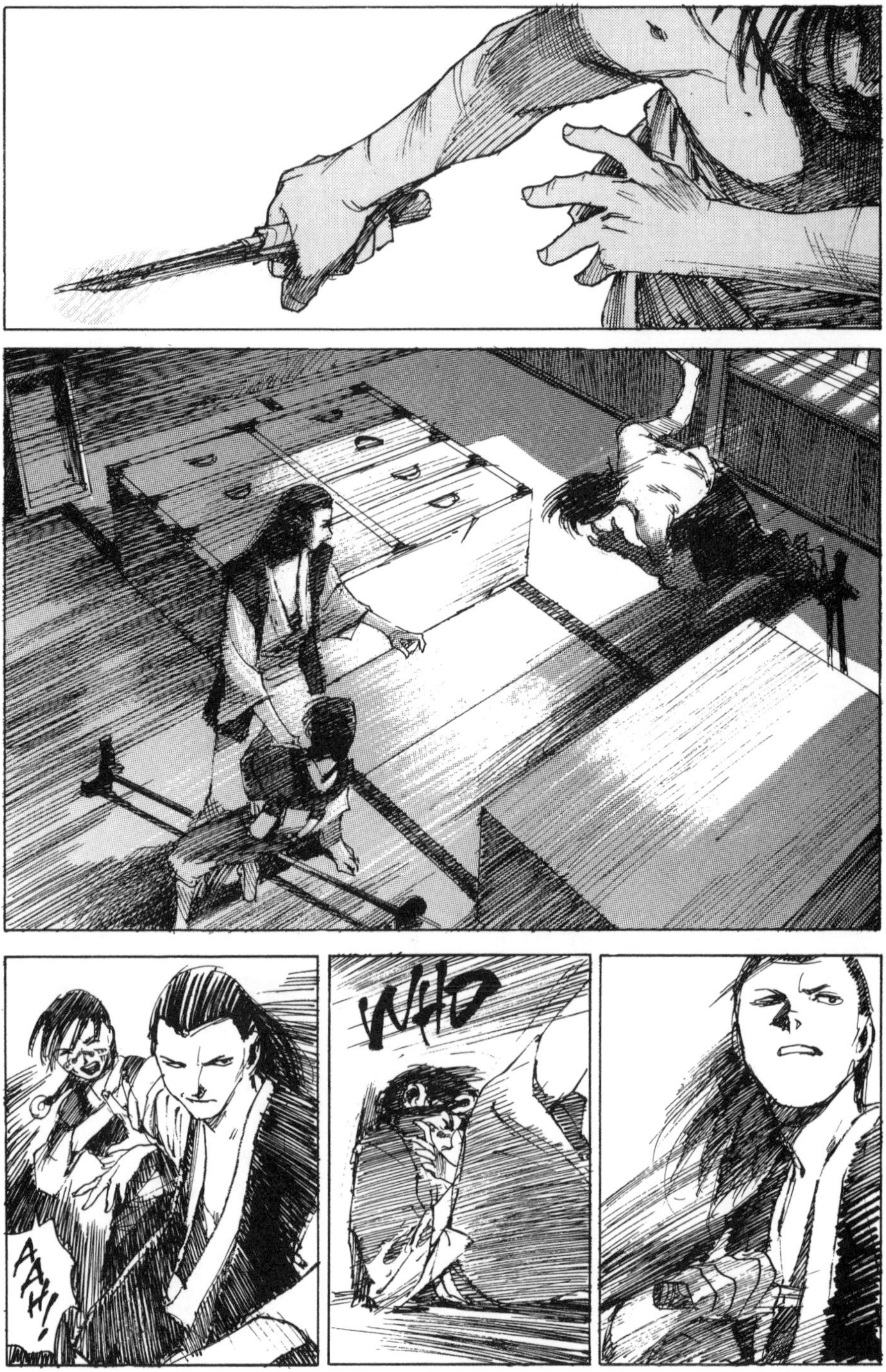
WHO
AAH!

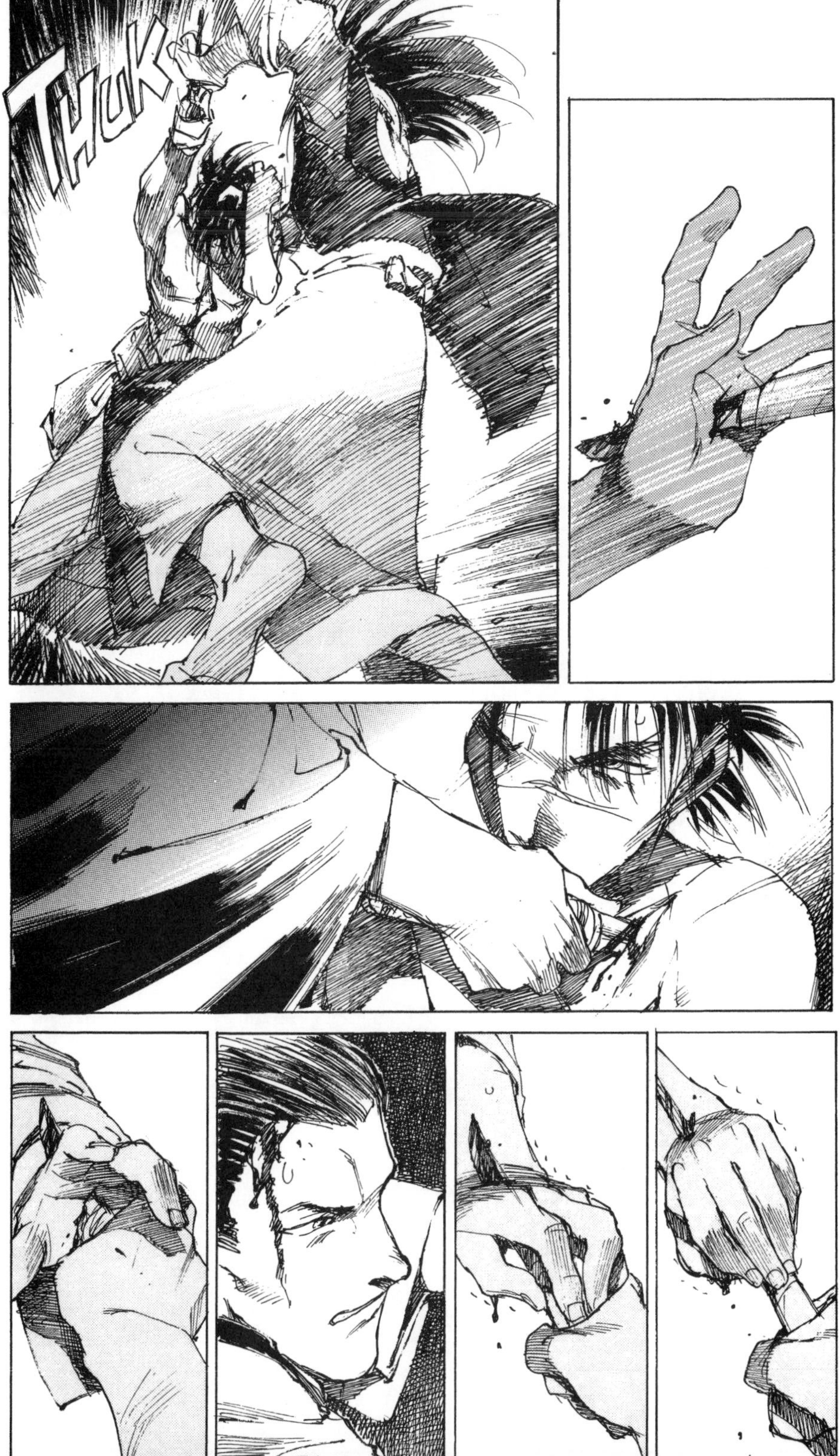
THUK!

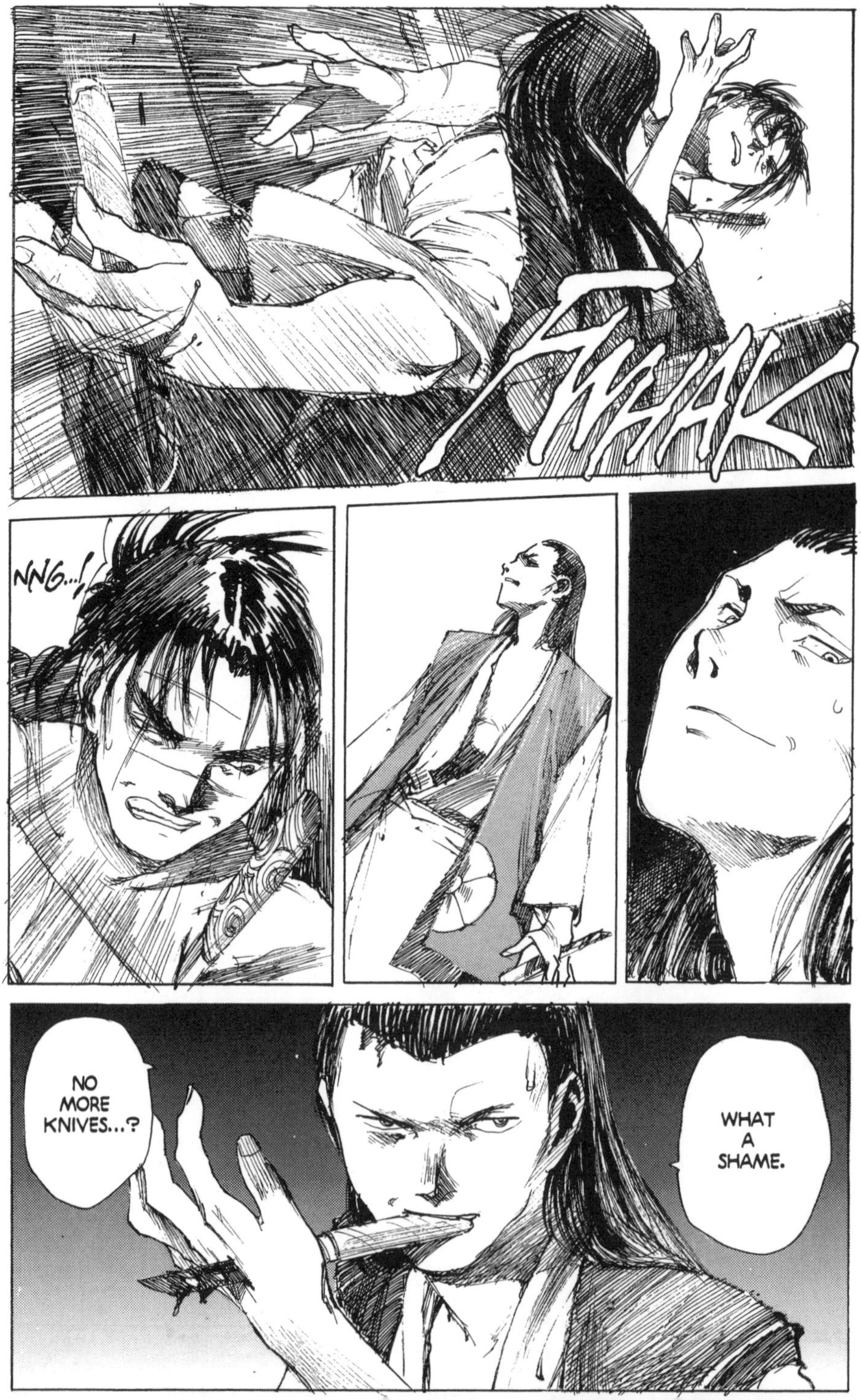
FWHAK
NNG...!
WHAT A SHAME.
NO MORE KNIVES...?

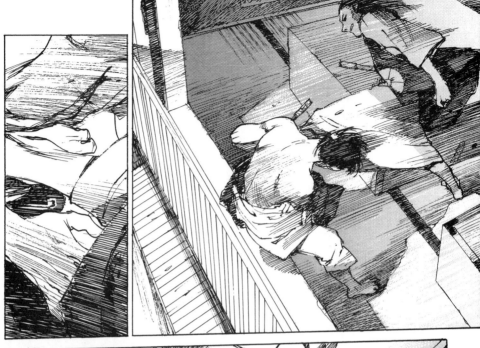

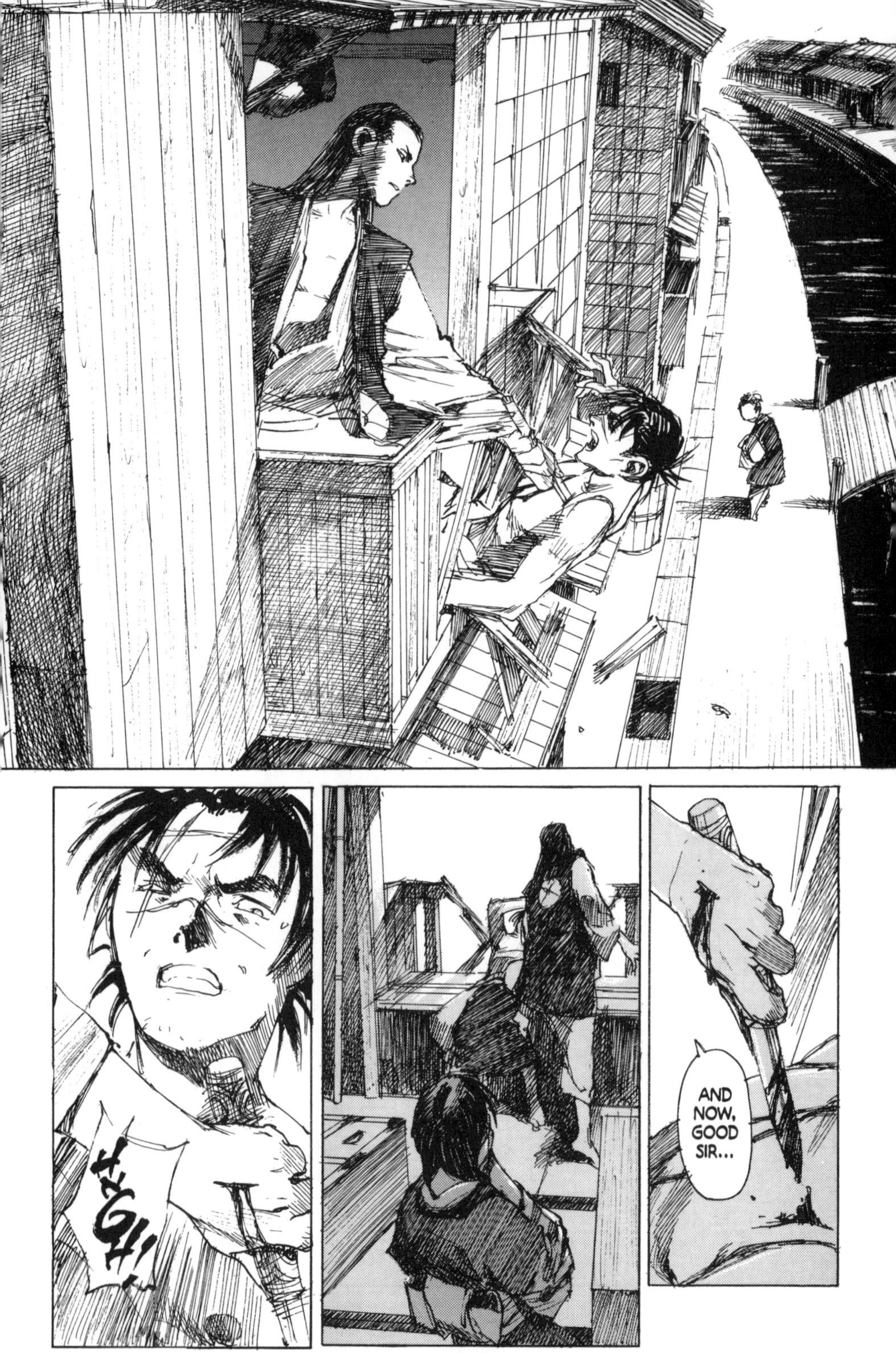
AND NOW, GOOD SIR...
HNGH!

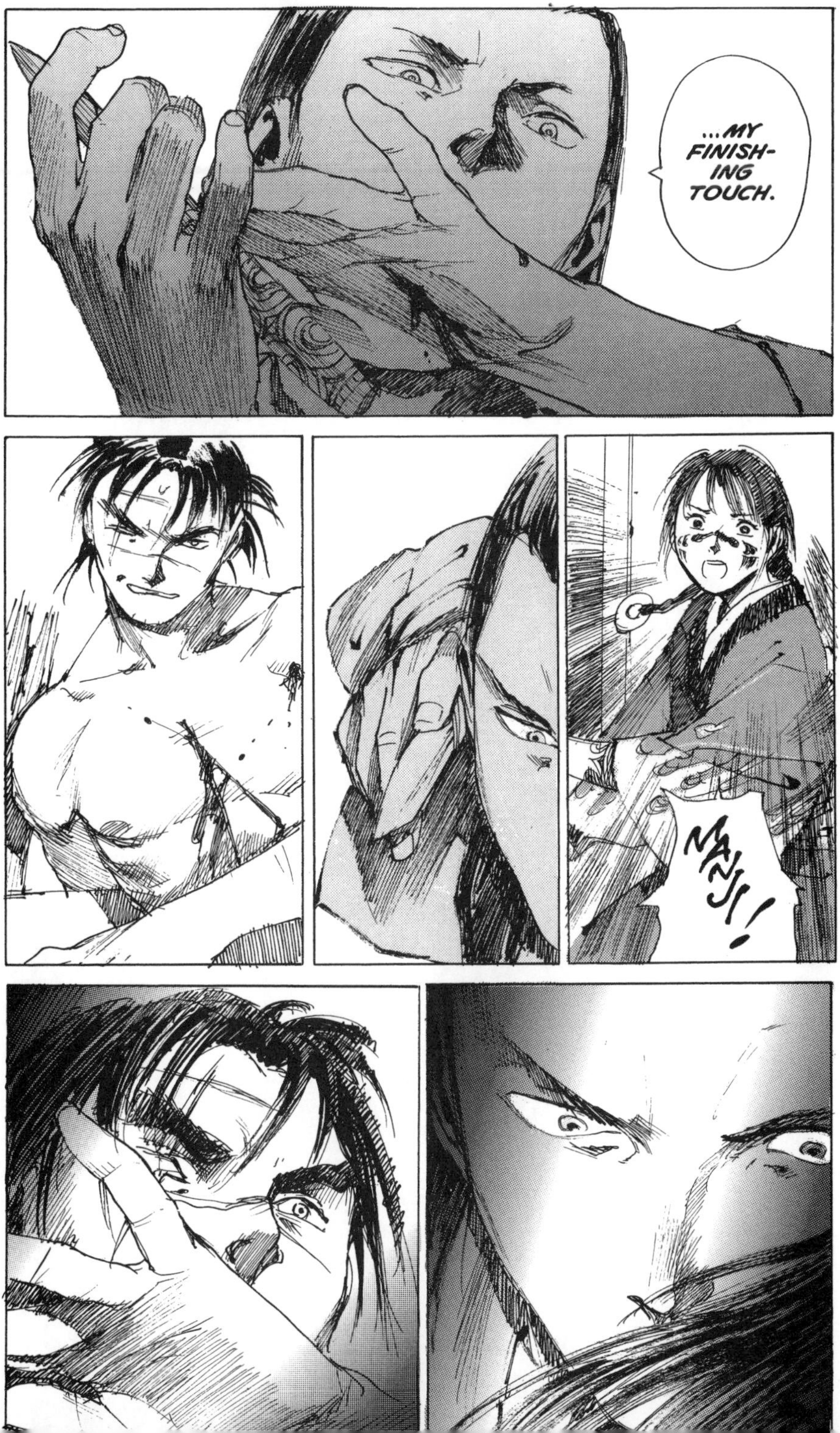
...MY FINISHING TOUCH.
MANJI!

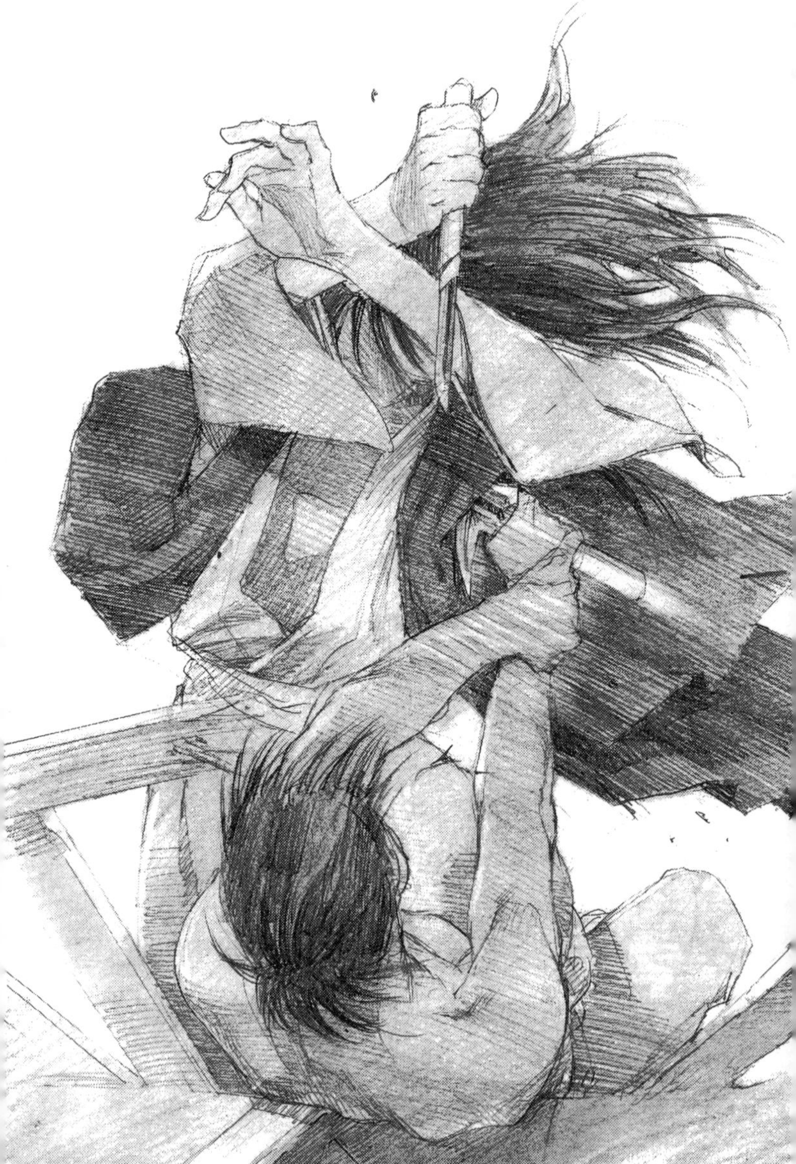

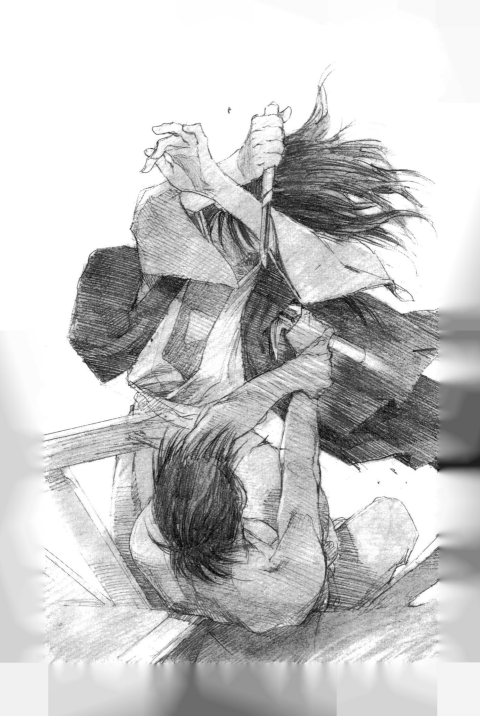

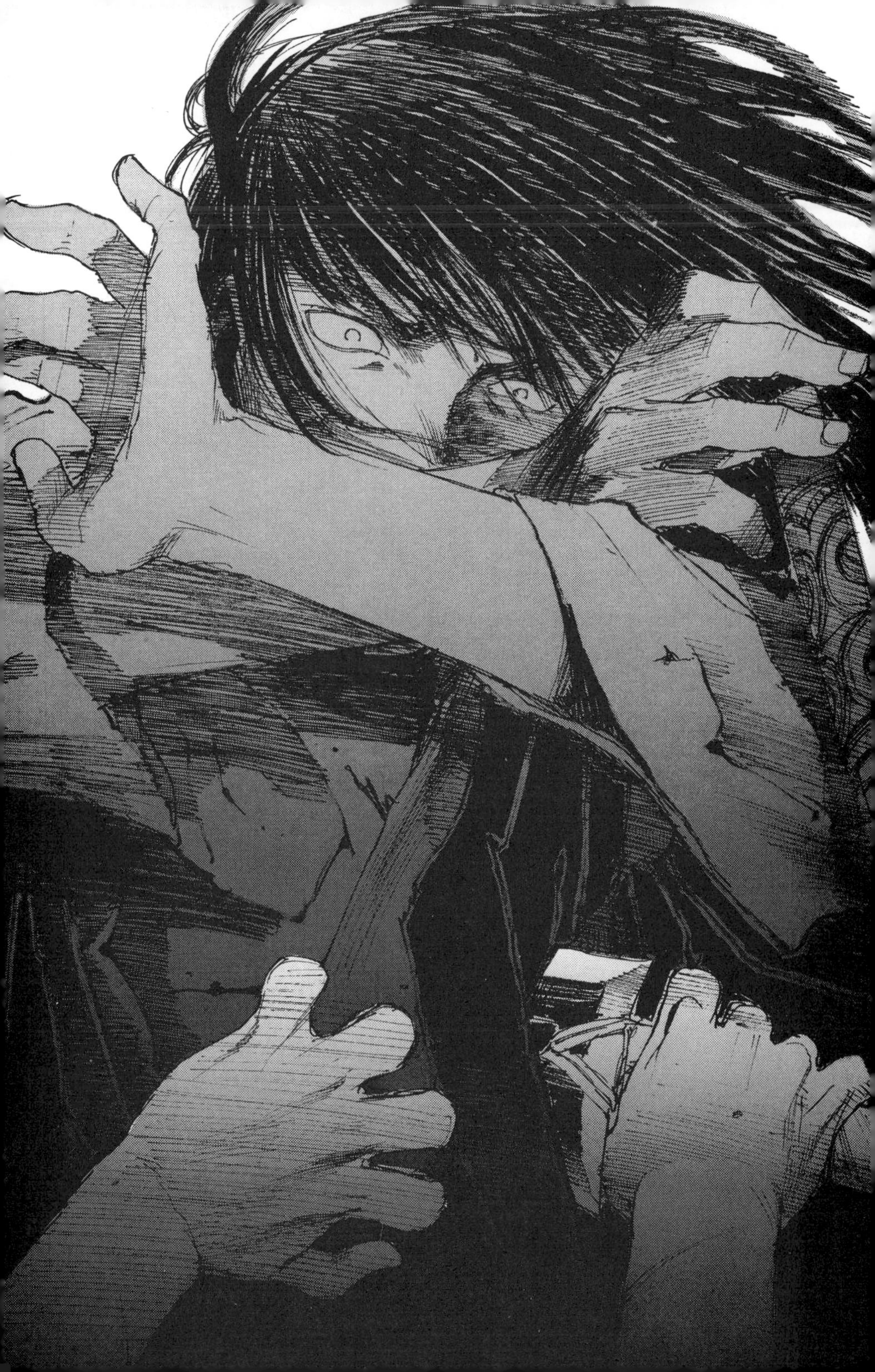

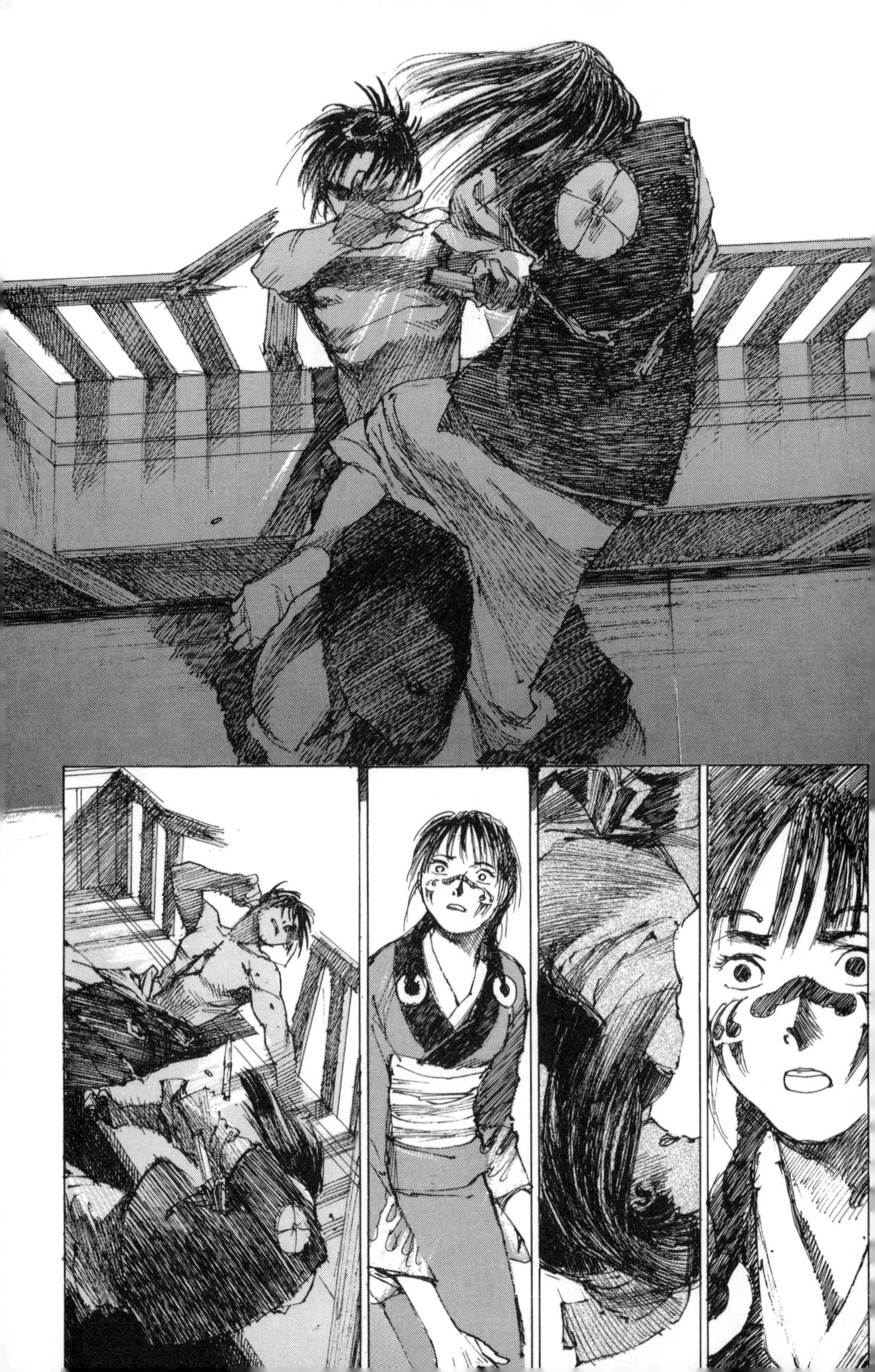

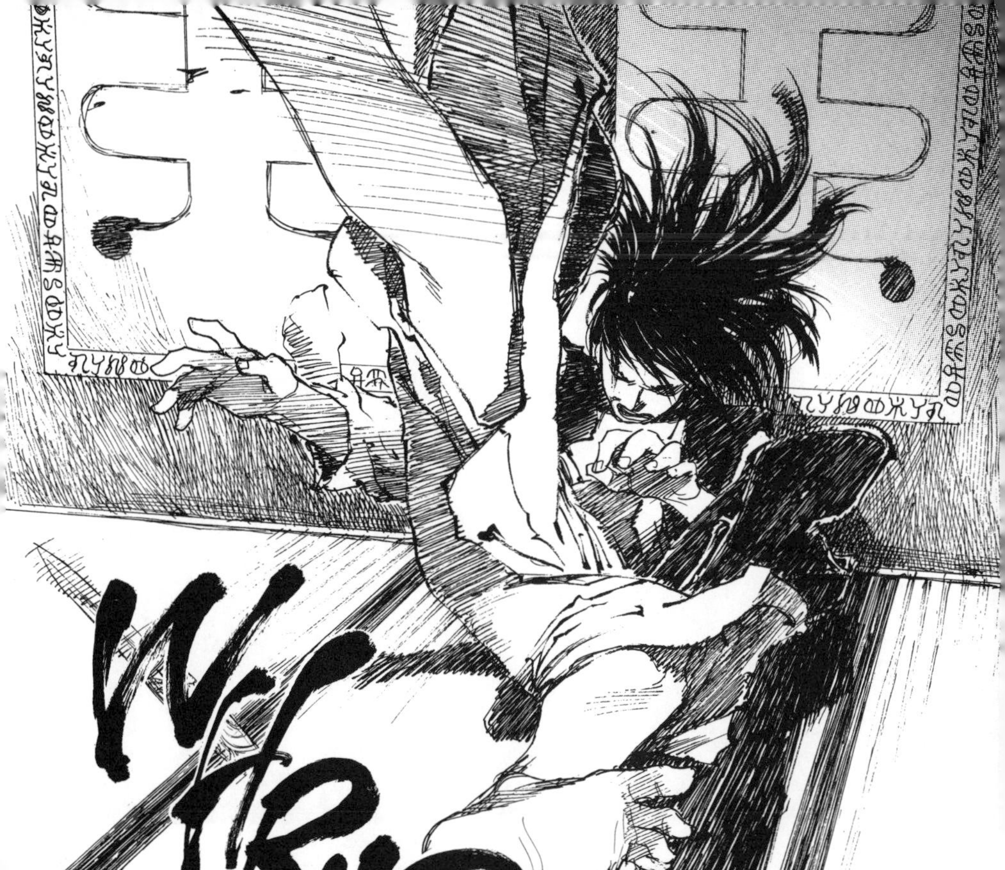

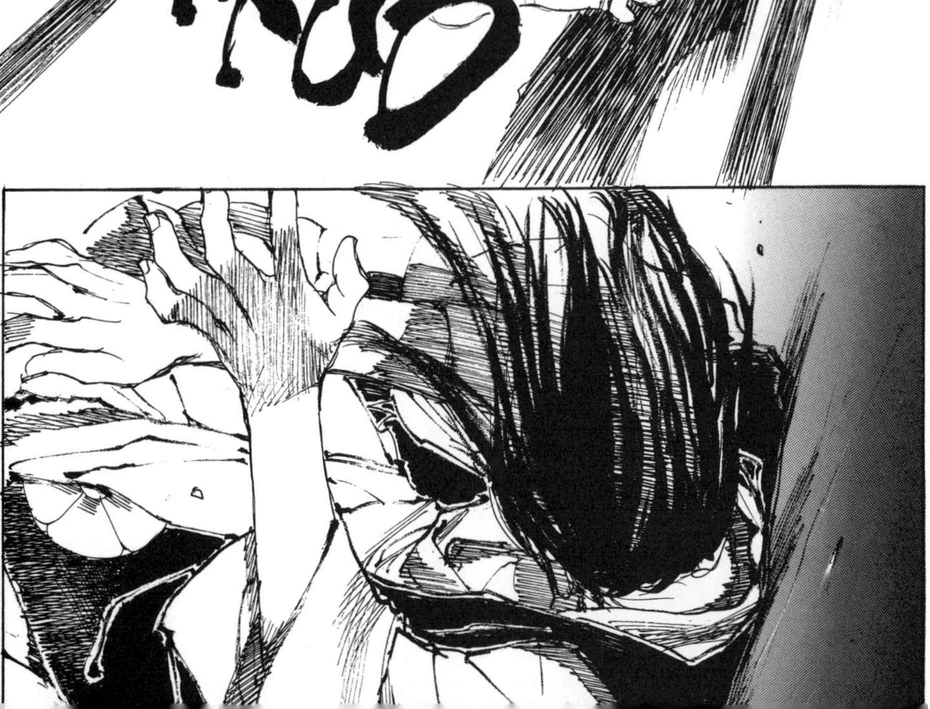

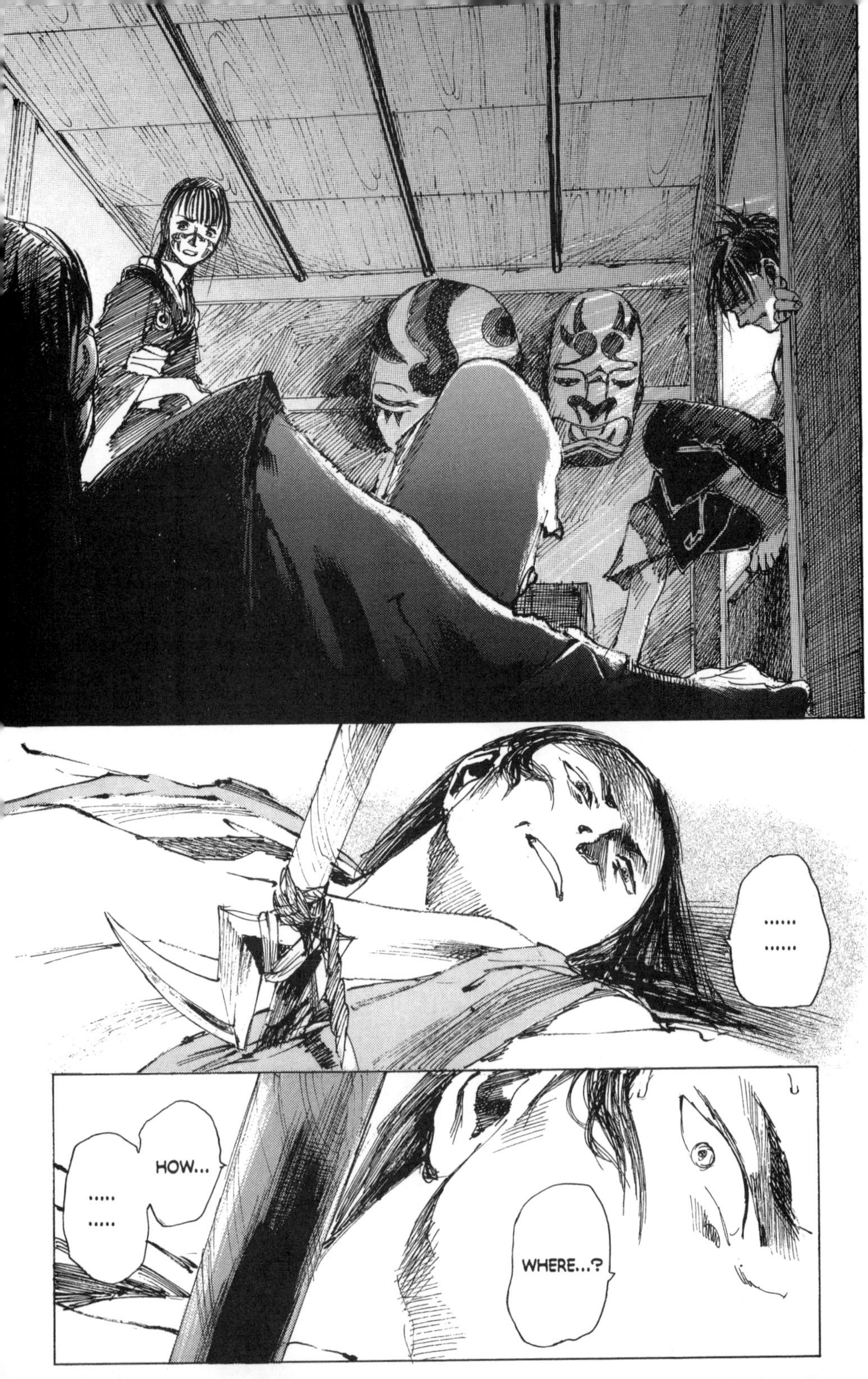
......
......
WHERE...?
HOW...
.....
.....

WELL, ARAYA...

KNOW HOW YOU DON'T GIVE A DAMN HOW DIRTY YOU FIGHT?

I FINALLY GOT WITH THE PROGRAM.

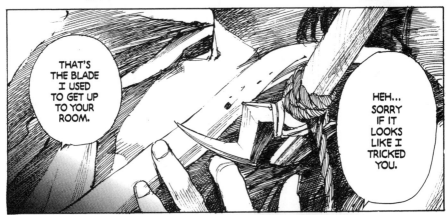

THAT'S THE BLADE I USED TO GET UP TO YOUR ROOM.

HEH... SORRY IF IT LOOKS LIKE I TRICKED YOU.

BUT I GOTTA TELL YA... I'D COMPLETELY BLANKED ON IT.

I LOOKED OVER AND THERE IT WAS, STILL STUCK IN THE WALL.

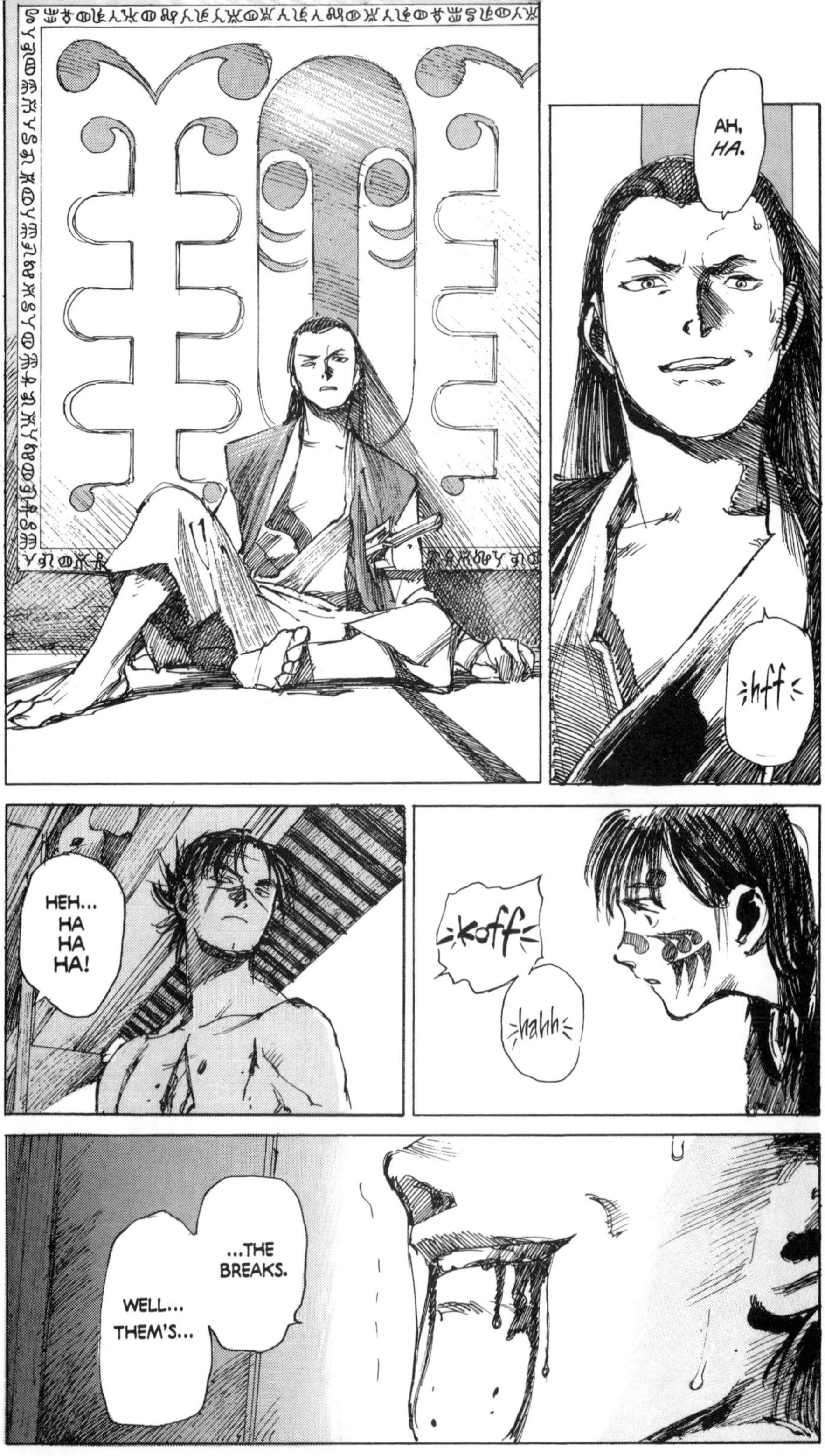
AH, *HA.*
hff
koff
hahh
HEH... HA HA HA!
WELL... THEM'S...
...THE BREAKS.

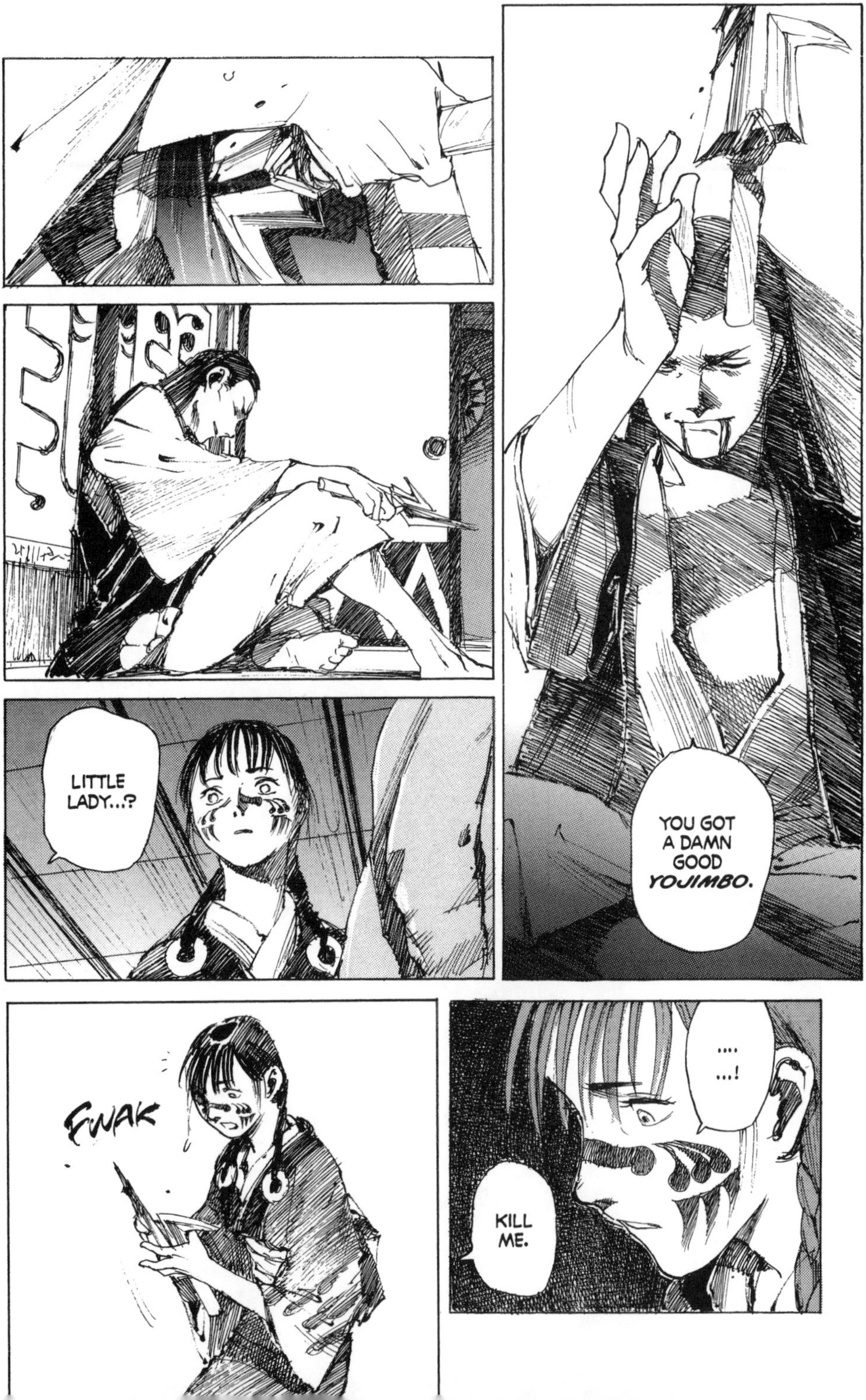
YOU GOT A DAMN GOOD *YOJIMBO*.
LITTLE LADY...?
....!
KILL ME.
FWAK

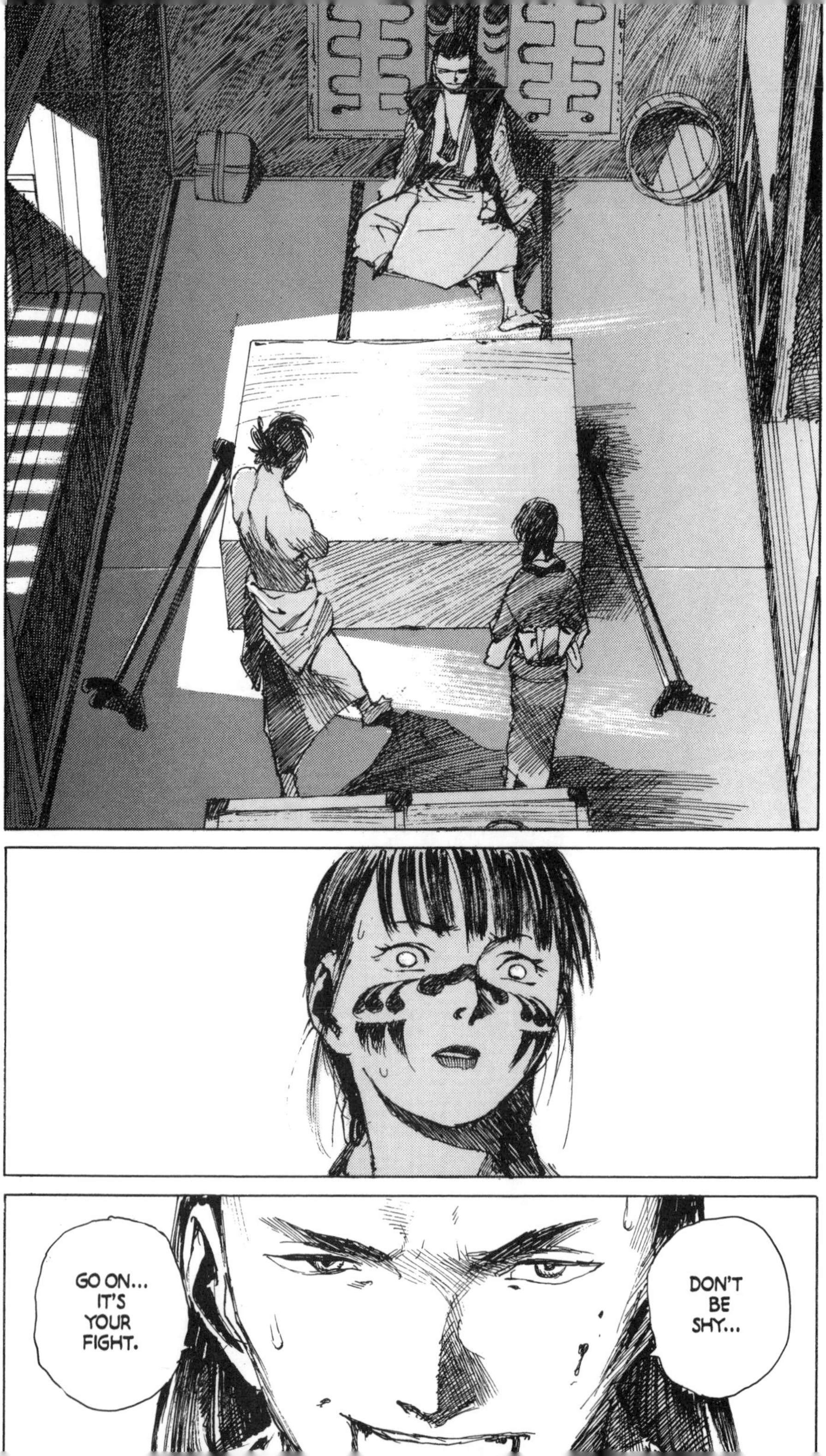
DON'T BE SHY...
GO ON... IT'S YOUR FIGHT.

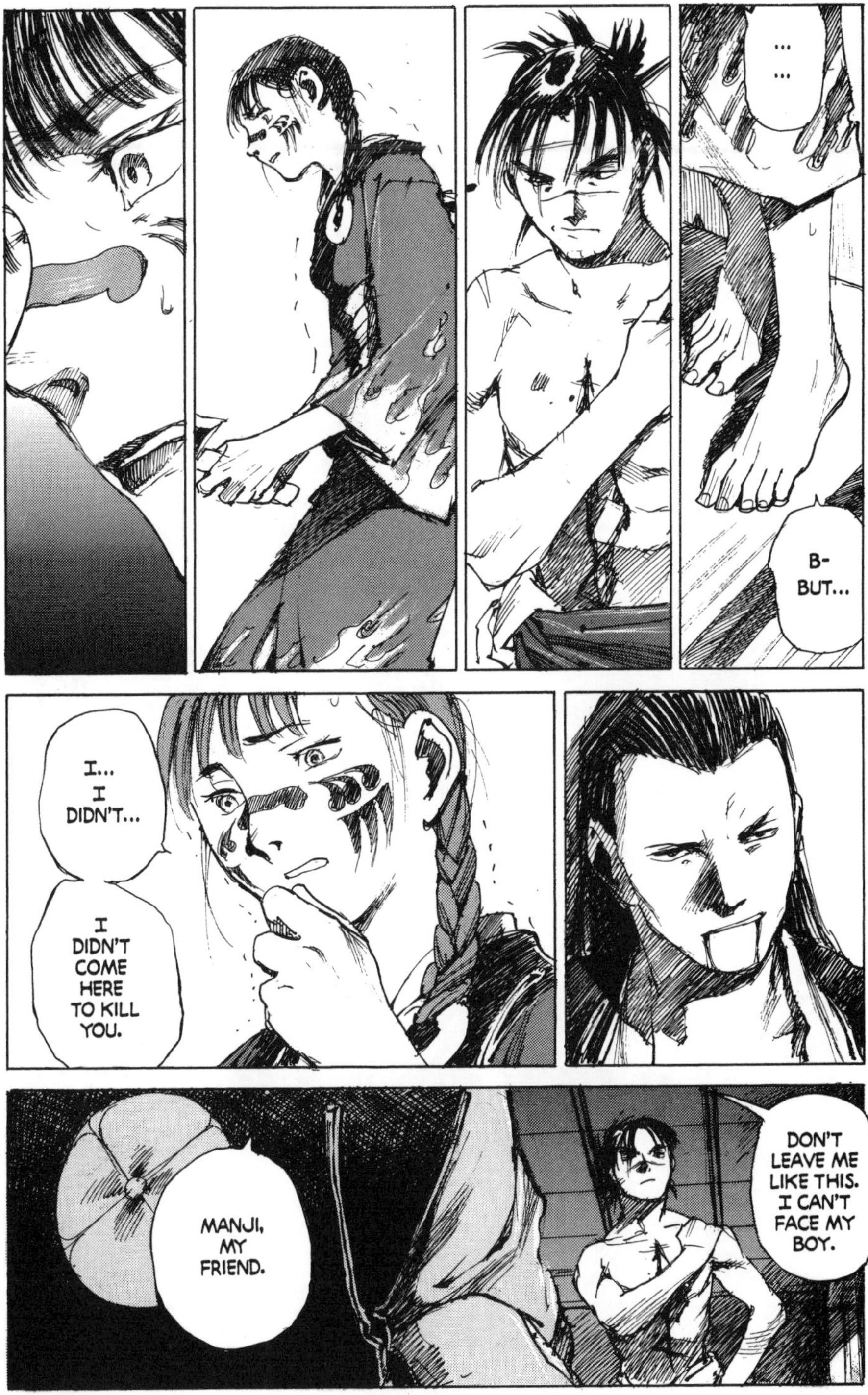
... ...
B- BUT...
I... I DIDN'T...
I DIDN'T COME HERE TO KILL YOU.
DON'T LEAVE ME LIKE THIS. I CAN'T FACE MY BOY.
MANJI, MY FRIEND.

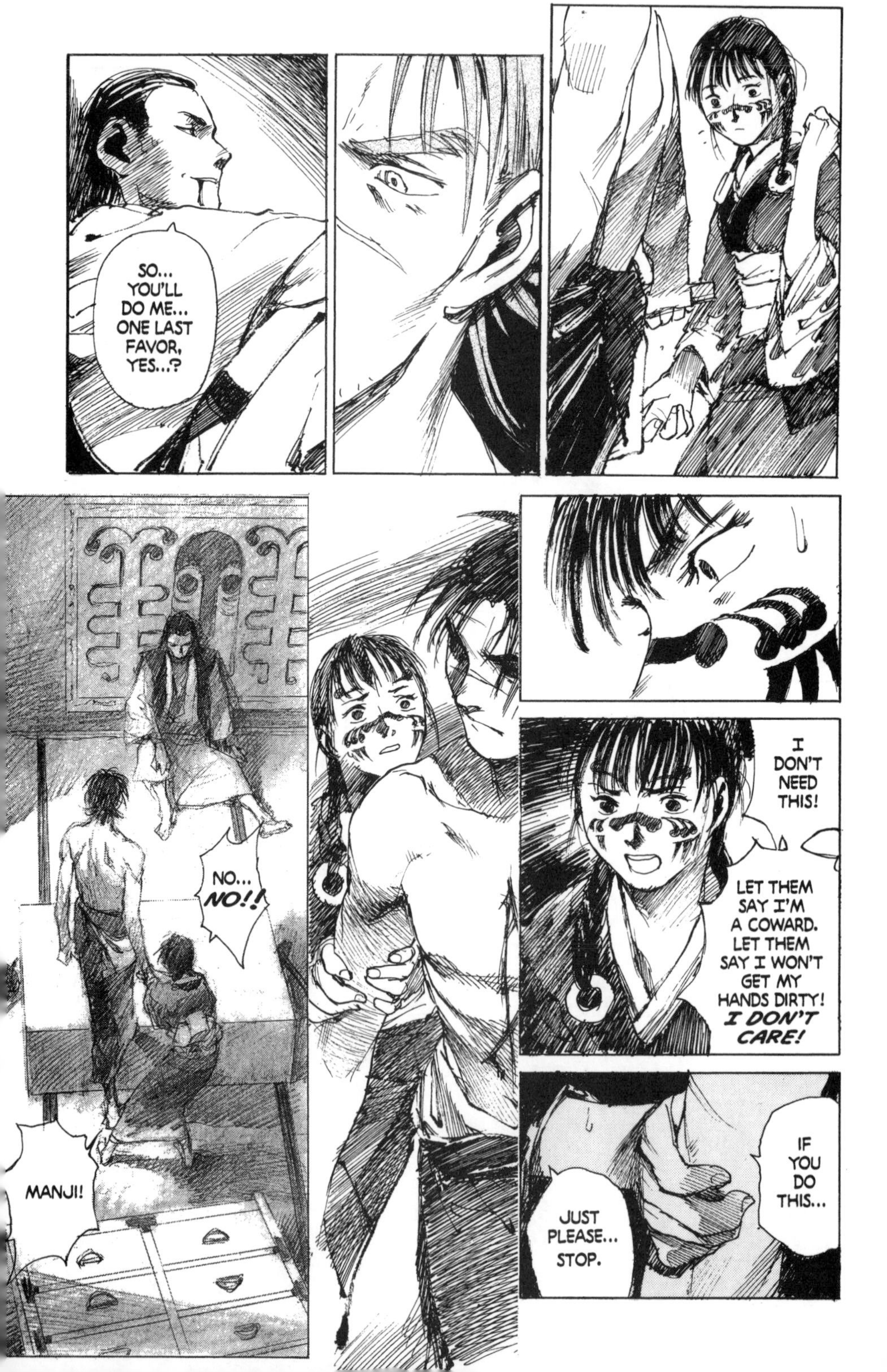
SO... YOU'LL DO ME... ONE LAST FAVOR, YES...?
I DON'T NEED THIS!
LET THEM SAY I'M A COWARD. LET THEM SAY I WON'T GET MY HANDS DIRTY! *I DON'T CARE!*
IF YOU DO THIS...
JUST PLEASE... STOP.
NO... *NO!!*
MANJI!

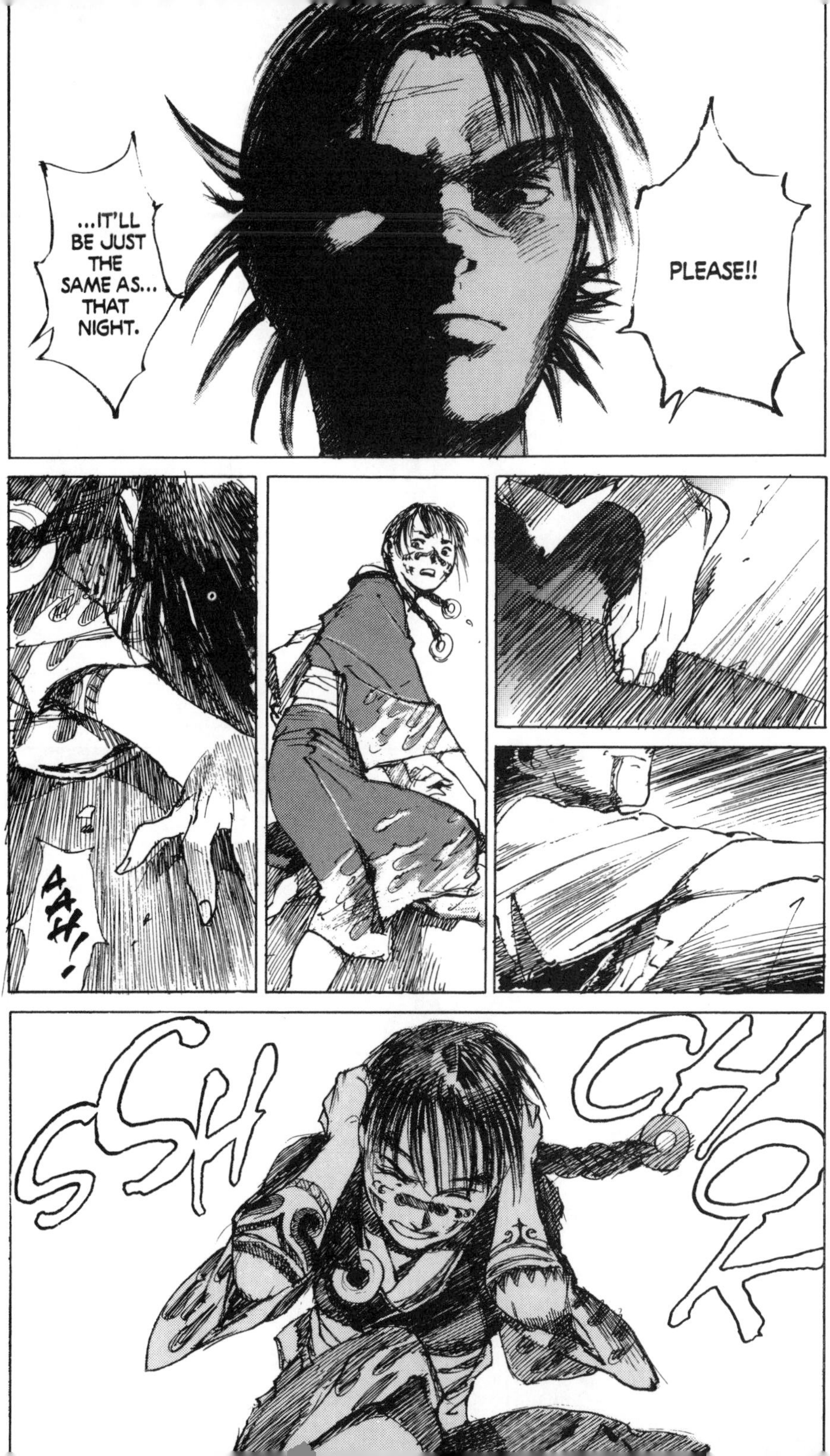
PLEASE!!
...IT'LL BE JUST THE SAME AS... THAT NIGHT.
AAH!!
CHOK
SSH

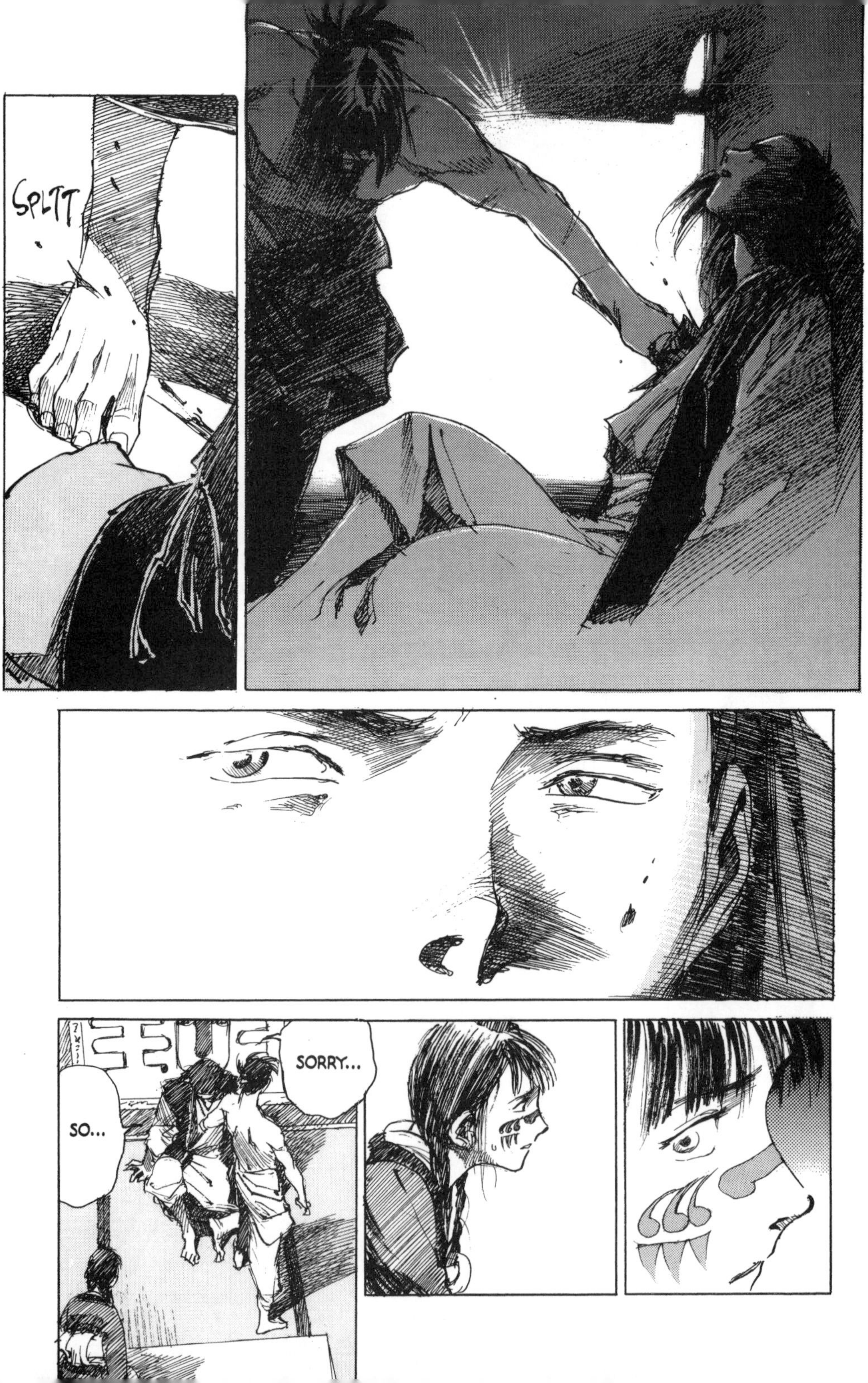
SPLTT
SORRY...
SO...

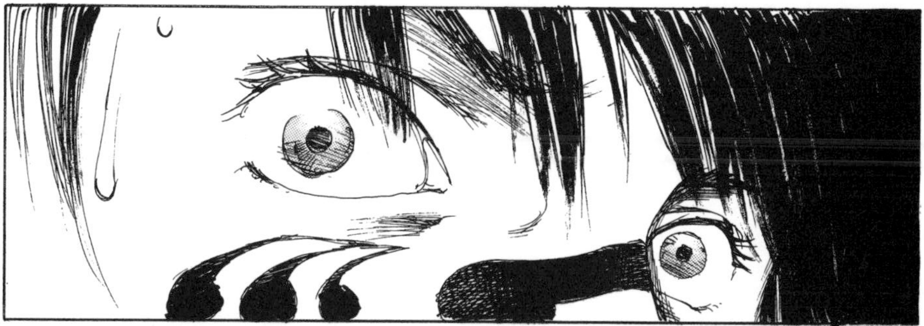
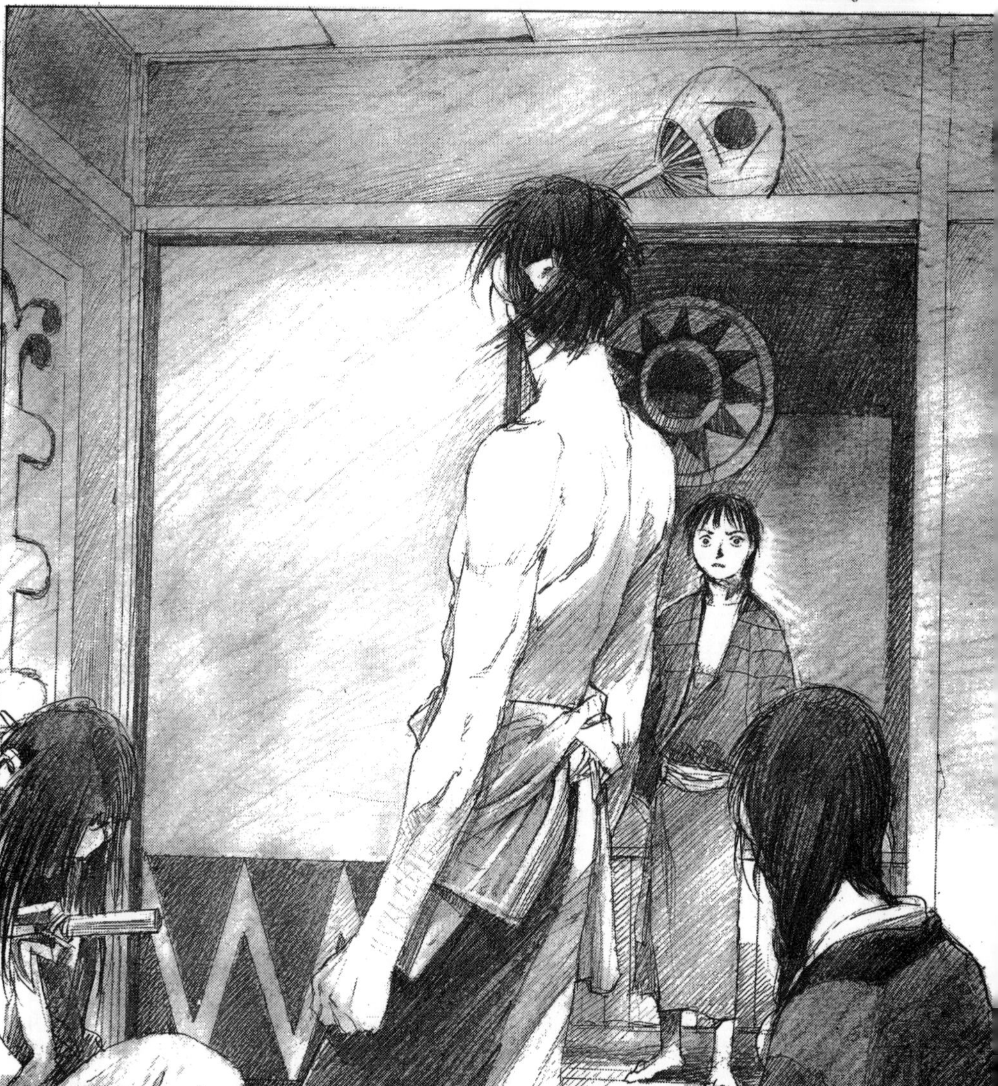

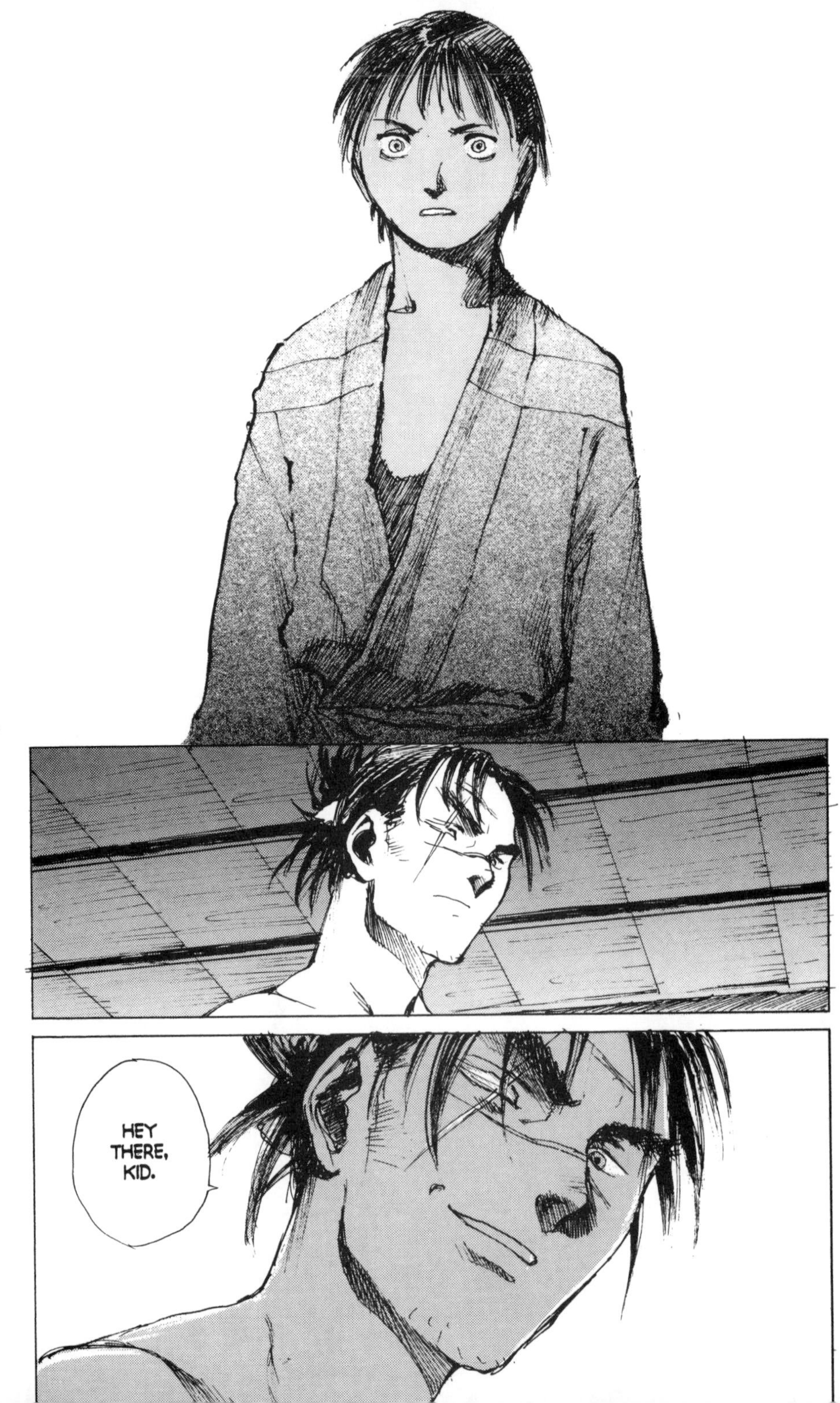
HEY THERE, KID.

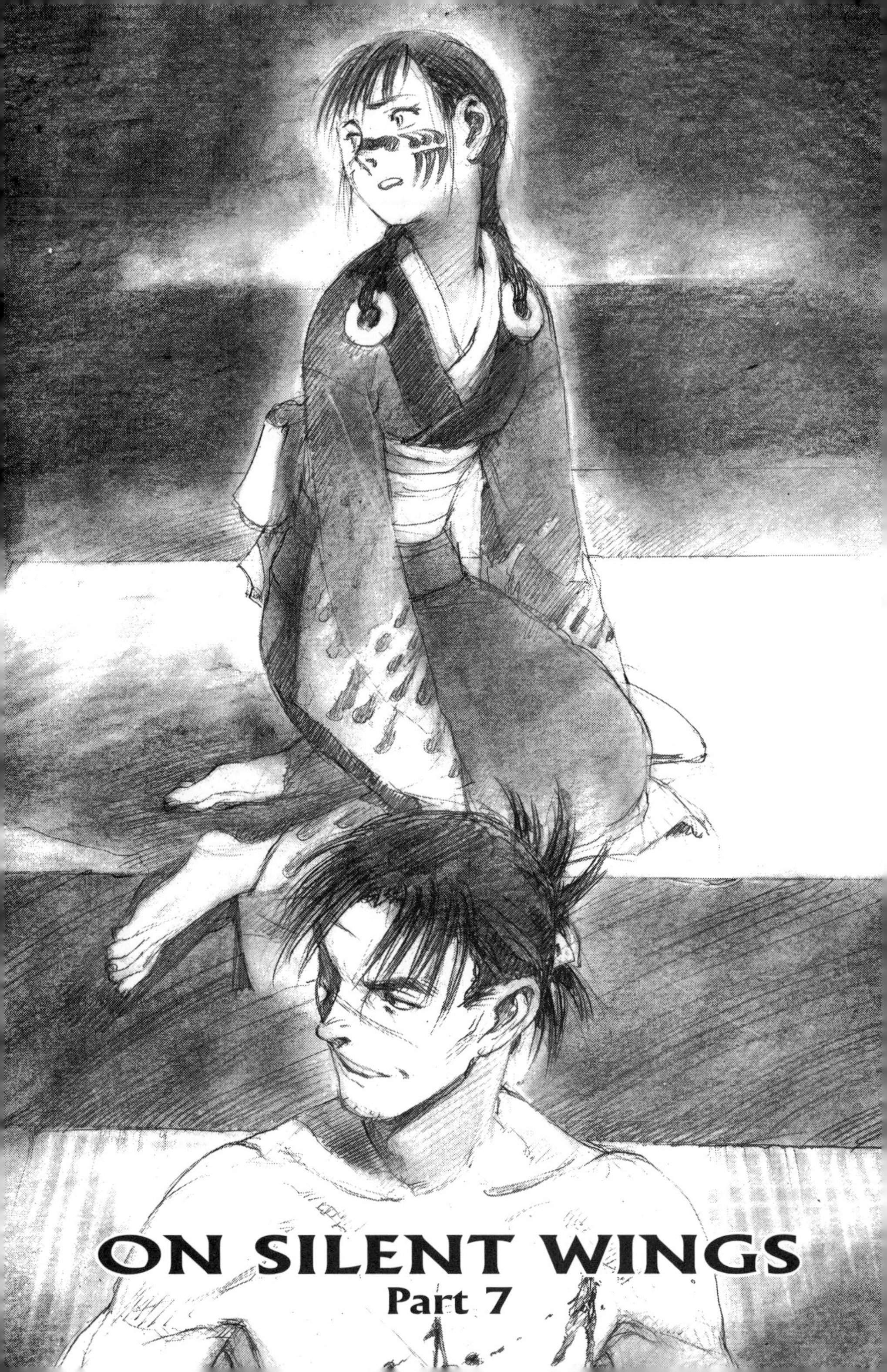

ON SILENT WINGS
Part 7

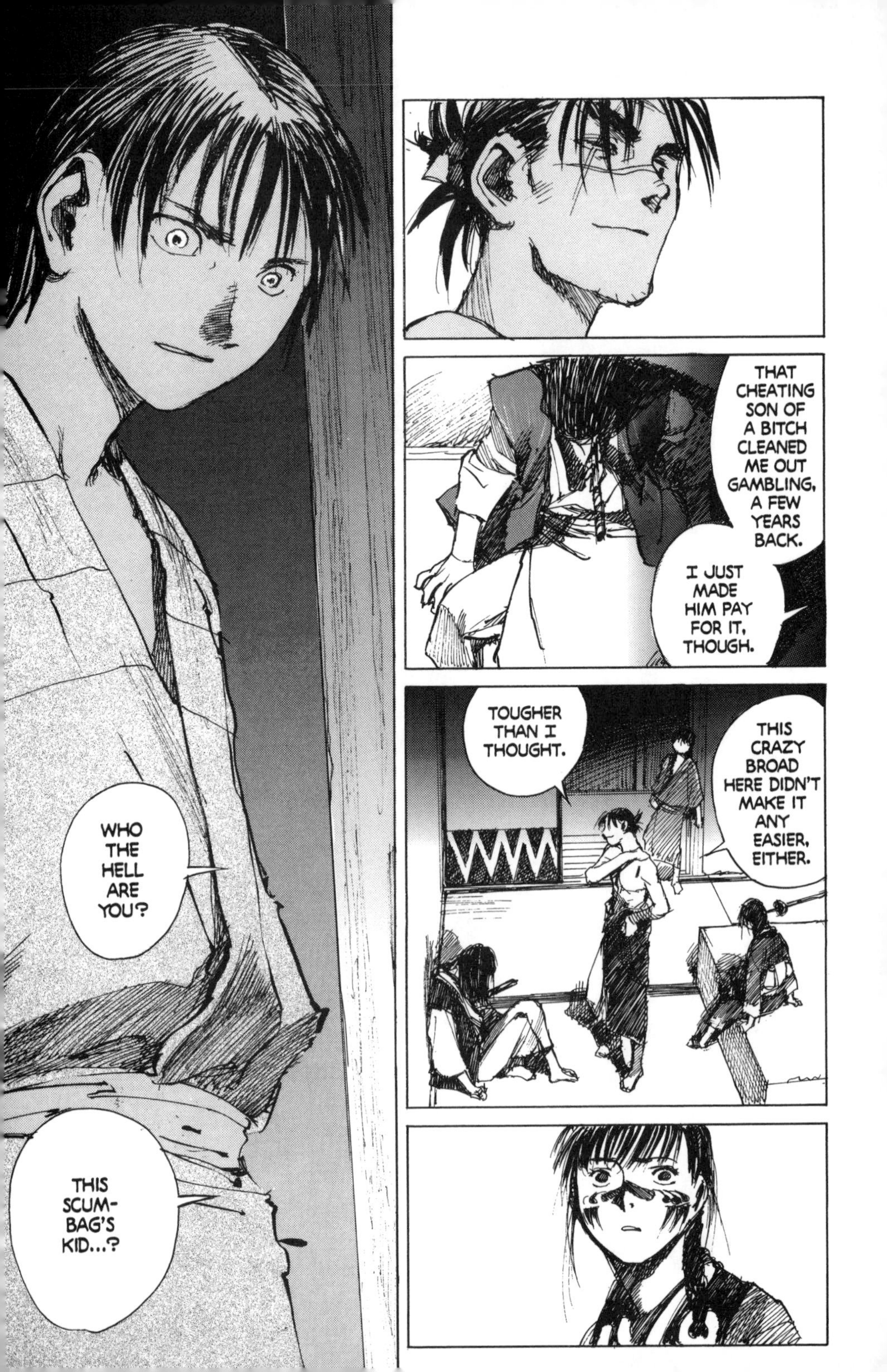
THAT CHEATING SON OF A BITCH CLEANED ME OUT GAMBLING, A FEW YEARS BACK.
I JUST MADE HIM PAY FOR IT, THOUGH.
TOUGHER THAN I THOUGHT.
THIS CRAZY BROAD HERE DIDN'T MAKE IT ANY EASIER, EITHER.
WHO THE HELL ARE YOU?
THIS SCUM-BAG'S KID...?

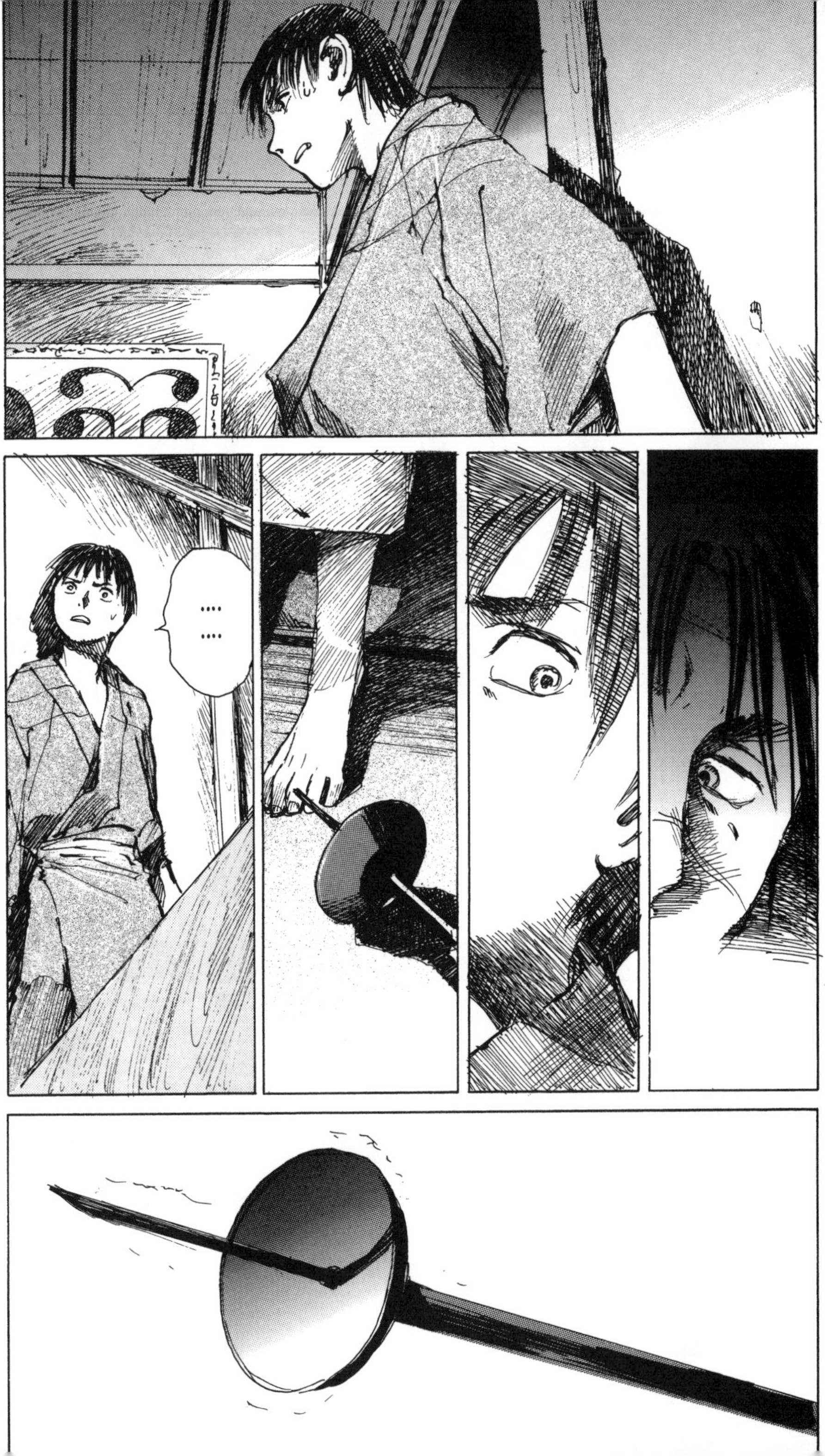
....

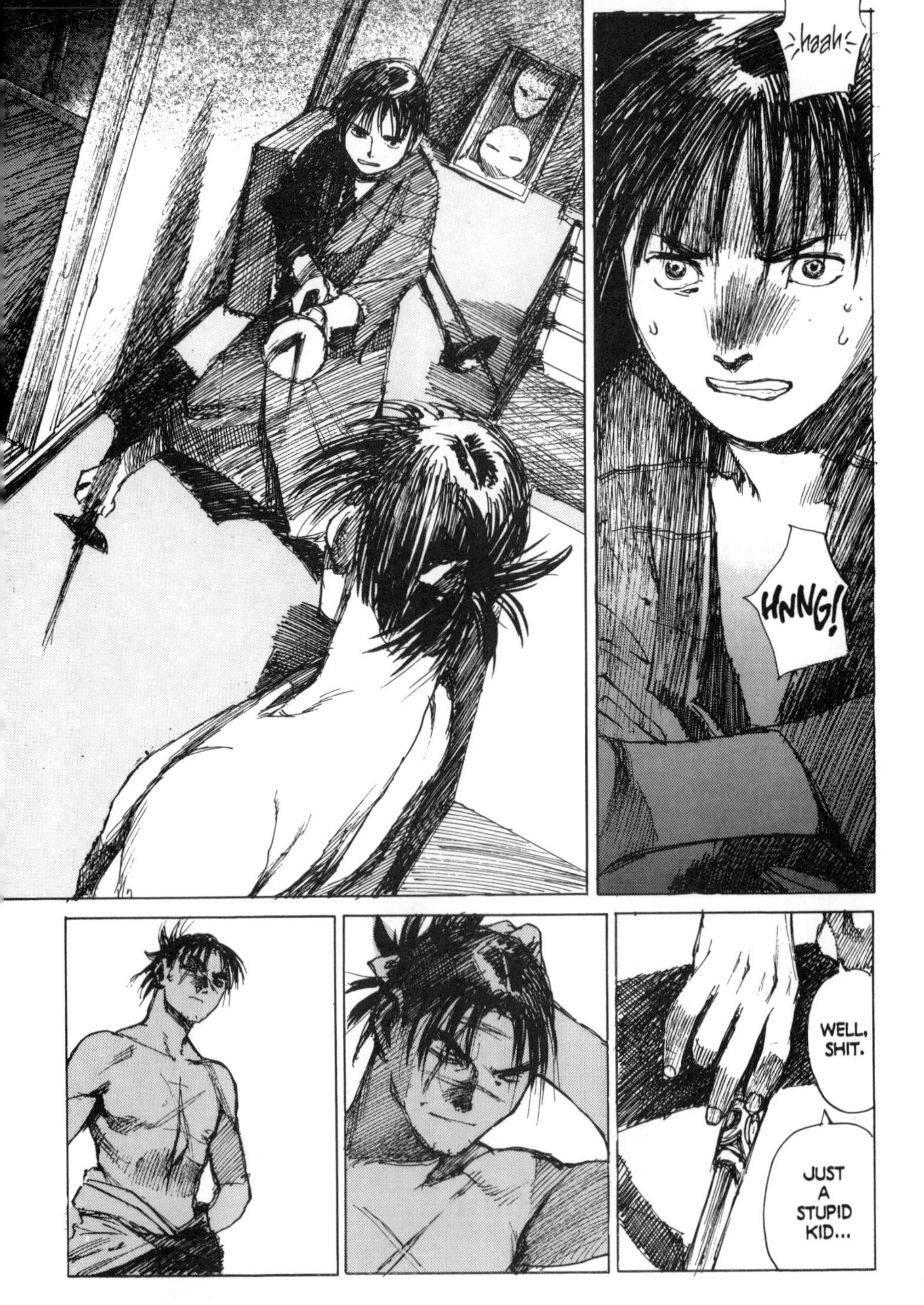
haah
HNNG!
WELL, SHIT.
JUST A STUPID KID...

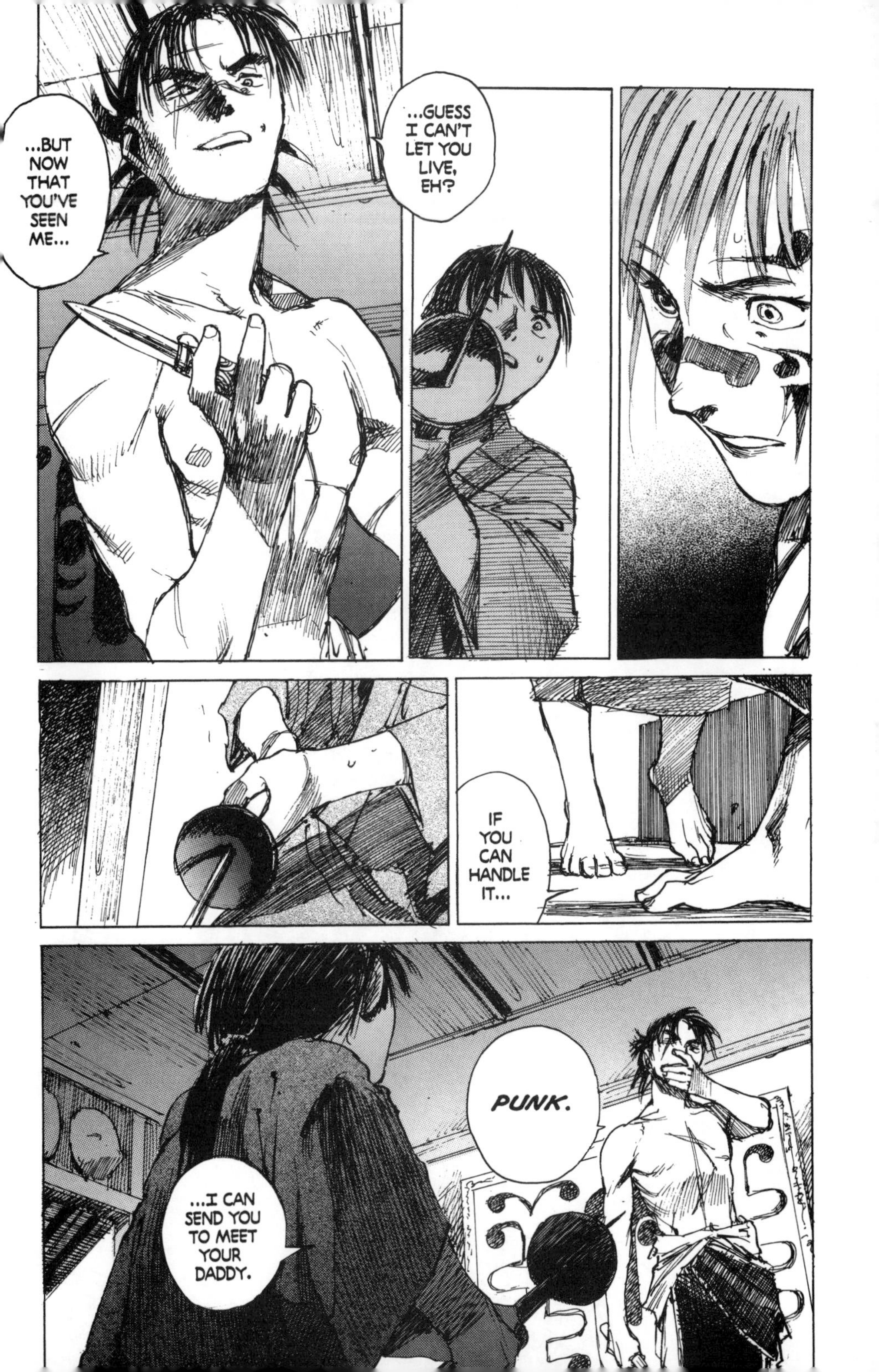
...BUT NOW THAT YOU'VE SEEN ME...
...GUESS I CAN'T LET YOU LIVE, EH?
IF YOU CAN HANDLE IT...
...I CAN SEND YOU TO MEET YOUR DADDY.
PUNK.

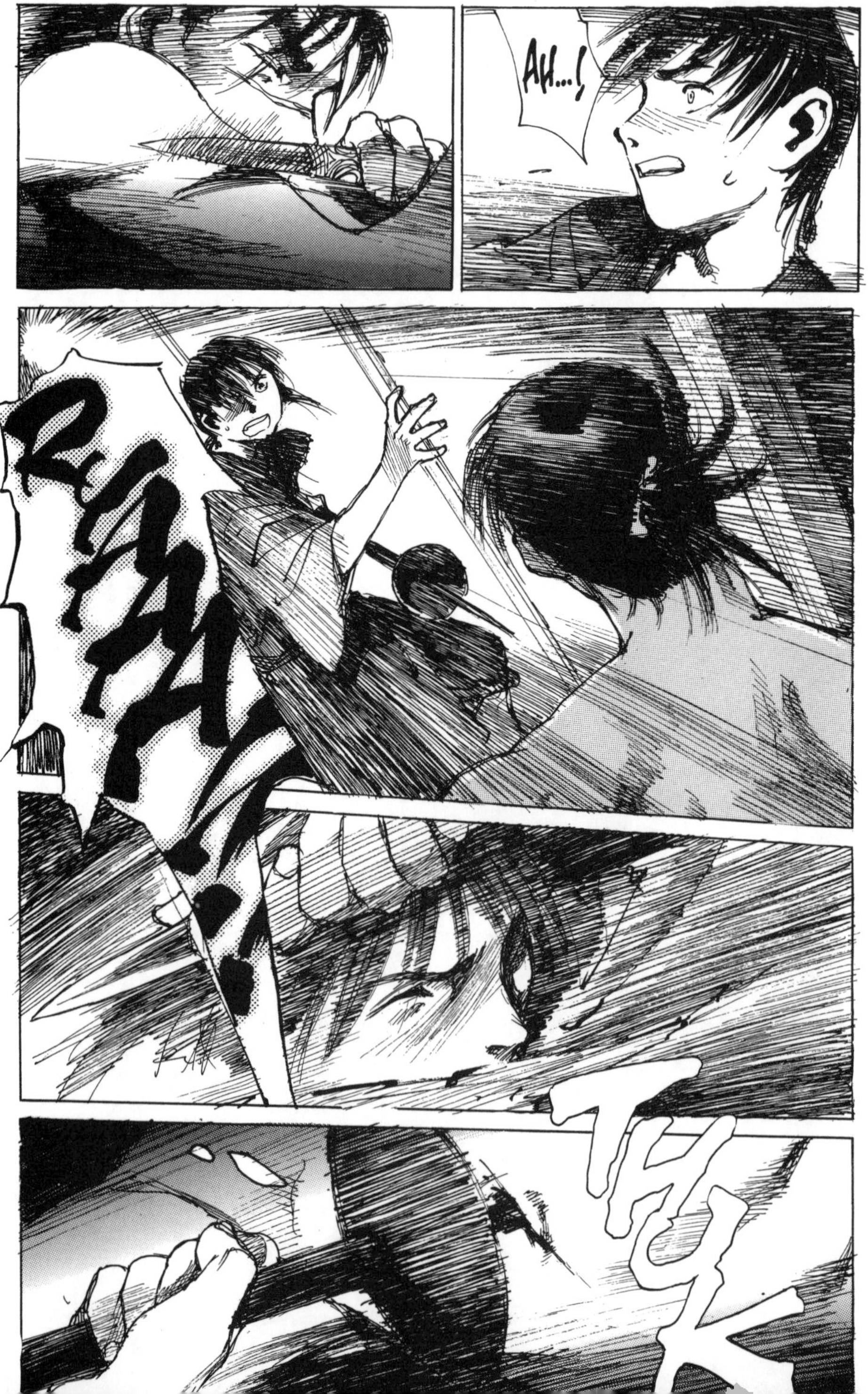
AH...!
RIIIP!
TCK

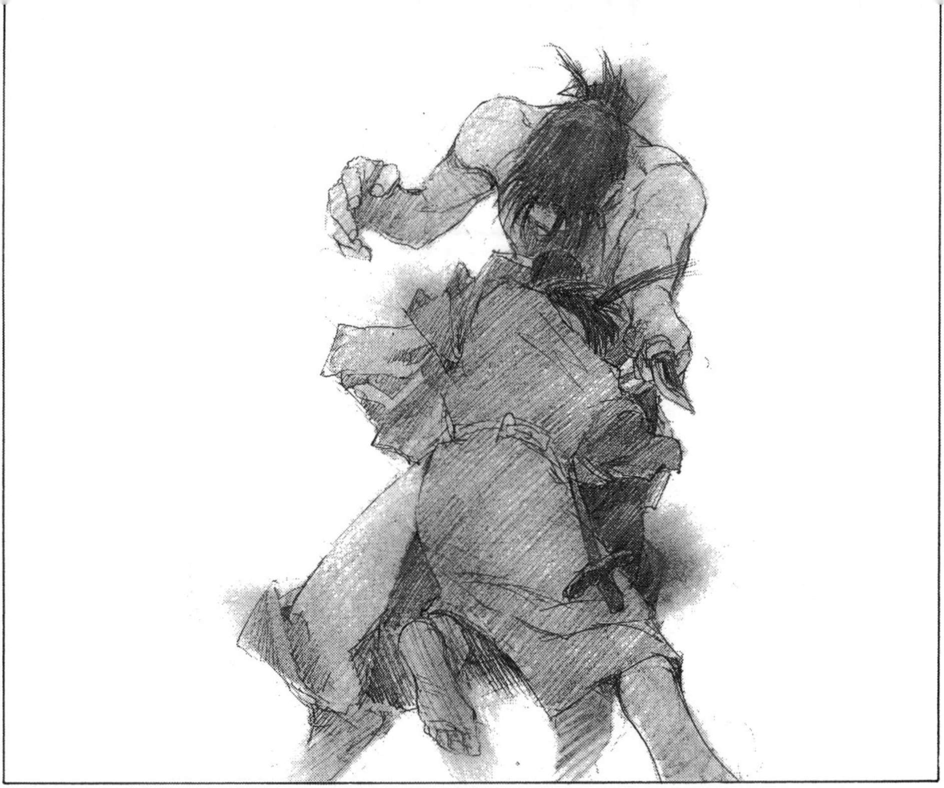
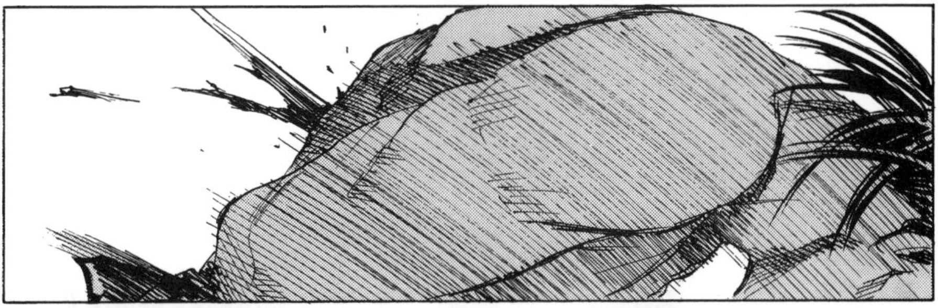
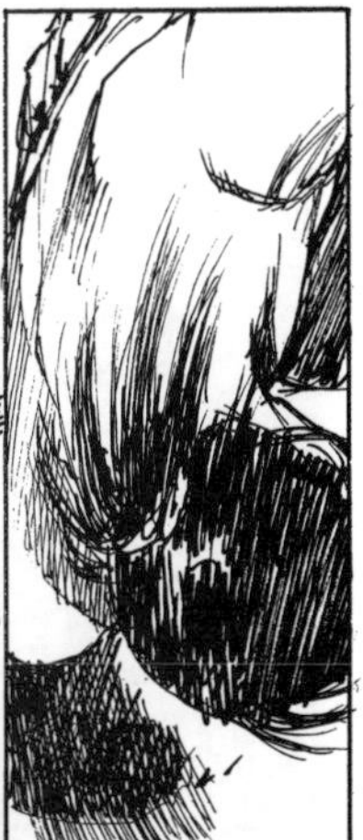
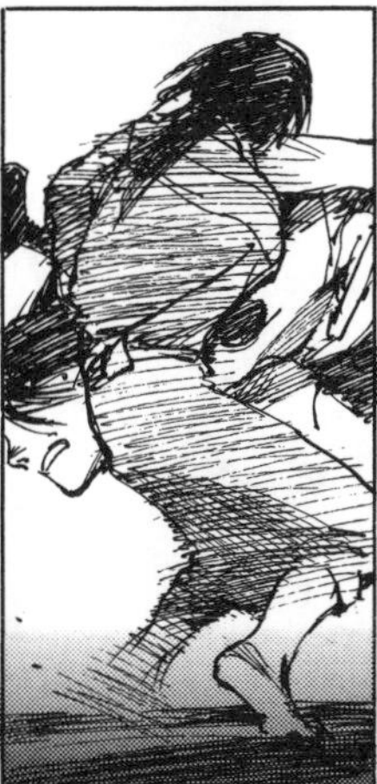
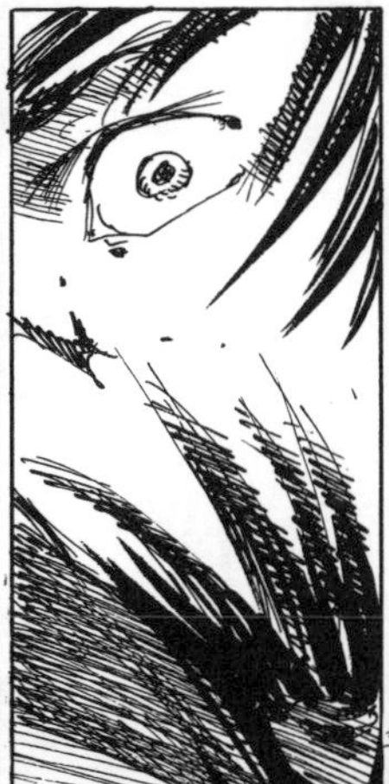
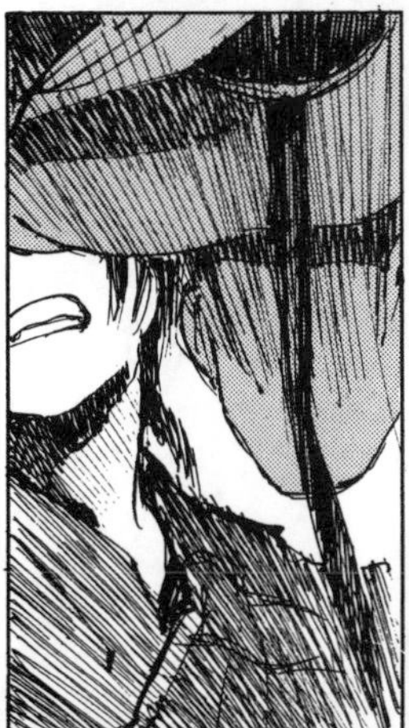

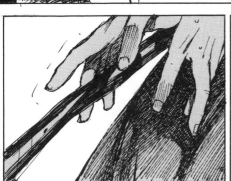

NNG...

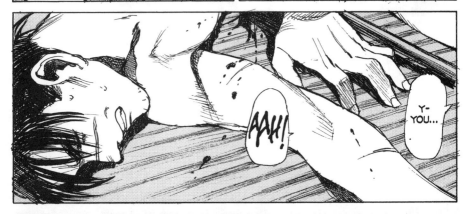

AAH!

Y-YOU...

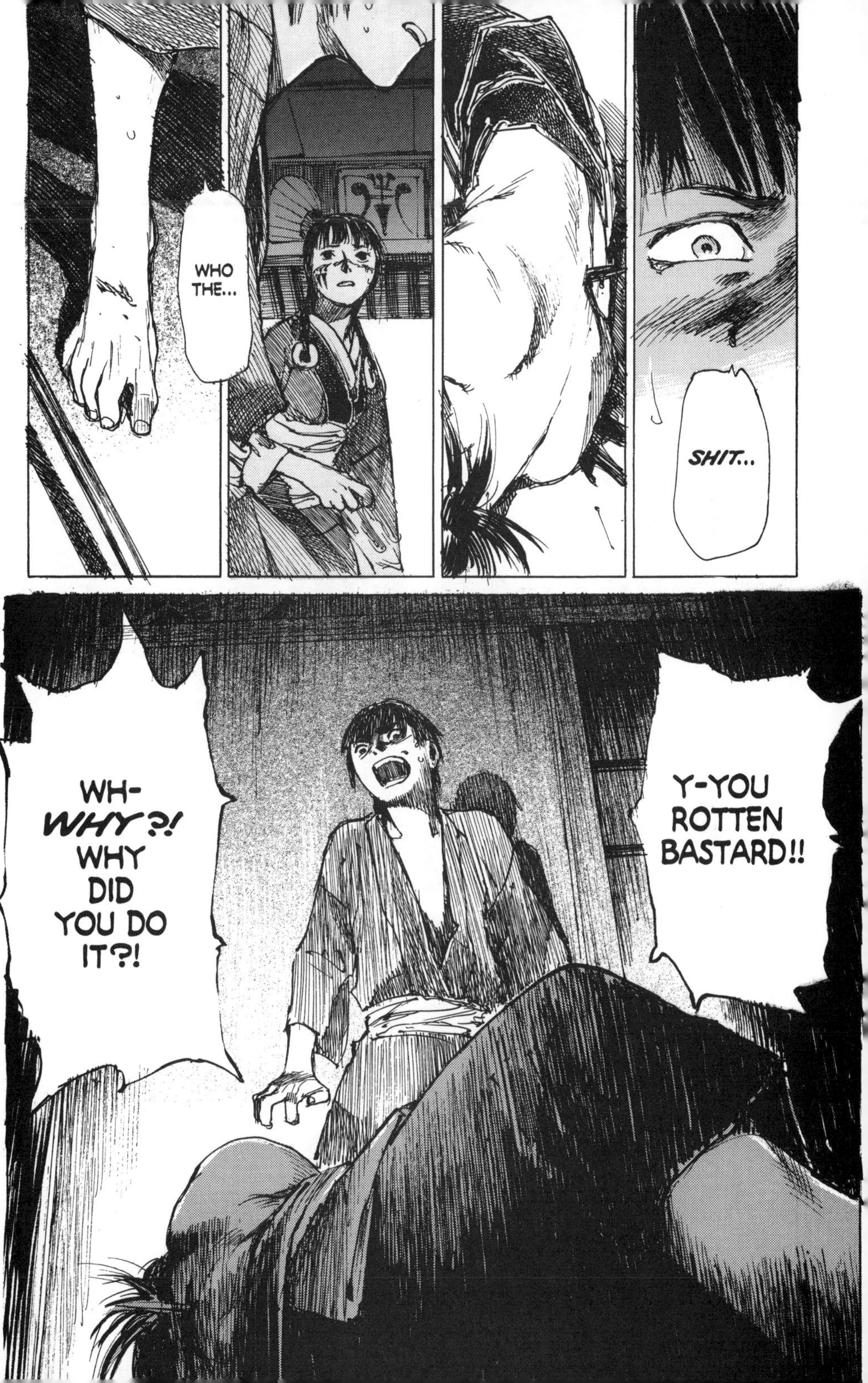
SHIT...
WHO THE...
Y-YOU ROTTEN BASTARD!!
WH- *WHY*?! WHY DID YOU DO IT?!

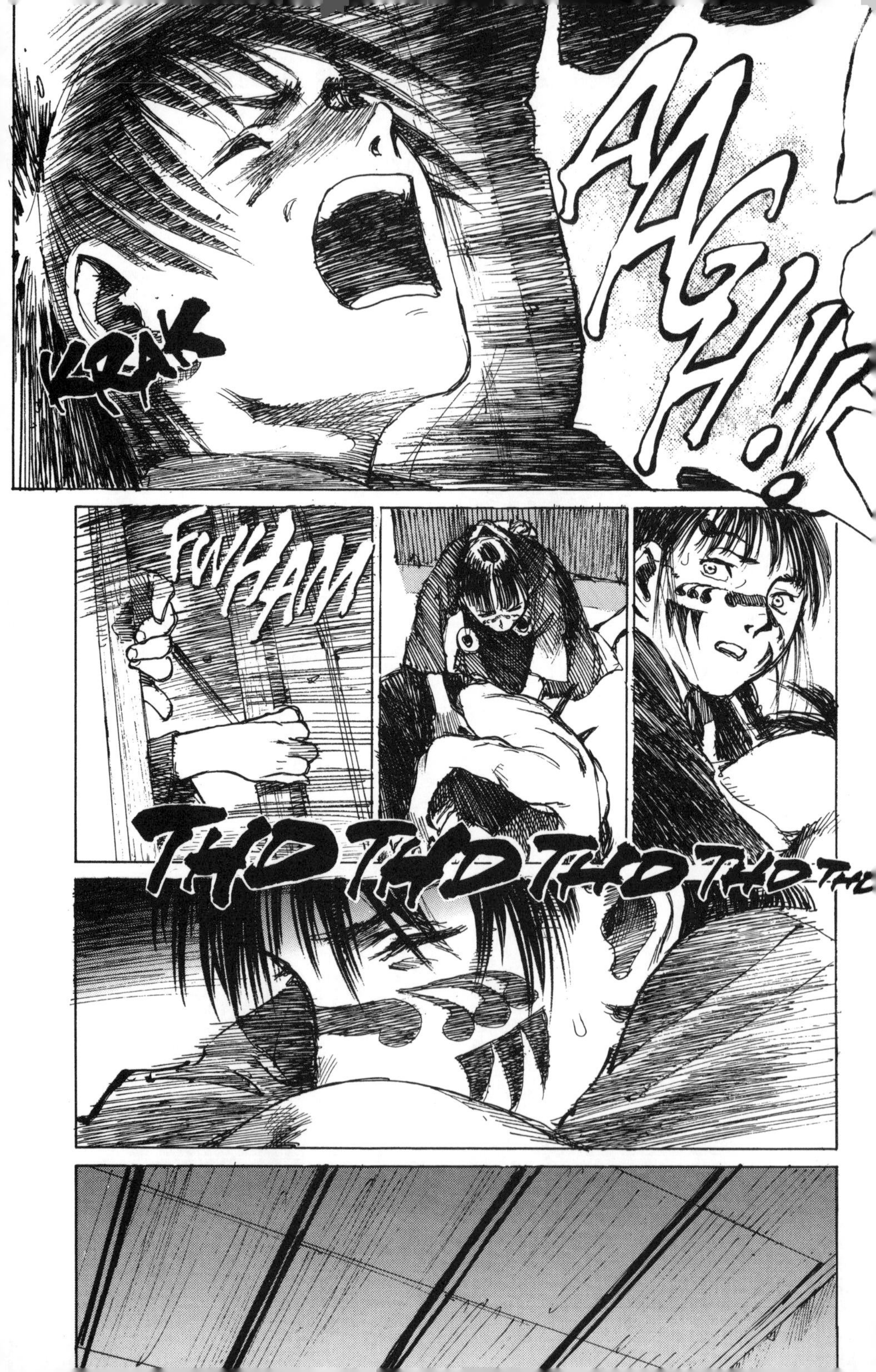
AAGH!!!
KRAK
FWHAM
THD THD THD THD THD

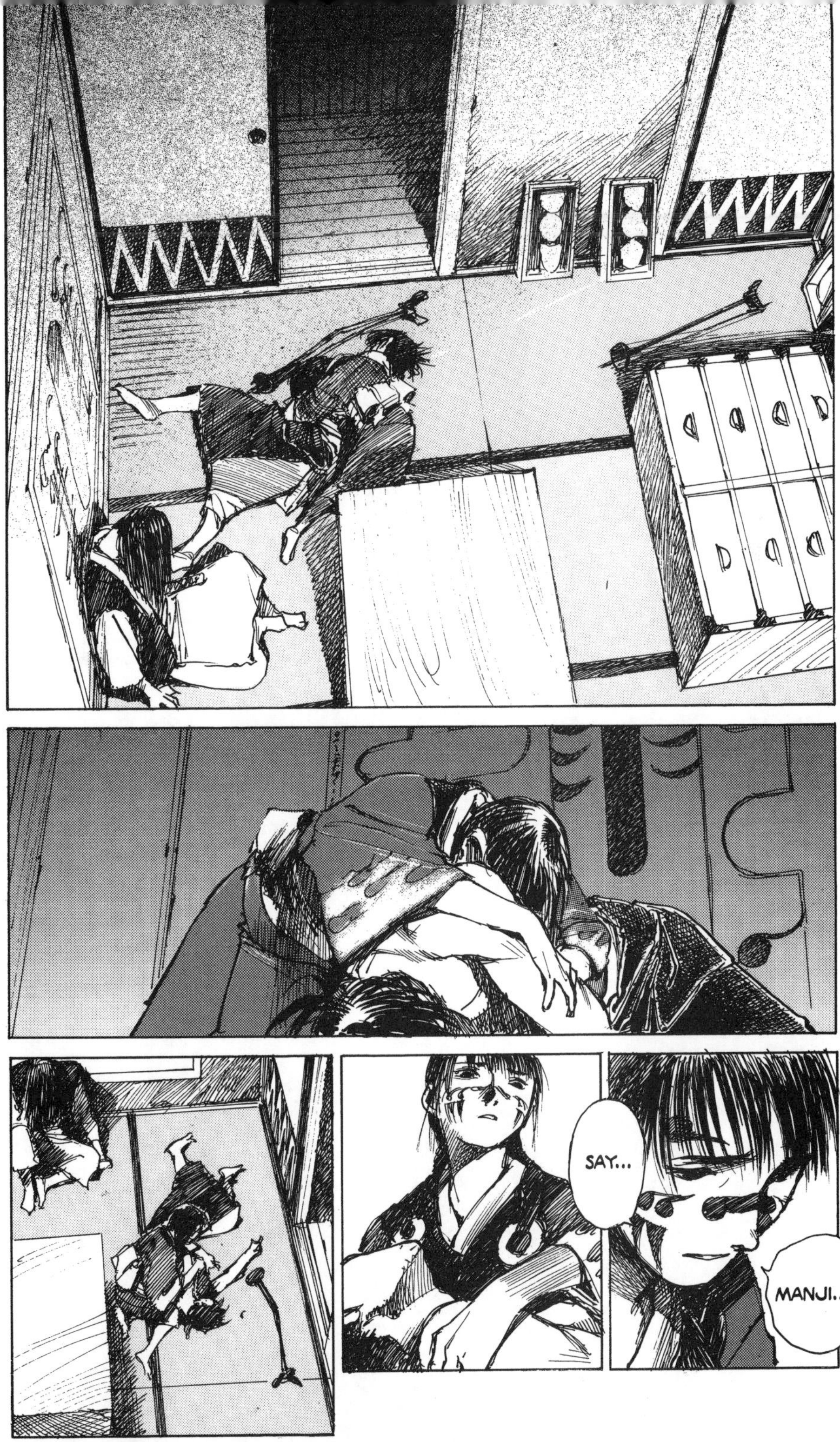
SAY...
MANJI...

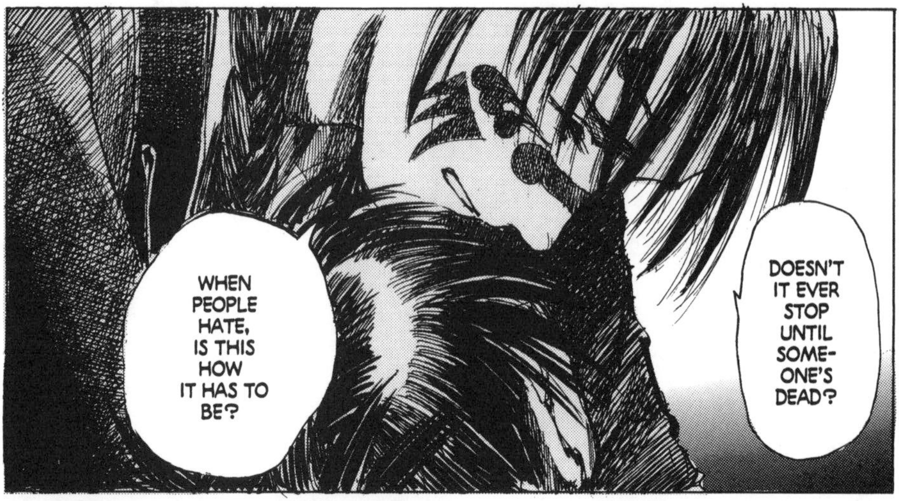
WHEN PEOPLE HATE, IS THIS HOW IT HAS TO BE?
DOESN'T IT EVER STOP UNTIL SOME-ONE'S DEAD?
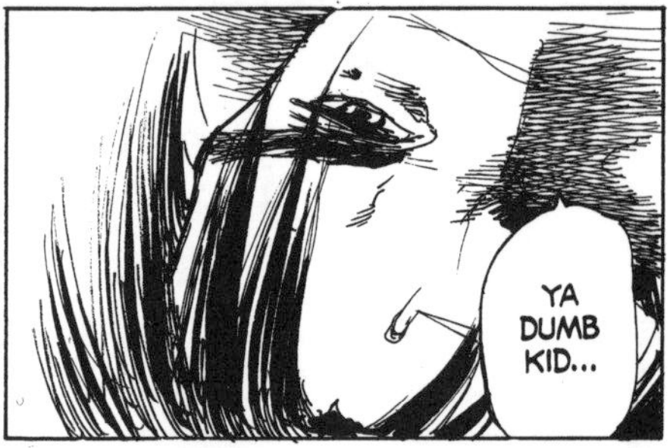
YA DUMB KID...
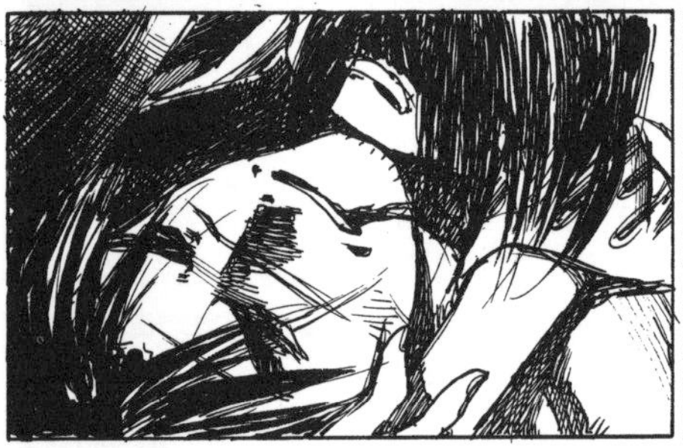
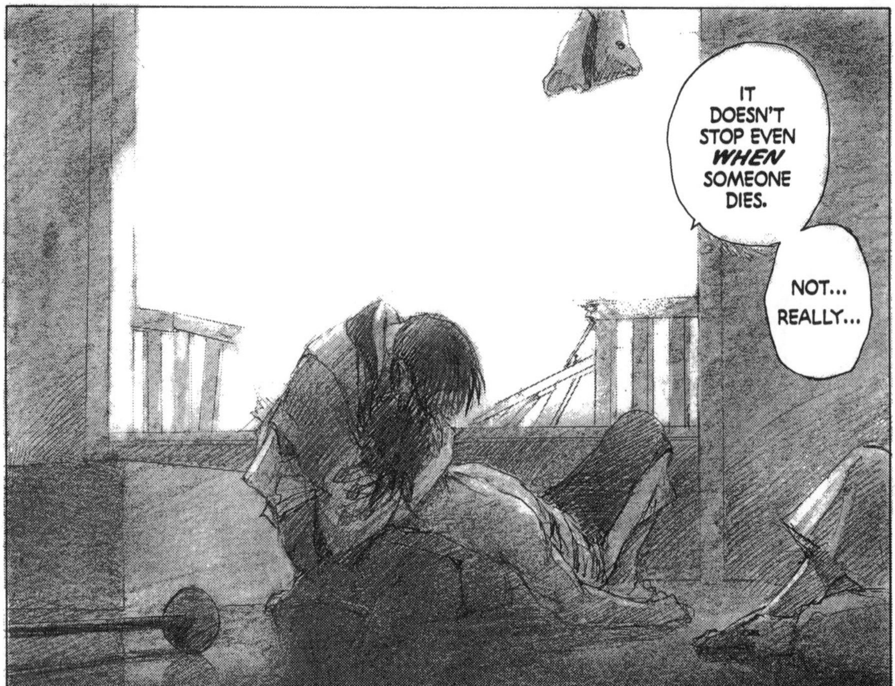
IT DOESN'T STOP EVEN *WHEN* SOMEONE DIES.
NOT... REALLY...

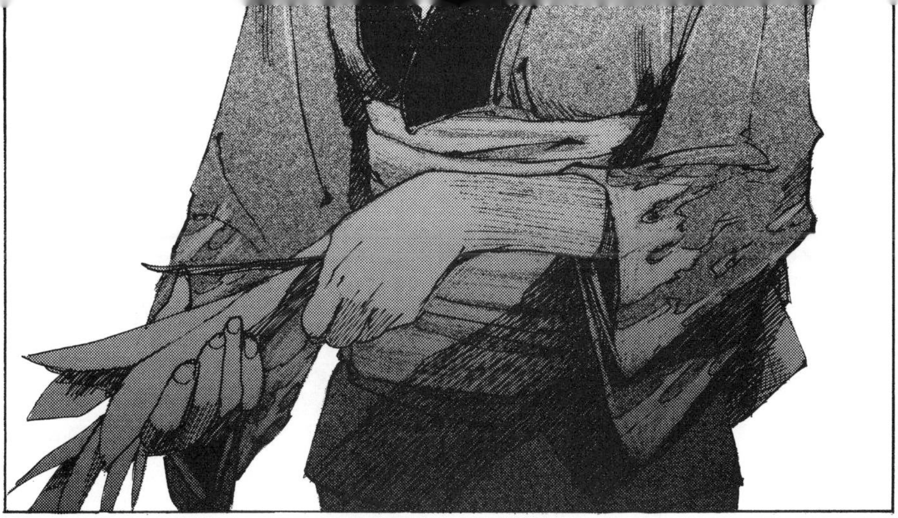

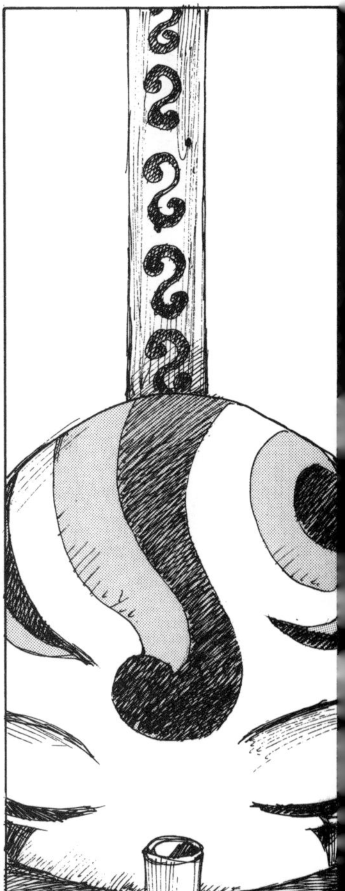

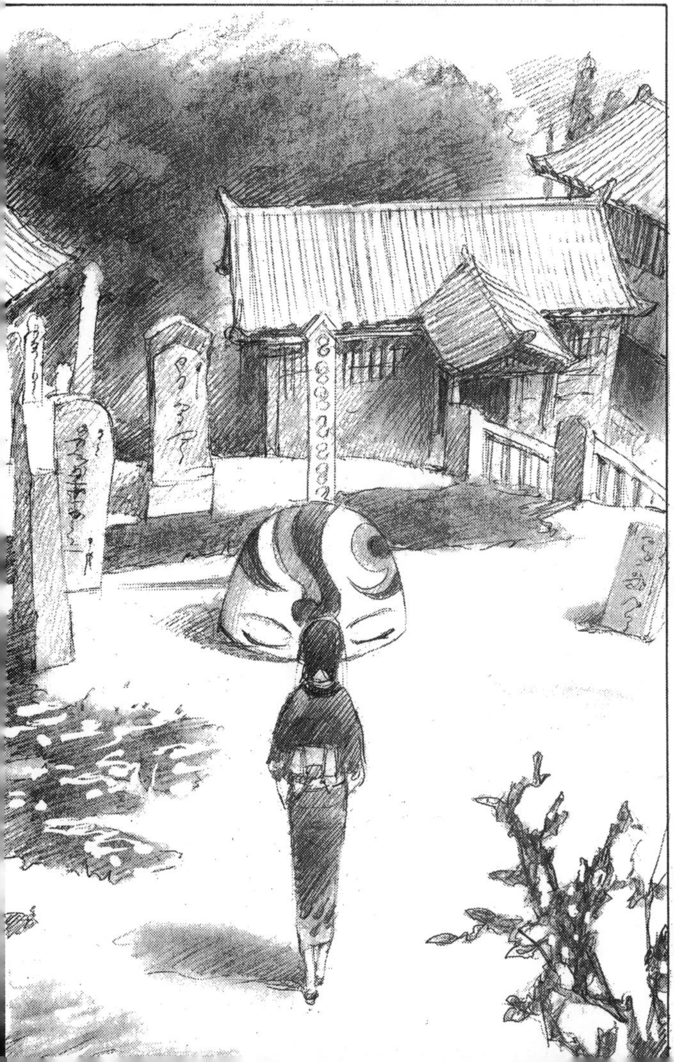

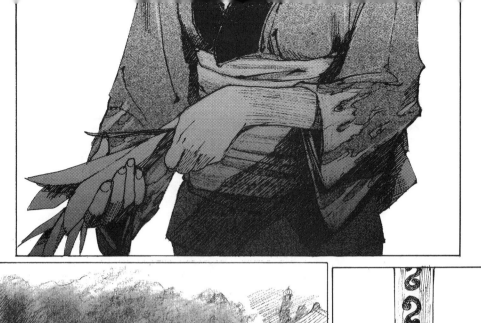

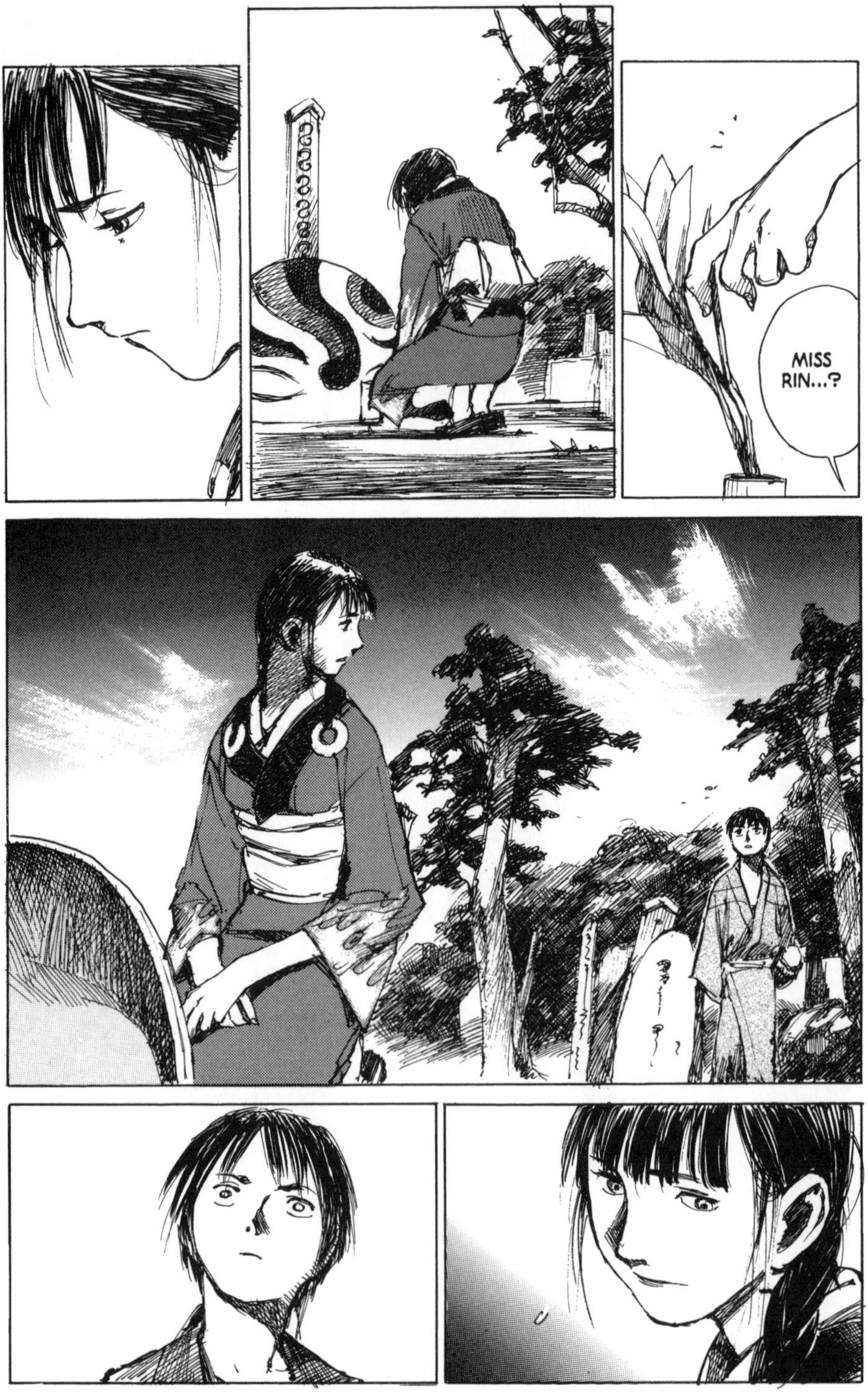
MISS RIN...?

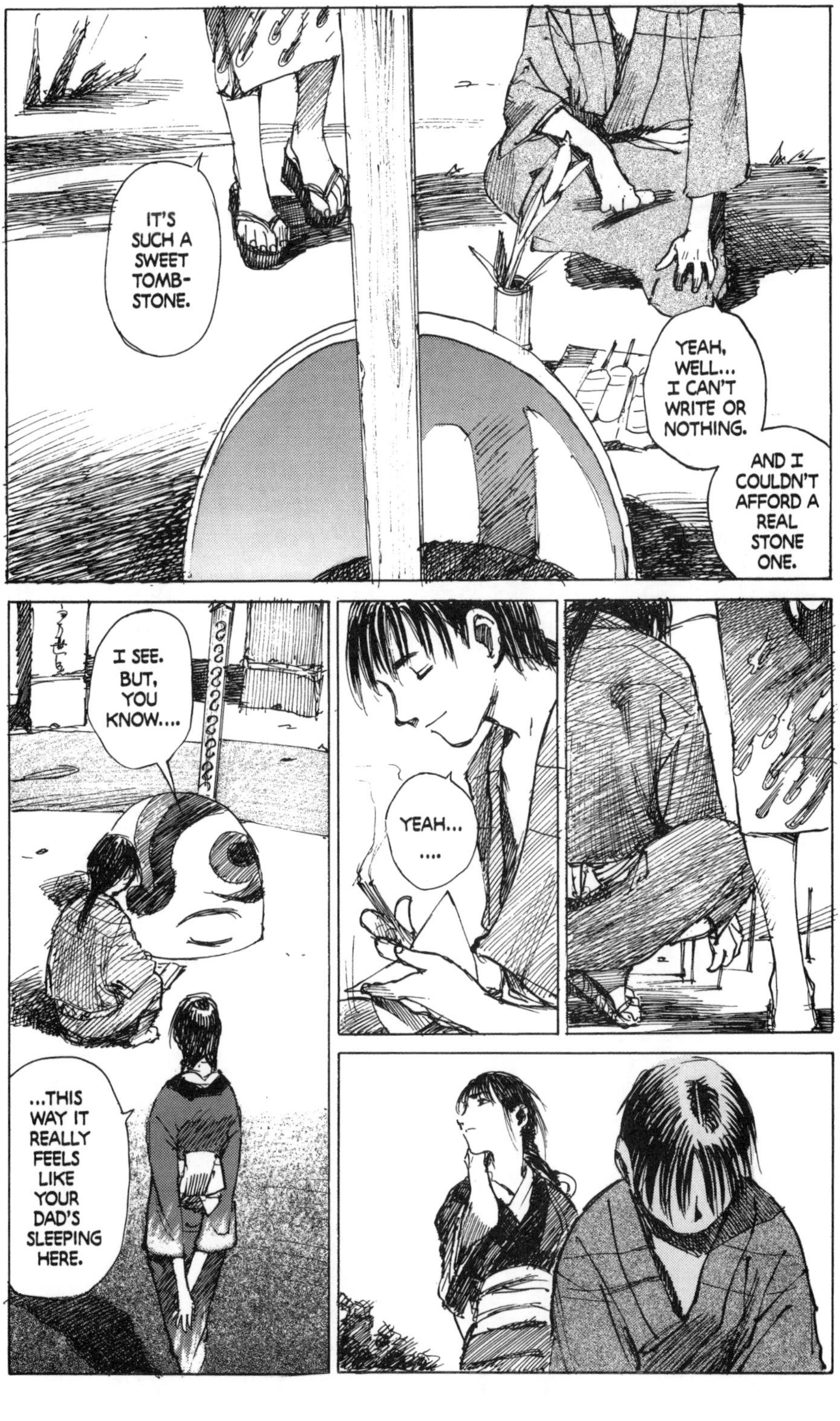
IT'S SUCH A SWEET TOMB-STONE.
YEAH, WELL... I CAN'T WRITE OR NOTHING.
AND I COULDN'T AFFORD A REAL STONE ONE.
I SEE. BUT, YOU KNOW....
YEAH... ....
...THIS WAY IT REALLY FEELS LIKE YOUR DAD'S SLEEPING HERE.

KNOW WHAT?

I'M HITTING THE ROAD TOMOR- ROW.

EH...?

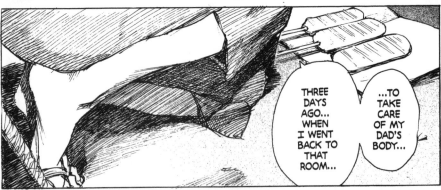

THREE DAYS AGO... WHEN I WENT BACK TO THAT ROOM...

...TO TAKE CARE OF MY DAD'S BODY...

HE WAS GONE.

I MEAN THAT GUY-- *HIS* BODY WAS GONE.

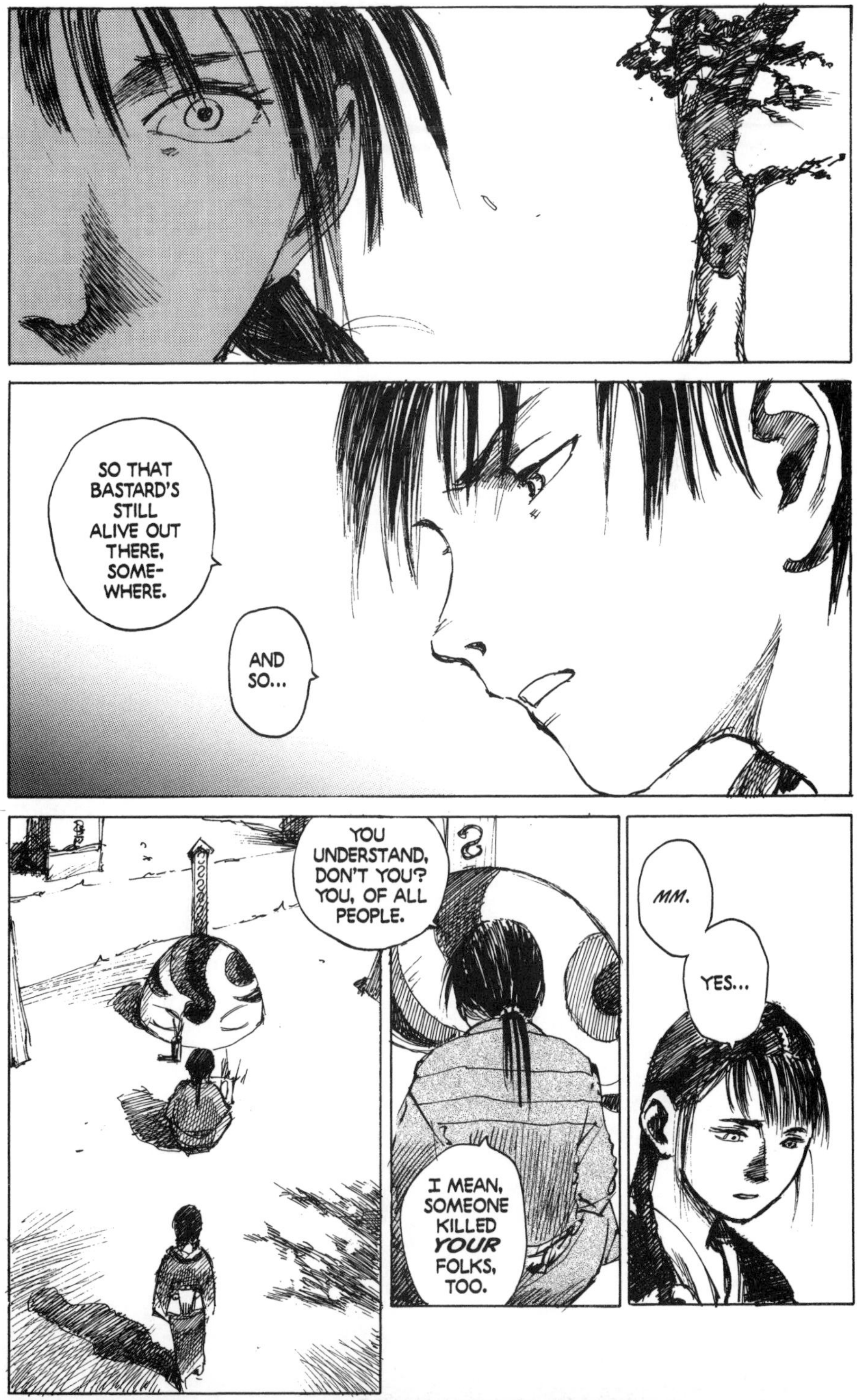
SO THAT BASTARD'S STILL ALIVE OUT THERE, SOME-WHERE.
AND SO...
YOU UNDERSTAND, DON'T YOU? YOU, OF ALL PEOPLE.
I MEAN, SOMEONE KILLED ***YOUR*** FOLKS, TOO.
MM.
YES...

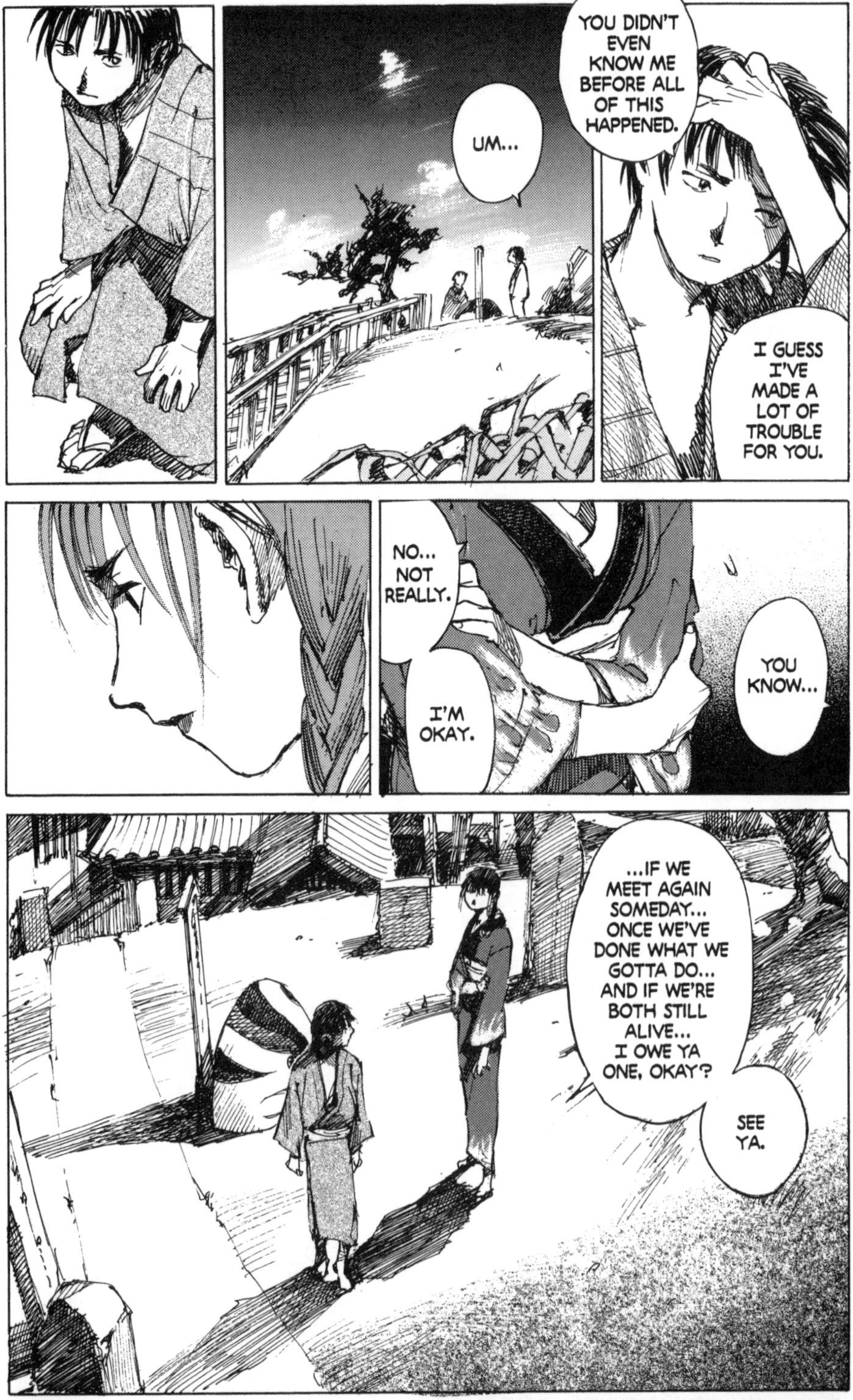
YOU DIDN'T EVEN KNOW ME BEFORE ALL OF THIS HAPPENED.
I GUESS I'VE MADE A LOT OF TROUBLE FOR YOU.
UM...
NO... NOT REALLY.
I'M OKAY.
YOU KNOW...
...IF WE MEET AGAIN SOMEDAY... ONCE WE'VE DONE WHAT WE GOTTA DO... AND IF WE'RE BOTH STILL ALIVE... I OWE YA ONE, OKAY?
SEE YA.

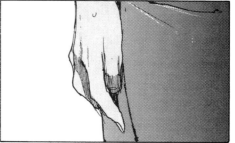

NO,
WAIT...

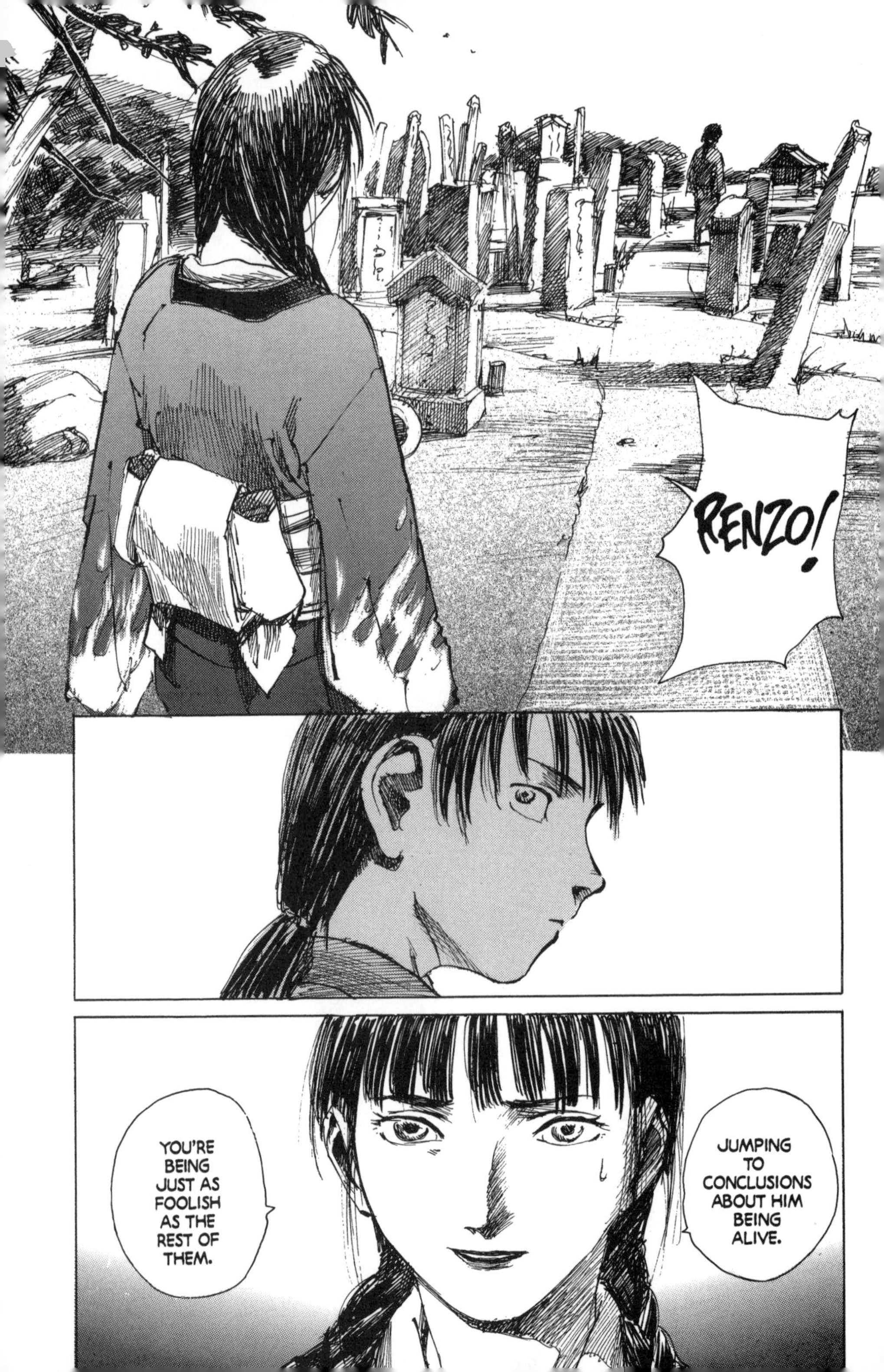
RENZO!
YOU'RE BEING JUST AS FOOLISH AS THE REST OF THEM.
JUMPING TO CONCLUSIONS ABOUT HIM BEING ALIVE.

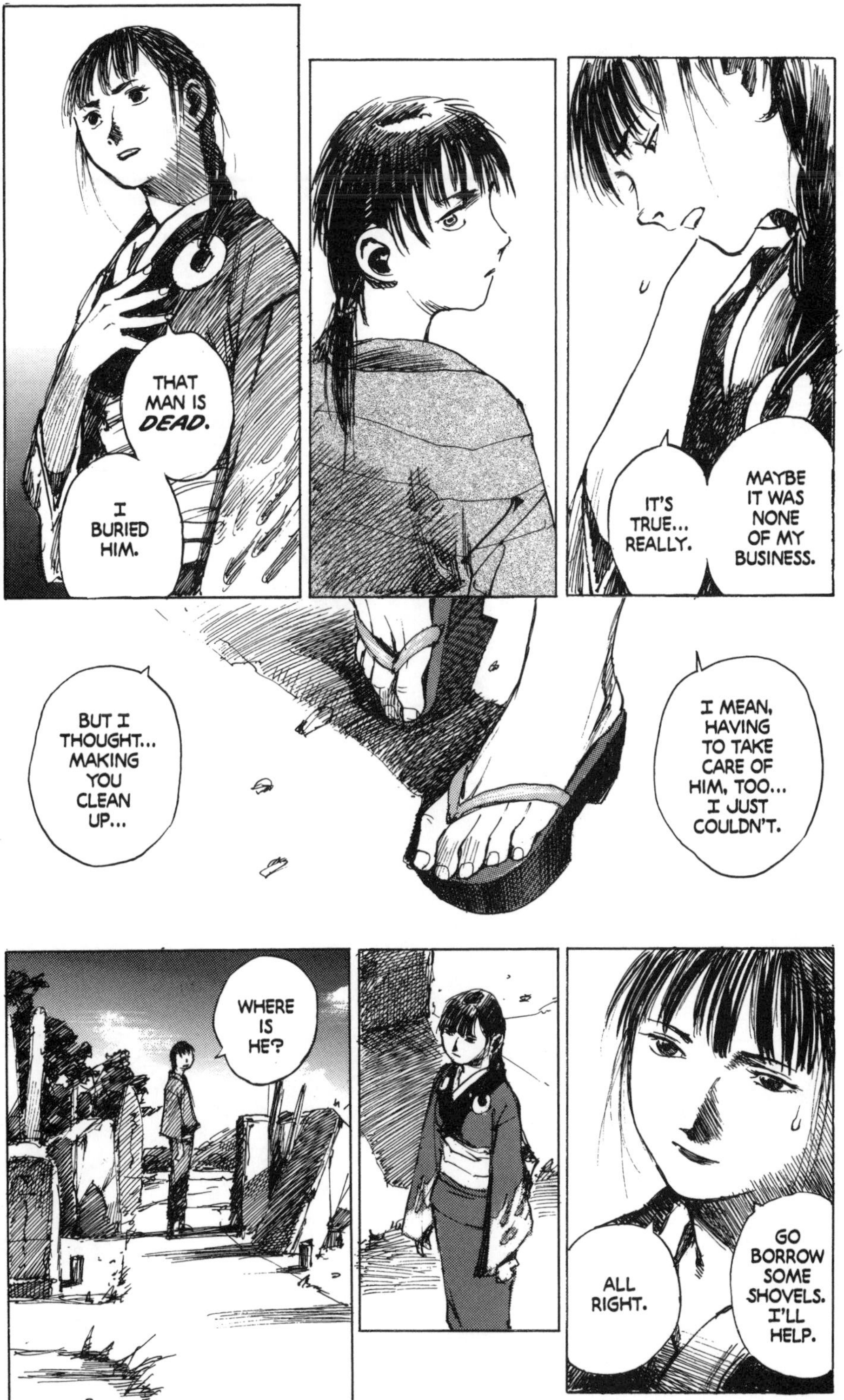
THAT MAN IS *DEAD*.
I BURIED HIM.
IT'S TRUE... REALLY.
MAYBE IT WAS NONE OF MY BUSINESS.
BUT I THOUGHT... MAKING YOU CLEAN UP...
I MEAN, HAVING TO TAKE CARE OF HIM, TOO... I JUST COULDN'T.
WHERE IS HE?
GO BORROW SOME SHOVELS. I'LL HELP.
ALL RIGHT.

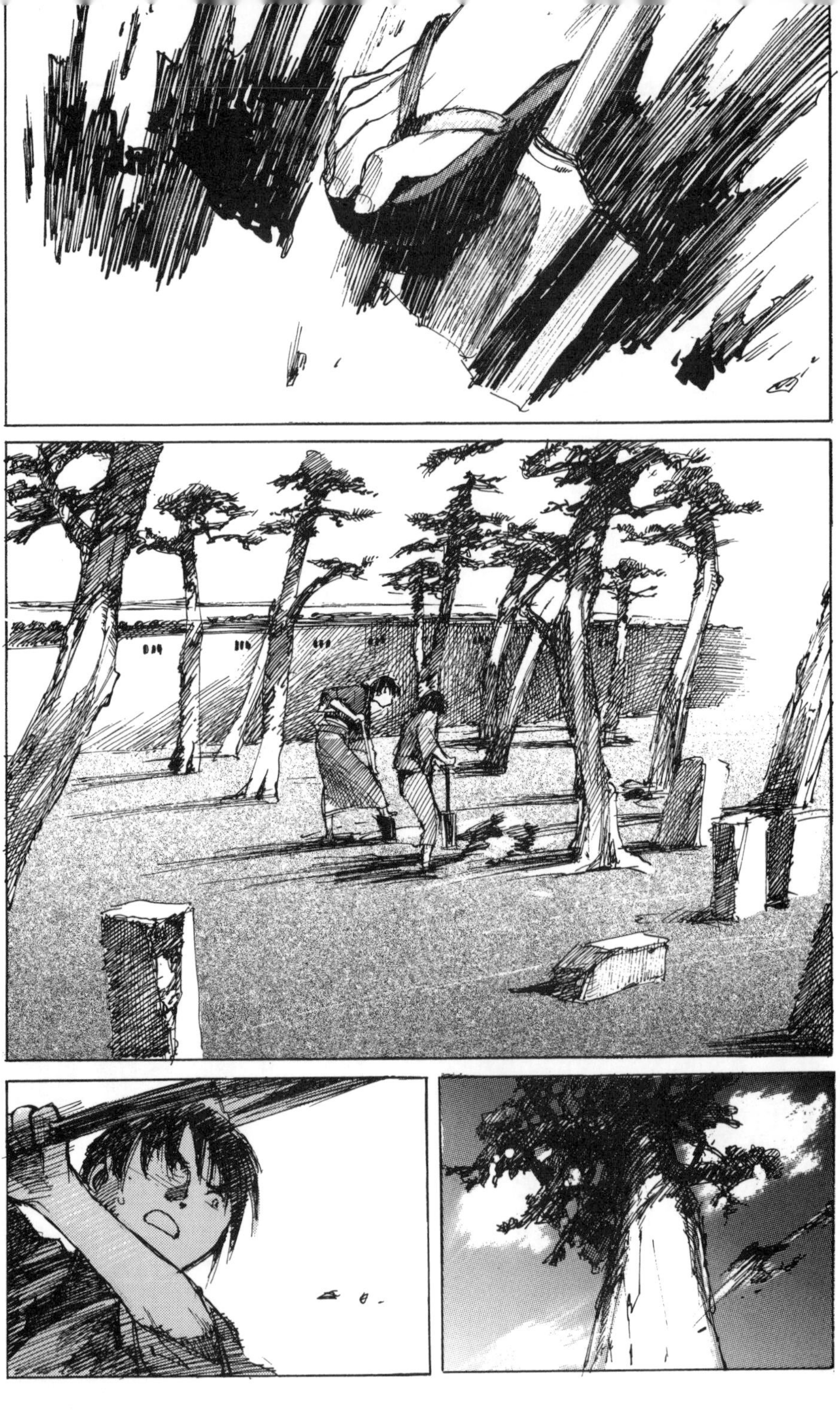

SHKK

CHNK

HOLD IT!

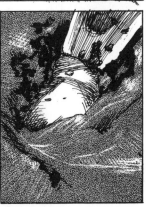

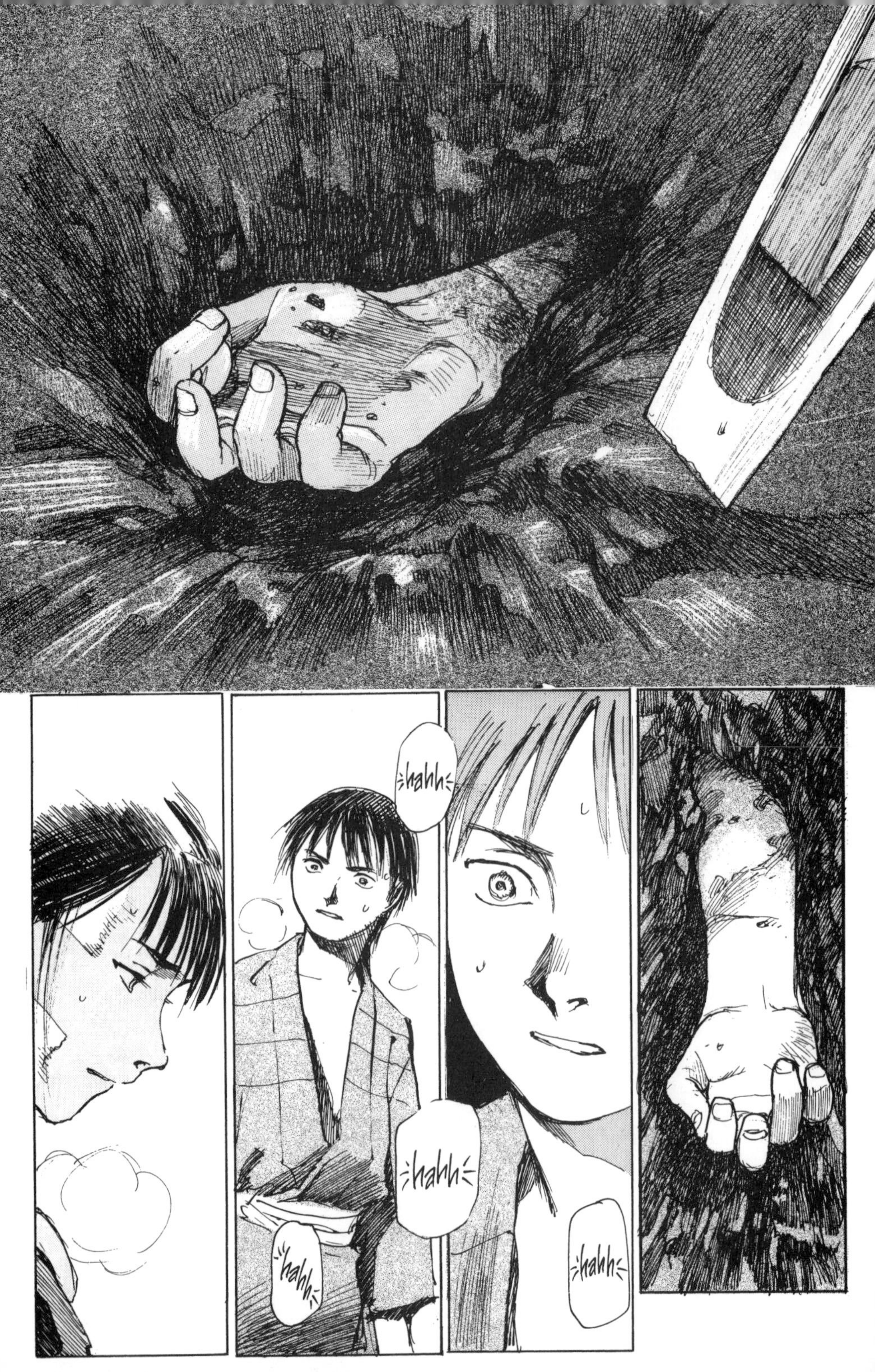
hahh
hahh
hahh
hahh

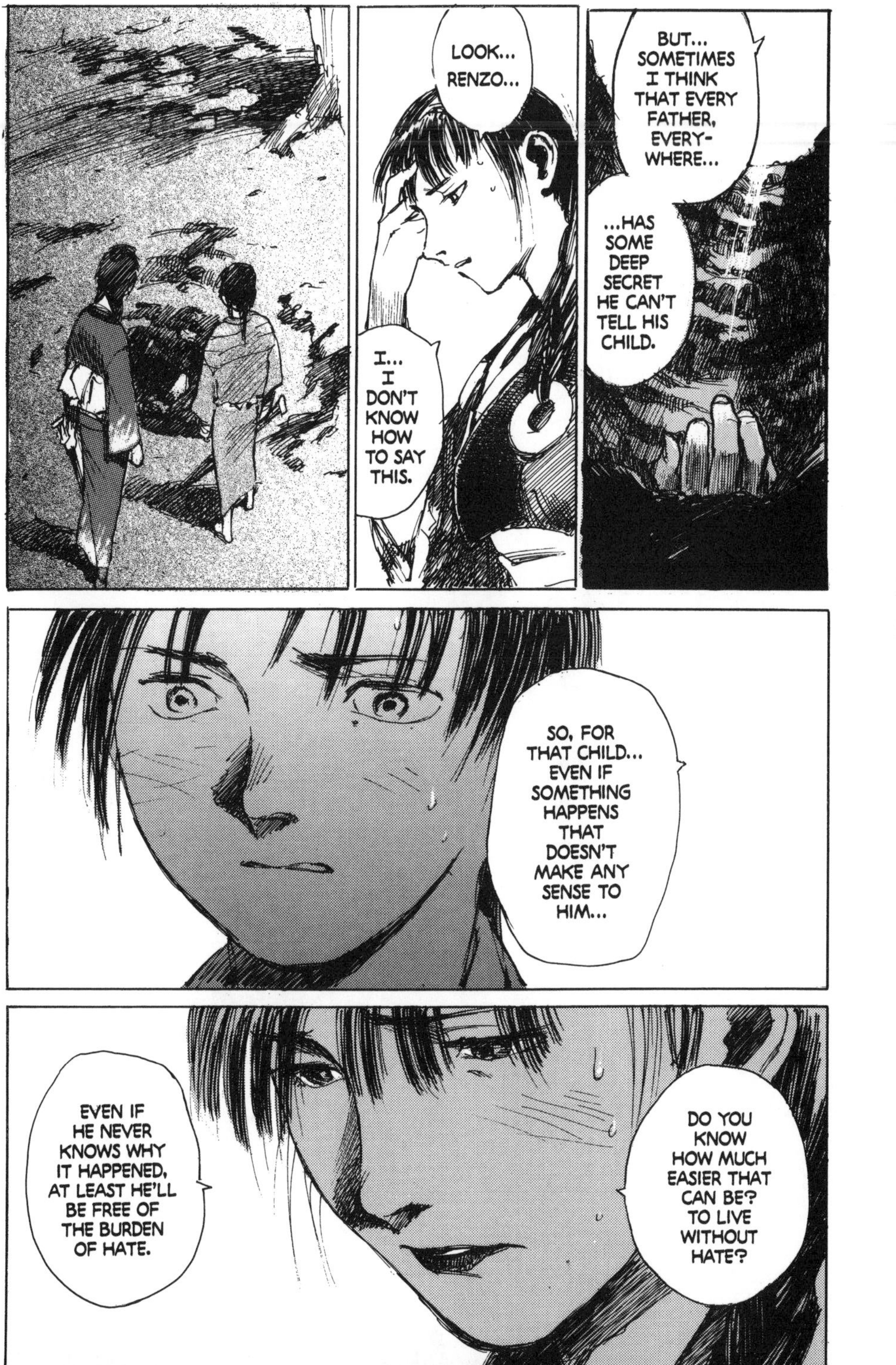
LOOK... RENZO...
I... I DON'T KNOW HOW TO SAY THIS.
BUT... SOMETIMES I THINK THAT EVERY FATHER, EVERY-WHERE...
...HAS SOME DEEP SECRET HE CAN'T TELL HIS CHILD.
SO, FOR THAT CHILD... EVEN IF SOMETHING HAPPENS THAT DOESN'T MAKE ANY SENSE TO HIM...
EVEN IF HE NEVER KNOWS WHY IT HAPPENED, AT LEAST HE'LL BE FREE OF THE BURDEN OF HATE.
DO YOU KNOW HOW MUCH EASIER THAT CAN BE? TO LIVE WITHOUT HATE?

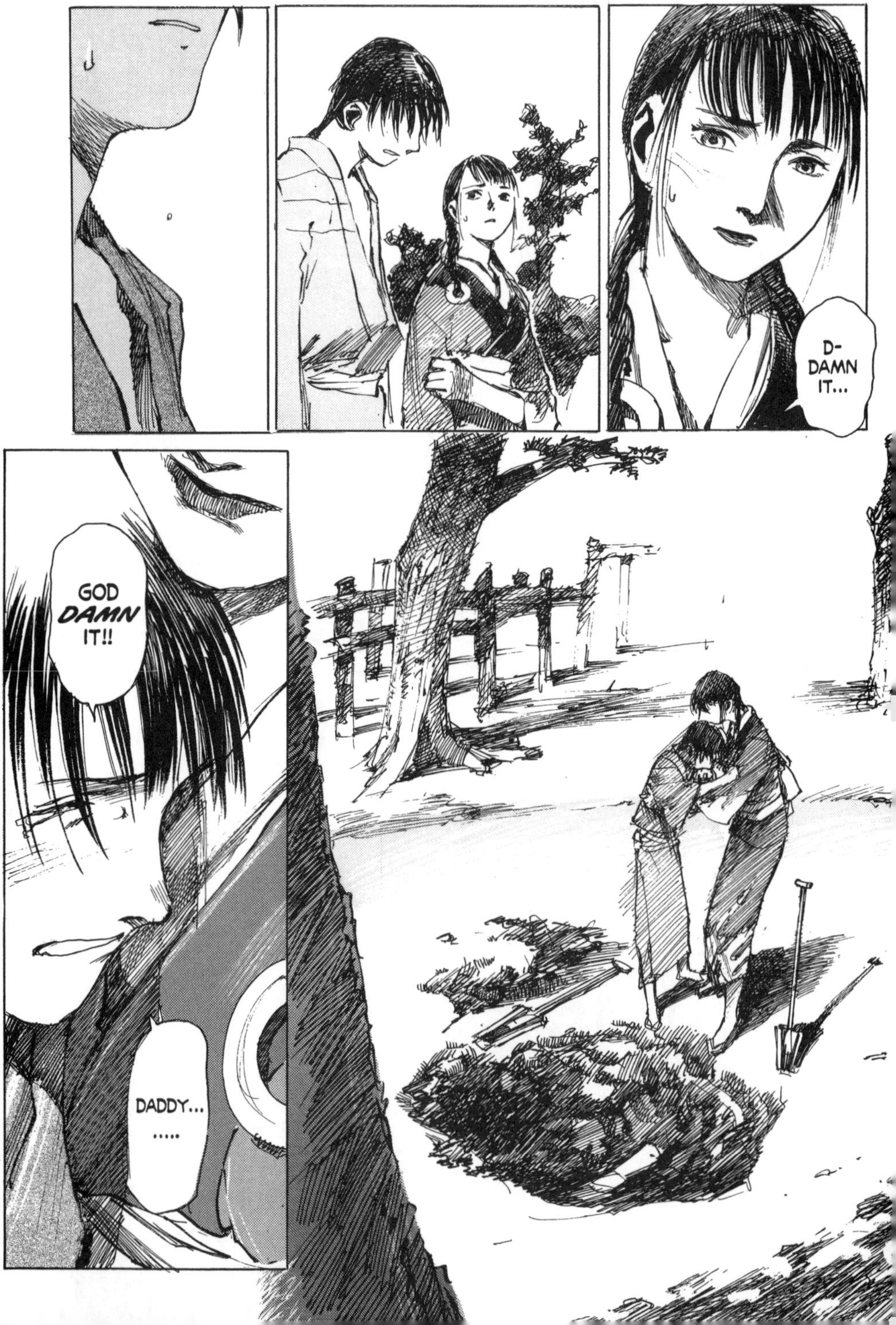
D-DAMN IT...
GOD *DAMN* IT!!
DADDY... ......

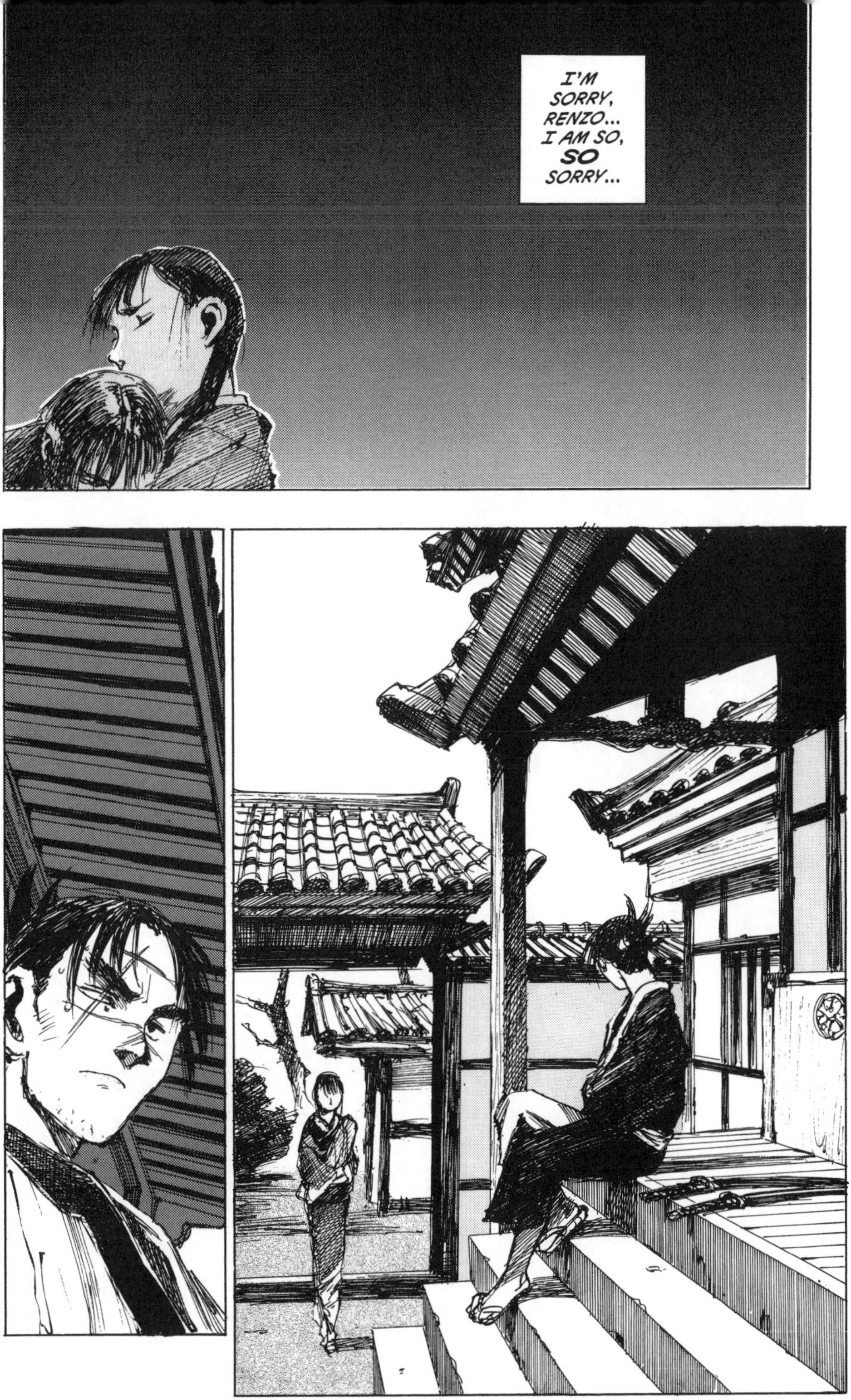
I'M SORRY, RENZO... I AM SO, SO SORRY...

MANJI...?

YEAH?

HE SAID "SORRY," RIGHT? AT THE END.

ARAYA...

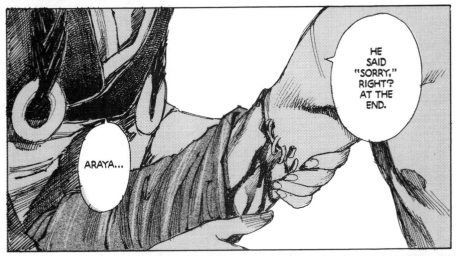

I DUNNO...

NOT LIKE HE APOL-OGIZED TO US.

.....
.....

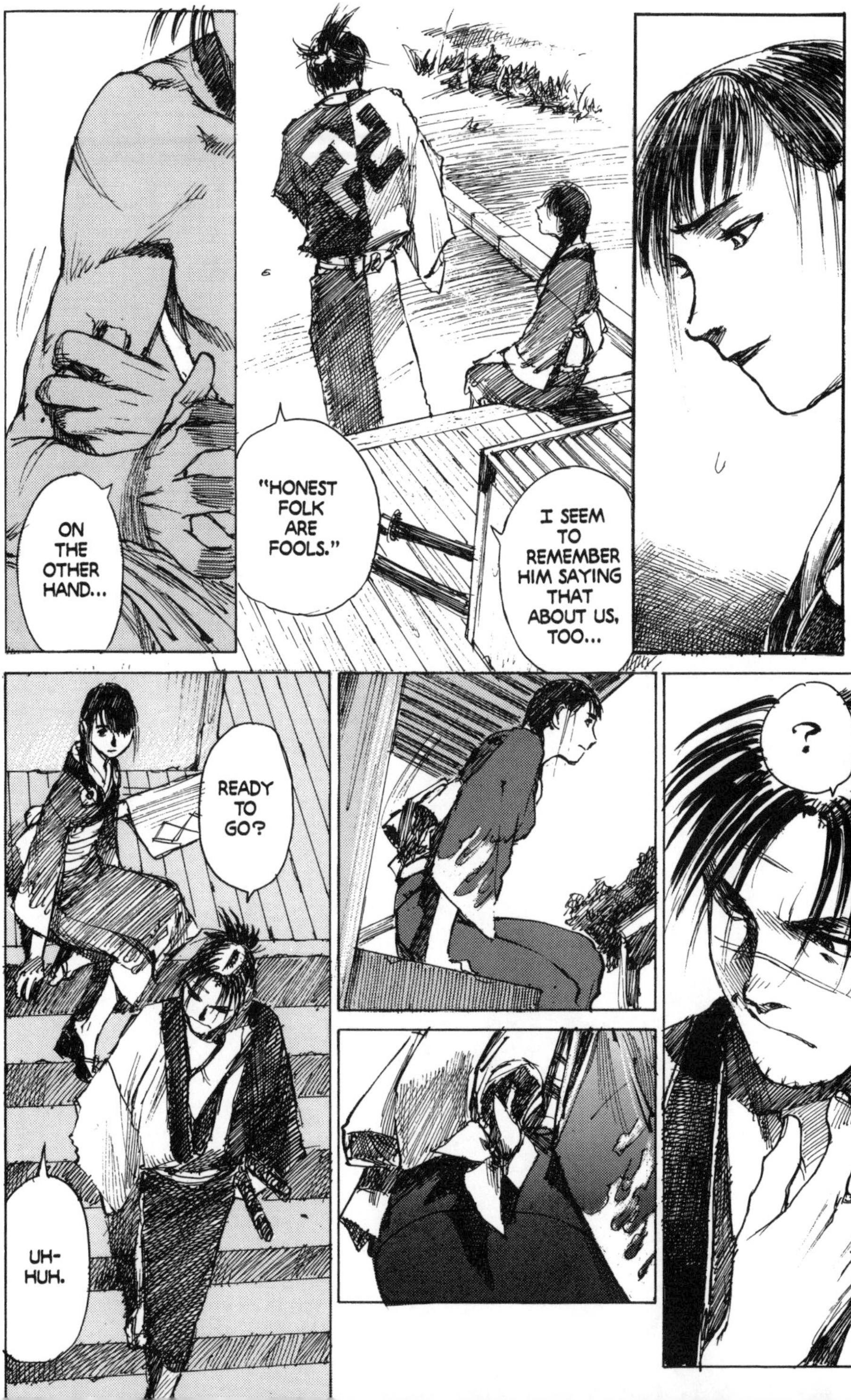
"HONEST FOLK ARE FOOLS."
I SEEM TO REMEMBER HIM SAYING THAT ABOUT US, TOO...
ON THE OTHER HAND...
?
READY TO GO?
UH-HUH.

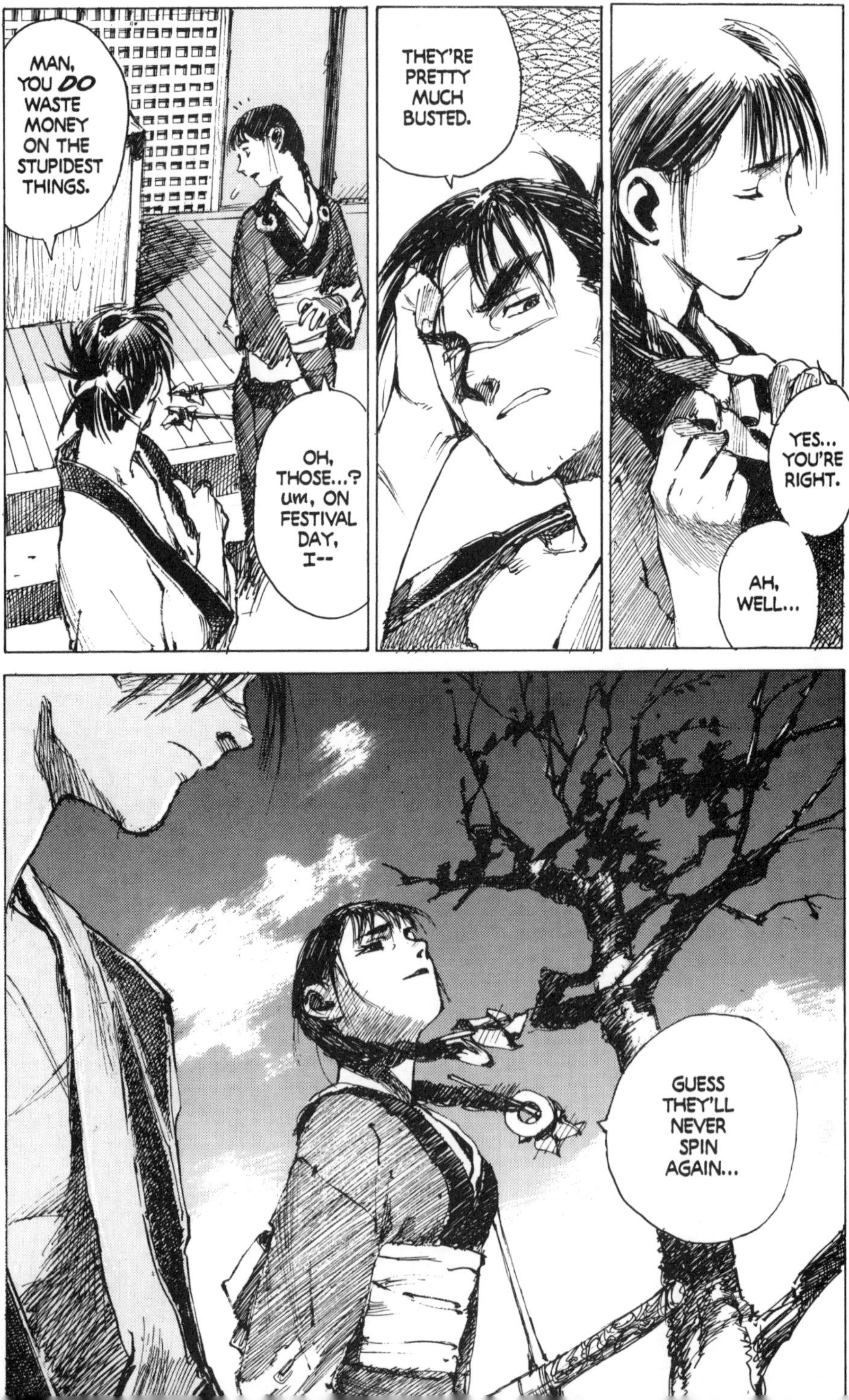
MAN, YOU DO WASTE MONEY ON THE STUPIDEST THINGS.
OH, THOSE...? UM, ON FESTIVAL DAY, I--
THEY'RE PRETTY MUCH BUSTED.
YES... YOU'RE RIGHT.
AH, WELL...
GUESS THEY'LL NEVER SPIN AGAIN...

GLOSSARY

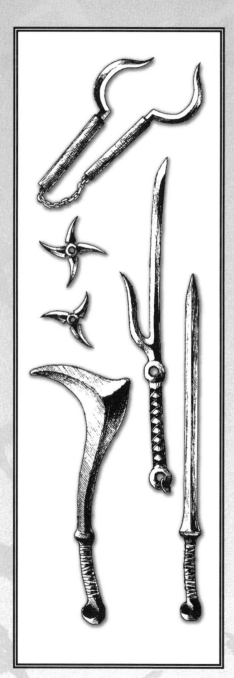

Bekkō-ame: a traditional sweet candy

Daimon: "Great Gate" — the great gate to the Asakusa Shrine, a famous landmark in old Edo still in existence today

Dōjō: training center for a sword school

Hamayumi: a bow accompanying the better-known *hakyuyumi* good-luck arrows still given out at shrine festivals today

Honjo: a place in central Edo

Ittō-ryū: the sword school of Kagehisa Anotsu

Kenshi: sword fighter

Kirisute: the right of a Samurai to kill a lower-caste person who has offended him

Mochi: a rice cake made a by pounding rice into a gooey mass

Mon: (1) literally, "a gate," used to designate all the members that pass the front gate to a *dōjō*: (2) a small unit of money

Mutenichi-ryū: sword fighting school led by Rin's father

Yojimbo: bodyguard

ABOUT THE CREATOR

HIROAKI SAMURA was born near Tokyo in Chiba Prefecture on February 17, 1970. After finishing college, Samura submitted work to *Afternoon Magazine*'s new talent contest and was ushered into the ranks of professional manga creators. Setting out to create an entirely new genre, his *Mugen no Junin* ("Inhabitant of Infinity," retitled *Blade of the Immortal*) drew critical acclaim for its brilliant draftsmanship and its daring and unconventional infusion of modernist sensibilities within the *jidai-geki* (period samurai drama) form. *Blade* was awarded Japan's prestigious 1998 Media Arts Award in the manga division. Administered by Japan's Agency of Cultural Affairs, the award praised *Blade* for "its graphic depictions, the power of its artwork, and its deep exploration of complicated human characters. *Blade of the Immortal* can rightly be called a work of great ambition that at once inherits the best traditions of the 'good old days' of Japanese storytelling manga, while taking the form to new heights of maturity and accomplishment." *Blade* has drawn similar accolades in the United States, garnering both Eisner and Harvey Award nominations.

ALSO AVAILABLE:

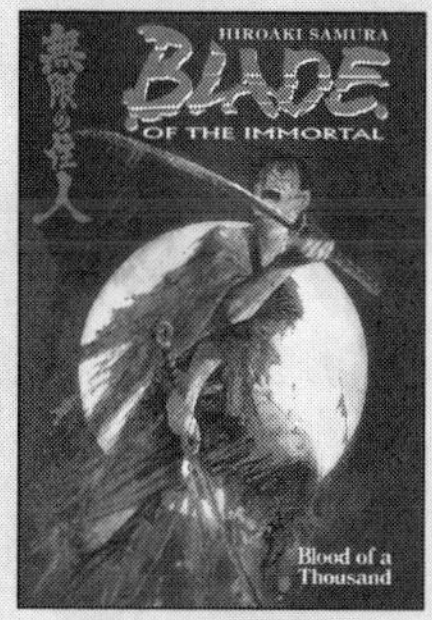
HIROAKI SAMURA
BLADE OF THE IMMORTAL
Blood of a Thousand

BLOOD OF A THOUSAND
ISBN: 1-56971-239-5 $14.95

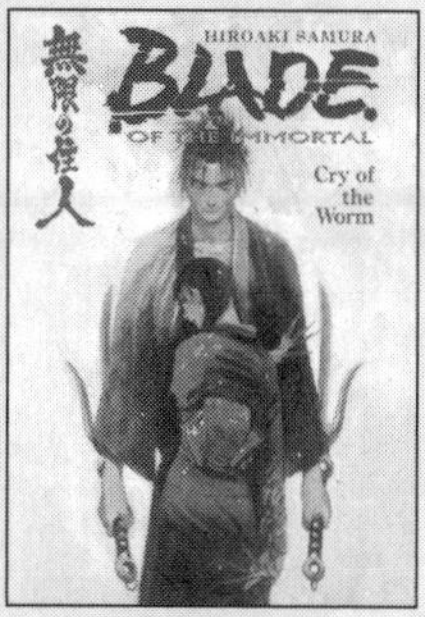
HIROAKI SAMURA
BLADE OF THE IMMORTAL
Cry of the Worm

CRY OF THE WORM
ISBN: 1-56971-300-6 $14.95

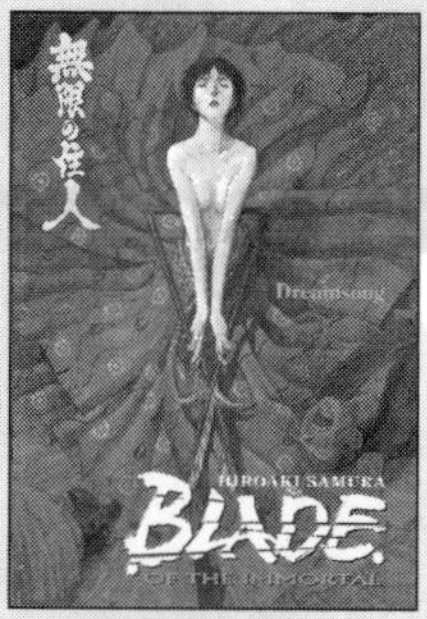
Dreamsong
HIROAKI SAMURA
BLADE OF THE IMMORTAL

DREAMSONG
ISBN: 1-56971-357-X $14.95

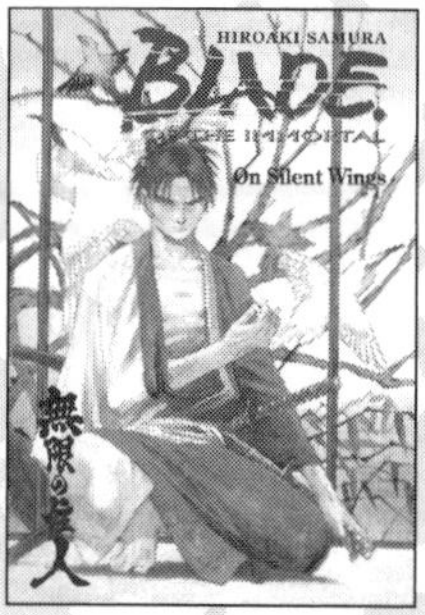
HIROAKI SAMURA
BLADE OF THE IMMORTAL
On Silent Wings

ON SILENT WINGS
ISBN: 1-56971-412-6 $14.95

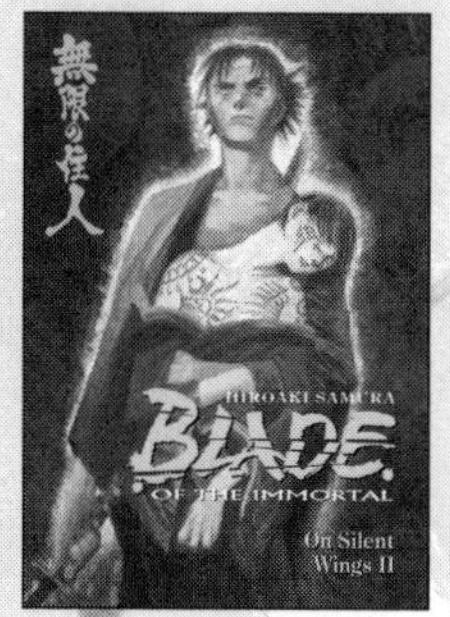
HIROAKI SAMURA
BLADE OF THE IMMORTAL
On Silent Wings II

ON SILENT WINGS II
ISBN: 1-56971-444-4 $14.95

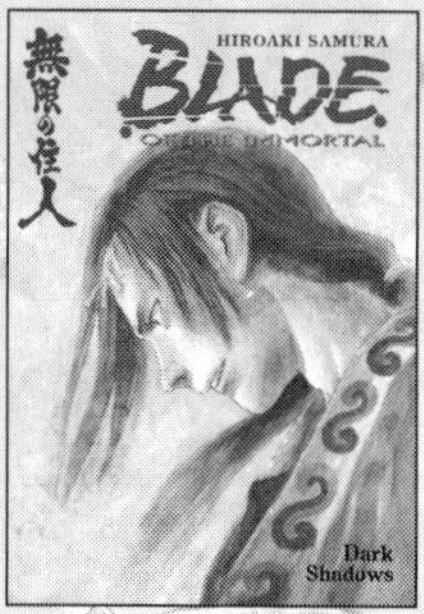
HIROAKI SAMURA
BLADE OF THE IMMORTAL
Dark Shadows

DARK SHADOWS
ISBN: 1-56971-469-X $14.95

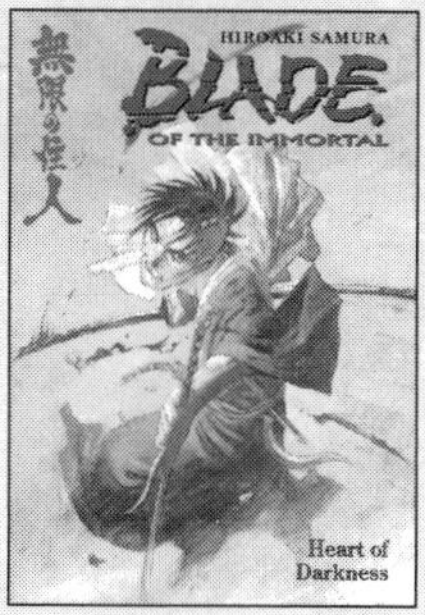
HIROAKI SAMURA
BLADE OF THE IMMORTAL
Heart of Darkness

HEART OF DARKNESS
ISBN: 1-56971-531-9 $16.95

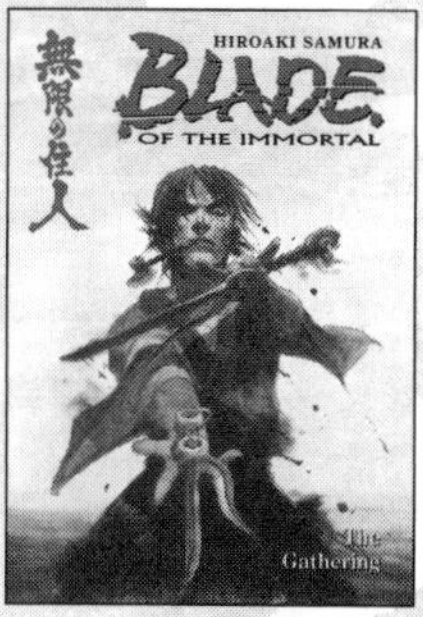
HIROAKI SAMURA
BLADE OF THE IMMORTAL
The Gathering

THE GATHERING
ISBN: 1-56971-546-7 $15.95

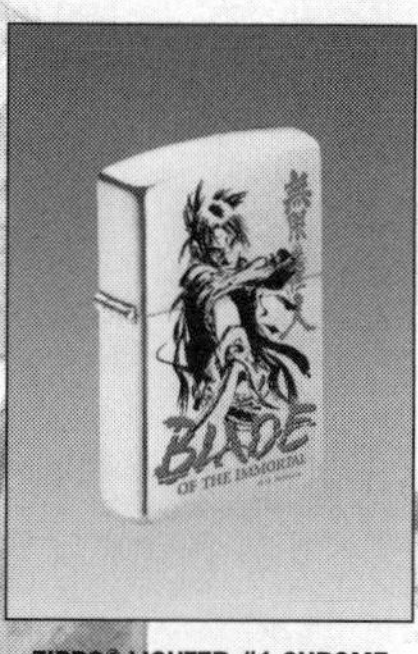
BLADE OF THE IMMORTAL

ZIPPO® LIGHTER #1 CHROME
#19-063 $29.95

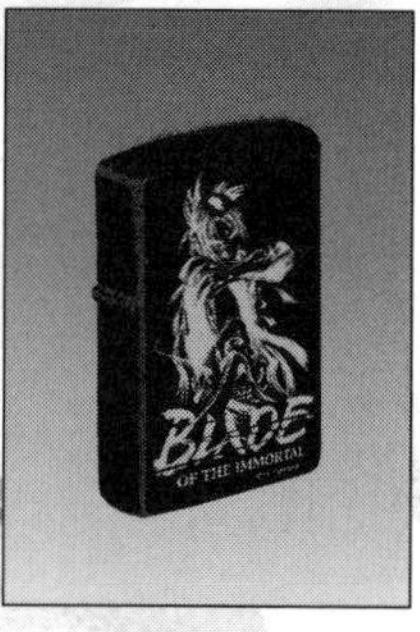
BLADE OF THE IMMORTAL

ZIPPO® LIGHTER #2 BLACK/BRASS
#19-169 $29.95

Prices and availability subject to change without notice.

To find a comics shop in your area, call 1-888-266-4226

For more information or to order direct: •On the web: www.darkhorse.com •E-mail: mailorder@darkhorse.com •Phone: 1-800-862-0052 or (503) 652-9701 Mon.-Sat. 9 A.M. to 5 P.M. Pacific Time

漫画 BACKLIST

A SAMPLING OF 漫画 GRAPHIC NOVELS FROM DARK HORSE COMICS

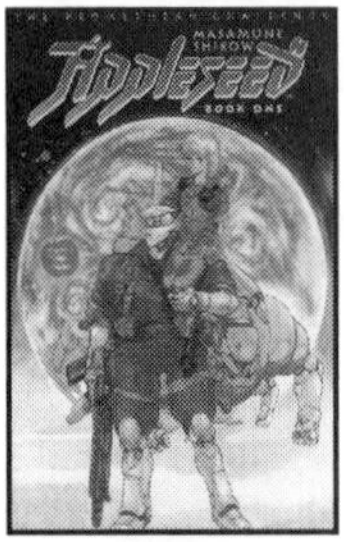
MASAMUNE SHIROW
Appleseed
BOOK ONE

BOOK ONE
ISBN: 1-56971-070-8 $14.95

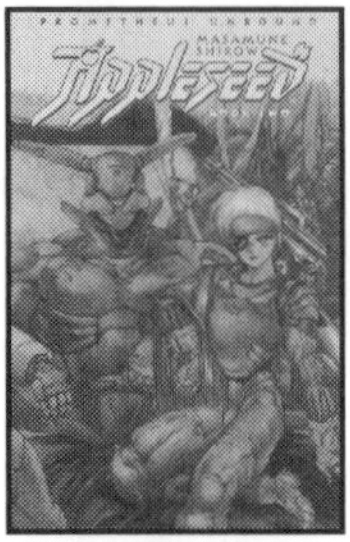
MASAMUNE SHIROW
Appleseed

BOOK TWO
ISBN: 1-56971-071-6 $14.95

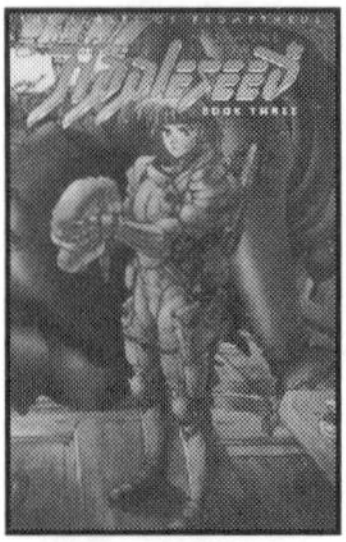
Appleseed
BOOK THREE

BOOK THREE
ISBN: 1-56971-072-4 $14.95

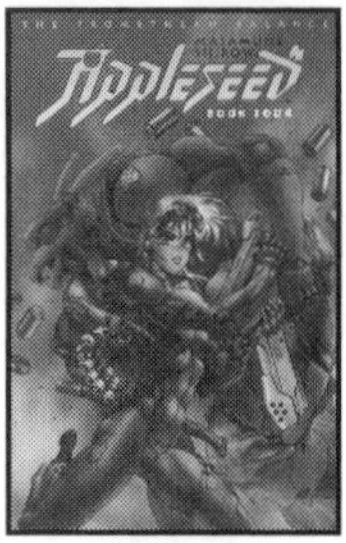
Appleseed
BOOK FOUR

BOOK FOUR
ISBN: 1-56971-074-0 $14.95

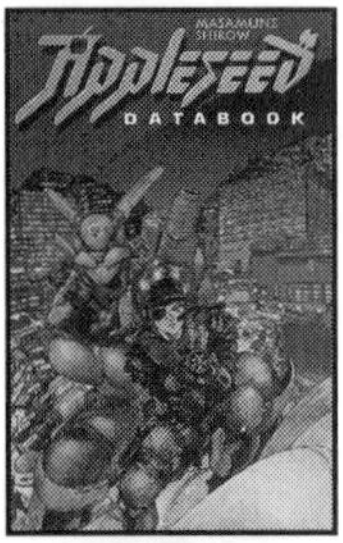
MASAMUNE SHIROW
Appleseed
DATABOOK

DATABOOK
ISBN: 1-56971-103-8 $12.95

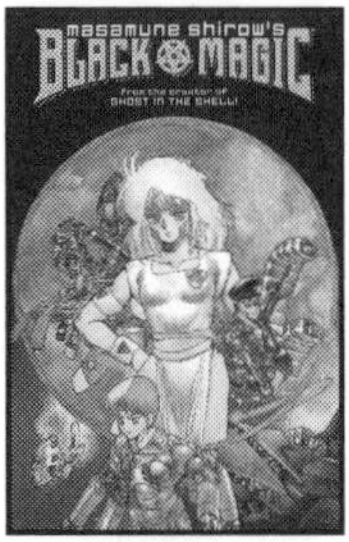
MASAMUNE SHIROW'S
BLACK MAGIC
From the creator of GHOST IN THE SHELL!

BLACK MAGIC
ISBN: 1-56971-360-X $16.95

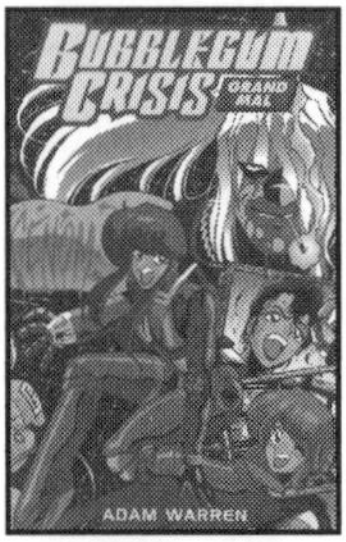
BUBBLEGUM CRISIS
GRAND MAL
ADAM WARREN

GRAND MAL
ISBN: 1-56971-120-8 $14.95

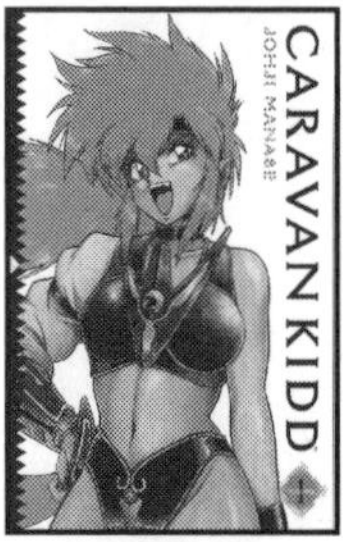
CARAVAN KIDD
JOHJI MANABE
1

VOLUME 1
ISBN: 1-56971-260-3 $19.95

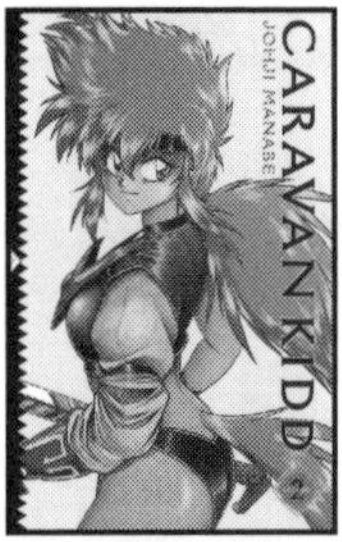
CARAVAN KIDD
JOHJI MANABE
2

VOLUME 2
ISBN: 1-56971-324-3 $19.95

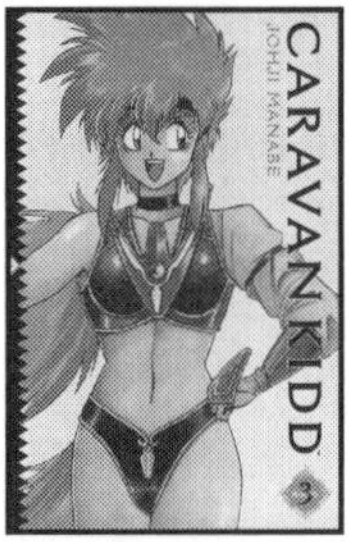
CARAVAN KIDD
JOHJI MANABE
3

VOLUME 3
ISBN: 1-5-6971-338-3 $19.95

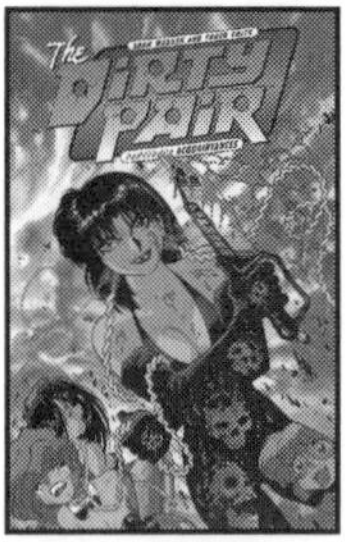
The Dirty Pair

DANGEROUS ACQUAINTANCES
ISBN: 1-56971-227-1 $12.95

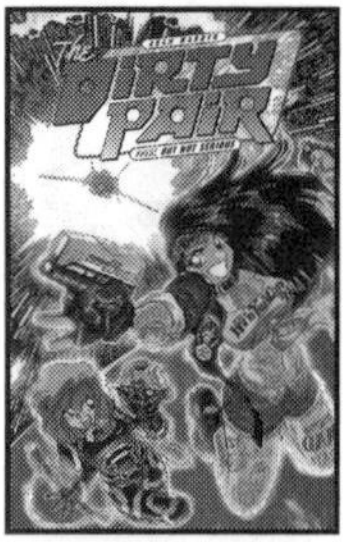
The Dirty Pair

FATAL BUT NOT SERIOUS
ISBN: 1-56971-172-0 $14.95

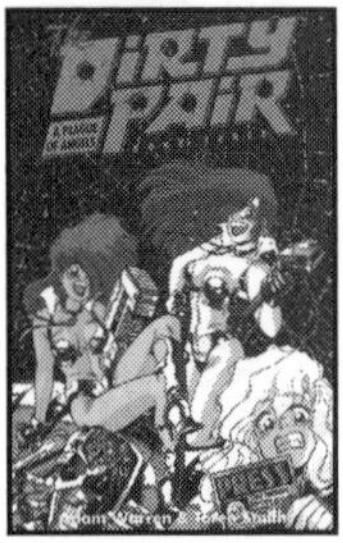
The Dirty Pair

A PLAGUE OF ANGELS
ISBN: 1-56971-029-5 $12.95

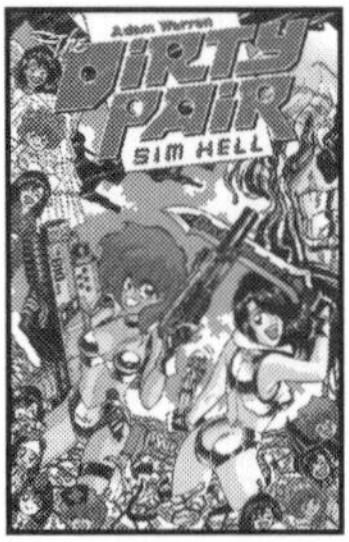
Adam Warren
The Dirty Pair
SIM HELL

SIM HELL
ISBN: 1-56971-159-3 $13.95

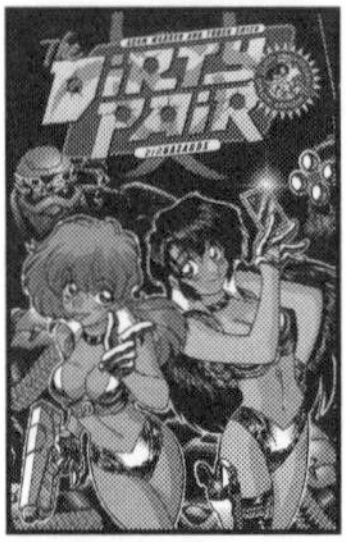
The Dirty Pair

BIOHAZARDS
ISBN: 1-56917-339-1 $12.95

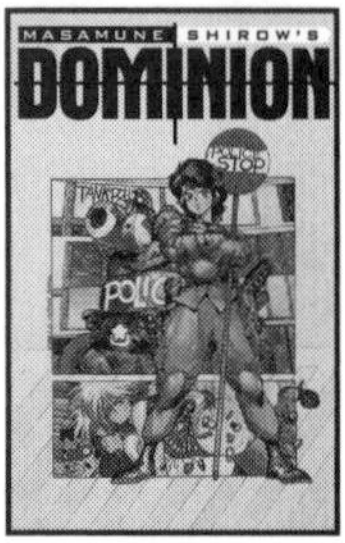
MASAMUNE SHIROW'S
DOMINION

DOMINION
ISBN: 1-56971-488-6 $16.95